'The MEN of 1914'

T. S. ELIOT
and early Modernism

'The MEN of 1914'
T. S. ELIOT
and early Modernism

Erik Svarny

OPEN UNIVERSITY PRESS
MILTON KEYNES · PHILADELPHIA

Open University Press
12 Cofferidge Close
Stony Stratford
Milton Keynes MK11 1BY

and
1900 Frost Road, Suite 101
Bristol, PA 19007, USA

First published 1988
Reprinted 1989

British Library Cataloguing in Publication Data
Svarny, Erik Michael
T. S. Eliot and 'the men of 1914'.
1. Eliot, T. S. – Criticism and interpretation
I. Title
821′ .912   PS3509.L43Z/
ISBN 0-335-150780 (pbk)

Library of Congress Cataloging-in-Publication Data
Svarny, Erik Michael.
T. S. Eliot and 'the men of 1914'/Erik Michael Svarny.
    p.   cm.
Bibliography: p.
Includes index.
ISBN 0-335-150780 (pbk)

1. Eliot, T. S. (Thomas Stearns), 1888–1965 – Criticism
and interpretation.   2. Eliot, T. S. (Thomas Stearns),
1888–1965 – Friends and associates.   3. Pound, Ezra,
1885–1972 – Influence – Eliot.   4. English poetry –
20th century – History and criticism.   5. World War,
1914–1918 – Literature and the war.   I. Title.
PS3509.L43Z8725   1988
821′ .912 – dc19

Typeset by Scarborough Typesetting Services
Printed in Great Britain by
St Edmundsbury Press, Bury St Edmunds

For Aranka Baum

Illustrations

Contents

Acknowledgements

As this book began its life as a doctoral thesis, the debts I have acquired in the process of bringing it to completion assume a corresponding longevity. Firstly, and primarily, I would like to thank Gabriel Josipovici, who supervised my thesis, and whose seminars on 'Dante, Eliot, and Beckett' initiated my interest in Eliot's poetry. I would also like to thank George Craig, who read and commented upon my doctorate while it was in progress. I would like to thank Graham Martin for recommending that work for publication; the Roehampton Institute for granting me a term's study leave to plan my revisions; and the Froebel Institute for financial assistance with the preparation of this manuscript. I would like to thank Brian Stimpson for his generous assistance with the poetry translations. Finally, I would like to thank my parents Walter and Gerda, and my sister Karen, for their encouragement throughout every stage of this project; and my friends, Emma Letley, Sarah Turvey, Jacob and Vanessa Frerichs, Kate Soper and Martin Ryle for their advice, interest and assistance.

For permission to quote copyrighted material I wish to express my thanks to: Faber and Faber Ltd and Farrar, Straus & Giroux for *Poems Written in Early Youth* by T. S. Eliot; Faber and Faber Ltd and Harcourt Brace Jovanovich Inc for 'Aunt Helen' and 'Whispers of Immortality' from *Collected Poems 1909–1962* by T. S. Eliot, copyright 1936 by Harcourt Brace Jovanovich, Inc.; copyright © 1963, 1964 by T. S. Eliot. Reprinted by permission of the publishers. Faber and Faber Ltd for *Collected Shorter Poems* by Ezra Pound, and to New Directions for *Personae* (copyright 1926 by Ezra Pound); Mrs Valerie Eliot and Faber and Faber Ltd for extracts from uncollected prose as indicated in the Notes and References. For permission to reproduce illustrations I wish to express my thanks to: the Victoria and Albert Museum; the Tate Gallery, Omar S. Pound and DACS; the Imperial War Museum; Southampton City Art Gallery; and the Ferens Art Gallery: Hull City Museums and Art Galleries.

Introduction: Critical Perspectives

The work is the death mask of its conception.

Walter Benjamin

i

The subject of this book is T. S. Eliot's poetic development between 1914 and 1922. I have concentrated in particular on the quatrain poems of 1920, which were originally published in England under the title *Ara Vos Prec*. 1914 was the year of Eliot's arrival in England and his entry into English literary society under the guidance of Ezra Pound; 1922 was the date of the completion of *The Waste Land* and its appearance in Eliot's own, newly launched magazine, *The Criterion*. This major poem was in many ways the final fruit of his poetic and critical co-operation with Pound, who had left England some two years previously.

The initial chapters of the book focus on a comment made by Pound in *The Criterion* of July 1932.

> [Mr. Eliot] displayed great tact, or enjoyed good fortune, in arriving in London at a particular date with a formed style of his own. He also participated in a movement to which no name has ever been given.
>
> That is to say, at a particular date in a particular room, two authors, neither engaged in picking the other's pockets, decided that the dilutation of *vers libre*, Amygism, Lee Masterism, general floppiness had gone too far and that some counter-current must be set going. Parallel situation centuries ago in China. Remedy prescribed 'Emaux et Camées' (or the Bay State Hymn Book). Rhyme and regular strophes.
>
> Results: Poems in Mr. Eliot's *second* volume, not contained in his first ('Prufrock', *Egoist*, 1917), also 'H. S. Mauberley'.
>
> Divergence later.[1]

Allowing for the elements of humour and rhetorical exaggeration in Pound's statement, the premise upon which this study is based is already implicit: that the work produced by Eliot between 1914 and 1922 has a specific historical consistency which can best be appreciated and analysed in the context of his association with Pound. As it has not been my intention to write a critical monograph with T. S. Eliot as the exclusive focus, I have included and interpolated critical discussion of those aspects of Pound's work which can be seen as being relevant to Eliot's and have included a separate chapter on the *Hugh Selwyn Mauberley* sequence mentioned above. This book attempts to situate Eliot's work within a complex of intellectual, cultural and historical co-ordinates, primarily those provided by his association with Pound, but not excluding the work of other contemporary writers, such as T. E. Hulme and Wyndham Lewis, whose writings can be seen as having some bearing on Eliot's work.

As a related aim I try to illuminate Eliot's work during this period not just by comparison with his contemporaries, but also by considering it in relation to those writers he used as textual sources and formal models. But Eliot's connection with his contemporaries and his uses of 'tradition' cannot be regarded as divergent or mutually exclusive. In attempting to understand Eliot's formal development I found that it was only by referring his work to contemporary tendencies and pressures that it was possible to explicate the various poetic modes by which he successively related his work to that of previous writers. This attempt to describe how Eliot's poetic employment of the work of previous writers and poets ('tradition') was inflected by contemporary interests is intended as a contrast to the majority of critical studies of Eliot's work, which, necessarily aware of the obtrusive intertextuality of his poetry, have tended to see in it a static, undynamic relation to the literary past, a relation more applicable to a neo-Classical poet than Eliot, the modernist, who wrote in his most famous essay that he did 'not find it preposterous that the past should be altered by the present as much as the present is directed by the past'.[2]

My title employs a phrase used by Wyndham Lewis in his autobiographical work *Blasting and Bombardiering* (1937) to describe Eliot, Pound, James Joyce and Lewis himself: 'the literary band, or group, comprised within the critical fold of Ezra Pound – the young, the "New", group of writers assembled in Miss Weaver's *Egoist* just before and during the War'.[3] The immediate and obvious reference of 'the Men of 1914', to those who fought in the First World War, is not inadvertent; nor do I think Lewis merely wishes to suggest a contingent historical conjunction. This military metaphor captures the antagonistic, often rebarbative, cultural posture of these writers, all of whom except Joyce, adopted anti-democratic and anti-humanist cultural stances; it indicates that Eliot's work can be sited within a context of oppositional avant-garde literature prevalent in the years during and immediately after the First World War. In order to describe these oppositional tendencies in my first chapter, 'The Moment of *Blast*', I shall give some attention to the Vorticist art movement and its short-lived propaganda magazine *Blast*, with which both Wyndham Lewis and Pound were closely associated. Close consideration of Eliot's work is intentionally deferred until I have provided an outline of its cultural and intellectual context.

Characteristically, in *Blasting and Bombardiering*, having offered us this resonant phrase, Lewis is at pains to distance himself from the arbitrary nature of literary groupings and, having acknowledged the connection that he, Eliot and Joyce had with Pound, and through him with the *Egoist*, he concedes that a more disparate group of individuals could scarcely be imagined. 'There is only one sense in which any such grouping of us acquires some significance – we all got started on our careers before the War. This was, I believe, an advantage.'[4] But Lewis was a writer with a strong sense of living in history, and before this remark he indicates, from the standpoint of 1937, what he thinks will be the future estimation of the achievement of 'the Men of 1914'.

> For forty years Shaw and Wells had been Fabians first and literary artists afterwards. Even Wilde had been a great outcast first and was never more than a minor poet. What I think history will say about 'the Men of 1914' is that they represent an attempt to get away from romantic art into classical art, away from political propaganda back into the detachment of true litera- ture: just as in painting Picasso has represented the desire to terminate the Nineteenth Century alliance of painting and natural science. And what has happened – slowly – as a result of the War, is that artistic expression has slipped back again into political propaganda and romance, which go to- gether. The attempt at objectivity has failed. The subjectivity of the majority is back again, as a result of that great defeat, the Great War, and all that has ensued upon it.[5]

Putting in parentheses the personal and period biases of Lewis's statement – par- ticularly his belief that 'the Men of 1914' represent 'classical' objectivity – the general historical distinctions he outlines are useful as a description of the sequen- tial phases of late nineteenth- and early twentieth-century English literary culture. Lewis distinguishes 'the Men of 1914', who emerged as a distinct force in the decade of the Great War, both from the aesthetes of the 1890s and the left-wing secular meliorists Wells and Shaw, whose work he regards as being marred by a predominance of 'ideas', and continues by suggesting that their dynamic achieve- ment was not sustained or responded to in the post-war period. 'We are not only "the last men of an epoch" (as Mr. Edmund Wilson and others have said): we are more than that, or we are that in a different way to what is most often asserted. *We are the first men of a Future that has not materialized.* We belong to a "great age" that has not "come off".'[6] Writing in 1937, with the hostile ideologies of Fascism and Communism contending for dominance, Lewis is aware that this decade represents a new and distinct cultural phase of political commitment: 'no one in 1937 can help being other than political. We are in politics up to our necks'. He describes a meeting with Auden in the late 1920s: 'I felt I was being interviewed by an emissary of some highly civilized power – perhaps over-civilized – who had considered that something had to be done about me and so one of its most able negotiators had been sent along to sound me out.'[7]

Lewis's schema is incomplete and partisan, but he does outline the major cultural and historical shifts which help us to place and comprehend T. S. Eliot's achievement in the period of 1914 to 1922. In terms of the development of English poetry and Eliot's career, the most significant emphases are firstly, the assimilation of Symbolist poetics into the English cultural environment, which went along with aestheticism in the 1890s; then the achievements of the decade of the Great War, which at least retrospectively can be characterized by the rivalry of the Georgian and Imagist 'schools' of poetry. Lewis subsequently describes the political and ideological commitments which characterized the 1930s, during which time Auden became a prestigious and influential figure. Beyond the period with which I am even indirectly concerned, and effectively almost beyond the active writing careers of Lewis and Eliot, came the emergence and consolidation of mass culture which marked the 1950s. Although mass culture achieved dominant expression only in the 1950s, it could be perceived as a threat to an exclusive literary and poetic culture far earlier; this was a development which Lewis, Pound and Eliot all explicitly disapproved of and feared. In the decade of the Great War a mediated response to the threat of mass culture can be perceived in many of their pronouncements, both in their general hostility to 'commercialism' and the rule of the majority, and in particular statements, such as that of Eliot in the *Egoist* of May 1918, that 'the forces of deterioration are a large crawling mass, and the forces of development half a dozen men'.[8] Although this is not an area with which I shall be directly concerned, the gradual emergence of mass culture is a central factor in assessing the anti-humanist and anti-democratic cultural and political stance of these and other major writers (such as W. B. Yeats) of the early twentieth century.

It is possible to relate the trajectory of Eliot's career as a poet to these general cultural emphases. The early poetry, culminating in 'The Love Song of J. Alfred Prufrock', written under the influence of Jules Laforgue, can be aligned with (though not assimilated to) late Victorian Symbolism, while the poetry of the years 1914 to 1922 leading up to the publication of *The Waste Land* belongs with the modernist achievements of the other 'Men of 1914'. Eliot's next major poem and stylistic shift comes with the publication of *Ash-Wednesday* in 1930. Here the effects of Eliot's reception into the Anglican Church in 1927 can be aligned with and seen to anticipate the intellectual and ideological commitments which were to characterize the following decade. Eliot's final major achievement as a poet, the *Four Quartets*, published between 1935 and 1942, does not, I think, represent a new stylistic phase, but is rather an integration of previous poetic modes within what is, as in *Ash-Wednesday*, a predominantly symbolist aesthetic. While a reading of Eliot's poetic career along the lines of this broad historical grid must necessarily be approximate, it is intended to supplement rather than replace a reading of his poetic development on its own terms.

The eccentricity of Eliot's achievement as a poet needs to be specified before the qualities of his poetry can be fruitfully engaged with. It is hard to think of any major poet who wrote fewer lines, or one who includes in the divisions of his

Collected Poems (1963) the categories of 'Unfinished Poems' and 'Minor Poems', both of which are kept distinct from the final dismissive rubric of 'Occasional Verses'. Eliot was a poet who found the production of poetry exacting and difficult, who compulsively reworked material and frequently felt that he had 'dried up'. Individual poems or sequences tend to achieve signficance in the context of Eliot's *oeuvre* not just because of the dense linguistic investment of his best poetry, but because they serve as markers for successive phases of his career. There is a critical tendency to view Eliot's career according to a retrospective teleology as a dialectical progression in which the 'thesis', the sceptical, ironic, social engagement of the early poetry up to *The Waste Land* (1922) is succeeded by the 'antithesis' of *Ash-Wednesday* in which the poet withdraws into the self-enclosed Symbolist universe of his spiritual concerns, to be completed by the final 'synthesis' of *Four Quartets* in which the poet achieves a range and ease of discourse which was not previously available to him and which marks the culmination (and conclusion) of his poetic career.

Since Eliot himself encourages this reading by the strategic lay-out of *Collected Poems* it is certainly justifiable as a means of grasping the total shape of his *oeuvre*; but as it is a reading by hindsight (even by the poet himself) it is attended by certain critical dangers, particularly that of reading Eliot's later poetry and ideological commitments (I am thinking of his religious commitment) into his earlier work. Though it is impossible not to do this to some degree, this tendency can obscure the historical particularity of individual poems and the various choices Eliot had open to him when those poems were written. While it would be a perverse exercise to try to read Eliot's poetry up to *The Waste Land* (1922) as if he had never written another line, there is, I think, some purpose in trying to view the work Eliot produced in the years 1914 to 1922 as belonging to a distinct cultural configuration (which I characterize in the next chapter as 'The Moment of *Blast*') and as being consistent with the work of the other 'Men of 1914', as well as representing a distinct stage in Eliot's personal poetic development.

In *Blasting and Bombardiering* Lewis is in no doubt about the particularity of this historical and cultural 'moment' and he justifiably relates it outwards to European rather than solely English culture. 'I have said "the Men of 1914". But we were not the only people with something to be proud about at that time. Europe was full of titanic stirrings and snortings – a new art coming to flower to celebrate or to announce a "new age".'[9] In retrospect, Lewis sees this new art as having been aborted by the effects of the Great War: 'the day was lost for art, at Sarajevo. World politics stepped in, and a war was started which has not ended yet: a "war to end war". But it merely ended art. It did not end war.'[10] This does not, however, obviate the significance of what was achieved.

A few arts were born in the happy lull before the world-storm. In 1914 a ferment of the artistic intelligence occurred in the west of Europe. And it looked to many people as if a great historical 'school' was in the process of formation. Expressionism, Post-impressionism, Vorticism, Cubism,

Futurism were some of the characteristic nicknames bestowed upon these manifestations, where they found their intensest expression in the pictorial field. In every case the structural and philosophic rudiments of life were sought out. On all hands a return to first principles was witnessed.[11]

In the literary sphere, the years during and immediately after the First World War witnessed an unprecedented concentration of literary masterpieces: major works by Proust, Valéry, Apollinaire, Kafka, Hofmannsthal, Pasternak and Mandelstam among many others – a tide of literary achievement which reached its high-water mark from the standpoint of English literature (though 'English' is strictly a misnomer), in 1922, with the publication of *The Waste Land* and Joyce's *Ulysses*. After this date it was as if a cultural and historical force had expended itself: little was produced on a scale to match the achievements of the past, allowing Lewis to suggest that 'by the end of this century the movement to which, historically, I belong will be as remote as predynastic Egyptian statuary'.[12] In the following chapters I wish to trace the development of Eliot's poetry within the focus provided by Lewis's phrase, 'the Men of 1914'; but before entering into that discussion I would like briefly to discuss certain aspects of the intellectual and critical genealogy of this study.

ii

Here then, in the revolt against exteriority, against rhetoric, against a materialist tradition, in this endeavour to disengage the ultimate essence, the soul of whatever exists and can be realized by the consciousness; in this dutiful waiting upon every symbol by which the soul of things may be made visible; literature, bowed down by so many burdens, may at last attain liberty, and its authentic speech. In attaining this liberty, it accepts a heavier burden; for in speaking to us so intimately, so solemnly, as only religion has hitherto spoken to us, it becomes itself a kind of religion, with all the duties and responsibilities of the sacred ritual.

> Arthur Symons, *The Symbolist Movement in Literature*.

[h]istory tells us that there is no such thing as a timeless essence of literature, but under the rubric 'literature' (itself quite recent, moreover) a process of very different forms, functions, institutions, reasons, and projects whose relativity it is precisely the historian's responsibility to discern.

> Roland Barthes, 'The Two Criticisms', *Critical Essays*.

When the first research and writing of this project was undertaken, it was conceived of as a socio-literary study – which is not the same as a study in the area defined as the 'sociology of literature'. I wished to both site and elicit the social intentionality of the literary text from within the text itself rather than by referring outwards to social and historical formations. Thus, I sought an inductive rather than a deductive method in which the text rather than its historical situation retained a conceptual priority. In attempting to achieve this aim the work of then contemporary radical literary theoreticians, such as Frederic Jameson, Pierre Macherey and Raymond Williams, was less helpful than two relatively unsophisticated and critically outmoded French post-war studies of the relation between literature and society: Sartre's *What Is Literature?* and Barthes's *Writing Degree Zero*, which is unashamedly indebted to Sartre's study.

Sartre's uneven polemic text was relevant largely on account of its third chapter, 'For Whom Does One Write?', in which he attempts to sketch out a brief history of the social situation of the writer, the necessary mediating term between literary text and social and historical formations. For Sartre, both the writer and the reader are 'situated' by their 'historicity'. 'Authors also are historical beings; and it is precisely for that reason that certain of them desire to escape history by a leap into eternity. Between those men who are involved in the same history and who equally contribute to making it, an historical contact establishes itself by the mediation of the book.'[13] Sartre emphasizes that the social situation of the writer (he uses the word 'situation' rather than the determinative term 'condition'), understood as the historic relation between the writer and his 'real' as opposed to 'virtual' public, and the ideological and financial nexus between the two, plays a crucial role in influencing the choice of values and ethics available to the writer. Thus, writing of French Classicism in the seventeenth century, Sartre describes a set of quasi-objective social and economic conditions which are to some degree common to the writers of this period and which influence the possible forms of expression in their work. 'There was no point in them deciding for each work what was the sense and the value of literature, since that sense and that value are fixed by tradition; strongly integrated into a hierarchical society, they knew neither the pride nor the anguish of singularity; in a word they were classicists.'[14]

To Sartre, during the Revolutionary period the writer was empowered to take up a more dynamic role as critic of society and spokesman for 'universal man'. 'Placed by an extreme chance between confused aspirations and an ideology in ruins, like the writer between the bourgeoisie, the Church and the Court, [literature] suddenly affirmed its independence: it no longer reflected the communal ties of the collectivity, it identified itself with the Spirit, that is to say with the permanent power to form and criticize ideas.'[15] During the Revolutionary period this served the purposes of the bourgeoisie; but subsequently the writer was abandoned in the role of impotent critic when, after 1848, the class society of the nineteenth century was stabilized and the bourgeoisie found that social criticism and speaking for the oppressed no longer suited their purposes. The link between the writer and the privileged classes was broken and the writer was set adrift in the literary 'market' of the nineteenth century with a problematic relation to an inevitably bourgeois readership. From the standpoint of the development of English literature it should be added that one fundamental aspect of the passage from a society of rank to one of class which received conclusive expression during the Revolutionary period was the final decline of the traditional patronage relation between writer and public; this is a crucial enabling factor behind many of the distinctive features of Romantic literature.

Sartre's achievement in the 'For Whom Does One Write?' chapter of *What is Literature?* was to employ the analysis of the writer's relationship to the public to define the broad ideological determinants operating in successive historical periods, determinants which can be regarded as influencing the range of social ethics available for the writer to espouse in his work. However, Sartre's treatment, as we might expect, extends far more to 'content' than to 'form'. Barthes's advance in *Writing Degree Zero* was to relate such influences and social signifi-cations to the area of genre, language and what can be broadly termed literary 'form'. In order to do this Barthes proposes the concept of *écriture*, which can be defined as the ethos of language a writer adopts in the face of his historical situ-ation. 'Now every Form is also a Value, which is why there is room, between a language and a style, for another formal reality: writing. Within any literary form, there is a general choice of tone, of ethos, if you like, and this is precisely where the writer shows himself clearly as an individual because this is where he commits himself.'[16] This ethos will be realized as much by the formal processes and allusive aspects of language as by the paraphrasable 'content' of the writer's work; in discussing it we must pay attention to connotational meanings: that which is implied by tone and literary form.

It is this conceptual proposition, rather than the details of Barthes's analysis and his historical schemas – which contain many ambiguities – that is of value to this study. (For example, he never engages with the question of how far the writer is free to choose his *écriture* within the limits of the broad, Sartrean, historical determinations he proposes.) However, among Barthes's formal and stylistic suggestions it is worth noting his belief that the late nineteenth- and early twentieth-century problematic of literature – seen as the writer's choice of attitude to the literary forms which comprise the institution of literature, with its implicit class biases – can be traced back to the disruption of bourgeois ideology which Barthes places in the 1850s.

> Until then, it was bourgeois ideology itself which gave the measure of the universal by fulfilling it unchallenged. The bourgeois writer, sole judge of other people's woes and without anyone else to gaze on him, was not torn between his social condition and his intellectual vocation. Henceforth, this very ideology appears merely as one among many possible others . . . It is at this moment that modes of writing begin to multiply. Each one, henceforth, be it the highly-wrought, populist, neutral or colloquial, sets itself up as the initial act whereby the writer acknowledges or repudiates his bourgeois condition.[17]

The general debt of this study to Sartre's and Barthes's books should not be exaggerated: it is certainly a critical debt, the details of which have been largely subsumed in the act of writing. While it would be possible to enter into a general critique of both works (which would mean contesting points that both writers themselves would later have disavowed) it is more relevant to the areas of debate engaged with in this study to consider a particular point, which is the exception, by both authors (Sartre explicitly, Barthes ambiguously), of poetry from the historical process they describe. In Sartre's case, the instrumentality of prose is opposed to poetry. 'In fact, the poet pulled back at one go from the instrumentality of language; he chose once and for all the poetic attitude which considers words as things and not as signs.'[18] This excepting of poetry from the 'committed' nature of literary language is convincingly replied to by Raymond Williams who, following Adorno, states that Sartre complicates his argument 'by an artificial distinction between poetry and prose, reserving the inevitability of commitment to the ''meanings'' of the prose-writer and seeing meaning and emotion in the poem as transformed into ''things'', beyond this dimension. Adorno's critique of this position is convincing. The artificial separation of prose reduces writing, beyond the reserved area of poetry, to a conceptual status, and leaves all questions of commitment *in writing* unanswered.'[19]

Barthes follows Sartre in claiming the radical autonomy of poetic language and in *Writing Degree Zero* the ensuing confusion is easy to demonstrate since Barthes attempts to integrate this literary absolutism *within* his historical analysis. In the chapter 'Is there any poetic *écriture*?' Barthes distinguishes categorically between 'classical' writing (both poetry and prose) and 'modern' poetry, which to Barthes begins with Rimbaud, on the basis that the relational, socialized nature of Classical poetry is entirely abandoned by modern poetry, which 'initiates a discourse full of gaps and full of lights, filled with absences and over-nourished signs, without foresight or stability of intention, and thereby so opposed to the social function of language that merely to have recourse to a discontinuous speech is to open the door to all that stands above Nature'.[20] Barthes concludes, 'At such a point, it is hardly possible to speak of a poetic mode of writing, for this is a language in which a violent drive towards autonomy destroys any ethical scope.'[21]

This is seeing and not seeing. It is strange for Barthes to be offering us what is to all intents and purposes an essentialist definition of the non-communicatory nature of modern poetry, although he has previously conceded the socialized nature of Classical poetry in writing that 'Classical poetry is felt to be merely an ornamental variation of prose, the fruit of an *art* (that is, a technique), never a different language, or the product of a particular sensibility'.[22] If Barthes's remarks are only applicable to modern poetry then it would surely be more consistent with his own argument in *Writing Degree Zero* to see this attempt by modern poetry to neutralize the communicatory, discursive elements of poetic discourse as having in itself a social and historic function. There is, to utilize Barthes's own terms, an implicit ethical gesture in that eschewal of 'ethical scope' which he considers removes the possibility of discussing a 'poetic mode of writing'. A linguistic practice which proclaims its own solitude proclaims that solitude as social fact.

This ambiguity or error is one that Adorno does not make. While Barthes's terms are adequate as a generalized description of modern poetry, as a prescriptive definition they fall foul of his own relativizing historical argument. Adorno, however, by grasping the significance of the Hegelian categories of 'negation' and 'contradiction' to cultural forms, is able to perceive the asocial in its more fundamental guise of social negativity: a social gesture rejecting the societal. Thus, in his essay 'Lyric and Society', Adorno claims, as Jameson puts it, that, 'the work of art "reflects" society and is historical to the degree that it *refuses* the social, and represents the last refuge of individual subjectivity from the historical forces that threaten to crush it'.[23] More generally, in the essay on 'Commitment', Adorno, agreeing with Sartre that the work of art is 'its own gesture towards reality', argues that

> It only remains to add that there is no straightforward relationship between this appeal and the thematic commitment of a work. The uncalculated autonomy of works which avoid popularization and adaptation to the market, involuntarily becomes an attack on them. The attack is not abstract, not a fixed attitude of all works of art to the world which will not forgive them for not bending totally to it. The distance these works maintain from empirical reality is itself partly mediated by that reality. The imagination of the artist is not a creation *ex nihilo*; only dilettanti and aesthetes believe it to be so. Works of art that react against empirical reality obey the forces of that reality, which reject intellectual creations and throw them back on themselves. There is no material content, no formal category of an artistic creation, however mysteriously changed and unknown to itself, which did not originate in the empirical reality from which it breaks free.[24]

Adorno's 'dialectical' position can be regarded as more than just a corrective to the stance adopted by Sartre and Barthes: I hope that it is consistent with the method employed here. But it is important to realize that Sartre's and Barthes's exclusion of poetry from the historical process is not a neutral intellectual decision, but is informed by the aesthetic and subsequent critical ideology which confirmed, and to some degree contributed to, the 'reified' aspect of modern poetry which they sought to describe. The aesthetic of Symbolism, formulated in the late nineteenth century, endorses their stance, and can be seen as underlying the dominant French and Anglo-American critical ideology and practice, especially as regards poetry, throughout the twentieth century and up to the present.

Symbolist aesthetics were initially formulated as a considered literary reaction against French nineteenth-century materialist, positivist theories of literary creation, which, as in Taine's *Philosophie de l'Art*, sought to reduce artistic creation to social and material determinants, 'laws' governed by such categories as 'Race', 'Milieu', and 'Moment'. This reactive background to Symbolist aesthetics is discussed in Lehmann's *The Symbolist Aesthetic in France (1885–1895)*,[25] in which he states that 'The first and most striking feature of the symbolist aesthetic was its attempt to establish art as an autonomous branch of human activity', and outlines how the Symbolists adopted the alternative intellectual tradition of German idealism, as represented by Kant, Fichte, Schelling, Hegel and Schopenhauer, in order to do so. However, Symbolist aesthetics were not just the concern of critics and theorists, but also an attempt by poets to formulate a working aesthetic which would, negatively, assert the dignity of their art by repudiating reductionist, determinist explanations of the literary work, and, as a more positive corollary, would confute the utilitarian, bourgeois ideology of the nineteenth century by claiming poetry as an autonomous preserve of the imagination. This leads, as Lehmann puts it, to 'a critical preoccupation with language as such, in the widest sense – the artist's peculiar field'.[26]

Symbolism's demand for the aesthetic autonomy of poetry – the poem as a self-sufficient, non-referential entity – has its place as a necessary reaction against the mechanical, reductionist tendencies of nineteenth-century positivism; but it also has a continuing history as a successful critical ideology, which has proved adaptable and able to meet more contemporary needs. General critical considerations cannot here be kept distinct from the subject of this study: for both Yeats, and perhaps even more influentially, T. S. Eliot (who learnt of Symbolism from Symons's *The Symbolist Movement in Literature* in 1908)[27] were instrumental in establishing and popularizing Symbolist aesthetics in the twentieth-century Anglo-American cultural environment. Moreover, it was the Symbolist premises of Eliot's early criticism that informed and empowered the 'New Criticism', according to (or at least not conflicting with) the tenets of which most available Eliot criticism has been written.

In so far as Eliot criticism has complied with the post-Symbolist demand for the self-referentiality of the text, it has, as in the 'New Criticism', elected to work under a set of intellectual paradoxes. For example, in claiming that the work has no discursive, conceptual content – the heresy of paraphrase – and at the same time contesting the mimetic, referential function of literary language (the heresy of extra-literary context), the 'New Criticism' should logically have elected total silence before the poem. Instead it employed paraphrase and other 'questionable' modes and exposed its fundamental contradictions (while achieving some useful criticism). As Gerald Graff suggests in *Literature Against Itself*,[28] a criticism which works with such disabling premises as 'a poem must not mean but be' (a caricatural but not entirely inaccurate portrayal of the New Critical stance) can be no more than atomistic and empirical; fleeing the demon of reductivism, it locks itself in a room where connections with social reality are made but are conceptual paradoxes.

The substance of what by now is a standard polemic against the 'New Criticism' is usefully and pertinently extended by Frank Lentricchia's *After the New Criticism*,[29] in which he argues that rather than responding to the challenge of the early semiotic work of Roland Barthes, American deconstructive criticism has, in embracing the work of Jacques Derrida, used it as an occasion to rework the formalist assumptions of the New Criticism while continuing to evade an engagement with the social functions and resonances of literary texts. Lentricchia's position can serve to suggest what from the standpoint of this study, is the main methodological flaw of the New Criticism (and, one might suggest, the Newer Criticism): a tendency to partition 'history' and 'text', defining history as 'context', instead of locating history *within* the text, in the meanings and forms it offers and allows. In focusing this book on Pound's *Criterion* statement, I intended

to write a comparative, historical study which would locate the social intentionality of a body of poetry notoriously resistant to any discussion of 'meanings'.
Previous Eliot criticism has fought shy of attempting this (largely because of the
methodological assumptions outlined above), and it is in the treatment of its subject area that the larger originality of this study resides. Thus, while I acknowledge my immense debt to previous Eliot criticism, which sets the boundaries for
any possible discourse, and concede that most of the material herein discussed has
been discussed before, I am not aware there is another critical text which attempts
to treat the same body of material in a similar way. Finally, I hope this book retains
something of its original intention, which was to open up critical issues rather
than to foreclose them in deference to cultural and critical orthodoxies.

1
The Moment of *Blast*

Really all this organized disturbance was Art behaving as if it were Politics
. . . It may in fact have been politics. I see that now.

Lewis, Blasting and Bombardiering

The purpose of this first chapter is to outline the cultural context in which Eliot returned to the writing of poetry after his arrival in England in August 1914 and his subsequent contact with Ezra Pound in September of that year. Eliot's work has its place within a larger formation of intellectual currents existing in the period immediately before and during the First World War, although some of these short-lived tendencies have not received due recognition in critical debate. In the first section of this chapter I shall discuss T. E. Hulme's anti-humanist philosophy and, in particular, his negative analysis of Romanticism, in order to elucidate its generic similarity to Eliot's own developing cultural and political stance. This analysis of Hulme's philosophy of art leads into a discussion of the practising cultural politics of the Vorticist propaganda magazine *Blast*, in which Wyndham Lewis and Ezra Pound made many significant aesthetic and cultural pronouncements. The third section is devoted to a consideration of Pound's post-Imagist poetics, which led directly to the adoption by both himself and Eliot of Théophile Gautier's 'sculptured' quatrains in 1916–17.

Eliot's initial literary alliances were formed swiftly enough to allow the first British publication of his poetry, that of 'Preludes' and 'Rhapsody on a Windy Night', to be in *Blast* (2), the final and war-time edition. Alone, this is little more than a contingent historical fact, but it does serve to introduce the larger argument of this chapter, which is that *Blast*, published in July 1914, represents a distinct and unreproducible 'moment' in British culture and that to fully comprehend the work that Eliot produced in the subsequent years it is necessary to consider the intellectual and artistic climate in which his work is consistent with a constellation of distinctively oppositional 'modernist' art. This chapter will not concentrate upon Eliot directly, but upon the specific cultural and intellectual milieu of the years leading into the First World War; and since the focus of the chapter is upon *Blast* and the cross-fertilization between the visual and literary arts that marked the co-operation between Wyndham Lewis and Ezra Pound, much of the discussion will centre upon the visual arts and the possibility of delineating a particular 'politics of style' within this period.

Wyndham Lewis produced *Blast* in 1914 to propagandize the work of the Vorticist artists and, in addition to various strident manifestos and articles in which he attempted to define the Vorticists as Britain's first abstract art movement, he also included literary material: manifestos and poems from his friend and associate Ezra Pound; his own harsh, ritualistic psychodrama *The Enemy of the Stars*; a short story by the young Rebecca West; and forthcoming chapters from Ford Madox Ford's ambitious modernist novel, *The Saddest Story*, subsequently entitled *The Good Soldier*. Lewis was later to complain of the diverse nature of the material that went into *Blast*, expressing the opinion that much of it did not conform with the harsh anti-traditionalist tone of the main manifestos and the art that was reproduced therein; but from a wider viewpoint *Blast* can be seen as drawing together various, not necessarily mutually compatible, avant-garde strands in a precarious moment of co-operation and synthesis.

Blast remained, however, primarily a means of publicizing and defining the Vorticist artists. The short but eventful history of the Vorticist movement had begun barely a year before the publication of *Blast* and can be conveniently dated by Lewis's quarrel with Roger Fry and abandonment of the Omega workshop scheme in October 1913. Previously, Lewis and his colleagues Etchells, Wadsworth and Cuthbert Hamilton had co-operated with a nucleus of Bloomsbury artists (Vanessa Stephens, Clive Bell and Duncan Grant) under the presiding influence of Roger Fry. Fry was the man who had introduced post-Impressionism and, in particular, the later work of Cézanne to England and he was therefore well placed to perceive the obvious analogies between these artists in their moves away from representational art towards 'pure form'.[1]

The period of co-operation was brief. Personal antagonisms between Fry and Lewis precipitated an acrimonious public parting which was underwritten by fundamental differences in artistic intention between Lewis's group, who were receptive to the influence of Marinetti and Italian Futurism, and the primarily decorative and domestic aims of the Omega group (see Figure 1). Lewis was to borrow from the Futurists their aggressive and strident propaganda techniques, their glorification of the machine age and dynamic approach to the possibilities of abstraction – elements that allowed Lewis to express his dissent from the pacific Omega group in unequivocal terms: 'This family party of strayed and Dissenting Aesthetes, however, were compelled to call in as much modern talent as they could find, to do the rough and masculine work without which they knew their efforts would not rise above the level of a pleasant tea-party, or command more attention.'[2]

However, emergent Vorticism wished to do more than distinguish itself from other native art movements/coteries: it wished to establish itself as independent of and distinct from the dominant continental abstractionist movements of this period, Italian Futurism (Figure 2) and French Cubism (Figure 3). It was particularly problematic for Vorticism to differentiate itself from Futurism since it had developed partly as a response to Futurism's urban dynamism and the pre-Dadaist aggression of Marinetti's art 'happenings'; but Lewis was able to make a crucial distinction in his independent catalogue introduction to 'The Cubist Room' in December 1913, in which he argued that

> All revolutionary painting today has in common the rigid reflections of steel and stone in the spirit of the artist; that desire for stability as though a machine were being built to fly or kill with; an alienation from the traditional photographer's trade and realization of the value of colour and form as such independently of what recognizable form it covers and encloses.[3]

Here, in his stress upon stability and rigidity, Lewis outlines the main point of dissent between Vorticism and Futurism, which glorified mechanical motion and speed and sought in its art to express movement through the fragmentation and displacement of lines, planes and surfaces.

At this point the Vorticists were to discover an influential champion in the person of the eccentric and pugnacious philosopher of art and polemicist T. E. Hulme. Hulme had played an important role in the early history of Imagism in 1908–9, a debt that Pound was to acknowledge by publishing 'The Complete Poetical Works of T. E. Hulme' (five poems) as an appendix to his *Ripostes* collection of 1912. However, Hulme was interested in wider cultural issues and just as he had predicted the downfall of Romantic poetry in his celebrated essay 'Romanticism and Classicism', he now used emergent Vorticism as the occasion to forecast, in 'Modern Art and Its Philosophy' (January 1914), the end of the Renaissance tradition of naturalism and the rebirth of an older tradition of geometrical art. Arguing with close reference to the work of Jacob Epstein and Lewis, Hulme distinguished the art he was concerned with from Futurism, which he regarded as 'the exact opposite of the art I am describing, being the deification of the flux, the last efflorescence of impressionism', and analytic Cubism with its 'theories about interpenetration'[4] to assert that 'the new "tendency towards abstraction"' will culminate not so much in the simple geometrical forms found in archaic art, but in the more complicated ones associated in our minds with the idea of machinery'.[5]

Hulme's lecture was followed by a series of partisan articles on 'Modern Art' in *The New Age*, in which he wrote on the work of Lewis, Bomberg, Wadsworth, Hamilton, Nevinson and the sculptor Jacob Epstein (Figure 4). Hulme, however, was a close personal friend of Epstein and was not happy with the move towards complete abstraction which some other Vorticist artists were making; he preferred figuration translated into harsh mechanical shapes. This was one reason why he did not participate in the fully fledged Vorticist movement when it arrived. Another is that Lewis, who had now established The Rebel Arts Centre as a clear retort to the Omega workshop, feared Hulme's influence and his preference for Epstein's work. He caused a violent quarrel with Hulme, centred upon their rivalry for the favour of the artist Kate Lechmere – who had financed the centre –

a quarrel which, according to Lewis, resulted in him being hung upside down by his trouser turn-ups from the tall iron railings in Soho Square.[6]

Lewis was able to establish the movement and provide it with an identity in June 1914 when Marinetti and his only notable English follower, Nevinson (Figure 5), issued a *Futurist Manifesto: Vital English Art* under the imprint of the Rebel Arts Centre, co-opting the names of the associated artists. This served to pull together a fractious and disparate group of individuals in opposition to Futurism and Lewis was able to issue *Blast* as a *Manifesto of the Vorticists* in July 1914. Here, in formulations which are essentially Lewis's own, Vorticism was defined as an austere Northern art which capitalized on Britain's industrial heritage, but which, in contrast to the sentimental and romantic celebrations of technology characteristic of Futurism, practised an attitude of classical detachment from the machine civilization it explored and exploited. Vorticism was defined as poised between the Futurist obsession with kinetics and the static, studio-based inspiration of the Cubists, seeking to produce an original synthesis that employed precise linear definition to produce an effect of tension and stasis that reflected the mechanical complexities of modern life (Figure 6). As Richard Cork writes, 'a typical Vorticist design shoots outwards in iconoclastic shafts, zig-zags or diagonally oriented fragments, and at the same time asserts the need for a solidly impacted, almost sculptural order'.[7]

The Vorticist artists were given barely a year to produce a body of work exemplifying Lewis's claims before active service in the First World War and critical neglect and incomprehension proved sufficient to destroy the movement's impetus. A second and final war number of *Blast* was issued in July 1915, with a suitably muted monochrome cover (Figure 7). In it, the death of the enormously gifted young sculptor, Gaudier-Brzeska, was announced at the foot of his second 'Vortex' manifesto in which, with what has become the most savage retrospective irony, he declared

THIS WAR IS A GREAT REMEDY.

IN THE INDIVIDUAL IT KILLS ARROGANCE, SELF-ESTEEM, PRIDE.

IT TAKES AWAY FROM THE MASSES NUMBERS UPON NUMBERS OF UNIMPORTANT UNITS, WHOSE ECONOMIC ACTIVITIES BECOME NOXIOUS AS THE RECENT TRADE CRISES HAVE SHOWN US.

'MY VIEWS ON SCULPTURE' REMAIN ABSOLUTELY 'THE SAME',

IT IS THE 'VORTEX' OF WILL, OF DECISION, THAT BEGINS.[8]

T. E. Hulme was killed in September 1917; but by that date the movement had already receded into the past and a commission from the Canadian War Memorial Fund in 1918 saw several of the artists retreating into what can be described as a highly stylized naturalism. Though Vorticism had actually contributed to the war effort through Wadsworth's development of abstract camouflage, it is hard to avoid the conclusion that mechanical aggression had lost its glamour for the Vorticist artists. The movement seemed to have passed into history as little more than a footnote, leaving Pound and Lewis to look back nostalgically upon an achievement that was destroyed almost at the moment it came to fruition: 'a Future that has not materialized'. It had seemed that the future might be very different when Hulme used his Quest Society lecture to predict the downfall of Renaissance humanism in January 1914.

i T. E. Hulme's 'new attitude of mind'

In 1914, in a paper on 'Modern Art and Its Philosophy' delivered to the Quest Society in Cambridge, T. E. Hulme argued, with reference to the new abstractionist art of the Vorticists, that 'the re-emergence of geometrical art may be the precursor of the re-emergence of the corresponding attitude towards the world, and so, of the break up of the Renaissance humanistic attitude'. Hulme's suggestion can be referred to the statement he made in 'Humanism and the Religious Attitude'.

> The questions of Original Sin, of chastity, of the motives behind Buddhism, etc., all part of the very essence of the religious spirits, are quite incomprehensible for humanism. The difference is seen perhaps most obviously in art. At the Renaissance, there were many pictures with religious subjects, but no religious art in the proper sense of the word. All the emotions expressed are perfectly human ones. Those who choose to think that religious emotion is only the highest form of the emotions that fall inside the humanist ideology, may call this religious art, but they will be wrong. When the intensity of the religious attitude finds proper expression in art, then you get a very different result. Such expression springs not from a delight in life but from a feeling for certain absolute values, which are entirely independent of vital things. The disgust with the trivial and accidental characteristics of living shapes, the searching after an austerity, a monumental stability and performance, a perfection and rigidity, which vital things can never have, leads to the use of forms which can almost be called geometrical. (Cf. Byzantine, Egyptian and early Greek art.) If we think of physical science as represented by geometry, then instead of saying that the modern progress away from materialism has been from physics through vitalism to the absolute values of religion, we may say that it is from *geometry through life and back to geometry*.[9]

While with the benefit of hindsight it is easy to perceive that Hulme was mistaken both in his belief in the intrinsic anti-vitalist bias of Vorticist art and his conviction that he was witnessing the supersession of Renaissance humanism, what remains is the sense Hulme gives of the hectic, almost frenetic intellectual and artistic excitement of the years that led into the First World War and the confidence with which he proclaims his belief in a fundamental cultural change. But, significantly, this was a cultural change based upon fundamentally reactionary premises.

Though it has been conceded in critical debate, often with dismay, that of the four 'Men of 1914' – Lewis himself, Pound, Eliot and Joyce – the first three display a conjunction between reactionary politics and avant-garde art, too little attention has been paid to the historic rationale of this phenomenon. Though Hulme's sche-matic cultural analyses do not have any wide historical generality, it is in this context that he becomes an interesting, if not representative, figure. Despite much previous critical confusion it is likely that Eliot's acquaintance with Hulme's ideas did not, as had been generally accepted, begin with the posthumous publication of *Speculations* in 1924, but much earlier. A. R. Orage, the former editor of *The New Age* had encouraged Herbert Read to undertake the editing of *Speculations*, the publication of which stimulated Eliot's first major writing on cultural politics in the April 1924 edition of his own magazine *The Criterion*, in which he declared that Hulme

> appears as the forerunner of a new attitude of mind, which should be the twentieth-century mind, if the twentieth century is to have a mind of its own. Hulme is classical, reactionary, and revolutionary; he is the antipodes of the eclectic, tolerant and democratic mind of the end of the last century. And his writing, his fragmentary notes and his outlines, is the writing of an individual who wished to satisfy himself before he cared to enchant a cultivated public.[10]

After this pronouncement Eliot consistently promoted Hulme's work, and that of other thinkers who accorded with his 'new attitude of mind', in the pages of *The Criterion*.[11] However, material included in the syllabus of Eliot's Oxford University Extension Lectures on 'Modern French Literature', given in 1916, the latter sections of which read very much like a primer on contemporary French re-actionary thought, makes it likely that Eliot knew of Hulme's views before that date.[12] From this perspective, Eliot's eager advocacy of Hulme's ideas in the 1920s was based not only on their congruence with his own stance, but upon prior knowledge and acceptance of a theorist who had eight years previously con-tributed to the formation of that stance.

While I would not wish to claim any facile equation between a political stance and the poetry Eliot produced between 1914 and 1922, and while the distance between Eliot and Hulme can be measured by the distance between the brash assertions of *Speculations* and the urbane Bradleyan obliquities of *The Sacred Wood*, evidence for Eliot's knowledge of Hulme's theories in this period does allow us to suggest that his philosophic, aesthetic and political views were being formulated long before the date when he had the confidence and authority to proclaim them openly in the pages of *The Criterion*. It is important, however, to realize that Hulme's ideas were not a necessary component of Eliot's thought and that Eliot's acceptance of Hulme's views (whether in 1916 or 1924) arose from a shared intellectual background from which both men derived their ideological choices: the writings of the theorists associated with the French reactionary political move-ment, the *Action Française*. Eliot, prepared by his contact with Babbitt's anti-democratic elitism at Harvard, and in particular the lectures which later formed his *Masters of French Criticism* (1912), had read Maurras's *L'Avenir de l'intelligence* by 1911[13] while Hulme openly declares his ideological allegiances in the initial section of his celebrated essay 'Romanticism and Classicism' (1911–12).

The writings and theories of the Catholic, monarchist, anti-democratic *Action Française*, formed by Charles Maurras after the Dreyfus case (1894–1906) to promote an authoritarian political solution, are of direct relevance to the work of Hulme, Eliot and, to a lesser extent, Lewis and can be regarded as a concealed influence on early Modernism. In particular the recurrent theme of 'Romanticism versus Classicism' in these writers (in the past generally dismissed as a critical red herring)[14] can only be fully understood by reference to this context. Significantly, in the early years of the decade of the Great War we find that Hulme, Eliot and Lewis follow a similar intellectual trajectory, from an enthusiasm for Henri Bergson's implicitly liberal, irrationalist and vitalist philosophy towards a gradual alignment with the authoritarian ideas of Maurras and the *Action Française*, which violently opposed everything Bergson stood for.[15] In a period of political and cultural turbulence we do not have to search far to discern the immediate attractions of the *Action Française*. Eugene Weber, in his *Action Française*, quotes Maurras to the effect that the origin of his ideas was literary and artistic rather than political. 'And so it was "by analysing the literary errors of romanticism that we were led, indeed dragged, to study the moral and political error of a State involved in revolution". There could be no beauty without order, no order without a hierarchy of values, no hierarchy without authority both to define and endorse it.'[16] The work of Charles Maurras was to provide Eliot with his most enduring cultural allegiance, a debt he was to acknowledge by the publication of *Homage à Charles Maurras* in 1948 – after Maurras, who had been a member of the Petain government, had been imprisoned for treason.

To return to Hulme's statement in 'Humanism and the Religious Attitude', we find that his commendatory definition of the 'religious attitude' is, when unpacked, as much a political as a metaphysical assertion.

> In the light of these absolute values, man himself is judged to be essentially limited and imperfect. He is endowed with Original Sin. While he can occasionally accomplish acts which partake of perfection, he can never himself *be* perfect. Certain secondary results in regard to ordinary human action in society follow from this. A man is essentially bad, he can only accomplish anything of value by discipline – ethical and political. Order is not merely negative, but creative and liberating. Institutions are necessary.[17]

This attitude, held in opposition to the 'humanist' confusion between the vital and the religious, can be located in a discourse reaching at least as far back as Joseph de Maistre, whose Christian conservatism contested what he regarded as the 'radically evil' premises of the French Revolution, employing arguments which have a family resemblance to Hulme's. As Ernst Nolte writes, glossing de Maistre's thought in an investigation of the roots of twentieth-century French reactionary politics, 'The protoreality of original sin is enough to condemn to failure the illusory dreams of the Enlightenment. If man were by nature good, he would in fact need neither authority, nor punishment.'[18] De Maistre's enemy is that utopian liberalism, conveniently located in the writings of Rousseau, which it was possible for French reactionary thinkers of the nineteenth and twentieth centuries to regard as the ideological premise not only for the Revolution's attack on social, political and religious hierarchy and authority, but also for the cultural phenomenon of Romanticism. Eliot locates himself in the same discourse as Hulme when he writes in the summary of his 1916 Oxford University Extension Lectures that 'Romanticism stands for *excess* in any direction. It splits up into two directions: escape from the world of fact, and devotion to brute fact. The two great currents of the nineteenth century – vague emotionality and the apotheosis of science (realism) alike spring from Rousseau.'[19]

Hulme's schematic 'theory of history' is based upon this contrast of the religious attitude with the humanist attitude which he sees as emerging as a new *Weltanschauung*, a new 'interpretation of life', during the Renaissance. It is not too much to say that Hulme equates the humanism of the Renaissance *with* the Renaissance. 'When a sense of the reality of these absolute values is lacking, you get a refusal to believe any longer in the radical imperfection of either Man or Nature. This develops logically into the belief that life is the source and measure of all values, and that man is fundamentally good'.[20] This anthropomorphism 'creates the bastard conception of *Personality*. In literature it leads to romanticism . . .'[21] From whence Hulme leaps to a broad historical generalization, distinguishing two periods, the first, when the dogma of original sin was dominant, 'the Middle Ages in Europe – from Augustine say, to the Renaissance', the second, when the humanist ideology is dominant, 'from the Renaissance to now'.[22] Following on from these cultural antinomies and integrating his ideas with those of the theorists of the *Action Française*, Hulme allows a subdivision in the 'modern' period: '*humanism* properly so called, and romanticism'.[23] The first 'heroic' stage, being represented by Donatello, Michelangelo or Marlowe, is conceded certain attractions; but it is ultimately to be rejected since it leads to Romanticism, which Hulme considers to be a degenerate humanism, 'spilt religion', as he puts it in a famous phrase from 'Romanticism and Classicism'.

As one would expect, Hulme's definition of Romanticism in 'Romanticism and Classicism' lies behind and is consistent with the broad lines of the original sin/humanism antithesis.

> these are the two views, then. One, that man is intrinsically good, spoilt by circumstance; and the other that he is intrinsically limited, but disciplined by order and tradition to something fairly decent . . . The view which regards man as a well, a reservoir full of possibilities, I call the romantic; the one which regards him as a very finite and limited creature, I call the classical.[24]

Hulme notes that the classical view 'is absolutely identical with the normal religious attitude', which is a belief in 'the sane classical dogma of original sin'.[25] However, in this essay Hulme explicitly concedes the polemical and political source of his definitions by stating that they 'conform to the practice of a group of polemical writers who have made most use of them at the present, and have almost succeeded in making them political catchwords. I mean Maurras, Lasserre and all the group connected with "L'Action Française".'[26] Stating that 'I make no apology for dragging in politics here; romanticism both in England and France is associated with certain political views' Hulme intends to commend his definitions by referring to a riot caused by the notorious 'Camelots du Roi' (a youth wing of the *Action Française*) in the course of a lecture in which Racine (the Classic) was disparaged. 'That is what I call a real vital interest in literature. They regard romanticism as an awful disease from which France has just recovered. The thing is complicated in their case by the fact that it was romanticism that made the revolution. They hate the revolution so they hate romanticism.'[27] Eliot, on the other hand, was rather more cautious than Hulme in commending the work of Maurras and Lasserre in his 1916 syllabus. 'Their reaction fundamentally sound, but/Marked by extreme violence and intolerance',[28] he notes in passing.

Hulme proceeds by following the French reactionary equation of Rousseau with Romanticism, though he is more crude than Eliot ever would be, in equating Romanticism with the Revolution. 'They had been taught by Rousseau that man was by nature good, that it was only bad laws and customs that had suppressed him.'[29] Thus, Hulme's definitions, by the aid of which he attempts to sort through literary history and offer a prognostication of the revival of 'dry and hard' Classical verse, are unashamedly political; and one finds Eliot, in the syllabus of his 1916 Extension Lectures, referring to the same political discourse with what is probably an implicit reference to Hulme in his final statement, when he writes that 'The beginning of the twentieth century has witnessed a return to the ideals of classicism. These may be roughly characterized as *form* and *restraint* in art, *discipline* and *authority* in religion, *centralization* in government (either as socialism or monarchy). The classicist point of view has been defined as essentially a belief in Original Sin – the necessity for austere discipline.'[30]

At this point it is worth noting how Frank Kermode in his *Romantic Image*,[31] in the course of an otherwise extremely valuable discussion of Hulme's place in the tradition of Symbolist aesthetics leading to Eliot in which he points out that Hulme's theory of history bears a family resemblance to Eliot's 'dissociation of sensibility' theory, fails crucially to appreciate the political, polemical tendencies of Hulme's later, post-Bergsonian writings. Having commented on the debt Hulme's Imagism owes to Bergson, from whom he takes his theory of 'intensive manifolds' (the intuition of an image composed of interpenetrating elements, which is not 'extensible' or discursive and which the poet has the ability to seize because he is not oriented towards the world, as are most men, in terms of 'action'), Kermode asserts that this is merely another version of the 'Romantic image', as the debt to Bergson's anti-positivism implies, and that despite Hulme's reputation as a 'Classicist', all that he is doing in 'Romanticism and Classicism' is offering a more austere version of the Romantic image – one that is finite and opposed to Romantic imprecision and striving after 'the infinite'. Kermode is correct. Hulme is substantially a Romantic thinker; what Kermode fails to do adequately is to realize the source of Hulme's antagonism to Romanticism. Instead of establishing a scholarly critique of Hulme upon the easily demonstrable fact that 'Hulme disastrously misrepresents Romantic philosophy',[32] and then being astonished by his ineptitude, it would be more to the point to acknowledge the polemical bases of Hulme's definitions, which he himself draws attention to, and note, as does his biographer, that despite his wider pretensions Hulme was attacking not Romanticism, but 'the utopian liberalism that very often went with romanticism'.[33] This is the same target as that attacked by the *Action Française* critic, Lasserre, in his *Le Romanticisme française*, which is the source for Hulme's polemical essay: 'Ces déités du romanticisme s'appelèrent l'un Nature, l'autre Progrès. Le Panthéisme en fut la synthèse.'[34] While it is essential to demonstrate, as does Kermode, that Hulme's historical generalizations are inadequate, we must first locate Hulme in the discourse to which he belongs. Despite Hulme's intentions, 'Romanticism and Classicism' is essentially a polemic with the veneer of a scholarly critique.

It is in this opposition to what is regarded as a dominant liberal-humanist ideology founded upon a belief in human perfectibility that a 'Classicist' aesthetic doctrine (which can be found in early Joyce) takes on a reactionary political inflection (which cannot be found in Joyce). Joyce, in *Stephen Hero* (1904–6), writes,

> Classicism is not the manner of any fixed age or of any fixed country: it is a constant state of the artistic mind. It is a temper of security and satisfaction and patience. The romantic temper, so often and so grievously misinterpreted and not more so by others than by its own, is an insecure, unsatisfied, impatient temper which sees no fit abode here for its ideals and chooses therefore to behold them under insensible figures. As a result of this choice it comes to disregard certain limitations. Its figures are blown to wild adventures, lacking the gravity of solid bodies, and the mind that has conceived them ends by disowning them. The classical temper on the other hand, ever mindful of limitations, chooses rather to bend upon these present things and so to work upon them and fashion them that the quick intelligence may go beyond them to their meaning which is still unuttered.[35]

Joyce's emphases are similar to those of Hulme in 'Romanticism and Classicism' (though one can discern a crucial difference of intention in the phrase 'their meaning which is still unuttered'). However in Hulme an aesthetic doctrine opposed to Romantic concentration upon temporality and historical process, with its concomitant striving after 'the infinite', takes on a definite political edge as soon as the 'finiteness' of human aspirations, and, by extension, the aesthetic image, are insisted upon.

A demand for the aesthetic 'stasis' of the art-object, is, in Stephen's purportedly neo-Aquinan definitions in *A Portrait*, a politically neutral statement; in Hulme, in 'The Philosophy of Modern Art', such views lead to anti-vitalist conclusions that elide with a political stance. Here, employing (and distorting) Worringer's recently published *Abstraction and Empathy*,[36] Hulme argues that the art of the Vorticists, being opposed to the romantic glorification of kinetics practised by Marinetti's Futurism, manifests that 'urge to abstraction' (rather than the naturalistic 'urge to empathy') which results in a divesting of the contingent, vital characteristics of living objects in favour of a mechanical, monumental 'dehumanization' of art. Hulme uses this to support his belief in the development of a new anti-humanist *Weltanschauung*. When Hulme says of one of Lewis's paintings that 'It is obvious that the artist's only interest in the human being was in a few mechanical relations perceived in it, the arm as a lever and so on. The interest in living flesh as such, in all that detail that makes it vital, which is pleasing, and which we like to see reproduced, is entirely absent',[37] he is descriptively accurate, but the political conclusions he draws from this, while they can with some qualification be applied to Lewis, cannot be generalized to apply to the Vorticist group as a whole. In general, we might well prefer the more neutral 'materialist' explanation which Hulme rejects, that 'an artist is using mechanical lines because he lives in an environment of machinery',[38] to Hulme's adaptation of Worringer's volition theory, by which the artist's primary impulse is to turn 'The organic into something not organic, it tries to change the changing and limited, into something unlimited and necessary'.[39] The 'materialist' explanation is adopted by Richard Cork in his two volume *Vorticism and Abstract Art in the First Machine Age*.[40]

More generally, as Hulme's anti-humanist emphasis on the dogma of original sin can be linked to political reaction and the theories of Maurras, Lasserre and *L'Action Française*, so his anti-vitalism, as evinced in his aesthetics, can also be seen as exhibiting a period reaction, in this case against the vitalist secularism which was prevalent in the major literature of the Edwardian period (which Richard Ellmann documents in his essay 'Two Faces of Edward'). Writing of the slippage of religious values into the secular realm, Ellmann comments,

> The Edwardians were looking for ways to express their conviction that we can be religious about life itself, and they naturally adopted metaphors offered by the religion they knew best. The capitalized word for the Edwardians is not God but life: 'What I'm really trying to render is nothing more or less than Life,' says George Ponderevo, when Wells is forty-three; 'Live,' says Strether to Little Bilham, when Henry James is sixty; 'O Life,' cries Stephen Dedalus to no one in particular when Joyce is about thirty-four; 'I am going to write a book about Life,' announces D. H. Lawrence, when he is thirty.[41]

One can discern just such a reaction against the 'religion of life' not only in Hulme's theories, but also in many of Lewis's pronouncements in *Blast* and in his first novel *Tarr*, where he takes Hulme's anti-vitalist aesthetic to its logical conclusion, to have his eponymous hero declare: 'Deadness is the first condition of art: the second is absence of soul, in the human and sentimental sense. With the statue its lines and masses are its soul, no restless inflammable ego is imagined for its interior: it has *no inside*: good art must have no inside: that is capital.'[42]

Like *Tarr* (which we will return to later), D. H. Lawrence's *Women in Love* was completed in the war years (being published in 1921; *Tarr* in 1918); the two make

a revealing comparison and contrast. In the writing of what eventually became
The Rainbow Lawrence had been influenced by Futurism, an influence he declared
in a famous letter to Edward Garnett of June 1914, where, disavowing what he
terms 'the old stable *ego* of the character', Lawrence suggests

> somehow, that which is physic – non-human in humanity, is more interest-
> ing to me than the old-fashioned human element, which causes one to con-
> ceive a character in a certain moral scheme and make him consistent . . .
> When Marinetti writes: 'It is the solidity of a blade of steel that is interesting
> by itself, that is, the uncomprehending and inhuman alliance of its molecules
> in resistance to, let us say, a bullet. The heat of a piece of wood or iron is in
> fact more passionate, for us, than the laughter or tears of a woman' – then I
> know what he means. He is stupid, as an artist, for contrasting the heat of
> the iron and the laugh of the woman. Because what is interesting in the
> laugh of the woman is the same as the binding of molecules of steel or their
> action in heat: it is the inhuman will, call it physiology, or like Marinetti
> physiology of matter, that fascinates me. I don't so much care about what
> the woman *feels* – in the ordinary usage of the word. That presumes an *ego*
> to feel with. I only care about what the woman *is* – what she IS –
> inhumanly, physiologically, materially . . .[43]

As with Lewis's practice in *Tarr*, or his Vorticist drama *The Enemy of The Stars*,
Lawrence wishes to dispense with the 'old-fashioned human element', which is
equated with sentimentality and conventional modes of understanding. But subsequently, in *Women in Love*, Lawrence's critical and cultural acumen having been
sharpened by the European war, we find what is at once a complex employment
of, and critical response to, such potentially dehumanizing tendencies. In the main
body of the text this issue is focused through Lawrence's treatment of the young
industrialist Gerald Crich and in the final chapters takes the form of a 'vitalist'
retort, delivered through Ursula's violently negative comments on the
abstractionist, dehumanizing sculptor, Loerke. The critique itself, however, must
remain fundamentally ambiguous, given Lawrence's own aesthetic commitment
to not entirely dissimilar modes of reification.

Before going on to the active cultural politics of *Blast*, it should be noted that
these sharp cultural frictions and antinomies are about more than questions of
intellectual fashion. While, on one level, such engagements with modes of
reification and anti-vitalism clearly demonstrate a mediated response to
technological change and the development of an urban and industrial 'mass'
society (the population of Britain had quadrupled in the nineteenth century and in
1911 stood at 45 million), they can also be seen as expressions of the profound
tensions of a society which was on the verge of engaging in a war which was to
prove apocalyptic in the scale of its futility and mechanical destructiveness. The
years leading into the Great War were also, to echo the title of George Dangerfield's classic history of this period, the years of *The Strange Death of Liberal
England*.[44]

ii The moment of *Blast*

In *Blasting and Bombardiering* (1937), Lewis writes of Hulme in the chapter entitled 'Hulme of Original Sin', offering a commendatory resume of his anti-humanist metaphysics, 'it was extremely original of this Mr. Hulme – especially living as he did in Mr. Polly's England – to pick out this stuffy old doctrine of Original Sin and rub everybody's nose in it'. As regards Hulme's theory of art, he comments, 'All the best things Hulme said about the theory of art were said about my art . . . What he said should be done, I *did*. Or it would be more exact to say that I did it, and he said it.'[45] As ever, it is difficult to gauge the veracity of Lewis's statements, especially as he acknowledges that Hulme preferred Epstein personally and Epstein's work of the period; and, as indicated, Hulme was not as fanatical an abstractionist as Lewis represents him to be. The convergence in views between the two men certainly extends however to Lewis's main statement that

> all this sort of thinking resulted in Hulme and myself preferring something anti-naturalist and 'abstract' to Nineteenth Century naturalism, in pictures and in statues. It must suffice for me to say that Man was not the hero of our universe. We thought he required a great deal of tidying-up before he became presentable; both he and I preferred to the fluxions in stone of an August Rodin (following photographically the lines of nature) the concentrated abstractions-from-nature of the Egyptians.[46]

However, moving from Hulme to Lewis's aesthetics, as promulgated in *Blast*, the quarto-size 'puce monster' Lewis produced to propagandize himself and the Vorticist movement, we find an anti-humanism which is not so much a purportedly metaphysical doctrine as a set of attitudes based on an implicitly Romantic glorification of the mystique of the artist and the power of the form imparting imagination, which is expressed through a self-conscious distaste for 'life' and a hostile stance towards the English public. In 'Life is the Important Thing' Lewis 'blasts' the professors of this sententious statement and equating 'life' with 'nature' comments

> NATURE IS NO MORE INEXHAUSTIBLE, FRESH, WELLING UP WITH INVENTION, ETC., THAN LIFE IS TO THE AVERAGE MAN OF FORTY, WITH HIS GROOVE, HIS DISILLUSION, AND HIS LITTLE ROUND OF HABITUAL DISTRACTIONS.[47]

Lewis continues

> For those men who look to nature for support, she does not care.
> 'Life' is a hospital for the weak and incompetent.
> 'Life' is a retreat of the defeated.
> It is very salubrious – The cooking is good –
> Amusements are provided.

As an extension, in 'Futurism, Magic and Life' Lewis states, 'The Artist, like Narcissus, gets his nose nearer and nearer the surface of life./He will get it nipped off if he is not careful, by some Pecksniff-shark sunning its lean belly near the surface, or other lurker beneath his image, who has been feeding on its radiance. /Reality is in the artist, the image only in life, and he should only approach as near as is necessary for a good view.'[48] The corollary is the statement made in the opening piece, 'Long Live the Vortex', where, in implicit contradiction to Hulme, Lewis asserts

> We believe in no perfectibility except our own. Intrinsic beauty is in the Interpreter and Seer, not in the object or content.[49]

What Lewis has done (more as a modernist extension of Stirner's radical egoism than a recasting of Hulme's ideas)[50] is to construct an art/life dichotomy, with the artist exploiting that which in circumadjacent 'reality' he finds is of use to him.

7. The Art-instinct is permanently primitive.
8. In a chaos of imperfection, discord, etc., it finds the same stimulus as in Nature.
9. The artist of the modern movement is a savage (in no sense an 'advanced,' perfected, democratic Futurist individual of Mr. Marinetti's limited imagination): this enormous, jangling, journalist, fairy desert of modern life serves him as Nature did more technically primitive man.[51]

The mystique of the artist becomes, in Lewis's terms, something belligerent, satiric and threatening, sharply delineating the artist as a superior individual, not to be confused with his fellow men.

5. Mercenaries were always the best troops.
6. We are Primitive Mercenaries in the Modern World.
7. Our *Cause* is NO-MAN'S.
8. We set Humour at Humour's throat.
Stir up Civil War among peaceful apes.[52]

Though Lewis declares that '*Blast* will be popular, essentially', and that '*Blast* represents an art of Individuals', such gestures towards the public are less significant than the negation of any sense of community that they imply: 'The moment a man feels or realizes himself as an artist, he ceases to belong to any milieu or time. *Blast* is created for the timeless, fundamental Artist that exists in everybody.'[53] While for those who fail to realize 'this timeless, fundamental Artist' in themselves when presented with *Blast*, Lewis declares:

> CURSE those who will hang over this
> Manifesto with SILLY CANINES exposed.[54]

Of course there is a heavy humour, almost playfulness, in Lewis's threatening posture. But it is interesting to note here how Hugh Kenner – a major critic of, and champion of, the Modernist writers – in seeking to elucidate the strategy of the manifesto, reveals the ideological premise he shares with Lewis in regarding *Blast* as 'an occasion for that tableau grimace of defiance that was Lewis's way of bringing home to his dozen or so sympathetic readers one of the essential facts in any modern cultural situation: their own isolation in a world of performing dolls'.[55] Kenner's comment is sufficiently close to Lewis's own elitist cultural premises – as when, for example, in 'The Code of a Herdsman' (July 1917), he states, 'Mock the herd perpetually with the grimace of its own garrulity or dead-ness'[56] – to suggest that it offers tautology rather than commentary; allowing replication rather than scrutiny of Lewis's assumptions.

Historically it is important to site Lewis's reaction against humanism and his aggressive and austere creed of the Vorticist artist within his perception of the condition of modern urban life. In 'The New Egos', writing of the inhabitants of the modern city, Lewis comments

> Promiscuity is normal; such separating things as love, hatred, friendship are superseded by a more realistic and logical passion.
>
> The human form still runs, like a wave, through the texture or body of existence, and therefore of art.
>
> But just as the old form of egotism is no longer fit for such conditions as now prevail, so the isolated human figure of most ancient Art is an anachronism.
>
> THE ACTUAL HUMAN BODY BECOMES OF LESS IMPORTANCE EVERY DAY.
>
> It now, literally EXISTS much less.
>
> Love, hatred, etc., imply conventional limitations.
>
> All clean, clear-cut emotions depend on the element of strangeness, and surprise and primitive detachment.
>
> Dehumanization is the chief diagnostic of the Modern World (Figure 8).[57]

For the inhabitant of the modern city, 'Impersonality becomes a disease with him'; but, as Lewis declares in 'The Exploitation of Vulgarity', he relishes this situation, particularly for the opportunities it gives to satiric art. 'The world may, at any moment, take a turn, and become less vulgar and stupid./ The great artist must not miss this opportunity.' Having previously asserted that 'the condition of our enjoyment of vulgarity, discord, cheapness or noise is an unimpaired and keen disgust with it', he suggestively concludes, 'This pessimism is the triumphant note in modern art.'[58]

In socio-literary terms, the median term between Blake, a politically radical first generation Romantic writer-artist with whom Lewis shares much (he is referred to as 'THE English Artist' in *Blast*) and Lewis himself, is the aesthete of the 1890s. The doctrine of art for art's sake has as one of its primary functions the rebuttal of a utilitarian, materialistic, bourgeoisie, the writer's inevitable public, from whom the writer or artist overtly detaches himself in order to form what is almost a priestly caste with those who share his refined, disdainful sensibility. (As with Wilde's aestheticism, or *Blast*, it is easy to discern that such apparent gestures of rejection can be, in reality, modes of self-advertising.) In other words, the writer regards himself as different *in kind* from his public, and his stance becomes antagonistic towards a society which he feels will not, or cannot, accommodate him. This development, a negative response to a stable class society, is intrinsic to the ethos of this mode of avant-garde art, an art which pursues formal innovation with an overt disinterest in its reception by a wide, rather than coterie, public. It is simultaneously the socio-literary premise for that gradual shift from a communicatory to a presentative function which can be seen as the underlying tendency of late nineteenth- and early twentieth-century avant-garde art and writing.

Pound acknowledges this heritage from the aesthetes in his 'Vortex' manifesto in *Blast*, where as 'Ancestry' he surrounds his own Imagist definition, 'An Image is that which presents an intellectual and emotional complex in an instant of time', with Pater's 'All arts approach the condition of music (sic)', and Whistler's 'You are interested in a certain painting because it is an arrangement of lines and colours.'[59] Both quotations have as their common ground the rejection of any extraneous, discursive, communicatory 'content' to art. Pater's is a characteristic Symbolist call for *poésie pure*, a poetry devoid of any discursive content, while Whistler exalts the formal qualities of painting and paves the way for an art devoid of any 'narrative' content or extraneous 'human interest'. It is not very far from these pronouncements to those Lewis makes in *Blast*, where to suit the conditions of modern life as he perceives them he purges the doctrine of any effete refinement or sentimentality, to emerge with such statements as 'At any period an artist should have been able to remain in his studio, imagining form, and provided that he could transmit the substance and logic of his invention to another man, could, without putting brush to canvas, be the best artist of his day.'[60] The combative tone of Lewis's and Pound's pronouncements reveal that such breaks with post-Renaissance norms of verisimilitude can be – though they are not necessarily – connected with a broadly anti-humanist cultural stance. This is an area which has hardly been explored, except somewhat schematically in Ortega's significantly entitled essay 'The Dehumanization of Art'.[61]

But Vorticist aesthetics did not seek to eradicate emotion from the work of art, provided that such emotion was generated by formal arrangement rather than by facile empathetic response to 'extraneous matter'. In an article in the *Fortnightly Review*, Pound commented on Lewis's mastery of design, singling out his series on Shakespeare's *Timon of Athens* for especial commendation. 'If you ask me what his "Timon" means, I shall reply by asking you what the old play means. For me his designs are a creation on the same *motif*. That *motif* is the fury of intelligence shut in by circumadjacent stupidity. It is an emotional *motif*. Mr. Lewis's painting is nearly always emotional' (Figure 9, cover illustration).[62]

If Pound could discern this as the *motif* suggested by the formal tensions within Lewis's *Timon* designs (indeed, a significant choice of subject in relation to the previous issues), then we are on even safer ground in seeing *Blast*, the literary product, as being an elaboration of the same *motif* of 'intelligence shut in by circumadjacent stupidity'. The new art propagandized by *Blast* was not produced or disseminated in a void: it was a self-consciously avant-garde art which could rely on incomprehension, if not intolerance, from a wide public. Of the three main theorists of *Blast*, Lewis, Gaudier and Pound, only Lewis had been educated in Britain and was (nominally) British and thus only Lewis could be assumed to have some implicit understanding of English culture and the English audience. A static socio-literary model of the interaction between writer and public would suggest that this accounts for the belligerence of *Blast* and the uncompromising truculence of the manifestos therein contained. As far as it goes this is helpful, but we can perhaps go further. Pound, in an article published in *The Criterion* of July 1937, 'D'Artagnan Twenty Years After', comments, 'Naturally Manchester took six months to discover the satiric propulsion of the Quarto *Blast*, 1914', and 'England was so smug in those days (as in 1937) that *Blast* was regarded as violent. So dynamic is ANY equation that attains any sort of justness whatsoever' (Figure 10).[63]

What was *Blast* a satire on? The answer is apparent: its own audience, the English public. As Lewis puts it in *Blasting and Bombardiering*, ' "Kill John Bull with Art!" I shouted. And John and Mrs. Bull leapt for joy, in a cynical convulsion.'[64] If *Blast* in its totality is seen as a satirical piece, this indicates that an awareness of the likely reception of the magazine and its art is compounded in its tone; that the work elects its own orientation *vis-à-vis* its audience and seeks to capitalize on its distance from a sympathetic public. In this way it is possible to appreciate the self-conscious, though aggressive, exclusivity of the Vorticist attitude as defined by Lewis.

Our Vortex is fed up with your dispersals, reasonable chicken-men.
Our Vortex is proud of its polished sides.
Our Vortex will not hear of anything but its disastrous polished dance.
Our Vortex desires the immobile rhythm of its swiftness.
Our Vortex rushes out like an angry dog at your Impressionistic fuss.
Our Vortex is white and abstract with its red-hot swiftness.[65]

The concept of *écriture*, of the value-bearing aspects of literary form, allows us to see the belligerence of *Blast* not only in terms of content or doctrine, as being an attack on cultural provincialism (which it certainly was), but to go further, to suggest that by a choice of literary form, of 'tone' or ethos of language, the magazine itself exemplifies what it preaches. The harsh typographic innovations, significantly reminiscent of the graphic shock tactics of the advertisement, the curt, compressed, explosive form of the various 'Blasts' and 'Blesses' and the cryptic, elliptical, almost reader-resistant formulation of the aesthetic doctrine all connote a choice of values within the limits set by history, a set of attitudes towards the social and cultural status quo in which the Vorticist artists were working. In terming *Blast* a satire upon its own audience, a separation is predicated between artist/writer and public, a separation which is internalized and made an occasion for response in the literary work. It is not a question of political or cultural presuppositions coming anterior to the art/literature and forming it, but more of the literature being in a dialectical relation to these attitudes, which are themselves largely a response to what is perceived as the situation of the artist. We should not talk of politics *and* literature, but of a politics *of* literature.

Eliot was fully exposed to these distinctive cultural and intellectual influences after his meeting with Pound in late 1914. At the same time as Pound was adapting his Imagist poetics to accord with his experience of contact with the Vorticist artists, Eliot was writing the first of his poems to be destined for publication since he completed 'La Figlia Che Piange' in 1912. Eliot's early, Laforguian poems had been written in relative intellectual isolation while he was still a Harvard student and from 1912 to 1914 he had concentrated his energies on the study of philosophy, being engaged in the writing of his doctoral thesis on the idealist philosophy of F. H. Bradley when he first met Pound. When his association with Pound began in 1914–15, he fell under the powerful influence of an older and intellectually more mature poet, who was fully engaged in oppositional cultural politics as well as the production of poetry. Lewis, in his 1948 memoir of Eliot, gives us his initial impression of Eliot sitting in Pound's triangular living-room in Notting Hill Gate at least ostensibly very much in the position of disciple in relation to ebullient master.[66] It is therefore necessary to consider the course of Pound's development within the context of contemporary English poetry in order to appreciate the specific emphases to which Eliot responded in his work. The last section of this chapter will consider Pound's development during the period of the Vorticist endeavour in order to illuminate his and Eliot's decision in 1916–17 to experiment with Gautier's 'sculptured' quatrains.

iii Pound's Vorticist Poetics

The immediate effect on Pound of contact with Lewis's uncompromising belligerence, coupled with his association with talented sculptors and artists whom he felt were not receiving their due, was to intensify and focus his hostility to the British public and then, more productively, to stimulate a refinement and redefinition of his Imagist poetics. As early as 1912, in his correspondence, Pound is writing of 'saving the public's soul by punching its face',[67] and between 1914 and 1915, the period of *Blast* and the launching of the Vorticist movement, he was given the opportunity to express his hostility in strident and unequivocal terms. Pound's position was that of an aesthetic elitism in which the artist and society are separated by a chasm, the artist having all the qualities of awareness that a hostile, intellectually inert society is held to lack. As he put it in his *Egoist* article on Wyndham Lewis, 'The rabble and the bureaucracy have built a god in their own image and that god is Mediocracy. The great mass of mankind are mediocre, and that is axiomatic, it is a definition of the word mediocre.' Thus, for Pound, 'In Mr. Lewis's work one finds not a commentator but a protagonist. He is a man at war.'[68] Some months previously, in the columns of *The Egoist*, he had encapsulated his view of the artist in giving his definition of 'the bourgeois': 'The bourgeois is, roughly, a person who is concerned solely with his own comfort and advancement. He is, in brief, digestive. He is the stomach and gross intestines of the body politic and social, as distinct from the artist, who is the nostrils and the invisible antennae.'[69]

For Pound, Vorticism allowed a focusing of hostility; the treatment of the movement itself and the artists concerned by the public did not induce a gradually revealed disillusion. In his very first article on art, 'The New Sculpture', published in *The Egoist* of February 1914, Pound is already writing in extreme terms that reveal the influence of Hulme, Lewis and the forgotten figure of Allen Upward (who at this period supplied the element of anti-humanism in Pound's ideas).[70]

> The artist has been for so long a humanist! He has been a humanist out of reaction. He has had sense enough to know that humanity was unbearably stupid and that he must try to disagree with it. But he has also tried to lead and persuade it; to save it from itself. He has fed it out of his own hand and the arts have grown dull and complacent, like a slightly uxorious spouse.
>
> The artist has at last been aroused to the fact that the war between him and the world is a war without truce. That his only remedy is slaughter. This is a mild way to say it.

Pound continues by recommending Hulme's assertion that 'the difference between the new art and the old was not a difference in degree but a difference in kind; a difference in intention'; but rather than expounding Hulme's aesthetic doctrine, he significantly bases this difference in intention upon the new, hostile attitude the contemporary artist, as opposed to his 'humanist' predecessors, has towards the public. 'The artist has no longer any belief or suspicion that the mass, the half-educated simpering general, the semi-connoisseur, the sometimes collector, and still less the readers of the "Spectator" and the "English Review" can in any way share his delights or understand his pleasure in forces (*sic*).' Pound sees the artist in a position of antagonism towards a society that misunderstands or ignores him, and states, 'There is a recognition of this strife in the arts – in the arts of the moment.' As expressed in sculpture, Pound sees this strife as resulting in work which 'with its general combat, its emotional condemnation, gives us our strongest satisfaction'. It is 'A sculpture expressing desire and aware of the hindrance, a sculpture recognising inertia and not trying to persuade us that there is any use analysing that inertia into seven and seventy sorts of mental and temperamental debility.' Pound concludes by stating:

> The artist has been at peace with his oppressors for long enough. He has dabbled with democracy and he is now done with that folly.
>
> We turn, we artists, to the powers of the air, to the djinns who were our allies aforetime, to the spirits of our ancestors. It is by them that we have ruled and shall rule, and by their connivance that we shall mount again the hierarchy. The aristocracy of entail and of title has decayed, the aristocracy of commerce is decaying, the aristocracy of the arts is ready again for its service.

Modern civilization has bred a race with brains like those of rabbits and we who are the heirs of the witch-doctor and the voodoo, we artists who have been for so long the despised are about to take over control.

And the public will do well to resent these 'new' kinds of art.[71]

That *Blast* was for Pound essentially an opportunity for a 'blast' at the public and the cultural status quo is clearly evinced in the poems he contributed to the first issue. In comparison to Lewis's poised cryptic aggression, Pound is embarrassingly blatant and hysterical when he chooses to attempt a direct satiric attack. His first poem, 'Salutation the Third', begins 'Let us deride the smugness of "The Times":/GUFFAW!' and the poem continues in this vein, with Pound finally offering his opponents, the 'detesters of Beauty' his boot, in order that they may, 'CARESS it, lick off the BLACKING'.[72] It is hard to dispute Aldington's verdict on Pound's contributions to *Blast*, when he states in *The Egoist* that they 'are quite unworthy of their author', and suggests that 'this enormous arrogance and petulance and fierceness are a pose. And it is a wearisome pose.'[73]

War had been declared between the publication of the first and the final, second edition of *Blast*; and in *Blast* (2), Pound in his 'Chronicles', commenting on the reception of the first *Blast*, dwells upon his hostilities. The general public is defined as 'homo canis', a race characterized by intellectual sterility and stupidity, the 'petrifaction of the mind' which Pound saw as the main characteristic of the British public. Pound does not propose any reconciliation with this animal. 'Does anything but the need for food drive the artist into contact with homo canis?' and he accounts for the hostility with which he believes *Blast* has been received in these terms: 'Because BLAST alone has dared to show modernity its face in an honest glass. 'While all other periodicals were whispering PEACE in one tone or another . . . BLAST alone dared to present the actual discords of modern "civilization", DISCORDS now only too apparent in the open conflict between teutonic atavism and unsatisfactory democracy.'[74] To Pound, the tenor of the modern can be accounted for thus. 'The present: a generation which ceases to flatter./Thank god for our atrabilious companions./and the homo canis?/Will go on munching our ideas. Whining.' Pound concludes this section by dividing the 'homo canis' into two groups, 'the snarling type and the smirking'. Of the latter he comments, 'The entrails of some people are not strong enough to permit them the passion of hatred.'[75] Even allowing for the licence that Pound undoubtedly felt that *Blast* afforded him, his stance in such pronouncements is excessive, artificial and melodramatic, a role assumed in default of any reliable sense of reality.

A more lasting and productive aspect of Pound's involvement with the Vorticist movement was the reformulation of his Imagist poetics which that involvement stimulated, a development which has a direct bearing on T. S. Eliot's poetic career. In order to appreciate the salient aspects of this redefinition, it is necessary to give a retrospective sketch of what those Imagist poetics entailed in order to appreciate Pound's new emphases. As in much of Pound's work, this can take the form of tracing the evolution and emphases he gives to a metaphor.

From its inception the Imagist movement employed the metaphor of 'hardness' to describe one of its primary poetic desiderata. It is there, almost obsessively, in Hulme (whom we may regard as a pre-Imagist, or Imagist, depending on whether we believe that his poetics are different in kind or degree from those of Pound), as in his insistence that the new Classical poetry he predicts will be 'dry and hard'.[76] Pound, in 1912, predicted in the pages of Harold Monro's *Poetry Review* that twentieth-century poetry 'will be harder and saner, it will be what Mr. Hewlett calls "nearer the bone". It will be as much like granite as it can be.'[77] Finally, Richard Aldington, writing in 1914, as a member of Pound's Imagist group, gives a useful brief definition of mature Imagist criteria in the 'Imagism' edition of *The Egoist*; a definition which, emphasizing as it does a shared (common) understanding, is more useful for our purpose than Pound's more specific comments and definitions. 'Hard, direct treatment, absolutely personal rhythm, few and expressive adjectives, no inversions, and a keen emotion presented objectively.' The third tenet in his list of fundamental objectives of the group, is 'A hardness, as of cut stone. No slop, no sentimentality. When people say that Imagist poems are "too hard," "like a white marble monument," we chuckle; we know we have done something good.' It becomes apparent that this desire for 'hardness' articulates with the aim of 'objectivity', the shunning of abstractions and stated emotions. As Aldington writes, 'Direct treatment of the subject. This I consider very important. We convey an emotion by presenting the object and circumstance of that emotion without comment.'[78]

To appreciate the historic rationale of such pronouncements, the purpose of this stress on 'hardness', it is necessary to realize the state of contemporary poetic production which induced this reaction. Eliot wrote many years later that, 'the situation of poetry in 1909 or 1910 was stagnant to a degree difficult for any young poet of today to imagine'. Pound characterized the situation more specifically and forcefully: 'The common verse in Britain from 1890 was a horrible agglomerate compost, not minted, most of it not even baked, all legato, a doughy mess of third-hand Keats, Wordsworth, heaven knows what, fourth-hand Elizabethan sonority blunted, half-melted, lumpy.'[79] The value of C. K. Stead's *The New Poetic*[80] is to give an accurate portrayal of the status quo against which Imagists (and also Georgians) were reacting. The public poetry of Newbolt, Watson, Austin, and to some extent, Kipling, was a 'popular' poetry in the most negative sense: it pandered to conservative, imperialist values; it was didactic and empathetic in that it merely versified values with which it knew the public would agree; it echoed commonplace sentiments and sentimentalities.

There was no vital minority poetry to set against this public verse. After the death of Swinburne in 1909, Yeats was, as he put it, 'king of the cats',[81] and before his gradual reorientation after the publication of *Responsibilities* (to some extent due to Pound's influence) he was not inaccurately seen as advancing the banner of the Symbolists and aesthetes of the 1890s into the twentieth century. Imagism was a reaction against the crude didacticism of this public poetry, but also against the diffuseness and suggestiveness of the incantatory late Romantic poetry produced by the English Symbolists and their successors. The emphasis on 'hardness' and precision was largely a reaction against this tendency: sonorous, incantatory poetry was regarded as achieving no engagement with quotidian reality; it was a mere subjective poetry of 'moods'. Pound wrote of Yeats in *Poetry*, 1912,

> Mr. Yeats has been subjective; believes in the glamour and associations which hang near words. 'Works of art beget works of art.' He has much in common with the French symbolists. Mr. Hueffer believes in an exact rendering of things. He would strip words of all 'associations' for the sake of getting a precise meaning. He professes to prefer prose to verse. You will find his origins in Gautier or in Flaubert. He is objective. This school tends to lapse into description. The other tends to lapse into sentiment.[82]

Pound was in favour of the work of Ford Madox Hueffer (subsequently better known as Ford Madox Ford) as a corrective and disciplinary measure.

A disciplinary or 'critical' aspect of Imagism was integral to Pound's aims. It was an attempt to wrest poetry from the creation of a 'subjective', Symbolist, verbal, hermetic universe, towards an 'objective' engagement with the circum-ambient world. He wished to realize an externalized, tangible, presentative poetry. It is possible to discern similar emphases in many of Eliot's critical comments of the years 1917 to 1920, although Eliot, arriving in England in 1914, picked up his Imagism directly from Pound, without being involved in the Imagist movement, which Pound was in the process of abandoning. We find what can be regarded as loosely (though not exclusively) Imagist criteria being applied, for example, in the 'Swinburne' essay, with its formulation that 'Language in a healthy state presents the object, it is so close to the object that the two are identified.' The grounds for Eliot's condemnation of Swinburne are very close to those used by Pound to criticize Symbolist verse:

> he uses the most general word, because his emotion is never particular, never in direct line of vision, never focused; it is emotion reinforced, not by intensification, but by expansion . . . it is not merely the sound that he wants, but the vague associations of idea that the words give him . . . It is, in fact, the word that gives him the thrill, not the object. When you take to pieces any verses of Swinburne, you find always that the object was not there – only the word.[83]

The obvious extrapolation of this Imagist emphasis on objectivity was Eliot's theory of the 'objective correlative', as outlined in the essay on 'Hamlet and his Problems'. 'The only way of expressing emotion in the form of art is by finding an "objective correlative"'; in other words, a set of objects, a situation, a chain of events which shall be the formula of that *particular* emotion; such that when the external facts, which must terminate in sensory experience, are given, the emotion is immediately evoked.'[84] However, in so far as Eliot's theory can be perceived to be ultimately expressive in its search for an objective metalanguage 'which shall be the formula of that particular emotion', it is Symbolist in tendency. Pound, on the other hand, inclines more to the full objectification of the poem, not making a schematic distinction between what Eliot terms 'the external facts' and the primary emotion to be expressed by the poet. 'An "Image" is that which presents an intellectual and emotional complex in an instant of time.'[85]

One of the doctrinal advantages of Pound's shift to Vorticism is that the very term 'Imagism' could give rise to confusion in the context of Pound's poetics, in that 'Imagism' could be compounded with the deployment of visual 'imagery'. There is no demand for visualization in this definition, only for presentation. The danger, to which Imagist poetry was to succumb after Pound had left the group, was that of a poetry of descriptive, visual 'images' which do not interact, but remain atomized units of perception. This helps us to appreciate why Pound does not employ the term 'image' in a unitary, visual sense in his Vorticist articles. 'Dante's 'Paradiso' is the most wonderful *image*. By that I do not mean that it is a perseveringly imagistic performance. The permanent part is Imagism, the rest, the discourses with the calendar of saints and the discussions about the nature of the moon, are philology.'[86] Thus, Pound writes,

> The image is not an idea. It is a radiant node or cluster; it is what I can, and must perforce, call a VORTEX, from which, and through which, and into which, ideas are constantly rushing. In decency one can only call it a VORTEX. And from this necessity comes the name 'vorticism'. 'Nomina sunt consequentia rerum', and never was that statement of Aquinas more true than in the case of the vorticist movement.[87]

The very term 'vortex' implies the dynamic interfusion and interrelation of constituent parts to form a single whole, one 'image', without implying that every element in the 'radiant node or cluster' be a visualizable 'image'. The term 'vortex' also suggests stillness in movement – 'The Vorticist is at his maximum point of energy when stillest' (*Blast*) – while 'image' suggests that which is solely static. This serves to distinguish Pound's Imagism from that developed previously by Hulme, who thought of the Image in terms of accurate but unfamiliar description, generated by fresh metaphors; and also from the standard poetic production of the Imagist group, particularly after Amy Lowell set about 'democratizing' it in 1914: after which Pound's term for the group became 'Amy-gism'.

What Pound insists on is that the Image is not discursive: it is both intensive and dynamic, and is intended to present an aesthetic monad. Here we move into the orbit of Pound's Vorticist definitions in *Blast*, where Imagism takes its place among the other dynamic Vorticist arts – the vortex being 'the point of maximum energy', and the Vorticist artist relying on what Pound terms, 'the primary pigment of his art'.

EVERY CONCEPT, EVERY EMOTION PRESENTS ITSELF TO THE VIVID CONSCIOUSNESS IN SOME PRIMARY FORM. IT BELONGS TO THE ART

OF THIS FORM. IF SOUND, TO MUSIC; IF FORMED WORDS, TO
LITERATURE; THE IMAGE, TO POETRY; FORM, TO DESIGN; COLOUR
IN POSITION, TO PAINTING; FORM OR DESIGN IN THREE PLANES, TO
SCULPTURE; MOVEMENT, TO THE DANCE, TO THE RHYTHM OF
MUSIC OR OF VERSES.[88]

These 'concentrated' arts, 'primary' arts, are contrasted with 'secondary' forms of expression.

Elaboration, expression of second intensities, of dispersedness belong to the secondary sort of artist. Dispersed arts HAD a vortex.

Impressionism, Futurism, which is only an accelerated sort of impressionism, DENY the vortex. They are the corpses of VORTICES. POPULAR BELIEFS, movements, etc., are the CORPSES OF VORTICES. Marinetti is a corpse.[89]

Pound sees the new Vorticist arts as moving parallel to his critical labour in the field of poetry. This labour was begun under the influence of Ford Madox Ford, who encouraged Pound to abandon the 'curial speech' of the 1890s and attempt to deal with the present in contemporary language, particularly through a Flaubertian search for *le mot juste*. 'As a "critical" movement, the "Imagism" of 1912 to '14 set out "to bring poetry up to the level of prose" . . . Flaubert and de Maupassant lifted prose to the rank of a finer art, and one has no patience with contemporary poets who escape from the infinitely difficult art of good prose by pouring themselves into loose verses.'[90] Pound considers that this process of a return to first principles can be discerned in the other arts.

Whistler said somewhere in the *Gentle Art*: 'The picture is interesting not because it is Trotty Veg, but because it is an arrangement in colour.' The minute you have admitted that, you let in the jungle, you let in nature and truth and abundance and cubism and Kandinsky, and the lot of us. Whistler and Kandinsky and some cubists were set to getting extraneous matter out of their art; they were ousting literary values. The Flaubertians talk a good deal about 'constatation'. The 'nineties' saw a move against rhetoric . . . I think all these things move together, though they do not, of course, move in step.[91]

As the painters were set on ousting 'literary values' – dependence on the mimetic or representational aspect of painting, by which the work appeals to values outside the formal satisfactions offered by an 'arrangement in colour' – so, in the field of poetry, Pound promoted a movement away from 'rhetoric' and appeal to 'popular beliefs', towards a precise registration of 'the image'.

The image is the poet's pigment. The painter should use his colour because he sees or feels it. I don't much care whether he is representative or non-representative. He should *depend*, of course, on the creative, not on the mimetic or representational part of his work. It is the same in writing poems, the author must use his *image* because he sees or feels it, not because he thinks he can use it to back up some creed or some system of ethics or economics.[92]

This emphasis on the artist's creativity introduces us to Pound's creed of the Vorticist artist, which was to prove of great importance in the composition of *Hugh Selwyn Mauberley*. In his *Blast* 'Vortex' Pound's initial statement includes this central antithesis.

> You may think of man as that towards which perception moves. You may think of him as the TOY of circumstance, as the plastic substance RECEIVING impressions.
> Or you may think of him as DIRECTING a certain fluid force against circumstance, as CONCEIVING instead of merely observing and reflecting.[93]

The first statement of this contrast is in Pound's 'New Sculpture' article, where it is attributed to a speaker who spoke after both Hulme and Lewis at the Quest Society lecture of January 1914. Pound cheekily deprecates all the speakers as being 'equally unintelligible', even though this third speaker was himself.

> A speaker got himself disliked by saying that one might regard the body either as a sensitized receiver of sensations, or as an instrument for carrying out the decrees of the will (or expressing the soul, or whatever you choose to term it). These two theories are opposed, and produce two totally opposed theories of aesthetic. I use the aesthetic paradoxically, let us say two theories of art.
> Finding this statement unfavourably received and wishing to be taken as a man of correct and orthodox opinions; trimming his words to the wind, he then said you could believe that man was the perfect creature, or creator, or lord of the universe or what you will, and that there was no beauty to surpass the beauty of man as conceived by the late Sir Lawrence Alma-Tadema; or that on the contrary you could believe in something beyond man, something important enought to be fed with the blood of hecatombs.
> This last seemed to cheer the audience. Mr. Hulme had also expressed it.[94]

The theory seems to stem from Worringer's distinction between the two modes of artistic volition, the 'urge to abstraction' and the 'urge to empathy', with which Pound would be familiar through his contact with Hulme. But Pound gives it an innovatory emphasis, which is more important than this possible derivation, in his 'Vortex' manifesto. The distinction is one between *passivity* – 'man as that towards which perception moves' – and *activity* – 'as CONCEIVING instead of merely observing and reflecting'. The Vorticist artist inclines to the latter alternative, which is associated with the 'creative', as distinct from the 'mimetic or representational part of his work'. In other words, the purely mimetic, 'reflective' artist is passive, mirroring the circumambient universe through the sensations he receives; while the creative, Vorticist artist, constructs form, perhaps utilizing nature, but fundamentally expressing his inner volition. This distinction can be seen to be, metaphorically, a sexual distinction: the passive-mimetic artist is 'female'; the form-imparting, 'creative' Vorticist artist is 'male'.

We can now appreciate how Pound conceives of the relation between the Vorticist artist and the 'forms' he creates.

> An organisation of forms expresses a confluence of forces. These forces may be the 'love of God,' the 'life-force,' emotions, passions, what you will. For example: if you clap a strong magnet beneath a plateful of iron filings, the energies of the magnet will proceed to organize form. It is only by applying a particular and suitable force that you can bring order and vitality and thence beauty into a plate of iron filings, which are otherwise as 'ugly' as anything under heaven. The design in the magnetised iron filings expresses a confluence of energy. It is not 'meaningless' or 'inexpressive'.[95]

This passage, using Pound's favourite metaphor of the magnet and the iron filings, reveals Pound's conception of the Vorticist artist as one who creates form by the application of directed force. In a subsequent 'Affirmations' article in *The New Age*, Pound attempts to apply these ideas as directly as possible to Imagism. 'In the second article of this series I pointed out that energy creates pattern. I gave examples. I would say further that emotional force gives the image.'[96] When Pound writes that 'The vorticist is expressing his complex consciousness', it is apparent that the vocabulary and the sentiment are similar to that of Gaudier's Vortex, from which Pound quotes the concluding line: 'Will and consciousness are our vortex.' It is easy to perceive that this conception of 'form' as being elicited by directed 'force' has obvious affinities in the sculptural practice of Gaudier-Brzeska, with whom Pound was in close contact during this period. Before indicating the more direct effects of Pound's contact with Gaudier upon his poetic theory and practice, it is worthwhile noting that it was in relation to Gaudier's sculpture that 'tradition' became a crucial issue for Pound (Figure 11).

In *Rude Assignment*, Wyndham Lewis retrospectively makes clear his basic disagreement with his erstwhile Vorticist colleagues.

> Gaudier-Brzeska, the sculptor, I regarded as a good man on the soft side, essentially a man of tradition – not 'one of Us'. To turn to literature (for theoretically my narrow criterion included that) I looked upon the Imagists (Pound, H. D., Aldington, Flint) as 'pompier'. About all that my first impulse would have been to shout, 'a la gare'!
> At this distance, it is hard to believe, but I thought of the inclusion of poems by Pound etc. in 'Blast' as compromising. I wanted a battering ram that was all of one metal. A good deal of what got in seemed to me soft and highly impure.[97]

Lewis, who had purged his prose style of any literary antecedents, and his painting style of any 'traditional' derivations, can be taken at his word here. It was not that he was against 'the past' – 'I heartily detested, and had violently combated, Marinetti's "anti-passéisme", and dynamism',[98] but that, as he states in *Blast*, 'Our vortex is not afraid of the Past: it has forgotten its existence . . . Life is the Past and Future. / The Present is Art.'[99] Lewis suggests this criticism in *Blast* itself, when in a brief, elliptical characterization, he sees Pound as 'Demon pantechnicon driver, busy with removal of old world into new quarters. In his steel net of impeccable technique he has lately caught Li Po. / Energy of a discriminating element.'[100]

Lewis's attitude was not true for Gaudier-Brzeska or for Pound, for both of whom the present was informed by a sense of the past and the vital traditions therein embodied. As Pound states in his 'Vortex',

> All experience rushes into this vortex. All the energized past, all the past that is living and worthy to live. ALL MOMENTUM, which is the past bearing upon us, RACE, RACE-MEMORY, instinct charging the PLACID, NON-ENERGIZED FUTURE.
>
> The DESIGN of the future in the grip of the human vortex. All the past that is vital, all the past that is capable of living into the future, is pregnant in the vortex, NOW.[101]

The emphasis upon 'RACE, RACE-MEMORY, and instinct', in this statement can be related to the influence of Gaudier, who adopted an instinctual primitivism in his behaviour;[102] but, more importantly, in his first *Blast* 'Vortex' contributed a formal history of sculpture, which analyses races and epochs, and the developments they wrought in 'form'. The piece is replete with racial references such as 'The PALEOLITHIC VORTEX', 'The HAMITE VORTEX of Egypt, the land of plenty', 'The SEMITIC VORTEX was the lust of war', each racial 'vortex' being related to a formal development. For example, on the 'HAMITE VORTEX': 'Religion pushed him to the use of the VERTICAL, which inspires awe. His gods were self made, he built them in his image, and RETAINED AS MUCH OF THE SPHERE AS COULD ROUND THE SHARPNESS OF THE PARALLELOGRAM.' Gaudier condemns, in Hulmian terms, the sculpture of the Greeks, and extends this condemnation to the 'SOLID EXCREMENTS in the quattro e cinque cento', concluding 'THIS is the history of form value in the West until the FALL OF IMPRESSIONISM.' He then deals with Chinese art, and that of 'other races inhabiting Africa and the Ocean islands', before returning to Europe, to comment on the renascent art of 'the moderns: Epstein, Brancusi, Archipenko, Dunikowski, Modigliani, and myself', of whom he asserts, 'The knowledge of our civilization embraces the world, we have mastered the elements.'[103]

Gaudier's 'Vortex' is an exhilarating piece of writing; but Pound claimed more for it. 'I repeat what I have said before; this Vortex Gaudier-Brzeska . . . will become the text-book in all academies of sculpture before our generation has passed from the earth.'[104] Here we can see why 'tradition' became such an issue for Pound in relation to Gaudier and his own work. If the Vorticist artist is a man whose 'force' brings to bear 'All the energized past . . . RACE, RACE-MEMORY, instinct', in the act of artistic creation in the present, then an awareness of tradition is implicit, indeed integral, to the 'vortex' of the present, and 'tradition' is necessary to focus and concentrate its energies. Following on from this, Pound can assert that an awareness of tradition is also necessary to *appreciate* this new art, which takes as its points of reference neither a local national tradition nor the products of the contemporary cultural status quo: The new art demands 'men of goodwill, considering art in terms of the world's masterwork'.[105] This breadth of reference is particularly necessary when considering Gaudier's work because the traditions he revives are outside the post-Renaissance norms. 'It is . . . exciting and interesting to find Epstein and Brzeska doing work that will bear comparison with the head of "An officer of rank" (of the XVII to XVIII dynasty); with Egyptian stone and with the early Chinese bronzes.'[106]

Hence, tradition becomes an issue not just in relation to the artist's attitude to his work, but also to the public. 'There are questions of taste and preference, but no dispute about art. So we find the "men of traditions" in agreement or in sympathy. We find the men of no traditions, or of provincial traditions, against us. We find the men whose minds have petrified at forty, or at fifty, or at twenty, most resolutely against us.' A live awareness of tradition, or traditions, is what differentiates the Vorticist artist from 'homo canis', and this issue can be employed to satirically berate those who suffer from 'petrifaction of the mind'. The analogy between the practice of poetry and that of sculpture was easy to make. As Gaudier needed an appreciation of *world* sculpture to make a true assessment of his work, so Pound (at this period involved in the Chinese translations which formed *Cathay*) required an awareness of world poetry to derive full satisfaction from his.

In 'Affirmations – Analysis of this Decade', Pound advances the belief that 'we live in a time as active and significant as the Cinquecento', and lists his own contribution to this new Renaissance as

> Myself, an active sense not merely of comparative literature, but of the need for a uniform criticism of excellence based on world-poetry, and not on the fashion of any one particular decade of English verse, or even on English verse as a whole. The qualitative analysis in literature (practiced but never formulated by Gaston Paris, Reinach in his Manual of Classical Philology, etc.). The Image.[107]

Without this exposition of the place 'tradition' assumed in Pound's Vorticist aesthetics, it would be difficult to appreciate the polemic force the term 'tradition' had, not only in Pound's writings of the period, but also in Eliot's critical pieces, such as 'Tradition and the Individual Talent'. Tradition became a focal issue for Pound and he passed on his belief in the importance of this issue to Eliot, who only began writing his literary essays and reviews in 1917, *after* Pound's Vorticist pronouncements. Both used it as a rubric under which they could combat what they saw as the forces of provincialism, insularity, intellectual entropy and 'petrifaction' at work in English society. Although each writer tended to give the term his own inflection, with Eliot increasingly employing it in a sense close to a Hulmian Classicism, and while they had little agreement on what the tradition was (even down to the question of whether European or world poetry was at issue), they could unite on what it was *not*, in terms of contemporary cultural practice.

Pound's contact with Gaudier stimulated further and more technical analogies between the arts of poetry and of sculpture. Just as the new sculpture wished to pare away all the redundant material that prevented the revelation of an essential complex of formal relationships, so Pound wished the poet to dispose of any 'ornamental' material ('Use no superfluous word, no adjective which does not reveal something.'), anything that 'dulls the image'[108] in the interests of precise verbal presentation. The care, control and craftsmanship that this new sculpture demanded could be seen by Pound in terms of the 'discipline' necessary to produce the poetry he desired: poetry of 'exact definition', like the new sculpture, had clear, precise outlines. During the period of his Vorticist involvement Pound's critical vocabulary becomes increasingly dominated by sculptural metaphors. To offer some examples from Pound's correspondence, E. L. Masters has 'some punch', but lacks 'sufficient hardness of edge'; Catullus is 'The most hard-edged and intense of the Latin poets'; some of McKail's poems were 'finely chiselled'; the imitators of Yeats and the Symbolists had 'Soft mushy edges'; and finally, in the same letter to Iris Barry, Pound suggests that the writing of poetry is 'as simple as the sculptor's direction: "Take a chisel and cut away all the stone you don't want." '[109] To Pound, the search for an exact outline meant that all superfluities had been purged away and only the essential configuration of relations remained. Writing to Amy Lowell in 1914, when she was 'democratizing' Imagism, Pound stated, 'I should like the name "Imagisme" to retain some sort of a meaning. It stands, or I should like it to stand for hard light, clear edges.'[110]

Such demands, while they do not entail for Pound the projection of a visualizable 'image', stress that the poem should be an objective 'presentation' (Pound's most frequent term) rather than a lyrical effusion. In other words, for Pound, the poem should be like an artefact rather than the vehicle of a communicatory utterance passing between poet and reader. Hence Pound demands aesthetic autonomy: that the poem should be a self-sufficient entity presenting in the most economic terms a set, or *Gestalt*, of objective relationships. In terms that can be related to (but not equated with) Eliot's later 'objective correlative', Pound sees the poem as an 'equation for the emotions'. 'By the "image" I mean such an equation; not an equation of mathematics, not something about *a, b,* and *c,* having something to do with form, but about *sea, cliffs, night,* having something to do with mood.'[111] The presentation of the dynamic interrelation between these elements in the poem should be capable of eliciting the appropriate response in the reader, without the mode of that response being stated by or referred back to the poet; just as the statue can elicit a response from the spectator by the formal interrelation of planes and masses. The exact analogy to Pound's emphases is provided by Gaudier's statement in his second *Blast* manifesto. 'I SHALL DERIVE MY EMOTIONS SOLELY FROM THE "ARRANGEMENT OF SURFACES", I SHALL PRESENT MY EMOTIONS BY THE ARRANGEMENT OF MY SURFACES, THE PLANES AND LINES BY WHICH THEY ARE DEFINED.'[112]

It is apparent that this reaction against the representational, in both the visual and literary arts, towards an insistence on art as 'formal arrangement' can be related forwards to Pound's subsequent utilization of Fenollosa's suggestions on the 'ideogrammic' method in *The Cantos*, wherein distinct and heterogeneous particulars are juxtaposed in the expectation that they will interrelate to form a new 'harmony'. This complex of analogies between poetry and abstractionist sculpture informs Pound's entire development, from 'Imagisme' through to his mature achievement, *The Cantos*. However, it was for Eliot a temporary bias, contained by and stimulated during his period of close association with Pound; it can to some extent be regarded as a diversion away from the primary Symbolist tendencies of his verse. At this point, in order to indicate how the synthesis of these analogies, the desideratum of 'sculptured verse' affected Eliot, it is necessary to anticipate the chronological narrative by looking beyond Eliot's first poetic production after his arrival in England (the Oxford poems and the poems in French) to the decision made in late 1916 or early 1917 by both Pound and Eliot, to adopt the quatrain form of Théophile Gautier: a decision which was to lead to Eliot's satiric *Poems* of 1920, and Pound's *Hugh Selwyn Mauberley* sequence.

For Pound, the instigator of this decision – a significant *volte face* in relation to his previous Imagist promotion of *vers libre* – the important feature of Gautier's use of the quatrain was its 'hardness'. In *Poetry*, 1918, he contributed an article entitled 'The Hard and the Soft in French Poetry', in which he discussed the application of these 'semetaphoric (sic) terms' – ('By "hardness" I mean a quality which is in poetry nearly always a virtue – I can think of no case where it is not.') – and commented, 'Anyone who dislikes these textural terms may lay the blame on Théophile Gautier, who certainly suggests them in *Emaux et Camées*; it is his hardness that I had first in mind. He exhorts us to cut in hard substance, the shell and the Parian.'[113] In this article, Pound suggests that Gautier's originality lay 'not in form, his hard, close-cut lines and stanzas', but in his modes of thought and attitudes. 'It is perhaps that Gautier is intent on being "hard"; is intent on conveying a certain verity of feeling, and he ends by being truly poetic . . . an intentness on the quality of the emotion to be conveyed makes for poetry. Another possible corollary is that the subject matter will very nearly make the poem'. Pound extends this discussion of 'hardness', judging the nineteenth-century French poets according to the commended norm of Gautier. 'Since Gautier, Corbière has been hard, not with a glaze or parian finish, but hard like weather-bit granite. And Heredia and Samain have been hard decreasingly, giving gradually smoothness for hardness . . . Tailhade is hard in his satire.'[114]

Here, Pound views Gautier's achievement of hardness as a consequence of his intentness on conveying a 'certain verity of feeling' rather than a product of his 'hard, close-cut lines and stanzas'; and in the context of the previous discussion and Pound's Vorticist emphasis that 'emotional force gives the image', it can be suggested that the 'quality of emotion' that is most likely to appeal to Pound as having a necessary 'hardness' will contain an implicitly oppositional, satiric element. But in Pound's retrospective 1932 *Criterion* comment, in which he provides us with the context for his and Eliot's decision to adopt Gautier's form, he emphasizes precisely that stanzaic form (rather than 'verity of feeling'); but emphasizes 'form' in oppositional, reactive terms. '. . . two authors . . . decided that the dilutation of *vers libre*, Amygism, Lee Masterism, general floppiness had gone too far and that some counter-current must be set going. Parallel situation centuries ago in China. Remedy prescribed 'Emaux et Camées' (or the Bay State Hymn Book). Rhyme and regular strophes.' Here, the decision to employ Gautier's 'hard, close-cut lines and stanzas' is seen as a literary corrective: 'Rhyme and regular strophes' are a 'counter-current' and implicit rebuke to the 'general floppiness' of second-rate *vers libre*.

That the adoption of a hard, sculptured, strophic verse suggests a primary oppositional bias within the contemporary cultural situation is also, and rather more surprisingly, made clear by Pound in a comment on Jules Laforgue in *Poetry*, 1917.

> He has done, sketchily and brilliantly, for French literature a work not incomparable to what Flaubert was doing for 'France' in *Bouvard and Pècuchet*, if one may compare the flight of the butterfly with the progress of the ox, both proceeding towards the same point of the compass. He has dipped his wings in the dye of scientific terminology. Pierrot *imberbe* has
>
> Un air d'hydrocephale asperge.
>
> The tyro can not play about with such things, the game is too dangerous. Verbalism demands a set form used with irreproachable skill. Satire needs, usually, the form of cutting rhymes to drive it home.[115]

The relevance of this comment to Eliot's poetry will be discussed in the next two chapters, while the outcome of Eliot's decision to employ the Gautier quatrain will be discussed in Chapter 4.

2

Eliot, Pound and Jules Laforgue

A dandy may be a man who is blasé, may be a man who suffers, but in the latter case, he will smile like a Spartan under the muzzle of a fox.

Charles Baudelaire

In August 1914, his plans to travel in Europe having been cut short by the recent declaration of war, Thomas Stearns Eliot, a graduate student in philosophy at Harvard University on a one year (renewable) Sheldon Travelling Fellowship, left Marburg in Germany and arrived in England. His purpose was to complete his study year at Merton College, Oxford, under Professor Harold Joachim, a disciple of the reclusive idealist philosopher F. H. Bradley, on whose epistemological treatise *Appearance and Reality* Eliot was engaged in writing his doctoral thesis. Aged 26, Eliot seemed set for, though not noticeably enthusiastic about, a career as an academic philosopher.

The body of poems which were to establish his initial reputation in the London literary world had all been composed at least two years previously, and his Harvard friend, Conrad Aiken, noted in 1915, regarding 'The Love Song of J. Alfred Prufrock', subsequently the most famous of these poems, that Eliot had been 'heartlessly indifferent to its fate'.[1] 'The Love Song of J. Alfred Prufrock' was almost the most recent of these poems, and had been completed in 1911; the fourth 'Prelude' and 'La Figlia Che Piange', the last of Eliot's pre-1914 poetic production to be regarded as worthy of publication, were probably completed in 1912. In 1915 Eliot wrote to Aiken that the poems which he had written subsequently, such as 'The Love Song of Saint Sebastian', were 'strained and intellectual', and added, 'I shan't do anything that will satisfy me (as some of my old stuff *does* satisfy me – whether it be good or not) for years.'[2] These latter poems remained unpublished and on Aiken's encouragement it was the earlier 'The Love Song of J. Alfred Prufrock' that Eliot had shown to the expatriate American poet, Ezra Pound, in September 1914. At the end of that month, Pound wrote to Harriet

Monroe, the editor of the Chicago magazine *Poetry*, expressing his enthusiastic reception of 'Prufrock'.

> He is the only American I know of who has made what I can call adequate preparation for writing. He has actually trained himself *and* modernized himself *on his own*. The rest of the *promising young* have done one or the other but never both (most of the swine have done neither). It is such a comfort to meet a man and not have to tell him to wash his face, wipe his feet, and remember the date (1914) on the calendar.[3]

In June 1917, after the publication of various of his poems in periodicals (including the second edition of *Blast*), *Prufrock and Other Observations* was published by the Egoist Press, containing all the poems that Eliot had written as a Harvard student which he wished to preserve, plus a group of poems he had written in Oxford in 1915: 'Aunt Helen', 'Morning at the Window', 'The Boston Evening Transcript', 'Cousin Nancy', 'Hysteria', and 'Mr. Apollinax'. The Harvard poems were all written in the period 1909 to 1912, and of them Eliot himself subsequently categorized 'Conversation Galante', 'Portrait of a Lady', 'The Love Song of J. Alfred Prufrock', and 'La Figlia Che Piange', as being written 'sous le signe de Laforgue',[4] leaving only 'Preludes' and 'Rhapsody on a Windy Night' unaccounted for. There is thus a gap of at least two years between the composition of Eliot's Laforguian poems and that of the Oxford poems, and in the interim Eliot had shifted stylistically so that he was never again to write poems which could be broadly classified as being 'under the sign of Laforgue'. To anticipate the end of the period with which we are concerned, in September 1920, after the publication of Eliot's quatrain poems in *Ara Vos Prec*, Pound, replying to William Carlos Williams's attack on 'exoticism' in American letters in the prologue to *Kora in Hell*, stated 'I certainly never put up translations of Provencal as "American"; and Eliot is perfectly conscious of having imitated Laforgue, has worked to get away from it, and there is very little Laforgue in his Sweeney, or his Bleistein Burbank, or his "Gerontion", or his Bay State Hymn Book.'[5]

Before considering the Oxford poems it is necessary to devote some attention to Eliot's debt to Laforgue, on the principle that we need to know where Eliot was coming from in order to appreciate where he was going to. But this is not the sole purpose, since Laforgue can also be regarded as a subsidiary influence on Pound's decision to adopt set forms and pursue a broadly satiric vein – a policy he communicated to Eliot, which resulted in the quatrain poems of *Ara Vos Prec*, as well as *Hugh Selwyn Mauberley*. Laforgue's influence can thus be viewed from a number of perspectives. There is first his direct influence on Eliot, which in the main was confined to the years 1909 to 1912, before he had met Pound or thought of settling in England. Then there is Laforgue's influence on Pound, which began after Eliot had drawn Pound's attention to the French poet's importance in his own early work; Laforgue exercised a subtle, never dominant, hence somewhat unquantifiable influence on Pound's poetry and critical theories from 1917 onwards. Then, and perhaps most interestingly, we can speculate from Pound's remarks on Laforgue about the context in which Pound viewed Eliot's early work. It will be argued that Pound's perspective on Eliot's early poetry exercised a definite influence on the direction Eliot's poetry was subsequently to take.

As a first stage, though, it is necessary to describe Eliot's debt to Laforgue in its own terms, and this requires a sharp move back in time and intellectual environment from Pound's twentieth-century modernist involvements to the lunar pierrots and hapless dandies of Jules Laforgue's *fin de siècle* world. Eliot's youthful encounter with the work of the French poet, whose promising career as a writer was cut short by his death from tuberculosis at the age of twenty-seven, in 1887, may be said to have stimulated the twenty-year old student and amateur poet into becoming a poet of potentially major stature.

i

The period of Laforgue's dominant influence on Eliot can be contained between 1908, when he learnt of Laforgue through Arthur Symons's *The Symbolist Movement in Literature*, and 1912, when he completed 'La Figlia Che Piange', the last of his Laforguian poems and in some ways more a retrospective acknowledgement of Laforgue's importance to the young poet than a dynamic exploitation of Laforguian compositional principles. The full extent of Eliot's debt to Laforgue is almost impossible to exaggerate: it is certainly rather more extensive than the usual generous critical acknowledgement, since the debt was personal to an extent that cannot be quantified by even the most acute critical techniques. Laforgue is certainly the writer Eliot was thinking of when he wrote of a mode of influence which differs from admiration leading to imitation, in an *Egoist* article of July 1919.

> If we stand toward a writer in this other relation of which I speak we do not imitate him, and though we are quite as likely to be accused of it, we are quite unperturbed by the charge. This relation is a feeling of profound kinship, or rather of a peculiar personal intimacy, with another, probably a dead author. It may overcome us suddenly, on first or after long acquaintance; it is certainly a crisis; and when a young writer is seized with his first passion of this sort he may be changed, metamorphosed almost, within a few weeks even, from a bundle of second-hand sentiments into a person.[6]

He goes on, 'if we had a genuine affair with a real poet of any degree we have acquired a monitor to avert us when we are not in love'. This relation, distinguished from the 'necessary snobbism' of 'admiration for the great', has a radical effect on the recipient. 'We do not imitate, we are changed; and our work is the work of the changed man; we have not borrowed, we have been quickened, and we become bearers of a tradition.'[7] In a letter to E. J. H. Greene of October 1939, specifying the four poems of his first volume written 'sous le signe de Laforgue', Greene tells us that 'Eliot spoke of the influence of Laforgue as of "a kind of possession by a stronger personality" like a demonic possession'.[8]

Laforgue's influence on Eliot's poetry proceeds in a number of stages, which can be seen as corresponding approximately to stages in Laforgue's own development. Eliot's earliest Laforguian poems (published as juvenilia in *Poems Written in Early Youth*),[9] were three pieces published in *The Harvard Advocate* in 1909 and 1910, 'Nocturne', 'Humoresque', and 'Spleen', none of which really rises above the level of pastiche. Although they are unsuccessful as original poetic statements, they mark a definite and abrupt technical advance beyond the derivative nineteenth-century lyrics Eliot had written previously, in which a straining for a suggestive Symbolist effect of mystery is wedded to an unusual precision of statement. 'Circe's Palace' is one of the most mature of these poems, and here the most apparent influences – if any particular influences are discernible in what is essentially a standard late nineteenth-century piece – are those of Dante Gabriel Rossetti and Edgar Allan Poe. It is worth noting, though, how the concluding line of the first stanza hovers on the edge of an ironic inflection, possibly prefiguring Eliot's later mode.

> Around her fountain which flows
> With the voice of men in pain,
> Are flowers that no man knows.
> Their petals are fanged and red
> With hideous streak and stain;
> They sprang from the limbs of the dead. –
> We shall not come here again.
>
> Panthers rise from their lairs
> In the forest which thickens below,
> Along the garden stairs
> The sluggish python lies;
> The peacocks walk, stately and slow,
> And they look at us with the eyes
> Of men who we knew long ago.[9]

The poetic lying behind this piece is that of the traditional expressive lyric: the poet communicates his impressions directly, without commentary, and without the construction of a persona. This self-expressive poetry is the technical analogue to Laforgue's early poetry, published posthumously as *Le Sanglot de la Terre*; the positive influence of Laforgue on Eliot begins with his presentational poetry of *Les Complaintes* and *L'Imitation de Notre-Dame La Lune*, in which Laforgue eschews eloquence and self-expression and attempts to achieve an ironic, sophisticated poetry which is 'refined', and in Laforgue's words, 'has only one aim: to be original at any cost'.[10] Here, forgoing engagement with the quotidian world, Laforgue projects a plethora of personae, the most famous of whom is Lord Pierrot, who exist in an alternative universe which Laforgue constructs with frenetic, virtuoso verbal artifice. Laforgue's 'lunar' pierrots have romantic entanglements with adoring women; but they are children of the moon, and committed to its sterility; their dialogues with women are imbued with the laconic, ironic fatalism Laforgue employs as an impassive mask to explore a painful failure of communication with the opposite sex. A central example is 'Autre Complainte de Lord Pierrot', which is quoted in full in Symons's chapter on Laforgue, and thus probably the first of Laforgue's poems that Eliot read. Here are the first two stanzas.

> Celle qui doit me mettre au courant de la Femme!
> Nous lui dirons d'abord, de mon air le moins froid:
> 'La somme des angles d'un triangle, chère âme,
> Est égale à deux droits.'
>
> Et si ce cri lui part: 'Dieu de Dieu que je t'aime!'
> – 'Dieu reconnaîtra les siens.' Ou piquée au vif:
> – 'Mes claviers ont du coeur, tu seras mon seul thème.'
> Moi: 'Tout est relatif.'[11] *

The connection of this poetry with the everyday world is achieved by inference. The pierrot's attitudes reflect on those of Laforgue; but the 'sordid realities' which engendered this ironic, virtuoso mode as a reaction are not mentioned directly.

> Life is gross, it's true – but, by God! when it's a matter of poetry, let us be as distinguished as carnations; let us say everything, everything (it is in effect above all the sordidness of life which must engender a melancholy humor in our verses), but let us say things in a refined manner. Poetry need not be an exact description (like a page of a novel), but drowned in dreams.[12]

Laforgue's next, and final development, was to achieve the *vers libre* of the thematically connected sequence *Dernier Vers*, in which he retained a persona, but the more worldly persona of a Hamletizing dandy, to succeed in achieving a poetry which combined the presentative aspects of his earlier verse with a more direct and mobile engagement with the everyday world.

Eliot's first Laforguian productions, before he followed Laforgue into the employment of *vers libre*, take from the French poet his mannerisms and themes, his cynical laconic tone, his self-parody, his self-conscious emphasis on *ennui*; but, more profoundly, they attempt to achieve something of Laforgue's presentational technique, which arises either from the use of a persona or from a doubling or splitting of consciousness, so that the scene or statements presented in the poem are always at one remove from the author. In 'Nocturne' the omniscient and omnipotent poet remains detached from the 'usual debate/Of love beneath a bored

---

* She who must put me in touch with Woman! We say to her firstly, in my least cold manner: 'The sum of the angles of a triangle, dear soul, is equal to two right angles.' And if this cry escapes her: 'God O God how I love you!' 'God will recognize his own.' Or stung to the quick: 'My keyboards have some heart, you will be my only theme.' Me: 'Everything is relative.'

but courteous moon,' conducted by his 'Romeo, *grand sérieux*,' and Juliet, and 'out of pity for their fate' arranges for a servant to stab Romeo.

> Blood looks effective on the moonlit ground –
> The hero smiles; in my best mode oblique
> Rolls toward the moon a frenzied eye profound,
> (No need of 'Love forever?' – 'Love next week?')
> While female readers all in tears are drowned:-
> 'The perfect climax all true lovers seek!'[13]

This self-conscious poem technically prefigures 'La Figlia Che Piange', the last of the Laforguian poems, in which the poet, commenting retrospectively and dramatically reliving the parting scene of a failed love affair, is at once the commentator *and* the male half of the couple. A phrase in the stanza above, 'in my best mode oblique', usefully encapsulates the immediate lesson Eliot learnt from Laforgue's *fin de siècle* poetry, which was to eschew overtly self-expressive, personalized poetry in favour of more sophisticated, oblique, inferential methods.

'Conversation Galante', the first of the Laforguian poems Eliot considered worthy of publication in *Prufrock and Other Observations*, is an urbane exploitation of Laforgue's central theme of a failure of communication between the sexes, a theme Laforgue had followed through the poems of *Les Complaintes* and *L'Imitation* to employ as the fundamental motif of *Dernier Vers*. This theme becomes Eliot's in his Laforguian poems; but also, as significantly, it offers an employment of the dandy persona, a facet of Laforgue's mature verse which was of incalculable importance to Eliot's personal and poetic development. Here it is necessary to divest the idea of the dandy of those connotations of frivolity and ostentatious display it acquired in the late nineteenth century and return it to its original meaning, the practice of austere, impassive elegance evinced by the early Regency examplars such as Beau Brummel. This is the mode theorized by Baudelaire in his remarks on 'The Dandy' in his *Salon de 1859*. Baudelaire sees the mode of the dandy not as an 'immoderate taste in dress and material elegance . . . to his eyes, taken above all with the idea of *distinction*, perfection itself consists in an absolute simplicity, which is, in effect, the best manner to distinguish himself.' Dandyism is an aristocratic, ironic cult of the self, 'It is above all the ardent need to be original, while remaining within the external limits of convention . . . It is the pleasure of astonishing and the proud satisfaction of never being astonished.' While Baudelaire regards wealth and leisure as necessary to free the dandy from a repugnant, mid-nineteenth century utilitarianism ('It is unfortunately true that without leisure and money, love can only be a commoner's orgy or the accomplishment of a conjugal duty') his real interest is in the dandy's ironic impassivity: 'The dandy's type of beauty consists above all in an air of coldness which comes from an unshakable resolution to never be moved; one speaks of a latent fire which can be divined, which could but which does not wish to shine forth.'[14]

While Baudelaire himself was too idiosyncratic and temperamental an individual to be able to live up to his own ideal of the dandy, by the late nineteenth century this ideal could be democratized and made the basis of a personal sense of style without the conspicuous wealth Baudelaire had regarded as necessary. Laforgue could be characterized as a *décadent* in his intellectual scepticism, if not nihilism; he had elements of the aesthete in his interest in fine art and disengagement from any notion of utilitarianism; but most profoundly he was a dandy in his combination of an extreme correctness of manner and appearance and a paradoxical disengagement from the social and cultural norms this correctness would seem to imply. As has often been remarked, Eliot's urbane Harvard style could easily be adapted to that of his mentor – described in Symons as 'very correct, with a high opera-hat, sober neck-ties, English jackets, a clergyman's overcoat, and by necessity, an immovable umbrella placed under his arm'[15] – but, more significantly, Laforgue's example opened up possibilities for ironic play, in life and art, which Eliot might never have discovered had he not read of Laforgue's 'art of the nerves' in Symons. The word 'ironist' is etymologically derived from the Greek *eiron*, meaning dissembler, and modes of irony presuppose a distance between expressed and intended meaning. As Baudelaire perceived, a social mask of overt conformity can be an implicitly ironic mode when combined with an inner conviction of 'opposition and revolt'; and, as pertinently, such irony is unstable since overt conformity gives no indication of what real convictions or opinions, if any, it may hide. In the terms of the epigraph that heads this chapter, Laforgue was 'a man who suffers' rather than 'a man who is blasé'; but he adopted the dandy's stance, using the mask of the smile to assume and conceal his social and affective marginality.

The central Laforguian theme of a failure of communication between the sexes is succinctly expressed by the counterpointing of conventional romantic expectations against the dandy's mode of wry, understated disengagement (as in 'Autre Complainte': '–"Mes claviers ont du coeur, tu seras mon seul thème."/Moi: "Tout est relatif." '). Seen less specifically as a 'failure of discourse', the ironic mode allows the poet to explore consequent, cognitive, ethical and emotional dilemmas, areas that Eliot was soon to explore more subtly and dynamically than his master. Finally, and perhaps less seriously, the theme itself may be regarded as offering a suggestive figural representation of the relation between the *fin de siècle* poet and his not always appreciative or comprehending audience.

In 'Conversation Galante', loosely based on Laforgue's 'Autre Complainte de Lord Pierrot', Eliot's form, rhymed symmetrical stanzas, aligns this poem with Laforgue's transitional verse; but Eliot stiffens the tone in comparison with the Laforguian models. In Laforgue's dramatic dialogues, the woman is generally the main speaker, forcing her sentimental ideals on the poet/persona, who deflects her claims ironically but remains implicated with her in a painful romantic dilemma. In Eliot's poem the burden of speech is taken by the poet/persona and the woman is no more than a somewhat obtuse listener, who is unable to follow his virtuoso 'mad poetics', and who presumably wishes he would say something more romantic and 'galante' to suit the moonlit scenery and the nocturne on the piano. The poet/persona would seem to wish to be elsewhere, free to consider his notional 'absolute' without distractions. Refusing complicity in favour of verbal cut and thrust, this poem does not have the 'singular pity of its cruelty' which Symons ascribes to Laforgue's 'Autre Complainte'.[16]

With 'Portrait of a Lady' and 'The Love Song of J. Alfred Prufrock' Eliot moved forward to an engagement with Laforgue's mature achievement, *Dernier vers*, the sequence of twelve poems Laforgue anticipated when he described his conception of poetry to Charles Henry in December 1881.

> I dream of a poetry which will be composed of psychology in the form of a dream, with flowers, wind, scents, inextricable symphonies with a phrase (a subject) which is melodic, of which the pattern reappears from time to time.[17]

The congruence between Eliot's practice in his two most ambitious Laforguian poems and that of his master is profound; but it is more a matter of creative adaptation rather than imitation. The first, and most important debt these two poems owe to *Dernier Vers* is that Eliot learnt how to employ *vers libre* through studying Laforgue. Laforgue's poems are built upon verse paragraphs as the fundamental structural unit, each paragraph being in general a single completed sentence. The individual verse lines may be phrasal interjections, but in metre they generally approach the standard twelve syllable alexandrine without maintaining a semblance of regularity for more than a few lines. In Eliot's poems the same structural principles are followed, with the iambic pentameter substituting for the alexandrine. From this practice Eliot subsequently generalized the remarks contained in 'Reflections on *Vers Libre*' (1917). 'We may therefore formulate as follows: the ghost of some simple metre should lurk behind the arras in even the "freest" verse; to advance menacingly as we doze, and withdraw as we rouse. Or freedom is only truly freedom when it appears against the background of an artificial limitation.'[18]

While Eliot certainly learnt from the Jacobean drama in achieving a 'free' use of iambics – as evinced by the examples he cites in this essay – a lesson he learnt exclusively from Laforgue was the advantage of using a self-reflexive structure in any extended exercise in *vers libre*. By this we mean the use of verbal and structural parallelisms (leitmotifs, isomorphic verse paragraph structures and formulaic lines which gather significance by repetition), in order to create a self-sufficient verbal context in which the poem can function. This is an important point because extended *vers libre*, unlike traditional symmetrical forms such as the sonnet, must create its own linguistic environment and establish precedents for its own functioning, since it cannot rely on pre-established formal limitations or conventions to supply a ready made context to mediate between poet and reader. Eliot's remark, quoted previously, concerning the necessity of 'limitation' to any true freedom, is of obvious relevance here: the poem in *vers libre* must establish its own forms of artificial limitation in order to counterpoint and valorize its freedom from formal restraint.

In Laforgue this often means the use of formulaic lines, by which is meant a line or phrase which by repetition becomes a verbal motif, which can be employed as a *point de repère*, a basic structural unit, from which the poet can develop his themes and variations. An example is the poem 'Solo de Lune', in which lines built around this and other phrases recur, and are used as a verbal springboard to launch the poet/persona into descriptions of the external scene or subjective reverie.

> La lune se lève,
> O route en grand rêve!
> O route sans terme,
> Voici le relais,
> Où l'on allume les lanternes,
> Où l'on boit un verre de lait,
> Et fouette postillon,
> Dans le chant des grillons,
> Sous les étoiles de juillet.[19]*

It is interesting to note that this mode of incantatory verbal play is the real precedent for the incantatory mode of 'Prufrock', where Eliot, as Kenner notes, 'exploits . . . the authorized sonorities of the best English verse, *circa* 1870'.[20]

At this point it is necessary to begin to specify the differences as well as the similarities between Eliot and Laforgue: for in aligning his work with Laforgue's most mature achievement, Eliot, at the same time, moves beyond him. Laforgue's *Dernier Vers* are at once more impressionistic tone-poems 'in the form of a dream' than is 'Portrait of a Lady', with its Jamesian quasi-narrative structure, and somewhat less mobile and oblique than 'Prufrock' – a poem which is radically decentred, being structured around an 'overwhelming question' that is never posed. The dominating Jamesian echoes in Eliot's two culminating Laforguian poems suggest that in 'crossing' his poetry with the example of James's work, and in particular his tales of middle age and the wasted life, such as *The Beast in the Jungle*, Eliot succeeds in achieving a detachment from the dandy persona, which he is able to employ and simultaneously subject to critical scrutiny. This is one way of measuring the distance between 'Conversation Galante' and 'Portrait of a Lady'.

In 'Portrait of a Lady' Eliot constructs a tripartite narrative and dramatic structure which relies on structural rather than phrasal repetitions. Each of the three seasonal scenes contains a structural parallelism, with the first section being devoted to the woman's words and the insistent personal claims that underlie her repetitive rhapsodic monologues; the second, terser and more succinct, concentrating on the young man's increasingly discomforted reactions. The climax of the poem is reached in the third section, with her sudden and significantly succinct admission on learning of the young man's decision to go abroad that 'we have not

---

* The moon rises, O road in the midst of a dream! O road without limit, Here is the relay, where the lamps are lit, and one drinks a glass of milk, and whips the postilion, amidst the song of crickets, under the July stars.

developed into friends', which destroys the fictive premise upon which their relationship, and the poem, is built.

> 'Perhaps you can write to me.'
> My self-possession flares up for a second;
> *This* is as I had reckoned.
> 'I have been wondering frequently of late
> (But our beginnings never know our ends!)
> Why we have not developed into friends.'
> I feel like one who smiles, and turning shall remark
> Suddenly, his expression in a glass.
> My self-possession gutters; we are really in the dark.

At this climactic point in the poem, the speaker loses his defining quality: his sang-froid, or in the terms of the poem, 'self-possession', which he had precariously retained at the conclusion of the previous section:

> I keep my countenance,
> I remain self-possessed
> Except when a street-piano, mechanical and tired
> Reiterates some worn-out common song
> With the smells of hyacinths across the garden
> Recalling things that other people have desired.
> Are these ideas right or wrong?

The effectiveness of Eliot's poems lies in the implication that the speaker's language, his dandy's idiom of restrained and restricted personal reactions and responses, is insufficient to deal with the situation in which he is implicated, and fails to engage with his disquieting new perception of the needs and desires of others. 'Are these ideas right or wrong?' – the generality of the terms, leaving us in doubt as to whether 'right' and 'wrong' are being invoked as ethical or intellectual categories, and what exactly these ideas are, is both comic and poignant in its inadequacy. His 'self-possession' is finally ruptured by a disturbing moment of self-objectification: 'I feel like one who smiles, and turning shall remark/Suddenly his expression in a glass.' Here, a sudden perception of the ethically questionable status, or at best sheer inappropriateness, of the polite, socially endorsed 'smile' to the situation in which he finds himself, serves to rob the young man of his repertoire of socially acceptable responses, thus effectively depriving him of his 'language'. He is, in imagination, reduced to the nightmarish, shifting, gestural expression of the animals of the circus or menagerie; hence, dehumanized.

> And I must borrow every changing shape
> To find expression . . . dance, dance
> Like a dancing bear,
> Cry like a parrot, chatter like an ape.
> Let us take the air, in a tobacco trance –

Over twenty years after the writing of 'Portrait of a Lady' Eliot was to describe Laforguian irony as a means 'to express a *dédoublement* [doubling] of the personality against which the subject struggles'.[21] In 'Portrait of a Lady' we find use of irony that serves to reveal a gulf between the public and private self which is not bridgable, but reduces the private self to incoherence. In Laforgue's *Dernier Vers*, the dandy persona functions relatively simply as a stylization of the self, allowing the poet to express an ironic and often anguished perception of the transience of the present; in 'Portrait of a Lady', combined with a Jamesian awareness of social nuances, it is seen as a social mask that can imply a crucial restriction of personal and intellectual response.

Eliot's Jamesian investigation of self-alienation and social forms is taken even further in 'The Love Song of J. Alfred Prufrock'. Here again Eliot can be seen as going beyond Laforgue, but it is his general reliance on Laforguian devices that allows him to do so. Even the use of brief verbal cameos, such as the celebrated couplet

> In the room the women come and go
> Talking of Michelangelo.

owes much to Laforgue's use of laconic presentative details, as in these lines from 'L'Hiver qui vient':

> Ah, nuées accourues des côtes de la Manche,
> Vous nous avez gâté notre dernier dimanche.[22]*

In 'Prufrock', having abandoned ostensible narrative, Eliot uses the entire battery of Laforguian devices to give coherence to his 'decentred' poem. He relies heavily on the use of formulaic lines, such as 'And indeed there will be time', with its biblical resonances, and 'And would it have been worth it, after all' from which to develop his thematic variations; and we find structural parallelism, as in the three stanzas which begin with the line 'For I have known them all already, known them all –' and end with the question 'And how should I begin?' But the most important device is the use of thematic leitmotifs, in particular, the 'over-whelming question' which is never asked or answered. Structurally, this question belongs in the brief five line section that succeeds the plea 'And how should I begin?'; but Prufrock's statement becomes the enactment of a failure to formulate what the question would be.

> Shall I say, I have gone at dusk through narrow streets
> And watched the smoke that rises from the pipes
> Of lonely men in shirt-sleeves, leaning out of windows? . . .

> I should have been a pair of ragged claws
> Scuttling across the floors of silent seas.

---

* Ah, clouds come from the Channel coast, you have spoilt our last Sunday for us.

Soon after this failed attempt the moment of confession or admission is allowed to become retrospective: 'And in short, I was afraid.' In leaving the nature of the question indeterminate Eliot suggests both a radical questioning of Prufrock's 'society' idiom, and the cognitive value of language itself; recounted experience, the 'lonely men in shirt-sleeves', fails to connect with any valid vocabulary by which it can be interrogated. Prufrock is left with the despairing, neutralized sibilants of the final couplet, in which the metrical regularity of the poetic form enacts a sad parody of poetic meaning: for the only clear and harmonious statement Prufrock can make is that of a preference for the mindless and regular automatisms of the crab over the fine discriminations of consciousness.

In earlier drafts of the poem there was a section entitled 'Prufrock's Pervigilium' which was to be placed where the previously quoted five line section now appears. In this section, during a night vigil, a metaphysical (Bergsonian) question about the meaning of accumulated experience is posed; but this section was apparently excised on Conrad Aiken's advice.[23] It seems likely, however, that the excision owed less to Aiken's advice than to Eliot's own critical acumen. He did, after all, reject Pound's opinion of the inferiority of the Hamlet passage in the final section of the poem; and Pound informed the sceptical Harriet Monroe that, 'I dislike the paragraph about Hamlet, but it is an early and cherished bit and T. E. won't give it up, and as it is the only portion of the poem that most readers will like at first reading, I don't see that it will do much harm.'[24] In deciding to remove 'Prufrock's Pervigilium' Eliot judged, I think correctly, that the poem would be enhanced rather than damaged by leaving the 'overwhelming question' indeterminate: for a radical pessimism concerning the possibility of communication becomes a more fruitful and suggestive epistemological dilemma when the speaker lacks the conceptual vocabulary to formulate his own unease. The poem we have circles around its absent centre, accommodating passages such as the Hamlet paragraph mentioned above, which cohere through formal poetic devices and tone, creating a work that inhabits a zone between reverie and recollection, without the linearity of narrative or the definition of precise conceptual focus.

If we look for the common denominator of the four poems Eliot declared as being written 'sous le signe de Laforgue' we will find it not in allusions and verbal borrowings – Eliot borrows as much directly from Laforgue in 'Rhapsody on a Windy Night' as he does in 'La Figlia Che Piange' – but in the employment of a persona which allows the poet to speak, but through the mediation of an ironic mask. Eliot declared that 'J. Alfred Prufrock was in part a man of about forty and in part himself.'[25] In this, Eliot's practice – employing Laforgue's hapless, self-parodic personae, but working at a further degree of detachment and ironic scrutiny – can be seen as according with Barthes's view of Flaubert, who, as he writes in *S/Z*,

in welding an irony fraught with uncertainty, brings about a salutary uneasiness in the writing: he refuses to halt the play of codes (or does so badly), with the result that (and this is no doubt the true test of writing as writing) one never knows whether he is responsible for what he writes (whether there is an individual subject behind his language): for the essence of writing (the meaning of the work which constitutes writing) is to prevent any reply to the question: who is speaking?[26]

By contrast with the Laforguian poems, the first person in 'Rhapsody on a Windy Night' and 'Preludes' – both written in the same period as the Laforguian poems – is depersonalized. In the former poem, a recording eye/I is buffeted by unrelated images, and seeks and fails to find some consistency between the present and memory; in the latter poem, the first person is almost entirely displaced and repressed, to appear only momentarily at the conclusion of the poem.

> I am moved by fancies that are curled
> Around these images and cling:
> The notion of some infinitely gentle
> Infinitely suffering thing.

What Barthes terms 'un malaise salutaire de l'écriture' is also the index of an acute historical dilemma. As Jeremy Lane states, in a perceptive essay on the modern writer's relation to authority, 'While the writer is unable to rely on the security of a general, social, classical code of authorization, he is equally unable to project with any confidence an individual personal Romantic voice which may authorize the world and himself.'[27] It can be seen that Laforgue helps Eliot surmount, with one rather breathtaking step, some of the disabilities which attend first person utterance in the post-Romantic period: the developed dramatic monologues of 'Portrait' and 'Prufrock' are profound questionings of the authority of personal experience which Eliot can conduct because he is not conducting them in his own 'voice'.

In this context it is worth citing one of the sources for 'Portrait of a Lady', where the woman's recollection of 'My buried life, and Paris in the Spring' seems itself to be a concealed reference to Matthew Arnold's mid-Victorian dramatic monologue, 'The Buried Life'.[28] Arnold's poem is a relatively straightforward profession of Romantic sentiment, addressed to a beloved, and conducted without the use of a persona. The buried life itself is metaphorically an underground river of spontaneous emotion, 'the mystery of this heart that beats/So wild, so deep in us', which is lost or suppressed by worldly distractions, except 'when a beloved hand is laid in ours' and 'a lost pulse of feeling stirs again:/The eye sinks inward, and the heart lies plain,/ And what we mean, we say, and what we would, we know.' Eliot's poem seems to function as an endless regress of ironic perspectives on Arnold's Romantic, if characteristically melancholy, certitudes. In place of Arnold's healing communion of souls, by which 'A man becomes aware of his life's flow', Eliot's speaker is left with a painful memory of non-communion, by which instead of 'what we mean, we say', the public and private selves have been pulled irreparably asunder, leaving a pervasive sense of doubt and unease: 'Not knowing what to feel or if I understand . . . And should I have the right to smile?'

Importantly, although Eliot is not the speaker in his dramatic monologues, the voice of the poems is close enough to the poet's to allow him to be at once implicated, and absolved, by what is said. Hence the implications of the title Eliot chose for his first volume of poems, *Prufrock and Other Observations*, where 'observation', in its sense of a polite social aside, draws Eliot into the orbit of Prufrock's social values, while the more overt sense of a detached scientific 'observation' radically distances him.

To conclude, it can be suggested that Laforgue's use of the dandy persona in *Dernier Vers* provided Eliot with one of his most useful devices. The figure of the dandy allows the poet to employ a stylized version of the self in the poem, rather than being driven back to unmediated personal expression or the removed fictionality of the nineteenth-century dramatic monologue, as employed by Tennyson and Browning. Laforgue's mode allows the poet to deal with contemporary personal concerns without incurring the loss of perspective and critical distance entailed by straightforward lyrical utterance; it allows the poet to present rather than state. In this respect, Eliot was well ahead of Pound, who used Browning as the poetic model for his early 'dramatic' verse, and whose early poetry the younger poet seems to have reacted to negatively. 'His verse is touchingly incompetent',[29] Eliot wrote to Aitken on making Pound's acquaintance; and at the end of his career he was to describe Pound's early work as 'old-fashioned cloak and dagger stuff'.[30] Pound, on the other hand, reacted to 'Prufrock' as being the kind of verse towards which, since 'Contemporania' (1913), his own work had been moving. 'He has actually trained himself *and* modernized himself *on his own.*'

ii

In late 1916 or early 1917 – the approximate date of Pound's and Eliot's decision to go over to 'rhyme and regular strophes' – the connection between Laforgue's and Eliot's verse was very prominent in Pound's mind. In June 1917, he had published his review of *Prufrock and Other Observations* in *Poetry*, a review which twice mentions Eliot in connection with Laforgue, and, taken in the context provided by his remarks on Laforgue in 'Irony, Laforgue, and some Satire', clearly demonstrates that he saw Eliot as being the beneficiary of certain lessons drawn from the French poet. For my purpose, it is best to approach Pound's perspective on Eliot's early work through his views on Laforgue. By doing so it is easier to grasp the premises on the Laforgue–satire connection, which can be seen as influencing the subsequent course of both poets' development.

In 'Irony, Laforgue, and some Satire', the aspect of Laforgue's poetry which attracts Pound's central commendation is his ironic sophistication. 'He is perhaps the most sophisticated of all the French poets, so it is not to be supposed that any wide public has welcomed or will welcome him in England or America. The seven hundred people in both those countries, who have read him with exquisite pleasure, will arise to combat this estimate, but no matter.'[31] Pound quotes from Laforgue's transitional presentative verse to exemplify this ironic sophistication, as in fairly untranslatable lines from the 'Complainte des bons ménages'.

> L'Art sans poitrine m'a trop longtemps bercé dupe.
> Si ses labours sont fiers, que ses blés decevants!
> Tiens, laisse-moi bêler tout aux plis de ta jupe
>   Qui fleure le couvent.*

This leads into Pound's historical estimation and appreciation of Laforgue, which is summed up in the simple statement, 'Laforgue was a purge and a critic.' Pound sees him in the tradition of Flaubert, but without 'the clogging and cumbrous historical detail'; while in French verse 'he marks the next phase after Gautier in French poetry. It seems to me that without a familiarity with Laforgue one cannot appreciate – i.e. determinate the value of certain positives and certain negatives in French poetry after 1890.'

Pound then broaches the satiric aspect of Laforgue's work as he perceives it.

> He is an incomparable artist. He is, nine-tenths of him, critic – dealing for the most part with literary poses and *clichés*, taking them as his subject matter; and – and this is the important thing when we think of him as a poet – he makes them a vehicle for the expression of his own very personal emotions, of his own unperturbed sincerity.

> Je ne suis pas 'ce gaillard-là!' ni Le Superbe!
> Mais mon âme, qu'un cri un peu cru exacerbe,
> Est au fond distinguée et franche comme une herbe.†

Pound distinguishes Laforgue's exquisite, light, ironic 'satire' from the 'strident and satiric voice of Corbière', whose 'hard-bitten' tone he relates to Villon; from the 'drawing with rough strokes' of Tailhade; and from the burlesque of George Fourest. Laforgue was not a 'red-blood', and he was 'a better artist than any of these men save Corbière'. He sees all these poets as being effectively contemporary with each other for the English reader: 'They "reached" England in the nineties. Beardsley's *Under the Hill* was until recently the only successful attempt to produce "anything like Laforgue" in our tongue.'[32]

It is apparent that Pound is placing Laforgue in relation to the aesthetes, that art for art's sake movement which rebuked the cumbrous stupidities of the bourgeoisie by refusing to allow art any social utility. The analogy drawn between Laforgue's *Moralités légendaires*, with its ironic, burlesque treatment of the legends of Salome, Perseus and Andromeda *et alia* and Beardsley's scurrilous *Under the Hill* is merely

---

* Flat-chested Art has cradled and beguiled me for too long. If the ploughing is proud, how disappointing is the wheat! Come, let me bleat everything into the folds of your skirt which smells of the convent.

† I am not 'that hearty chap there!' nor The Haughty One! But my soul, which is irritated by a shout that is a little coarse, is at bottom distinguished and fresh as a herb.

baffling unless it is seen in the context of the aesthetes' negative definition – both are exquisite, almost effete productions which refuse the lure of seriousness. It is, however, questionable whether Pound is justified historically in describing Laforgue as an aesthete. Laforgue's extremely self-aware, self-lacerating manner does not permit the ascription of such generalized categories, and though he claimed to be a 'dilettante' there is a difference between a claim and a reality. While Laforgue's late verse has been seen as employing the stance of the 'dandy' – in Baudelaire's terms, 'an unemployed Hercules' – this term has been used to emphasize the reactive aspect of Laforgue's stance, his choice of this stance as a stylized gesture against 'the sordidness of life'. It is this reactive dimension that Pound does not seem to fully appreciate.

However, it is within the context of aestheticism that we can grasp the rationale of Pound's categorization of Laforgue as a satirist. Pound sees Laforgue as a writer whose irony exposes literary and existential clichés, in the tradition of Flaubert's *Bouvard et Pécuchet*.

> Chautauquas, Mr. Eddys, Dr. Dowles, Comstocks, societies for the preven-tion of all human activities are impossible in the wake of Laforgue. And he is therefore an exquisite poet, a deliverer of the nations, a Numa Pompilius, a father of light. And to the crowd this mystery, the mystery why such force should reside in so fragile a book, why such power should coincide with so great a nonchalance of manner, will remain forever a mystery.[33]

This last statement reveals that Pound sees Laforgue as exemplifying an appeal to minority values, the values of 'the intelligent': 'The ironist is one who suggests that the reader should think, and this process being unnatural to the majority of mankind, the way of the ironist is beset with snares and with furze-bushes.' Indeed, at the level of social intentionality Pound considers sophisticated irony to be implicitly satirical because of the effect it has on the average reader. Quoting a passage from one of the *Complaintes* he comments 'The red-blood has turned away, like the soldier in one of Plato's dialogues. Delicate irony, the citadel of the intelli-gent, has a curious effect on these people. They wish always to be exhorted, at all times no matter how incongruous. . .' In other words, for Pound 'delicate irony', excluding and exposing the inadequacies of the average reader, was tantamount to satire *on* the average reader. Laforgue's irony is seen as a satiric medium; but without overt vituperative comment or rhetoric, according to the practice of the 'movement against rhetoric' Pound saw at work in the 1890s.

From the perspective of Pound's own development, the lesson he draws from Laforgue's poetic example is of great significance.

> I do not think one can too carefully discriminate between Laforgue's tone and that of his contemporary French satirists. He is the finest wrought; he is the most 'verbalist'. Bad verbalism is rhetoric, or the use of *cliché* unconsciously, or a mere playing with phrases. But there is good verbalism, distinct from lyricism or imagism, and in this Laforgue is a master.[34]

This formulation was to remain a constant for Pound. In the 1928 'How to Read' essay he offers a definition of the distinction between verbalism, lyricism, and imagism, and uses Laforgue to exemplify the verbalist mode. He distinguishes 'three kinds of poetry': 'melopoeia', which is equivalent to lyricism, 'wherein the words are charged, over and above their plain meaning, with some musical property, which directs the bearing or trend of that meaning'; 'phanopoeia', which is a restricted and restrictive definition of imagism, 'a casting of images upon the visual imagination'; and 'logopoeia', verbalism,

> 'the dance of the intellect among words', that is to say, it employs words not only for their direct meaning, but it takes count in a special way of habits of usage, of the context we *expect* to find with the word, its usual concomitants, of its known acceptances, of ironical play. It holds the aesthetic context which is peculiarly the domain of verbal manifestation, and cannot possibly be contained in plastic or in music. It is the latest come, and perhaps most tricky and undependable mode.[35]

Pound makes it clear that he is thinking of Laforgue when he describes this mode. 'Unless I am right in discovering *logopoeia* in Propertius . . . we must almost say that Laforgue invented *logopoeia* observing that there had been a very limited range of *logopoeia* in all satire . . . At any rate Laforgue found or refound *logopoeia*.'[36]

It is apparent that at the latest by 1917 Pound was seeing Laforgue's ironic verbalism, his play with 'habits of usage', and socially conditioned idioms, as offering a supplementary mode to Imagism, and one by means of which poetry could best attain a satiric edge. It would be an error to see Pound's recommendation of logopoeia as being a rejection of Imagism, rather Pound is discovering precedents and offering a theoretical formulation for practices he was already in the process of developing. The terse epigrammatic poems he had written from the Greek or the Chinese as early as 1913 or 1914 were already employing an urbane irony, which accentuates a tone of voice, rather than relying on a realizable, visual image. What this means in relation to Pound's post-Imagist poetics is that the phase of Imagism as a technical discipline – the concentration upon 'Don'ts' and injunctions such as 'Direct treatment of the "thing" whether subjective or objective' – has been superseded, and Pound is willing to allow ironic ambivalence, connotation, a calculated precision in imprecision, based on the exposure of clichés, of 'known acceptances', into his verse.

In practice this means that Laforgue provides Pound with a precedent by which he can engage with contemporary mores; for the 'usual concomitants' of the word are socially conditioned, and as Pound saw in Laforgue, ironic play with received ideas is a method of achieving an oblique satiric exposure of common assumptions. One of Pound's first extended exercises in this mode is the sequence 'Moeurs Contemporaines';[37] and as indicated in the 'How to Read' essay, such methods are of great relevance to 'Homage to Sextus Propertius' and also to *Hugh Selwyn Mauberley* where the use of cliché serves as an ironic commentary on English norms, while being in a more profound sense a mode of satiric accusation. For

Pound, who had had the experience of watching the Vorticist sculptors, the lack of precision and exactitude he seeks to exploit and expose is an index of decadence. As he puts it towards the close of 'Homage to Sextus Propertius',

> For the nobleness of the populace brooks nothing below its own
>   altitude.
> One must have resonance, resonance and sonority . . . like a
>   goose.[38]

The sense of exact outline, of precise delineation, is, to Pound, an index of cultural health: a proof which is most effectively manifested in a culture's artistic and literary productions, while a lack of this sense is an index of cultural decline. Thus, we can appreciate that for Pound verbalism had to be a mode of satiric exposure – Laforgue is a 'purge and a critic' to Pound because the verbalist mode reveals ambivalences, vaguenesses and stupidities that a healthy society would not tolerate.

Before linking the previous remarks with Pound's perspective on Eliot's early work, it is necessary to make a brief but important point. When Pound reconciles Gautier's 'hard' strophes with Laforgue's verse by the statement, 'Verbalism demands a set form used with irreproachable skill. Satire needs, usually, the form of cutting rhymes to drive it home', he reveals that his understanding of Laforgue is based on a partial estimate of his verse: he ignores the *vers libre* of *Derniers Vers* which was of such importance to Eliot. Nowhere in his remarks on Laforgue does Pound mention him in connection with *vers libre*. This is extremely surprising given the extent of Pound's interest in Laforgue in the years 1917 and 1918, in which, in addition to giving Laforgue as much publicity as was feasible in the columns of *The Little Review*, he translated a story from *Moralités légendaires*, ('Salomé'), and one of the pierrot poems, under the pseudonym John Hall, and introduced a selection of his verse in the February 1918 'A study of Modern French Poets' edition – but significantly the six poems he introduced are all taken from *Les Complaintes* and *L'Imitation de Notre-Dame la Lune*. We must presume that Pound had access to the poems of *Derniers Vers*. He almost certainly read Laforgue's work in the four volume Mercure de France edition of *Oeuvres complètes* (1902–3), which had established Laforgue's reputation, and had been purchased by Eliot soon after he first read the poet in Symons's *The Symbolist Movement in Literature*.[39] The most feasible explanation for this neglect is at best hypothetical – that Pound, according to Gautier's practice primary importance during this period, was not receptive to the technical innovations of the man who can perhaps be regarded as the originator of *vers libre*; Pound thus concentrated exclusively on the body of Laforgue's work which used symmetrical forms. It seems likely that the 'verbalism' Laforgue practised in *Derniers vers*, which relies on impressionistic techniques, an exploitation of rhythmic sonorities and incantatory modes (which was so useful to Eliot in the composition of 'Prufrock') was not temperamentally congenial to Pound, whose irony remains terse, epigrammatic and focused outwards, even when dealing with cultural ambivalences, as in *Hugh Selwyn Mauberley*. Pound was in reaction against vague sonority, and fundamentally Laforgue could only deflect him from his primary aim, which was to achieve precision rather than to be suggestive. But if Pound can be held to have made a partial estimate of Laforgue, does he also make a partial estimate of the early work of T. S. Eliot?

Pound prefaced his review of *Prufrock and Other Observations* (1917) with an epigraph from Rémy de Gourmont, which encapsulates the essential significance of Eliot's early work as Pound perceived it, and also reveals the connection Pound made between Eliot and Laforgue. 'Il n'y a de livres que ceux où un écrivain s'est raconté lui-même en racontant les moeurs de ses contemporains – leurs rêves, leur vanités, leurs amours, et leurs folies.'[40]* It is this focus upon the contemporary scene which is the distinctive aspect of Eliot's work for Pound.

> I should like the reader to note how complete is Mr. Eliot's depiction of our contemporary condition. He has not confined himself to genre or to society portraiture. His
>
> > lonely men in shirt-sleeves leaning out of windows
>
> are as real as his ladies who
>
> > come and go
> > Talking of Michelangelo.
>
> His 'one night cheap hotels' are as much 'there' as are his
>
> > four wax candles in the darkened room,
> > Four rings of light upon the ceiling overhead,
> > An atmosphere of Juliet's tomb.[41]

Pound is quick to mention Laforgue, stating that 'It is quite safe to compare Mr. Eliot's work with anything written in French, English or American since the death of Jules Laforgue.' He proceeds from this statement to a characteristic condemnation of cultural insularity and we can be confident that Eliot's debt to Laforgue strengthened Pound's resolve to combat national versions of 'the tradition'. He continues by praising Eliot's work in the same terms he was to use in praising Joyce's *Ulysses*: Eliot had succeeded in the Aristotelian aim of capturing the universal in the particular. 'His men in shirt-sleeves, and his society ladies, are not a local manifestation; they are the stuff of our modern world, and true of more countries than one. I would praise the work for its fine tone, its humanity, and its realism; for all good art is realism of one sort or another.'[42]

As further evidence that Pound was seeing Eliot in the same terms as he saw Laforgue, we have the employment of the epigraph from de Gourmont, but applied to Laforgue, in Pound's introduction to his selection from Laforgue's work in the February 1918 'French Poets' edition of *The Little Review*. 'He,

---

* The only books are those where a writer has spoken of himself in recounting the mores of his contemporaries – their dreams, their vanities, their loves, and their follies.

Laforgue, satirizes inimitably Flaubert's heavy "Salammbô" manner. But he manages to be more than a critic, for in the process of this ironic summary he conveys himself, *il raconte lui-même en racontant son âge et ses moeurs*, he conveys the subtle moods and delicate passion of an exquisite and rare personality . . .'[43] Pound praises Eliot in roughly the same terms as he was to praise Laforgue; arguing for the inextricability of intelligence and emotion, he concentrates upon Eliot's modernity and his ironic delineation of the contemporary condition, seeing this 'realism' as primary: 'The vision should have its place in due setting if we are to believe its reality.' Finally, as regards the technical qualities of Eliot's work, Pound describes Eliot in terms which can be related directly to his remarks on Laforguian 'verbalism', subsequently defined as 'logopoeia'.

> Were I a French critic, skilled in their elaborate art of writing books about books, I should probably go to some length discussing Mr. Eliot's two sorts of metaphor: his wholly unrealizable, always apt, half ironic suggestion, and his precise realizable picture. It would be possible to point out his method of conveying a whole situation and half a character by three words of a quoted phrase; his constant aliveness, his mingling of a very subtle observation with the unexpectedness of a backhanded cliché.[44]

The first sort of metaphor we can appreciate as being Laforguian 'verbalism' or 'logopoeia', according to Pound's terms; the second, 'Imagism' in the stringent sense of 'phanopoeia'.

It can thus be suggested that Pound viewed Eliot as he viewed Laforgue: not merely as an ironist, but as a satirist. For Pound the distinction between the two modes was not particularly discernible; from our point of view the distinction is likely to be more apparent. It is not easy to see Laforgue's ironic mode, from which Eliot learnt so much in the writing of 'Portrait of a Lady' and 'Prufrock', as essentially satiric: we are more likely to see Laforgue's irony and Eliot's irony in his Laforguian poems as being predominantly self-reflexive. The sophisticated, but defeatist and hapless persona that Laforgue projects in *Derniers Vers* (and Eliot adapts in 'Portrait' and 'Prufrock') employs irony, but it is an irony that reflects back on the inadequacies of the speaker at least as much as it offers an indictment of *moeurs contemporaines* – prevalent vices and follies. Aware of the extremely personal basis of Laforgue's art (in *Derniers Vers* particularly) and retrospectively aware of Eliot's subsequent development, in particular his exploration of states of accidie in poems such as *The Waste Land* and 'The Hollow Men', we read Eliot's early poems as being at least as much an exploration of personal dilemmas as externalized societal satire.

But reading a knowledge of Eliot's subsequent development into these early poems does not help us appreciate how they appeared to the contemporary audience. The reception accorded to *Prufrock and Other Observations* indicates that, if not bewildered and hostile, readers were likely to regard a poem like 'Prufrock' as a light-hearted *jeu d'esprit*, latter day *vers de société*. As regards Pound's perspective, it seems likely that with his knowledge of, and early enthusiasm for, the dramatic monologue as derived from Browning, he was disposed against seeing a poem such as 'Prufrock' as being even obliquely a personal statement. He compares Eliot favourably with Browning in his 1917 review: 'Since Browning there have been very few good poems of this sort. Mr. Eliot has made two notable additions to the list. And he has placed his people in contemporary settings, which is much more difficult than to render them with medieval romantic trappings.'[45] It is very significant that in writing to Harriet Monroe, who was being refractory about the publication of 'Prufrock' (which it is apparent she lamentably failed to understand), Pound states: 'Now as to Eliot: "Mr. Prufrock" does not "go off at the end." It is a portrait of failure, or of a character which fails, and it would be false art to make it end on a note of triumph . . . For the rest: *a portrait-satire on futility* can't end by turning that quintessence of futility, Mr. P. into a reformed character breathing out fire and ozone [author's emphasis].'[46]

However, there is a difference between appreciating Eliot's early poems as dramatic monologue, and appreciating that the mode of functioning of that dramatic monologue is derived from the Laforgue of *Derniers Vers*, where the ironic, Hamletizing speaker is at once Laforgue *and* a persona: a dandy, a stylized version of the self. There are good grounds for considering that Pound's partial view of Laforgue's achievement colours his view of Eliot's work. When Pound mentions Eliot in connection with Laforgue in the *Egoist* review, it is to commend his use of set forms: 'If the reader wishes mastery of "regular form" the "Conversation Galante" is sufficient to show that symmetrical form is within Mr. Eliot's grasp. You will hardly find such neatness save in France; such modern neatness, save in Laforgue.'[47] The *vers libre* of *Derniers Vers* is, in practice, outside Pound's province; whether this is through aversion to Laforgue's use of sonorous incantatory modes, or through a less likely oversight, is not of immediate importance. What is important is that he commends the virtuoso, ultra-sophisticated 'presentative' Laforgue of *Les Complaintes* and *L'Imitation*, without engaging with the Laforgue who wrote at the conclusion of 'Simple agonie', what Symons terms his own 'solemn and smiling' epitaph.

> Il prit froid l'autre automne,
> S'étant attardé vers les peïnes des cors,
> Sur la fin d'un beau jour.
> Oh! ce fut pour vos cors, et ce fut pour l'automne,
> Qu'il nous montra qu' 'on meurt d'amour'!
> On ne le verra plus aux fêtes nationales,
> S'enfermer dans l'Histoire et tirer les verrous,
> Il vint trop tôt, il est reparti sans scandale;
> O vous qui m'écoutez, rentrez chacun chez vous.[48]*

It is this Laforgue who was of overwhelming importance to the young T. S. Eliot.

---

* He caught a cold the other autumn, lingering after the sorrow of hunting horns, towards the end of a fine day. Oh! it was for your horns, and it was for the autumn, that he showed us that 'one dies of love'! One will see him no more at public holidays, shut himself in History and pull the bolts, he arrived too early, he has returned without scandal; O you who listen to me, return each one of you to your homes.

3
The Oxford Poems and the Poems in French

i

Pound's bias in reading Laforgue, seeing him more as a critic of *moeurs contemporaines* than, as Eliot saw him, a uniquely personal poet, and his view of Eliot according to the same bias, would be of slight importance, except as evidence of the tendency of Pound's criticism and poetics in this period, were it not that we can hazard that his views influenced the direction that Eliot's work was to take after 1914. It also gives us clues towards the solving of what could be regarded as a literary conundrum: how is it that, if Pound was so active in publicizing and praising Laforgue's work after meeting Eliot, and so well aware of the relation between Eliot and Laforgue, and so willing to promote ironic 'logopoeia' as a means of exposing *moeurs contemporaines* – how is it that Laforgue effectively disappears as the predominant influence on Eliot's work after 1912, and was never reinstated as an active influence despite Pound's eager proselytization?

Here we must beware of suggesting that the primary reason for Eliot's stylistic shift away from Laforgue has anything to do with Pound. Eliot had ceased writing Laforguian poems in about 1912, and when he resumed the writing of poems which were destined for publication (the Oxford poems of 1914–15) we cannot doubt that in a sense Eliot had grown out of Laforgue. It is certainly apparent that he came to see Laforgue as a 'youthful influence' to whom he owed a great deal, but an influence it was necessary to supersede. This seems to be the reasoning behind Pound's remark in a 1928 letter to René Taupin: 'Je crois que Eliot, dont les premières poésies ont montré influence de Laforgue, a moins de respect pour Laf. que le respect que j'ai pour Laf.'[1] But we may still wonder how it is that Pound's enthusiasm, which certainly leaves some mark on *Hugh Selwyn Mauberley*, even if that influence is subsumed under the dominant influence of Gautier, so completely failed to re-excite Eliot's interest. It is worth suggesting here that in so far as Eliot was capable of being interested by Laforgue after 1914 that interest would be in Laforgue's mature achievement: the *vers libre* of *Derniers Vers* and

Laforgue's employment of the persona. Eliot does not return to those facets of Laforgue's work, but he does move towards modes that Pound could regard as being loosely 'Laforguian': ironic engagement with contemporary mores; use of sophisticated, pseudo-scientific vocabulary; and, after 1916, the use of symmetrical forms. But these characteristics are not really the aspects of Laforgue's achievement that interested Eliot; and Laforgue was no longer the dominant influence on his work.

If Pound's excited commendation of Eliot to Harriet Monroe in 1914 was as one who had 'modernized himself *on his own*', which in Pound's terms means engaging with the contemporary scene in contemporary language, we can assume that the aspect of Eliot's work that he especially commended to the author in 1914 was that which remained as the keynote of the 1917 *Egoist* review: 'I should like the reader to note how complete is Mr. Eliot's depiction of our contemporary condition.' This is a natural judgement for Pound to make, given the trajectory of his own work from the 'Contemporania' series of 1913, through to the work contained in *Lustra* (1915); the 'Moeurs Contemporaines' sequence (1917); and finally, *Hugh Selwyn Mauberley* (1920). As previously mentioned, this development of Pound's work was initially stimulated by his contact, at the inception of Imagism, with Ford Madox Ford, who, according to Pound, laughed uproariously at his archaisms, and encouraged him to make his work deal with the contemporary scene in the language of the present. We can argue that the terms of Pound's appreciation did have some positive effect on Eliot's work, and that effect was not to turn him back to Laforgue, but towards Pound himself.

The Oxford poems, here so named because Eliot wrote them while at Oxford in 1914–15, engaged in studying for and producing his doctoral thesis on F. H. Bradley, are more like certain of Pound's poems of the period than they are like anything Eliot had previously produced. The immediate relationship is to the series 'Contemporania', which Pound described to Harriet Monroe by writing 'I don't know that America is ready to be diverted by the ultra-modern, ultra-effete tenuity of Contemporania.'[2] Pound himself believed his influence to be visible in Eliot's work of 1914–15; writing to John Quinn in 1918, as an aside, he comments, 'T. S. E. first had his housemaids drooping like the boas in my "Millwins", and it was only after inquisition of this sort that he decided to the improvement of his line, to have them sprout.'[3] (The comment is interesting in that it demonstrates that Eliot was accepting Pound's critical suggestions as early as 1914–15.) 'Les Millwins' (published in *Poetry*, November 1913), is one of a number of poems Pound wrote in this period, when he was first to attempt to achieve an 'ultra-modern, ultra-effete tenuity', in which he gives a laconic, ironic, exteriorized cameo picture of *moeurs contemporaines*, in which personal comment is almost totally eschewed in the interests of 'presentation'. These poems, very much the fruit of Pound's Imagist endeavour, are far from being the dominant element in his production (and it is hard to see them as being 'modern', except in that Pound was working hard to purge his verse of archaisms); they are, however, the finest of his Imagist poems, those in which he best succeeds in keeping his own personal concerns and obsessions out of the poem. Representative examples to which Eliot would have had access are, in addition to 'Les Millwins', 'The Garden', 'The Bellaires', and 'Albâtre', which can be quoted in full.

> This lady in the white bath-robe which she calls a peignoir,
> Is, for the time being, the mistress of my friend,
> And the delicate white feet of her little white dog
> Are not more delicate than she is,
> Nor would Gautier himself have despised their contrasts in
> whiteness
> As she sits in the great chair
> Between the two indolent candles.[4]

The poem accords finely with Imagist desiderata, being a terse, spare presentation, in which no word could be sacrificed without a diminution of effect. We recall Aldington's one sentence definition: 'Hard, direct treatment, absolutely personal rhythm, few and expressive adjectives, no inversions, and a keen emotion presented objectively.' The poem's irony establishes itself in the first two lines with the woman calling her bath-robe 'a peignoir' and being 'for the time being' the mistress of his friend (thus socially placing the woman); and that irony underwrites the entire poem's effects, from the wry comparison between the whiteness of the dog's feet and the whiteness of its mistress, to the laconic suggestiveness of the two 'indolent' candles. The reference to Gautier, who wrote the poem 'Symphonie en blanc majeur', predicates the poet's social and aesthetic sophistication, a quality of fine art connoisseurship that sets him apart from the scene which he beholds. The poem achieves its effect in a few spare strokes, and no comment or expansion is desired or necessary.

Eliot's Oxford poems, 'Morning at the Window', 'The Boston Evening Transcript', 'Aunt Helen', 'Cousin Nancy', 'Mr. Apollinax' and 'Hysteria', all, except for the prose-poem 'Hysteria', pursue a similar policy of ironic, laconic exteriorization, which eschews personal comment or involvement in favour of a terse presentation of an existing social milieu. The obvious comparison is between 'Les Millwins' and 'Morning at the Window', which is a particularly good example of Pound's Imagism in that it attempts to record an interacting complex of impressions occurring in a moment of time, 'the precise instant when a thing outward and objective transforms itself, or darts into a thing inward and subjective,'[5] as Pound commented on his poem 'In a Station of the Metro'. The other Oxford poems are less overtly Imagistic than ironic presentations of vitiated cultural norms, like 'Aunt Helen'.

> Miss Helen Slingsby was my maiden aunt,
> And lived in a small house near a fashionable square
> Cared for by servants to the number of four.
> Now when she died there was silence in heaven
> And silence at the end of the street.

> The shutters were drawn and the undertaker wiped his feet –
> He was aware that this sort of thing had occurred before.
> The dogs were handsomely provided for,
> But shortly afterwards the parrot died too.
> The Dresden clock continued ticking on the mantelpiece,
> And the footman sat on the dining-table
> Holding the second housemaid on his knees –
> Who had always been so careful while her mistress lived.[6]

While we cannot help being aware of the slightness of this type of poetry in comparison with Eliot's previous verse – the almost clumsy straining for ironic effect in lines such as 'He was aware that this sort of thing had occurred before', which detracts from the more balanced, off-hand irony of the conclusion – this poem, though not the best of the Oxford group, usefully demonstrates the direction Eliot's poetry was to take after his Laforguian phase. In sloughing off Laforgue's influence, Eliot moves towards the oracular disappearance of the poet/persona, who cedes place to an exteriorized presentation of *moeurs contemporaines*. All four of the poems written 'sous le signe de Laforgue', and included in *Prufrock and Other Observations*, obliquely implicate the poet through the medium of a persona; while 'Preludes' and 'Rhapsody on a Windy Night' present a depersonalized 'I', which is in a sense constituted, certainly implicated, by the aggregate of sordid, fragmentary images it perceives. The difference in the Oxford poems is that for the first time we have a more radical ironic detachment; Eliot manipulates the elements that constitute the poem allowing almost no reference back to the subjectivity of the author.

Moreover, in moving away from Laforgue Eliot abandoned the use of rhythmic sonority in favour of a deliberate flatness of tone. The Oxford poems have almost no verbal resonance in comparison with the parodic playing with rhythms and phrases that helps make 'Prufrock' so memorable: 'I grow old . . . I grow old . . ./I shall wear the bottoms of my trousers rolled.' This kind of formulaic, nursery-rhyme playing with language, which Eliot derived from Laforgue (lines like 'Moi, je ne vais pas a l'église,/Moi, je suis le Grand Chancelier de l'Analyse,')[7] is abandoned in favour of a willed terseness of phrase which is in line with Pound's practice. If we disapprove of Pound's poetics we can characterize this mode of verbal functioning as being 'flat', 'thin', and rhythmically inert; if we are in sympathy, even while we concede the deficiencies of these particular poems, we can regard them as a commendable seeking for exactness and precision, the 'clear outline' Pound desired. Leaving aside the issue of Pound's influence on Eliot, these poems are, in their 'hardness', their eschewal of expansiveness (of rhythm or comment), in their 'objectivity', closer to Imagist practice, whether that of H. D., Aldington, or Pound, than they are to the rhetorical grandiloquence of 'Prufrock', a poem which does not so much 'present an intellectual and emotional complex in an instant of time', as embody an *état d'âme* (state of the soul) – an embodiment that has no necessary beginning or ending. This is not to say that these poems are Imagist, but that Imagism, particularly as practised and promul-gated by Pound, who did not demand pictorial images, provides the necessary context for comprehending the direction of Eliot's development.

Without any doubt the Oxford poems are a lesser achievement than Eliot's Harvard poems; and undoubtedly even Pound did not accord them the importance he accorded to Eliot's earlier work (though it is worth noting that in his corres-pondence he described the first batch, 'The Boston Evening Transcript', 'Aunt Helen' and 'The Death of St. Narcissus', which Eliot withdrew from publication, as 'three jems',[8] mentioning a 'forthcoming Cousin Nancy'). However, they are Eliot's first sustained attempt at poetic composition after a considerable interval devoted to his philosophic studies. It seems worth suggesting that Eliot, who had entrusted 'Prufrock' some years earlier to Conrad Aiken who showed the poem to Harold Monro, the editor of *Poetry and Drama*, to receive the opinion that it 'bordered on insanity',[9] would have been more than a little pleased and overawed by the ready reception his work was accorded by Pound. Eliot was unknown; Pound was already established as an avant-garde poet of some notoriety, who numbered among his acquaintances most of the period's 'names', and had acted as secretary to the redoubtable W. B. Yeats. While not suggesting that the Oxford poems were written 'to please' Pound, it seems logical that the first fruits of Eliot's renewed poetic impulse should accord with the practice of the man to whom Eliot was very much in the position of protégé to master. Eliot was subse-quently to prove himself a very independent disciple as regards his poetic practice and his criticism; but there are good reasons why Eliot, taking up the threads of poetic composition in 1914 to 1915, should have immediately resorted to modes in line with Pound's reading of his previous verse and the tendency of Pound's own. It is worth noting that the irony of the Oxford poems is indeed close to satire; and it is worth reading these poems in relation to Pound's later sequence 'Moeurs Contemporaines', where the modes employed are very similar to Eliot's, the rela-tive lateness of Pound's sequence being discernible in a strengthening of satiric attack. These poems provide the most relevant points of reference for Eliot's poems of 1914–15.

'Mr. Apollinax' has a breadth of implication beyond that of the other Oxford poems because in this poem alone the satiric portrayal of a vitiated, emotionally anaemic New England milieu is counterpointed against an ambiguous positive: Mr Apollinax himself. Eliot would undoubtedly have sympathized with Joyce's declared intention in writing *Dubliners*, 'to betray the soul of that hemiplegia or paralysis which many consider a city';[10] there is a similar intention behind the Oxford poems. Mr Apollinax, based on the priapic figure of Bertrand Russell (whom Eliot had met as a Harvard student in 1914, and who was to play an ambiguous role in the early history of his marriage to Vivienne Haigh-Wood in 1915) is a disturbing presence. He is at once attractive by virtue of his vitality – 'I heard the beat of a centaur's hoofs over the hard turf/ As his dry and passionate talk devoured the afternoon', this voracity of appetite being contrasted with the desic-cation of 'dowager Mrs. Phlaccus, and Professor and Mrs. Cheetah', of whom 'I remember a slice of lemon, and a bitten macaroon' – yet disturbing by emphasis on his extra-human, mythic dimension. He is at once Priapus, the old man of the sea, and a centaur: in all, a not quite human figure. 'He laughed like an irresponsible foetus': the image hovers in an unresolved tension between approval and alarm, as does the entire poem. The constant emphasis upon Mr Apollinax's amusement and laughter, is, as ever in Eliot's early poetry, an emphasis upon a phenomenon of ethically dubious status (see 'Hysteria', 'Portrait of a Lady', and 'Preludes'). It seems that for Eliot, as for Baudelaire, laughter was more likely to evince cruelty than innocence. 'It is certain, if one wished to put it from the point of view of the orthodox spirit, that human laughter is intimately allied to the mischance of an ancient Fall, a physical and moral degradation',[11] as Baudelaire put it in 'Of the Essence of Laughter'. However, Mr Apollinax, being an extra-human figure, escapes any direct human assessment of his behaviour; he is quite simply a phenomenon.

> I looked for the head of Mr. Apollinax rolling under a chair
> Or grinning over a screen
> With seaweed in its hair.

The studied neutrality of 'its' rather than 'his' emphasizes this extra-human dimension. The anti-heroic employment of myth for ironic purposes, as in the reference to John the Baptist, is one of the lessons Eliot learned from Laforgue, and in particular from the short stories of *Moralités légendaires*,[12] from which Eliot also culled the anti-heroic references to John the Baptist and Hamlet which he had deployed so effectively in 'Prufrock'.

The overall significance of the poem is, however, anticipatory, in that it establishes one of the major thematic polarities upon which Eliot was to articulate the later quatrain satires: a contrast between a sexually based, unreflective vitality, which in the figure of Sweeney becomes a caricatural form of brutality, and a hyperconscious emotional and sexual desiccation. The author's relation to these externalized extremes is, as in 'Mr. Apollinax', one of detachment, but a detachment fraught with ambiguity and tension. He is at once able to recognize and thus condemn anaemic desiccation – here epitomized by the New England milieu – while at the same time implying a compound of attraction and repulsion towards the sexually based vitality of a Mr Apollinax, which, as in the later quatrain poems, is regarded as being inhuman. In the case of Mr Apollinax, it is regarded as superhuman, of mythic dimensions; in Sweeney's case it is regarded as subhuman, hence animal, as, for example, in the poem 'Sweeney Erect'.

Eliot, the poet, is committed to neither extreme – he manipulates these irreconcilable attitudes to create a thematic dynamic for his satire. However, through the Laforguian persona of the emotionally ineffectual, sophisticated dandy, a 'pâle et piètre individu/Qui ne croit à son Moi qu'à ses moments perdus',[13]* which Eliot adapted to good effect in his four Laforguian poems, Eliot can be seen as having

---

* A 'pale and wretched individual who only believes in his Self at forgotten moments'.

associated himself with the hypercivilized, sexually ineffective pole of these attitudes − hence his mixture of fascination and repulsion when he considers the
contrary extreme. If the poet is present at all in 'Mr. Apollinax' it is as 'Fragilion,
that shy figure among the birch-trees', in contradistinction to the gaping Priapus
in a Fragonard tableau; while, in the later 'Burbank with a Baedeker: Bleistein
with a Cigar', it is the ineffectual Burbank who is closer to the poet while Bleistein
attracts his fascinated animus. However, in externalizing and satirizing the New
England milieu, Eliot is asserting his detachment from an environment with
which he is implicated: the mode of treatment predicates the author's 'difference'.
This is Eliot's oblique answer to Pound's comment to Carlos Williams in 1920.
'There is a blood poison in America . . . Eliot has it perhaps worse than I have −
poor devil.'[14]

This was to be a characteristic procedure in Eliot's verse: the purgation of an
attitude or set of responses which are close to the poet's own, by the adoption and
deployment of those attitudes and an exploration of their effectual limits in verse.
As in a dramatic monologue, the poet's independence of the aesthetic structure is a
testimony to his autonomy towards the attitudes deployed. In writing 'Portrait of
a Lady' and 'Prufrock' Eliot has at once absorbed and understood from within the
full implications of the Laforguian attitude, but he has also, by the creation of a
poem employing a persona, asserted his detachment. This process of 'mastery by
absorption' is one of the fundamental dynamics of Eliot's dramatic monologues.
The implications of this procedure are to be seen in 'Gerontion', which will be
read in the context of Eliot's reading of *The Autobiography of Henry Adams* − a
displaced Boston 'aristocrat' like James and Eliot, whose failures and attitudes
Eliot comes to terms with by writing a poem that *uses* these attitudes and hence
masters them.

ii

We can confidently speculate that after the writing of the Oxford poems there was
an interval in Eliot's poetic production of six months to a year, which was
terminated by the writing of the poems in French (1916−17), which were
produced immediately before the first of the quatrain poems, both groups being
published in *Ara Vos Prec* (1920). Eliot himself tells us that,

> At that period I thought I'd dried up completely. I hadn't written anything
> for some time and was rather desperate. I started writing a few things in
> French and found I could, at that period. I think it was that when I was
> writing in French I didn't take the poems so seriously, and that, not taking
> them seriously, I wasn't so worried about not being able to write. I did these
> things as a kind of *tour de force* to see what I could do. That went on for some
> months. The best of them have been printed. I must say that Ezra Pound
> went through them, and Edmond Dulac, a Frenchman we knew in London,
> helped with them a bit. We left out some and I suppose they disappeared

completely. Then I suddenly began writing in English again and lost all desire to go on with French. I think it was just something that helped me to get started again.[15]

Of this group of poems, four were printed in *Ara Vos Prec*: 'Le Directeur', 'Mélange Adultère de Tout', 'Dans le Restaurant', and 'Lune de Miel'; they need not detain us except in so far as they reveal elements helpful to an understanding of Eliot's subsequent poetic practice.

The first two poems, 'Le Directeur' and 'Mélange Adultère de Tout' are both slight and Corbièresque. They can almost be regarded as the *quid pro quo* Pound returned for the interest in Laforgue that Eliot had aroused in him. Here, it is as if Pound had returned the compliment by emphasizing the quality of Corbière to the younger writer. To Pound, Corbière had qualities that made him especially useful to a satiric critic of *moeurs contemporaines*; Pound consistently emphasizes his affinity with Villon, while in 'The Hard and Soft in French Poetry', Corbière is singled out as a successor to Gautier as a practitioner of 'the hard'. In the context of Eliot's association with Pound, the fact of his passing interest, testified to in these two rather whimsical poems, is almost more interesting than the poems themselves. Both display their affinity with the work of Corbière less in the adoption of a vehement, hard-bitten irony, *à la* Villon, than in the formal employment of short lines, and obtrusive, opportunist rhymes, and a superficial reference to Corbière's themes. In 'Le Directeur', the social gulf between 'Le directeur/Conservateur/Du Spectateur', and 'Une petite fille/En guenilles', who stands in the gutter and 'Regarde/Le directeur/Du Spectateur/Conservateur/Et crève d'amour',[16]* reflects lightly back to Corbière's awareness of social inequalities; while in 'Mélange Adultère de Tout', Eliot, again lightly, adapts Corbière's personal theme of the shiftless traveller who reconciles seemingly incompatible qualities. Yet, though Eliot may have appreciated the Laforguian echoes in Corbière's questioning of personal identity, such as in the lines, [he] 'Ne fut *quelqu'un*, ni quelque chose/Son naturel était la pose . . .' ('Épitaphe'),† insofar as Pound is justified in perceiving affinities between Corbière and Villon, it is apparent that Eliot was reluctant to associate himself with Corbière's socially low, Villonesque stance – unwilling to associate himself, as does Corbière in 'Le Crapaud' with the 'rossignol de la boue.'[17]‡ These two poems which display the influence of Corbière are urbane, detached, virtuoso exercises, which employ elements of Corbière's work, but do not adopt the harsh personal involvement (which can easily lapse into self-pity) that is intrinsic to the author of *Les amours jaunes*: a *poète maudit* as well as a dandy.

The other two poems in French, 'Lune de Miel' and 'Dans le Restaurant', display no single dominant influence (though a knowledge of Corbière, Laforgue,

---

* 'The Conservative director of *The Spectator*' and 'a little girl in rags', who stands in the gutter and 'looks at the Conservative director of *The Spectator* and dies of love'.
† He 'was neither *someone* nor something, his natural state was the pose . . .'
‡ 'The Frog', 'the nightingale of the mud'.

and in 'Dans le Restaurant', a previous reading of Rimbaud is apparent), and both are more ambitious pieces, less easily comprehended by the category *tour de force*. 'Dans le Restaurant' is interesting as an obliquely personal poem: if we discount 'Hysteria' it is the first poem since Eliot's Harvard verse in which the poet figures significantly within the poem as narrator, rather than under the guise of a persona; while 'Lune de Miel' can be seen as anticipating the presentative, satiric techniques of the quatrain poems.

In dealing with 'Dans le Restaurant'* first (although it is extremely unlikely that it was composed before 'Lune de Miel'), the discussion can concentrate on two points, a textual allusion and a textual revision. The first, the narrator's interjection 'Mais alors, tu as ton vautour', reveals that the dramatic situation and the central image of the poem owes much to Gide's novel, or as he categorized it, *sotie*[18] (an ironic or didactic narrative) *Le Prométhée mal enchaîné*,[19] a work that Eliot was much later to draw on for the composition of the Christian allegory of section IV of 'East Coker'. Eliot also mentions the book in *The Use of Poetry*. 'As Andre Gide's Prometheus said . . . Il faut avoir un aigle',[20] though Eliot does not mention that Gide's Prometheus ends up by eating his pet bird. In Gide's book Prometheus enters a Parisian restaurant where he shows his eagle to a *garçon*, and two other mythic diners, after they have insisted that he reveal his 'distinctive trait'. Prometheus's eagle could as well be a vulture (as in the original myth), and in Prometheus's reply.

– What have I got, Gentlemen? – What have I got, well! it's an eagle.
– A what?
– An eagle – or perhaps a vulture . . . it's hard to decide.[21]

Prometheus and his vulture-eagle (the vulture becomes an eagle after Prometheus decides to love it) are in the Romantic tradition, as in, for example, in Shelley and Goethe, symbols of the Christ-like artist, whose art is paid for by his suffering. Gide, in his ironic use of the myth, which displays obvious similarities to Laforgue's use of myth in *Moralités légendaires*, is well aware of this heritage. His

---

* 'In the Restaurant'. The run down waiter who has nothing to do except scratch his fingers and lean on my shoulder: 'In my country it will be the rainy season, wind, full sun, and rain; it's what they call the beggars' washing-day' (Garrulous, slobbering, with a rounded rump, I beg you, at least, don't slobber in the soup.) 'The willows soaked, and buds on the blackberry bushes – it's there, in a sudden shower, that one shelters. I was seven years old, she was younger. She was soaked through, I gave her some primroses.' The stains on his waistcoat add up to the sum of thirty-eight. 'I was tickling her to make her laugh. I felt a moment of power and delirium.'
But come now, old lecher, at that age . . . 'Sir, life is hard. A big dog came to paw us: I was afraid, I left her half-way. It's a pity.' But then, you have your vulture! Go away and clean out the wrinkles of your face; here, my fork, scour out your skull. By what right do you pay for experiences like I do? Come, here are ten sous, for the public baths.
Phlebas, the Phoenician, drowned for five days, forgot the cries of the seagulls and the Cornish sea-swell, and the profits and losses, and the cargo of tin: A deep-sea current took him far away, he relived the stages of his past life. Imagine it so, it was a painful fate; nevertheless, he was once a fine man, tall of stature.

Prometheus answers the *garçon*'s inquiries as to his occupation by declaring that he used to make matches, an obvious allusion to the theft of fire; but the waiter, unable to rest content with this declared occupation decides, 'Then let us put: man of letters'[22] – a man of letters, or words. Thus Prometheus becomes the incarnate Word, a bringer of illumination, combining the Titan and Christ in the figure of the artist.

Hence in 'Dans le Restaurant', after the run down waiter has finished his tale of childhood trauma, the narrator exclaims, 'Mais alors, tu as ton vautour!', the narrator's surprise that the waiter, a 'vieux lubrique', has a vulture, being mitigated by a knowledge of Gide's text, where in his public lecture, Prometheus lays down two definite propositions. 'First point: it is necessary to have an eagle. Second point: Besides, we've all got one.'[23] However, the narrator of Eliot's poem is not quite willing to allow the waiter parity of experience – 'De quel droit payes-tu des expériences comme moi?' – and he offers the waiter punning, allusive advice which prepares for the final verse paragraph, presenting the posthumous career of 'Phlébas, le Phénicien' (later adapted to form the 'Death by Water' section of *The Waste Land*). He tells the waiter to 'décrotter les rides du visage' ('to clean away his tears'), *rides* being both wrinkles and the ripples of water; to 'décrasse-toi le crâne' with a fork, as would the vulture, but also as would happen to a drowned man; and he finally gives him 'dix sous' for the public baths, directly anticipating the fate of Phlébas, who returns the compliment by 'repassant aux étapes de sa vie antérieure', as the waiter does in relating this childhood story.

In less immediate terms, Eliot's employment of the Prometheus myth, mediated through Gide, in 'Dans le Restaurant' indicates his profound affinity with that aspect of the Romantic tradition which saw such mythic figurations as accurate depictions of the situation of the artist. Laforgue, though somewhat more subversive than Gide in his use of myth in *Moralités légendaires*, was at the same time obsessed with the myth of Philoctetes, the Argive bowman whose power was intimately connected with the suppurating wound which necessitated his isolation on Lemnos. The adoption of these myths is one aspect of the theme Frank Kermode treats in *Romantic Image*, where he accurately describes the situation of the Romantic writer in terms by which the artist's search for 'the image' involves chosen isolation and the abandonment of the normal human orientation towards action. However subversive and ironic the Laforguian use of particular myths may be in a poem like 'Prufrock', the underlying myth of the artist is still profoundly Romantic and relatively straightforward: the artist as solitary creator attended by the opportunities and disabilities that define this condition, under which he pursues a quest for the image.

The second textual point is a revision, which can serve to reveal the deeper significance of the waiter's tale. In the September 1918 edition of the *Little Review* in which the poem was first published (between Yeats's 'Major Robert Gregory' and a chapter of *Ulysses*), and also in *Ara Vos Prec*, the line which in Eliot's *Collected Poems 1909–19* reads 'J'éprouvais un instant de puissance et de délire' ('I felt a moment of power and delirium'), reads instead as 'Elle avait une odeur fraiche qui m'était inconnue-' ('She had a fresh scent which was unknown to me-'), [24] a possible echo of some lines in Rimbaud's 'Les Poëtes de sept ans'. By strengthening the line after 1920, through a less oblique transcription of the waiter's reactions, Eliot, perhaps inadvertently, makes apparent the relation between this episode, 'Elle était tout mouillée, je lui ai donné des primevères' . . . 'Je la chatouillais, pour la faire rire./J'eprouvais un instant de puissance et de délire', and the culmination of the second verse paragraph of *The Waste Land*, the elements of which are exactly parallel.

> 'You gave me Hyacinths first a year ago;
> 'They called me the hyacinth girl.'
> – Yet when we came back, late, from the hyacinth garden,
> Your arms full, and your hair wet, I could not
> Speak, and my eyes failed, I was neither
> Living nor dead, and I knew nothing,
> Looking into the heart of light, the silence.
> *Oed' und leer das Meer.*[25]

The two incidents, though parallel in kind, are not in any way equal in emotional weight. In the passage from *The Waste Land* the weight of reiterated negatives constructs a precarious positive, until in the statement 'I knew nothing', 'nothing' is almost a substantive, a state to be known. This state, leading to the Buddhist calm of 'Looking into the heart of light, the silence', is a twilight, indeterminate condition, verging on vacancy or plenitude, before the sudden Wagnerian recall to an actuality of implied failure, *'Oed' und leer das Meer.'* The waiter's tale, however, is constantly counterpointed by satiric comments on his present condition; and it has a burlesque dénouement when, as a ludicrous Actaeon, he admits to being scared away by a big dog. 'Moi, j'avais peur, je l'ai quittée à mi-chemin.' However, even aside from the duplication of details (spring flowers, moisture), the two incidents demonstrate a more profound parallelism in being depictions of a crucial erotic incident, characterized by a loss of the sense of self-identity: an experience which is ambiguously positive, but which cannot be sustained, and is followed by aridity and failure. These erotic instants can be regarded as nodal points of experience, almost in the sense that Lawrence (a writer with whom Eliot shared little) would have comprehended. The waiter, now a 'vieux lubrique', is obsessed by his juvenile fiasco; the moment and his subsequent cowardice have assumed incommensurate importance for him; while in *The Waste Land*, a delayed commentary on the incident in the hyacinth garden (and the other modes of sexual and personal surrender in the poem) seems to be offered in 'What the Thunder Said':

> DA
> *Datta*: what have we given?
> My friend, blood shaking my heart
> The awful daring of a moment's surrender

Which an age of prudence can never retract
By this, and this only, we have existed
Which is not to be found in our obituaries
Or in memories draped by the beneficent spider
Or under seals broken by the lean solicitor
In our empty rooms.[26]

Eliot's transcription of these states always emphasizes their briefness and transience: 'un instant de puissance et de délire', 'the awful daring of a moment's surrender', and behind all these references which provide parallelisms both in text and signification it is possible to trace the influence of some lines in a passage in Tourneur's *The Revenger's Tragedy* which had great personal import for Eliot. He quotes the lines and discusses them in the 1930 essay on Cyril Tourneur; but more relevantly, in a period context, he quotes the entire passage in 'Tradition and the Individual Talent'. The relevant lines have been italicized.

And now methinks I could e'en chide myself
For doating on her beauty, though her death
Shall be revenged after no common action.
Does the silkworm expend her yellow labours
For thee? For thee does she undo herself?
Are lordships sold to maintain ladyships
For the poor benefit of a bewildering minute?
Why does yon fellow falsify highways,
And put his life between the judge's lips,
To refine such a thing – keep horses and men
To beat their valours for her?[27]

The significance these lines had for Eliot is made clearer in a letter from Eliot to Stephen Spender of 1935, in which he writes,

You don't really criticize any author to whom you have never surrendered yourself . . . Even just the bewildering minute counts; you have to give yourself up, and then recover yourself, and the third moment is having something to say, before you have wholly forgotten both surrender and recovery. Of course the self recovered is never the same as the self before it was given.[28]

Obviously, Eliot is here applying to the process of criticism a reference to a passage which has its primary significance as a description of extra-literary matters (though considering the effect of Eliot's youthful encounter with the work of Jules Laforgue, in practice such demarcations are somewhat arbitrary); but the terms used are helpful in clarifying what might remain implicit in Eliot's 'poetic' reading of Tourneur's lines. The 'bewildering minute' (detached from the revulsion and disgust of the Jacobean context) is a moment of sexual surrender; the word 'bewildering' – so much 'richer' than the alternative reading 'bewitching',

Eliot commented in 1930[29] – emphasizes the loss of self-identity induced by powerful, almost involuntary, sexual and personal attraction. Perhaps a final metamorphosis of these lines from Tourneur can be discerned behind the lines in section I of *Ash-Wednesday*, where the poet declares that he will forgo 'The infirm glory of the positive hour . . . The one veritable transitory power', which is associated with the Edenic 'There, where trees flower, and springs flow . . .' The experience of 'the bewildering minute' is always presented in Eliot's poetry as a transient temporal phenomenon. In *Ash-Wednesday* such sensory, temporal experience, as represented by the temptation of the 'broadbacked' flautist in section III of the poem, is rejected by the poet in order to transcend profane and secular values.

This might seem to have taken us a long way from 'Dans le Restaurant', but we will return, and conclude, by suggesting that Eliot's post-1920 revision of the line to read 'J'éprouvais un instant de puissance et de délire', was made to emphasize the fundamental significance of the waiter's tale as an instant of self-surrender followed by failure and guilt; an emphasis that textually and semantically relates this section of 'Dans le Restaurant' to the passages in Eliot's work that have been instanced, all of which to some degree relate back to the lines in Tourneur's *Revenger's Tragedy*. The telling of this experience is sufficient for the narrator to allow, 'Mais alors, tu as ton vautour!', but the ludicrous denouement of the tale, which prompts the waiter's tears, does not impress the narrator beside his own memories: 'De quel droit payes-tu des expériences comme moi?'

'Lune de Miel',* almost certainly written before 'Dans le Restaurant', can be regarded as the first poem in which Eliot was to employ the satiric methods of the quatrain poems, though in loosely rhymed alexandrines rather than Gautier's tetrameters. The advance this poem makes over the earlier Oxford poems is that of a move towards the aesthetic autonomy of a more economical presentative technique, which relies not on social tone or nuance – which refers the poem back to the poet – but has ironic contrasts and juxtapositions integrated within the aesthetic structure of the poem as elements of a presented scene. We can contrast the lines in 'Aunt Helen', 'Now when she died there was silence in heaven/And silence at her end of the street', in which the satiric juxtaposition of spiritual and mundane depends on an ironic inflection (almost a tone of voice) which hovers close to comment by the poet, with the relatively depersonalized presentation of the lines:

---

* 'Honeymoon'. They have seen the Low Country, they return to the High Ground; but one summer night, here they are at Ravenna, at ease between two sheets, at home with about two hundred bed-bugs; the summer sweat, and a strong smell of bitch. They lie on their backs spreading the knees of four soft legs all swollen with bites. They lift the sheet to scratch better. Less than one league from here is St. Apollinaire En Classe, a basilica known to connoisseurs of capitals [of columns] decorated with acanthus where the wind swirls.

They are going to take the eight o'clock train to prolong their miseries from Padua to Milan where one can find The Last Supper, and a cheap restaurant. He thinks about the tips, and draws up his balance sheet. They will have seen Switzerland and crossed France. And St. Apollinaire, stiff and ascetic, old factory unused by God, still holds in its crumbling stones the precise form of Byzantium.

Ils vont prendre le train de huit heures
Prolonger leurs misères de Padoue à Milan
Où se trouve la Cène, et un restaurant pas cher.
Lui pense aux pourboires, et rédige son bilan.[30]

The difference is that whereas the assertion 'there was silence in heaven' in the earlier poem is a reference outside the scope of the scene presented, introduced purely to establish a somewhat arch ironic effect, here there is little that we cannot accept as plausible at the level of fact, and little that overtly impresses us as the poet claiming a complicity between himself and the reader. The ironic juxtaposition between 'la Cène', the Last Supper, and 'un restaurant pas cher', in which the husband is concerned with material rather than spiritual accounting, gives the impression of existing in the poem independent of both poet and reader (though it is important to realize that it is only an *impression* of aesthetic autonomy that is achieved, especially for the English reader who is not placed to appreciate the awkwardnesses and errors of Eliot's French). The implied comment of 'Lui pense aux pourboires, et rédige son bilan', reveals that despite its 'realistic' plausibility, we are far from being in the realm of phenomenological reporting.

The newly weds are created with an ironic dispassion that permits them to attain to the status of the representative, while employing a maximum of specificity.

Mais une nuit d'été, les voici à Ravenne,
A l'aise entre deux draps, chez deux centaines de punaises;
La sueur aestivale, et une forte odeur de chienne.

The approximate specificity of the number of bed-bugs (which is made ludicrous by its pretence to precision) immediately qualifies the previous 'A l'aise' and prepares us for

Ils restent sur le dos écartent les genoux
De quatre jambes molles tout gonflées de morsures.
On relève le drap pour mieux égratigner.

The couple, absorbed by their physical discomfort, are reduced to the irritation of their limbs: 'quatre jambes molles tout gonflées de morsures'; their particular brand of physical absorption (inappropriate for a 'lune de miel') forming an ironic contrast with the monumental stillness of the Church of St Apollinaire, 'basilique connue des amateurs/De chapitaux d'acanthe que tournoie le vent.' At the conclusion of the second stanza, the appropriateness of the contrast of this particular church with the physical and material concerns of the honeymooners is made apparent.

Et Saint Apollinaire, raide et ascétique,
vieille usine désaffectée de Dieu, tient encore
Dans ses pierres écroulantes la forme précise de Byzance.

The lines can refer both to St Apollinaire, and his church, now secularized, 'dés-affectée' (a laconic comment on the 'amateurs', connoisseurs, and such tourists on their Baedeker tours); but the form, 'raide et ascétique', 'la forme précise de Byzance', remains, despite crumbling stones, an implicit reminder of spiritual austerity in a world of 'pourboires' and 'bilans'. While it would be extravagant to suggest that Eliot chose this particular church as a conscious reference to the rele-vance of Byzantine formal, linear art to the Vorticist endeavour, there can be little doubt that T. E. Hulme would have immediately appreciated the appositeness of this choice of non-vital, non-empathetic art to form a satiric contrast with the material concerns of the newly weds who are more absorbed by train timetables than the 'absolute' realm of ethical and religious values.

Thus Eliot's satiric technique establishes itself in this poem as a mode of presentation by which values are asserted obliquely through ironic juxtapositions, eschewing commentary and allowing these juxtapositions to achieve the desired satiric effect unaided. Though in 'Lune de Miel' much remains at the level of in-tention (rather than realization) it is apparent that to achieve this presentative satiric mode the newly weds must be maintained at the level of caricature, indeed dehumanized, being little more than an aggregate of itchy limbs and appetites; for we cannot be permitted to enter into an empathetic relation with them, we must only be allowed to register their physicality and circumscribed perspectives in order to appreciate the satiric contrast with St Apollinaire, 'raide et ascétique'. This mode of treatment asserts values, but the values are implicit, generated by the poem's formal techniques, rather than being stated or achieved through discursive comment.

In a perceptive discussion, commenting on the 'appropriate method' of 'Lune de Miel', Hugh Kenner asserts,

> This is a more important critical point than the fact that its personages are treated with no special compassion. They are bodies circulating within the sufficient system of the poem itself, which does not appropriate them for ridicule but contains them as elements in its own economy. Its objectivity is more efficacious than the studied insensibility of
>
>> The worlds revolve like ancient women
>> Gathering fuel in vacant lots
>
> (the prologue to which is 'Wipe your hands across your mouth, and laugh').[31]

Kenner's comment, which hovers uneasily between analysis and evaluation, takes the 'objectivity' of Eliot's poem at face value, and does not consider whether this 'objectivity' is itself dependent on a mode of treatment which promotes and estab-lishes certain values. The 'studied insensibility' of the conclusion of 'Preludes' has its effect because it is indeed 'studied', which implies a complexity of response: the inability of the poet to entirely dissociate himself from the scenes of sordidness and deprivation that the poem has disclosed. The less overtly problematic 'objectivity' of 'Lune de Miel' perhaps involves a more troubling 'insensibility', in that to achieve its formal efficacy a level of human response has been abandoned in favour of detached satiric scrutiny. The 'objectivity' of 'Lune de Miel' is in fact only a quasi-objectivity: the mode of treatment predicates non-humanist values in its very achievement of overt 'objectivity'. This Kenner is not in a position to appreciate, for identifying himself with the cultural premise upon which this poem is written (the 'isolation' of those like Wyndham Lewis and 'his dozen or so sympathetic readers . . . in a world of performing dolls'), he is unlikely to consider a number of issues that this very premise might raise. This is, of course, not to suggest that 'Lune de Miel' is an objectionable poem: rather that within the context of Eliot's development its witty dispassion provokes rather than closes discussion of certain issues.

Kenner, however, accurately comments, 'its suggestiveness inheres in the materials liberated by the aridity of expression, not in the auras and resonances of words'.[32] It is true that, in the attempt to achieve a precise, dispassionate satiric scrutiny, Eliot has entirely abandoned the incantatory verbalism of the Laforgue of *Derniers Vers*: irony is created more through the materials which are brought into contact than the ironic inflection given to a social usage. The poet does not mediate, even via a persona; he is not overtly implicated in the structure he projects. It will be appreciated how well, in a general sense, the poem complies with Imagist strictures. Although Pound's Imagism did not require an appeal to 'visual' values, this is the first of Eliot's poems to which terms like 'caricature', 'montage', and 'juxtaposition' can be usefully applied, while it is apparent how accurate Pound's 'semetaphorical' (sic) desideratum of 'hardness' is, as a description of the poem's overall effect. The next step in Eliot's development was to adopt the quatrain stanza of Gautier; to set a 'counter-current' going against the 'general floppiness' of *vers libre* in the hands of Amy Lowell and her 'bunch of goups'.

With 'Dans le Restaurant' and 'Lune de Miel' we bring Eliot's poetic production up to 1917–18. The latter poem was published with the other two French poems, and the first of the quatrain poems, 'The Hippopotamus', in the July 1917 edition of *The Little Review*; 'Dans le Restaurant', which Eliot presumably worked on for longer, was published with the more important quatrain poems in the September 1918 edition of that periodical. We can assume that in late 1916 or early 1917 the decision to turn to set forms was made, and in the next two years or so, Eliot was to write and publish the seven extant quatrain satires which were the fruit of that decision, while Pound's major contribution, the *Hugh Selwyn Mauberley* sequence, was published in 1920. In the following two chapters I shall examine both Eliot's and Pound's use of the Gautier quatrain.

4
Eliot and Théophile Gautier

In July 1917, the first of Eliot's quatrain poems, 'The Hippopotamus', was published in *The Little Review* with the bulk of the poems in French. Eliot, in the *Paris Review* interview given late in his life, saw the decision to employ 'rhyme and regular strophes' as primarily an attempt to experiment with Gautier's 'form', presumably for the disciplinary reasons Pound specifies, rather than because he was inspired by the absolute admiration, or 'demonic possession' he had experienced after first reading Laforgue. In the *Paris Review* interview, Eliot is asked to comment on Pound's statement that they had both adopted quatrains as a 'counter-current' against the 'dilutation (sic) of *vers libre*':

> ELIOT: I think that's something Pound said. And the suggestion of writing quatrains was his. He put me on to 'Emaux et Camées'.
>
> INTERVIEWER: I wonder about your ideas about the relation of form to subject. Would you have chosen the form before you knew quite what you were going to write in it?
>
> ELIOT: Yes, in a way. One studied originals. We studied Gautier's poems and then we thought, 'Have I anything to say in which this form will be useful?' And we experimented. The form gave the impetus to the content.[1]

This is obviously not quite the entire story. As indicated previously, Gautier's 'sculptured' verse appealed to Pound for more than just its quatrain structure, and he lauded Gautier's 'hardness' as being more a product of the quality of the emotions deployed in *Emaux et Camées* than merely a function of his use of a symmetrical form. While Pound's relation to Gautier will be discussed in further detail in the next chapter, Eliot's comment does serve to indicate that for him it was 'form' rather than 'content' that gave the initial impetus. That form, the octosyllabic rhyming quatrain, was maintained in seven of Eliot's poems published in the years 1917 to 1919 (though only in the first of these poems, 'The Hippopotamus', did he keep to Gautier's rigorous alternating rhyme; the other poems rhyme only the second and fourth lines). In the entire course of Eliot's poetic development this was the only instance where he was to maintain for more than a single poem a symmetrical form. The quatrain poems thus have a certain significance in Eliot's *oeuvre* by virtue of being a sustained formal achievement in a literary career where the verse pattern of each individual poem is as a rule *sui generis*.

As has been suggested, there is an implicit oppositional impulse behind the adoption of this austere form, requiring craftsmanship and discipline from the poet; the form itself was intended to constitute an indictment of the 'general floppiness' of what passed as *vers libre*. Here we can see in the most direct and uncomplicated manner possible a means by which 'form' can connote value when viewed historically within an actual social and literary context. Neither Pound nor Eliot needs to state that they have attained a level of technical competence, and can employ a demanding medium, which, like the sculptor's marble, presents formal difficulties to the artist; their employment of the form does this for them, while their professionalism is manifested in the ease and brilliance with which the quatrain is manipulated. As Eliot states, with reference to poetic technique, in an *Egoist* article, 'Professional, Or', in which he berates the British lack of, and suspicion of, professionalism in the arts, 'Technique is more volatile; it can only be learned, the more difficult part of it, by absorption. Try to put into a sequence of simple quatrains the continual syntactic variety of Gautier or Blake, or compare these two with A. E. Housman. Surely professionalism in the arts is hard work on style with singleness of purpose.'[2] It is this syntactic or rhythmic variety that distinguishes Gautier's or Eliot's use of the quatrain, and removes it from Housman's or Eliot's own immediate imitators (such as Robert Nichols in the pages of *Coterie*).[3] However, it is not just the employment of the quatrain structure, but the structure itself which suggests discipline and professionalism when seen within the context of a burgeoning literary production of second rate *vers libre*. That Pound, the poet most closely associated with the development of English *vers libre* through pre-Amy Lowell 'Imagisme', should a few years subsequently turn to the production of quatrain poems bespeaks a concern with maintaining literary standards which led him to note in 'Vers Libre and Arnold Dolmetsch' (1918), 'It is too late to prevent vers libre. But, conceivably, one might improve it . . .'[4]

That hard, strophic verse should constitute an implicit condemnation of formless *vers libre* can be readily appreciated. The very appearance of these compact blocks of verse incarnates the values of precision, concision and definite contours, as opposed to the formless, 'soft', and slack; the primacy of the artist's will is suggested by the manner in which he has imparted 'form' to his material. These values are explicit in Gautier's adoption of the form, as he states in the final stanza of his manifesto poem 'L'Art'.

> Tout passe. – L'art robuste
> Seul a l'éternité.
>   Le buste
> Survit à la cité.

Et la médaille austère
Que trouve un laboureur
    Sous terre
Révèle un empereur.

Les dieux eux-mêmes meurent.
Mais les vers souverains
    Demeurent
Plus fort que les airains.

Sculpte, lime, cisèle;
Que ton rêve flottant
    Se scelle
Dans le bloc résistant![5]*

As Gautier states earlier in this poem, and comments in his 'Salon' of 1845, 'Marble and verse are two materials equally hard to work, but the only ones that eternally retain the form which one confers to them.'[6] Hence, the 'rêve flottant' is removed from its transience and eternalized by being 'sealed' in the resistant material of sculptured verse; the fluid 'content' must accommodate itself to the austere 'form'. The Romantic basis of Gautier's poetry is apparent in the terms of this definition. We can go on to suggest that 'form' as practised by Gautier necessitates a certain epigrammatic concision: the 'rêve flottant' achieving precise definition through the beneficent friction between a 'fluid' content and a 'static' form. By comparison, in a poem like 'The Love Song of J. Alfred Prufrock', the 'rêve flottant' is accorded primacy and takes its own distinctive and unreproducible form. (Pound, perhaps, would regard the Laforguian 'Prufrock' as an example of 'impressionist' art, incarnating passive receptivity, as opposed to form-giving Vorticist art.) The rather simple point to be made is that the 'formed' quality of the Gautier quatrain is apparent immediately, before the reading process, to the visual sense. The eye perceives that the verse is 'formed' because it is presented with discrete blocks of typescript in a simple, unvarying symmetry. This could be seen as an aspect of what Joseph Frank, in the title of his influential article, terms the desire for 'Spatial Form in Modern Literature';[7] regarding this phenomenon as an attempt to capture in the literary medium something of the instantaneous perception which is possible in the visual arts.

Frank is well aware of the problems involved in maintaining this proposition, for he bases his discussion on Lessing's *Laocöon*, itself partly an attack on pictorial poetry, in which Lessing argues that,

> Form in the plastic arts . . . is necessarily spatial, because the visible aspects of objects can best be presented juxtaposed in an instant of time. Literature,

---

* Everything passes.– Only strong art possesses eternity. The bust outlives the city. And the austere medal found by a labourer beneath the earth reveals an emperor. The gods themselves die. But sovereign lines of verse remain stronger than brass. Carve, file, and chisel; let your hazy dream be sealed in the hard block (translated by Hartley).

on the other hand, makes use of language, composed of a succession of words proceeding through time; and it follows that literary form, to harmonize with the essential quality of its medium, must be based primarily on some form of narrative sequence.[8]

Thus, following Lessing, Frank realized that the reading process is indeed a 'process' and, as such, time dominated: the possibilities for instantaneous perception in literature are severely curtailed by the nature of the medium. Rather than seeing the phenomenon as being primarily 'pictorial', he dwells on the opportunities for synchrony (as opposed to diachrony) which are presented by the metaphoric/paradigmatic axis of the novel, as in Joyce's *Ulysses* or Proust's *Remembrance of Things Past*, and the compounding of past and present he considers is achieved in poems such as *The Waste Land* and Pound's *Cantos*.

As is implicit in the terms in which I have posed Frank's concerns, these topics anticipate areas of interest characteristic of emergent structuralist debate; and without the theoretical background provided by structuralism, Frank is unsure of the status of the phenomenon with which he is dealing. Stating acutely, if with some exaggeration, that 'language in modern poetry is really reflexive: the meaning-relationship is completed by the simultaneous perception in space of word-groups which, when read consecutively in time, have no comprehensible relation to each other',[9] Frank, after some consideration of T. E. Hulme's employment of Worringer's aesthetic theories in the latter's *Abstraction and Empathy*, goes on to regard this denial of sequence and temporality as serving an attempt (both in poetry and the novels he considers) to 'maintain a continual juxtaposition between aspects of the past and the present, in such a way that both are fused in one comprehensive view'.[10] When Frank, in a more judicious formulation, suggests that 'past and present are seen spatially, locked in a timeless unity which, while it may accentuate surface differences, eliminates any feeling of historical sequence by the very act of juxtaposition',[11] we have to state that in a poem like *The Waste Land* it is precisely these 'surface differences' (which connote an implicit sense of historical perspective) that are accentuated, and which impede the achievement of any confident 'comprehensive view'. We will return to these issues at the end of this chapter.

More particularly, in realizing, as is apparent in any discussion of Imagism, that such a drive towards the concrete, visual medium can only be maintained at the level of analogy, Frank largely ignores this movement. Thus, he fails to perceive the usefulness of the term 'spatial form' to describe the impulse away from the time-orientated, musical analogies characteristic of nineteenth-century Symbolism towards the attempt to achieve objective form, instantaneous, predominantly 'visual' perception, which Imagism constituted. Similarly, the musical analogy dear to Symbolism is finally subject to the limitation that even a rhetorical distinction between form and content is specific to literature. Once it is perceived that the impulse towards 'spatial form' is analogic, and the term itself an aesthetic metaphor, certain direct and pertinent applications become apparent.

As we saw in the discussion of Imagism, a fundamental desideratum of the movement was towards 'objectification', the aesthetic autonomy of the art-work:

as the sculpture is independent of its creator, so the poem should not need to be referred back to the subjectivity of the poet. This demand for 'impersonal' aesthetic autonomy can be seen to be relevant to Pound's and Eliot's adoption of the Gautier quatrain, for once the writer eschews a communicatory aesthetic and begins to regard the poem as an artefact, it becomes possible that the increased 'detachment' of the poet *vis-à-vis* the poem will encourage him to regard it in spatial terms, as a self-sufficient entity to be appreciated by the reader in terms analogous to the manner in which a painting or statue is viewed by the spectator. Criticism that acknowledges the importance of the 'silence' of the blank portions of the page to Mallarmé's poetry, or the exploitation by Pound of the typographic possibilities of presenting his verse in *The Cantos*, stimulated by his fascination with the hieroglyphic aspect of the Chinese ideogram, should readily accept that blocks of quatrains can connote aesthetic autonomy, and manifest an appeal to visual values which is rather more discreet than the excesses of 'concrete poetry'. Gautier, who was concerned to stress the craftsmanlike, volitional attributes necessary to the 'true' artist – the primacy of 'artifice' in art – demanded of the literary arts an approach towards the plastic, concrete qualities of the visual arts, and declaring himself to be 'plus plastique que littéraire', set about the construction of sculptured quatrains that declared their plastic values not only in content but also by their form: the crystalline quatrain.[12]

Gautier, in fact, manifested all the impulses and attributes we regard as being distinctive of Imagism some sixty or more years before that movement which is so integral to our understanding of the historical specificity of Modernism. Boschot informs us that

> In one letter, he said that he wished to write 'having things before his eyes'. In another, where he asks a friend to take notes for him, he advises, like a classicist (or rather like a reasonable chap) submission to the object:- 'Less reflections, verbiage and synthetic ideas; but *the thing, the thing*, and *always the thing*.' And that, as early as 1837, at the age of twenty-six.[13]

Here, the position of *Emaux et Camées* (1852) in Gautier's development is of some relevance. He began producing these quatrain poems as a conscious reaction against the effusive, self-expressive Romantic excesses of his earlier poetry (*Poésies* 1830, 1832, *Albertus* 1832). This turning away from the claims to cosmic significance, and the total moral and political commitment of the poets of French Romanticism, such as Hugo, Lamartine or Vigny, is realized in *Emaux et Camées*, which marks a development in French poetry away from the overtly rhetorical and declamatory towards the aesthetic, objective, detached Parnassian manner: the proclamation of the superiority of 'art' over 'life'. Previously, this tendency had been displayed in that first manifesto for *l'art pour l'art* aestheticism: Gautier's 1834 'Préface' to *Mademoiselle de Maupin*. This adoption of the aesthete's stance is embodied in the poems of *Emaux et Camées* by a detached, ironic manner, the willing eschewal of expansiveness and claims to philosophic significance, in favour of an art which models itself on the art of the miniature (Gautier referred to the genre of *Emaux et Camées* as the 'médaillon') – a form which emphasizes stylization, compactness, and aesthetic self-sufficiency. The rejection of 'engagement' which aestheticism was designed to manifest is implicit in these poems, with reference to the title of which Gautier stated,

> Enamels, Cameos, Caryatids, Festoons, Astragales, Amethysts, things which are painted, engraved, sculptured, designed, replace in the titles of poetry collections Voices, Songs, Meditations, Harmonies, Consolations, Thoughts, and all outpourings of the soul. Everything is plastic and picturesque.[14]

The relevance of this aspect of Gautier's development to the themes under discussion should be apparent. Gautier's reaction against the over-ambitious claims of French Romanticism (which could be aligned with Shelley's claim that the poet is the 'unacknowledged legislator of mankind') manifests the very tendencies that we have been examining in relation to Pound and Eliot: a movement away from a self-expressive, communicatory art (in the sense of discursive communication of 'ideas' and emotive communication of 'mood' through incantatory rhythms) towards a poetry of detached, 'impersonal' observation, which emphasizes the status of the poem as aesthetic artefact, rather than as expressive vehicle. In relation to Eliot, it needs to be stressed that it is these 'spatial' tendencies, as manifested in *Emaux et Camées*, rather than the poetry itself, which were of primary importance. Pound's radical over-valuation of Gautier, as, for example in his suggestion that Laforgue 'marks the next phase after Gautier in French poetry',[15] was not shared by the younger poet, who was well able to perceive that Gautier's epigrammatic concision often amounts to little more than preciosity. For Pound, also, these 'spatial' tendencies were of great importance and help to explain his otherwise somewhat inexplicable elevation of a minor poet. However, it does need to be pointed out that the leap Pound makes from Gautier to Laforgue omits Baudelaire, Rimbaud, and Mallarmé, and is, in relation to the values of nineteenth-century French poetry wilfully, almost perversely, selective. While Eliot dutifully followed Pound's interest in *Emaux et Camées*, he did not aggrandize Gautier's literary stature. This is demonstrated by the almost parodic manner in which he treats Gautier as a textual source; Eliot's direct relation to Gautier amounts largely to a relation with his formal emphases.

It is significant in relation to these themes that Gautier has been accused of the 'dehumanization' of art; his emphasis on the formal properties of the poetic art, as against lyrical or declamatory 'outpourings of the soul' anticipates tendencies which might have been considered exclusively Modernist, and indicate the existence of similar socio-literary tendencies. That Gautier should be considered to have written a cold, elitist poetry, and regarded himself as attempting to do so – 'Nothing is more insupportable than the word "me"' . . . We reduce ourselves as far as possible to being only a detached gaze'[16] suggests that this poetry of Parnassian austere withdrawal can be seen as presenting parallels with Eliot's and Pound's development. Gautier's aestheticism, established in the 1830s, is undoubtedly a romantic reaction against Romanticism; an analogous, though not equivalent reaction, can be perceived in the development of Eliot and Pound. Behind Pound's interest in Gautier's 'sculptured' verse, and the 'ironism' of Laforgue, there is the premise that the poet should be separate, hostile and alienated from his inevitable audience, the bourgeoisie, and the social and political status quo it maintains. We can suggest that in post-Romantic societies, a presentative art is likely to supersede a communicatory art when the situation of the writer is biased towards ideological isolation, and a disenchanted view of all the classes of the society in which he works. Sartre, writing of nineteenth-century French literature in general, comments of the writer: 'He spoke voluntarily of his *solitude* and, rather than ac-knowledging the public which he had craftily chosen for himself, he contrived that one writes for one's sole self or for God; he made writing into a metaphysical occupation, a prayer, an examination of conscience, everything except a com-munication.'[17] That Sartre's observation is underpinned by political assumptions as to the 'correct' relationship between writer and public does not, of course, mean that the observation is invalid.

The profound shift from the radicalism of French or English early Romanticism to the right-wing politics of a Pound or Eliot cannot be explained simply in these terms. We have to take into account the unquantifiable, but undoubtedly import-ant, influence of both poets' position as *émigrés* and estimate the effect of this on their attitudes and their verse. In a sense their true 'foreignness' compounds the in-creasing social isolation of the poet throughout the nineteenth century: for both poets were working in an environment which they could not help but be more radically detached from than even the most 'alienated' native poet, who would have an intuitive social comprehension. Within the development of post-Romantic poetry it can be suggested that once the poet accepts his art as a minority art, having little social effectiveness in a stabilized class society, an elitism (as mani-fested in the tendencies of Gautier or Baudelaire) becomes possible, and if a social diagnosis is sought, it becomes conceivable that democracy will be equated with levelling, debasing tendencies and various 'aristocratic' solutions will be preferred. Populism, the mob, 'homo canis' become the discernible enemies of the arts which require sophisticated appreciation, an awareness of tradition beyond that attained by the 'man in the street', who is berated as the lowest common denominator of the democratic ideal. Thus, hierarchy, authority, order, a sense of 'distinctions', become appealing concepts, and ironically, these Romantic (because condemned to Romanticism by the objective social and literary conditions of their period) poets and writers begin to develop nostalgic versions of aristocratic Classicism. In this context, Pound's abortive 1922 Bel Esprit scheme is particularly revealing. The scheme which Pound floated was to realize a form of subscription patronage, the first aim of which was to release Eliot from his exhausting labours in a bank. (Eliot, embarrassed, declined the invitation.) By this attempt and the terms in which he posed the project Pound reveals his desire to return to the patronage sys-tem which was the socio-literary basis of Classicism. In the outline of the scheme which he sent to William Carlos Williams, Pound begins by stating,

There is no organized or coordinated civilization left, only individual scattered survivors.

Aristocracy is gone, its function was to select.

Only those of us who know what civilization is, only those of us who want better literature, not more literature, better art, not more art, can be expected to pay for it. No use waiting for masses to develop a finer taste, they aren't moving that way.[18]

However, having strayed from Gautier, we must return to acknowledge that, despite the status of *Emaux et Camées* as a reaction against early French Romanticism, and its reputation as a cool, impersonal collection of poems, the modern reader is not likely to perceive this impassiveness, except in relative terms. *Emaux et Camées* is a subjective and essentially lyrical collection of poems, having for its inspiration personal events and circumstances in the life of the poet, who, unlike Eliot, has no real diffidence about employing the personal pronoun in his verse. A sizable number of the poems are love poems; and while the form prevents expansiveness and helps the poet to achieve obliquity and decorative rendition, despite the evocation of a gamut of moods and emotional registers, ranging from the ironic and sensual to the personal and moving, it is difficult to associate the dominant tone of this collection, that of the aesthete's religion of beauty, with the harsh satire of Eliot's *Poems* of 1920. Nor need we do so. But it will be easier to discuss both the similarities and the distinctions between Gautier and Eliot through a more particularized analysis and comparison of individual poems.

Eliot's first quatrain poem, 'The Hippopotamus', has as its central reference Gautier's 'L'Hippopotame', not one of *Emaux et Camées*, but from *Poésies diverses*; it is a poem which it is likely that Pound brought to Eliot's attention, since he had admired it for some years.[19] More than in any other of the later quatrain poems we find here a direct relation between Eliot's poem and a Gautier original. What is in the other poems generally a passing reference is here a direct borrowing of the central image/symbol; but, as commentators have noted, there are more dissimilarities than similarities between the two poems. It is worth quoting Gautier's poem in full in order to briefly consider the direction that Eliot has taken.

L'Hippopotame au large ventre
Habite aux Jungles de Java,
Où grondent, au fond de chaque antre,
Plus de monstres qu'on n'en rêva.

Le boa se déroule et siffle,
Le tigre fait son hurlement,
Le buffle en colère renifle,
Lui dort ou paît tranquillement.

Il ne craint ni kriss ni zagaies,
Il regarde l'homme sans fuir,

Et rit des balles des cipayes
Qui rebondissent sur son cuir.

Je suis comme l'hippopotame:
De ma conviction couvert,
Forte armure que rien n'entame,
Je vais sans peur par le désert.[20]*

The Gautier of 'L'Hippopotame' is the balanced, witty, ironic Gautier, whom Eliot was to compare with Baudelaire in these terms.

> In minor form he never indeed equalled Théophile Gautier, to whom he significantly dedicated his poems: in the best of the slight verse of Gautier there is a satisfaction, a balance of inwards and form (*sic*) which we do not find in Baudelaire. He had a greater technical ability than Gautier, and yet the content of feeling is constantly bursting the receptacle.[21]

In this admittedly slight poem of Gautier's the balance of form and feeling is indeed perfect: there is no sense of strain. However, Eliot, in adopting the dandyish irony of Gautier's 'conceit', and by applying it to a more external and formidable subject has crossed the boundary between self-reflexive irony and satire, and there is equally no sense of strain in the more ambitious and extensive poem he has constructed.

The most important distinction is the most obvious: Gautier's poem is presentative, but it finally reflects back on the poet's subjectivity: 'Je suis comme l'hippopotame/De ma conviction couvert', an obvious representation of the poet in 'the desert' of bourgeois society; while Eliot's poem functions at a further remove of objectivity, comparing the hippo, here *l'homme moyen sensuel*, with the church for parodic purposes, and not introducing the poet into its presentative scheme. Once we have acknowledged the borrowing of the central image, the use of equivalent rhythms based on a distich structure (though it is worth noting how Eliot's rhythm tightens when the hippo begins his apotheosis in stanza seven), we must go on to recognize in Eliot's poem a far greater breadth of comic invention. The comparison between the hippo and the church seems to allow a certain slippage between the two terms, so that the Church becomes a mode of superior hippo, less 'Susceptible to nervous shock' (a fine comic inversion of Gautier's original stress on the hippo's impassivity). The point of association is reached in stanza five, where the 'But' is rhythmically crucial yet also supererogatory: the hippo and the Church have attained a perilous unity, until the hippo is given his just apotheosis, preparing us for the final distich, which leaves us in no doubt about the difference

---

* The hippopotamus with a large belly lives in the jungles of Java, where growl, from the back of every cave, more monsters than one has ever dreamed of. The boa uncoils and hisses, the tiger roars, the buffalo snorts in anger, he sleeps or grazes tranquilly. He fears neither daggers nor assegais, he looks at man without fleeing, and laughs at the bullets of the sepoys, which rebound from his hide. I am like the hippopotamus: wrapped in my conviction, strong armour which nothing breaches, I go without fear through the desert.

between the righteous hippo and the 'True Church . . . Wrapt in the old miasmal mist.'[22] This element of almost dramatic development removes Eliot's poem from Gautier's, which is relatively lyrical and static in conception; there is no friction or osmosis between the two terms – the poet and the hippo are equivalent – their real inequivalence being the ironic premise upon which Gautier relies to achieve the desired effect. His joke is much simpler than Eliot's.

However, viewed in a broader perspective, we can perceive Eliot's poem as being a development as much as a departure from Gautier's example. Both poems have a presentative, pictorial quality, which in Eliot's poem suggests caricature or primitive art; and while 'The Hippopotamus' works at a further degree of objectification and separation between poet and poem, we can appreciate that Gautier's presentative irony, as best represented by *Emaux et Camées*, was an innovatory step in the direction that Eliot, and less radically Pound, were subsequently to take. Thus, if Pound's 'semetaphorical term' of 'hardness' is considered for its suggestive potential, it can be appreciated that Gautier's aesthetic theory and practice, which in the manifesto poem 'L'Art' still accords a place to the 'rêve flottant', is taken to a logical conclusion by Eliot, who expels all overt traces of the poet and his fluid reveries from the poem in the interest of defined satiric presentation. Although Eliot is usually and accurately represented as an auditory poet, in contrast to Gautier's 'plastic' sensibility, in adopting Gautier's form as a vehicle for exteriorized satire, Eliot was accepting a bias towards pictorial representation which suggests a detour away from the predominantly Symbolist tendency of his temperament and poet development. The verbal universe of *Ash-Wednesday* is in many ways closer to the incantations of 'The Love Song of J. Alfred Prufrock' than it is to 'Sweeney Among the Nightingales'. The quatrain form itself, biased as it is towards epigrammatic concision and allowing little opportunity for rhythmic expansiveness, is, if it is to be employed successfully, a more suitable vehicle for what Pound would term 'constatation' than introspective musing. It works well when employed to evoke definite quantities and sharp ironic contrasts; tangibles, preferably with 'clear contours', to suit the sharp outlines of the verse. This Gautier realized when he adopted the form for 'plastic' expression; and Eliot, in advancing the practice of 'hardness' a step further than Gautier's example, follows his lead in realizing that the most 'hard', tangible, flow-resistant counter in the poet's arsenal of effects is the evocation of a precise visual image. Auditory effects, whether we term them 'verbalism', 'incantation', or 'logopoeia' must by contrast be fluid and suggestive rather than precise, Symbolist rather than Imagist, emotive-empathetic rather than 'hard', 'spatial' and presentative.

While it might be possible to contest the statement that Eliot's mode in the quatrain poems is predominantly pictorial, it cannot be denied that they are more so than the poems of any other phase of Eliot's development. While the precise modes of Eliot's pictorialism will be discussed subsequently, it is worth pointing out that in allowing these poems a certain objectified dramatic quality, we indicate that a 'scene' is projected for our scrutiny. This is true of all the quatrain poems, however much they may substantiate that scene and develop the poem thematically by use of previous literature, allusions, and references to what may be considered exclusively literary values. Indeed, we are on safer ground if we suggest that there is a 'spatial' and pictorial quality to the manner in which quotations and allusions are employed, torn as they are from their original context and used to construct a linguistic collage. However, Eliot's employment of pictorial modes and conventions is generally more direct and ascertainable, as in, for example, the iconographic references of 'Mr. Eliot's Sunday Morning Service'; the caricatural, dramatic mode of 'Burbank with a Baedeker: Bleistein with a Cigar'; the caricatural, visual, descriptive method of 'The Hippopotamus', 'Sweeney Erect' and 'Sweeney Among the Nightingales'; and the pervasive use of such 'visual' techniques as juxtaposition and contrast, as in 'Whispers of Immortality', where a shift of tone is effected by a shift of attention from the fleshless skeletons of Donne and Webster to the fleshly 'Grishkin', herself a caricature of Gautier's 'Carmen'. The term 'caricature' is one that recurs in referring to the quality of Eliot's pictorial modes. This is not a term we would employ when discussing Gautier's 'plastic' explorations of reality. Even in his morbid, Gothic poems, such as 'Bûchers et tombeaux', or disenchanted and mundane, such as 'La Mansarde', Gautier is always more concerned with the picturesque and decorative, with fulfilling the aesthete's criteria of beauty, however eccentric (as, for example, in 'Étude de mains')[23] than with the depiction of the brutal and dehumanized, as in Eliot's 'Sweeney Erect'.

'Whispers of Immortality' makes an interesting comparison with Gautier's poetry, since it is the only one of the quatrain poems, aside from 'The Hippopotamus' that contains extensive references to Gautier's work. The initial four quatrains owe something to Gautier's 'Bûchers et tombeaux', while the second section is an adaptation of 'Carmen'. In his 1921 essay on 'Andrew Marvell', Eliot was to refer to the opening lines of 'Bûchers et tombeaux' in the course of an attempt to define wit: an

> alliance of levity and seriousness (by which the seriousness is intensified) is a characteristic of the sort of wit we are trying to identify. It is found in
>
> > Le squelette était invisible
> > Au temps heureux de l'art païen!
>
> of Gautier, and in the dandysme of Baudelaire and Laforgue.[24]

If we add the next two lines of the quatrain: 'L'homme, sous la forme sensible,/Content du beau, ne cherchait rien,'* we have the likely point of departure for Eliot's 'witty' disquisition on contrasting modes of corporeal perception in 'Whispers of Immortality'. Gautier's lines provide Eliot with a starting point, but it is important to realize that the entire drift of Eliot's poem is an ironic reversal of Gautier's poem. Gautier's recommendation of classical contentment with exterior,

---

* The skeleton was invisible in the happy time of pagan art! Mankind, content with beauty, searched for nothing beneath perceptible form.

palpable form in this initial quatrain is developed into a nostalgic contrast between classical, pagan serenity, where death, the skeleton, did not exist, and the febrile, medieval, death-oriented perceptions of Christian eschatology, symbolized by the *danse macabre*.

> Des dieux que l'art toujours révère
> Trônaient au ciel marmoréen;
> Mais l'Olympe cède au Calvaire,
> Jupiter au Nazaréen;
>
> Une voix dit: Pan est mort! – L'ombre
> S'étend. – Comme sur un drap noir,
> Sur la tristesse immense et sombre
> Le blanc squelette se fait voir . . .[25]*

Pound, in the crucial third section of *Hugh Selwyn Mauberley*, characteristically gives us a version of this which echoes Gautier's meaning as well as his form, and uses it as the basis for his denunciation of contemporary civilization.

> Christ follows Dionysus,
> Phallic and ambrosial
> Made way for macerations;
> Caliban casts out Ariel.[26]

Eliot, on the other hand, has taken a hint from Gautier, and coolly reversed the current of the French poet's perceptions. In the first section of 'Whispers of Immortality', the Christian, post-mediaeval, death-obsessed perception of a Webster or a Donne is established with dispassionate interest; it is not established to be condemned by reference to a serene, pagan ideal.

> Webster was much possessed by death
> And saw the skull beneath the skin;
> And breastless creatures under ground
> Leaned backward with a lipless grin.
>
> Daffodil bulbs instead of balls
> Stared from the sockets of the eyes!
> He knew that thought clings round dead limbs
> Tightening its lusts and luxuries.
>
> Donne, I suppose, was such another
> Who found no substitute for sense,
> To seize and clutch and penetrate;
> Expert beyond experience,

---

* The gods which art always reverences were throned in a marble heaven; but Olympus cedes to Calvary, Jupiter to the Nazarene; A voice says: Pan is dead! – shadows stretch forth. – Like on a black pall, on the immense and sombre sadness, the white skeleton appears . . .

> He knew the anguish of the marrow
> The ague of the skeleton;
> No contact possible to flesh
> Allayed the fever of the bone.[27]

These four quatrains, which have been taken as a commendatory text on 'undissociated sensibility',[28] presumably because Webster and Donne figure as exemplars of these mortuary perceptions, are less elucidated by reference to Eliot's 1921 essay on 'The Metaphysical Poets'[29] than they are by reference to Gautier's 'Bûchers et tombeaux'. Eliot's belief that 'The poets of the seventeenth century, the successors of the dramatists of the sixteenth, possessed a mechanism of sensibility which would devour any kind of experience',[30] helps us rather less in defining the mode of functioning of Eliot's poem, than the realization that Eliot is giving us a deadpan rendition of the very kind of 'Christian' perception that Gautier condemned. The point to be made is that Eliot 'states'; he does not, like Gautier, overtly condemn or recommend; and if we discern a current of commendation when this first section is brought into ironic collision and contrast with Grishkin's trivial world, that current is mitigated by the lively horror of the 'visual' imagery of this opening section. Depth of perception in this first section brings a terrifying awareness of 'the anguish of the marrow'; but emphasis on the fleshly superficies, as in Grishkin's section, brings a pervasive triviality, and a, perhaps involuntary, sense of repulsion that is if anything more acute than in the previous lines.

> Grishkin is nice: her Russian eye
> Is underlined for emphasis;
> Uncorseted, her friendly bust
> Gives promise of pneumatic bliss.
>
> The couched Brazilian jaguar
> Compels the scampering marmoset
> With subtle effluence of cat;
> Grishkin has a maisonette;
>
> The sleek Brazilian jaguar
> Does not in its arboreal gloom
> Distil so rank a feline smell
> As Grishkin in a drawing-room.
>
> And even the Abstract Entities
> Circumambulate her charm;
> But our lot crawls between dry ribs
> To keep our metaphysics warm.[31]

If the last two lines, which are semantically and rhythmically flawed by comparison with the sureness of tone of the rest of the poem, are intended to commend Grishkin's charms by comparison with the devolved, arid metaphysics of 'our lot', then that commendation does not really detract from what is predominantly a satiric portrayal. It is as if Eliot could not quite manage a positive to round off a poem composed of a double negative. Eliot's bathetic, tawdry epithets – 'Grishkin is nice', 'her friendly bust' – and his fixed concentration upon odours, sweat glands and secretions, reveals itself in a term indicative of loathing, 'so *rank* a feline smell', which serves to align Grishkin with Fresca, the *demi-mondaine* in a deleted Popian pastiche in *The Waste Land*:

> Odours, confected by the cunning French,
> Disguise the good old hearty female stench.[32]

Grishkin is based upon Gautier's Carmen, and presents us with another instance of ironic, satiric reversal of a Gautier original:

> Carmen est maigre, – un trait de bistre
> Cerne son oeil de gitana.
> Ses cheveux sont d'un noir sinistre,
> Sa peau, le diable la tanna.
>
> Les femmes disent qu'elle est laide,
> Mais tout les hommes en sont fous,
> Et l'archevêque de Tolède
> Chante la messe à ses genoux . . .[33]*

Eliot's debt to Gautier's poem is extensive. But once we have acknowledged the pervasive and particular similarities – the abrupt opening, the rhythm of which Eliot duplicates with a slightly more pronounced satiric inflection, the ironic cameo of the 'archevêque de Tolède' who 'Chante la messe à ses genoux', which parallels the obeisance of the 'Abstract Entities' in Eliot's poem, and the obvious similarity that Eliot's poem, following Gautier's, focuses upon a woman who exercises a sensual fascination – we are left with the duty of stating that Eliot's Grishkin is a satiric pastiche of Gautier's Carmen, and that Gautier's poem is a tribute to the slightly sinister fascination of Carmen, who in the final stanza is aligned with the 'âcre Vénus du gouffre amer', while Eliot's is a disenchanted portrayal of 'tawdry cheapness': 'Grishkin has a maisonette'. Thus, Eliot has constructed a poem which, having some of its main points of reference in the work of Gautier, has elected for its satiric mechanism an ironic reversal of Gautier's terms. In Gautier's work, a Carmen (or a Grishkin) is accorded an ambivalent approval, while the mortuary eroticism of a Webster or a Donne would be condemned in comparison to the 'healthy' exteriorized, Classical ideal, which these 'pagan' sensual women to some degree embody. Gautier's poems are implicitly didactic, even if that didacticism is mitigated by a developed ironism. Eliot inverts Gautier's poems to construct a satiric mechanism, which does not to anything like the same

---

* Carmen is skinny, – a line of bistre circles her gypsy eyes. Her hair is sinister-black, her skin, the devil tanned it. The women say that she is ugly, but all the men are mad about her, and the archbishop of Toledo chants the mass kneeling before her at her feet. . . .

degree choose to accord approval: it exists, almost hovers, in a negative ambivalence.

The late Elizabethan perceptions of a Donne or a Webster, imbued with their period's equation of sex with death, so that their febrile thought was at once 'possessed' (sexually and obsessionally) by death, and could 'possess' death (by a combination of sense and intellect so complete that it is almost sexual) – 'He knew that thought clings round dead limbs/Tightening its lusts and luxuries' – have a feverish intensity and starkness, an 'authenticity' that does not extend to Grishkin's world. Without this dichotomy the satiric contrast would fail. The distinction is tonal: the sombreness and Elizabethan Jacobean *gravitas* of the first section creates an emphatic discontinuity when we reach the jaunty 'Grishkin is nice . . .' But this dominant awareness of the *memento mori*, the death's head in an Elizabethan portrait, while recreated by Eliot with a grim, mordant relish, is still, surely, not offered for our approbation. Though it permits an undivided, totalized quality of perception which we could align with 'undissociated sensibility' – 'A direct sensuous apprehension of thought'[34] – the 'penetration' of these writers' sexual-intellectual perceptions disposed of the sensory conditions and limitations of actual existence – in Eliot's terms, 'No contact possible to flesh/Allayed the fever of the bone'. They penetrated too far, while Grishkin and her peers remain too content with the superficialities. The satiric friction of the two sections articulates this contrast between two partial, though not equivalent, modes of perception, each sited within a historical period, which are brought into abrupt juxtaposition, and not orientated *vis-à-vis* each other; which, indeed, are allowed to co-exist for the satiric friction of their propinquity. The effect sought after is that of collage, which, of course, eschews commentary. This is analogous to the mode Walter Benjamin was to develop in his collecting of quotations, by which he would place a German lyric of the seventeenth century next to a short newspaper report of the Nazi era, in the full knowledge that they would not illuminate each other, but by their very incompatibility exist in greater particularity, while implying a radical historical discontinuity or incoherence.

It is apparent from Eliot's adoption of Gautier's verse form, and use of some of Gautier's poems as points of reference for his own quatrains, that Eliot's relation to Gautier is to take him as a point of departure as well as a precedent to sanction the modes and ethos of his satiric verse. It is difficult to distinguish formal development from departure and any positive or negative conclusions are bound to be somewhat arbitrary, since they are necessarily dependent on the breadth of the historical perspective one chooses to apply. If we correlate *Emaux et Camées* and the *Poems* of 1920 on one broad historical grid, we can state that both manifest, though to differing degrees, the move away from the didactic, self-expressive, introspective tendencies of Romanticism in favour of an externalized 'objectivism'. More particularly, we are struck by the degree to which Eliot's satiric poems have erased any obtrusive trace of what is still apparently a personal, lyric inspiration in Gautier's *Emaux et Camées*. Gautier's asethete's perceptions and cameos seem sentimental beside Eliot's harsh, non-empathetic satiric delineations;

and this can be seen as the index of an historical development from 'disengage-ment' to cultural opposition. Then, viewed according to an even wider, perhaps more profound, historical perspective, we can suggest that the roots of Eliot's poetic, though less overtly than in the case of Gautier, must still be fundamentally Romantic. His 'objective correlatives' have the function of externalizing a personal vision of the poet's, and his voice does not have access to an overreaching Classical authority to relieve him of the burden of *individual* vision and judgement, which he disparagingly refers to as the 'Inner Voice'[35] in the 1923 essay 'The Function of Criticism'. This Eliot was to admit later in his career by conceding that 'a poet in a romantic age cannot be a "classical" poet except in tendency'.[36] Once this problem is specified, the phenomenon we have to examine in relation to Eliot's poetry is that of a necessarily Romantic poetry which simultaneously dis-guises and exploits its origins.

At this point it must be conceded that neither the generalized aesthetic category of 'spatial form', nor even the more neutral genre designation of 'satire', ade-quately decribe Eliot's quatrain poems. While the argument of this chapter has suggested that a term such as 'spatial form' is necessary to indicate certain repre-sentative features of the trajectory of Eliot's development away from the Symbolist, musical tendencies of his earlier verse towards a more objectified, societal focus – even if we use the term more loosely than Frank does – it must be admitted that this 'objectification' refers us back to the peculiar perceptions of Eliot, the poet, at least as much as it leaves us securely in possession of an aesthetic artefact, embodying an 'impersonal', satiric vision of society. That this is not entirely the necessary effect of those post-Romantic social and literary conditions mentioned previously can be ascertained by the manner in which in the earlier quatrain poems Eliot refuses to allow the reader to place himself in a secure relation to the poem's concerns. He uses an obscure narrative framework (the identity of Pipit in 'A Cooking Egg', upon which much critical debate has been expended, is a case in point), while in the later quatrains, Eliot seems to accentuate and at the same time disguise his personal perspective through what is often a wilfully idio-syncratic deployment of allusions and literary modes.

If we consider the specific terms of Frank's thesis in relation to 'Whispers of Immortality', we find that the general aim that he believes such self-reflexive poetic structures serve, maintaining 'a continual juxtaposition between aspects of the past and present, in such a way that both are fused in one comprehensive view',[37] is almost entirely alien to the effect of Eliot's poem. The Jacobean and the contemporary sections of Eliot's poem are riven by internal tensions which do not allow us to posit an attitude of approval or disapproval to either the past or the present, and their articulation, the one with the other, is in terms of satiric friction rather than the compounding of a 'comprehensive view'. The importance of this is not as a caveat to Frank's thesis – a suggestion that in practice such an omniscient perspective is difficult to achieve – but rather to assert that Eliot has constructed a poem which, in intentionally denying the achievement of a comprehensive view, must inevitably turn us back, often in puzzlement, to the viewpoint of the poet.

The lyrical element in these poems becomes important as we find ourselves searching for a coherent basis on which to organize the societal-satiric elements. In an *Athenaeum* article, 'Beyle and Balzac', of 1919, Eliot wrote,

Stendhal's scenes, some of them, and some of his phrases, read like cutting one's own throat; they are a terrible humiliation to read, in the understanding of human feelings and human illusions of feelings that they force upon the reader.

The exposure, the dissociation of human feeling is a great part of the superiority of Beyle and Flaubert to Balzac . . . But the patient analysis of human motives and emotions, and human misconceptions about motives and emotions, is the work of the greatest novelists, and the greatest novelists dispense with atmosphere. Beyle and Flaubert strip the world, and they were men of far more than the common intensity of feeling, of passion.

It is this intensity, precisely, and consequent discontent with the inevitable inadequacy of actual living to the passionate capacity, which drove them to art and to analysis . . . they suggest unmistakably the awful separation between potential passion and any actualization possible in life. They indicate also the indestructible barriers between one human being and another.[38]

Something of this sense of 'the inevitable inadequacy of actual living to the passionate capacity' inheres in 'Whispers of Immortality', and the other quatrain poems, and it is to discern the precise quality of Eliot's disillusion, articulated not in didactic generalizations but in sharply delineated satiric cameos, that we return to the quatrain poems. Eliot too, 'strips the world' of its clichés and condolences; and if we look for a personal statement in 'Whispers of Immortality', it is surely integrated with the title of the poem, which referring us back to Wordsworth's 'Ode. Intimations of Immortality from Recollections of Early Childhood', reads as Eliot's laconic disavowal of 'faith that looks through death', and the 'years that bring the philosophic mind'.[39]

In this context, it is worth considering 'A Cooking Egg' in its entirety. Here, in the only one of the quatrain poems in which the poet employs the first person and figures directly in the poem's presentative schema, the epigraph from the opening lines of Villon's 'Testament', 'En l'an trentiesme de mon age/Que toutes mon hontes j'ay beues . . .' ('In the thirtieth year of my life/Having undergone all my humiliations . . .') prepares us for a vision of 'the indestructible barriers between one human being and another' in which the terms of a previous, or possible intimacy – 'the penny world I bought/To eat with Pipit behind the screen' – is contrasted with an actuality composed of the trivial properties of Pipit's contemporary existence – '*Views of Oxford Colleges*/Lay on the table, with the knitting.' However, the poet is not unimplicated; through the epigraph and the project of the 'penny world' he is involved in the failure suggested by the first lines of the poem, 'Pipit sate upright in her chair/Some distance from where I was sitting', where the stiffness of 'upright' validates the real 'distance' between the two. In the central section of the poem, a satiric litany, figures from the past and present are appropriated to drive home the affective inadequacy of Pipit's world, but without suggesting the real possibility of an alternative existence (in 'tradition' or spiritual realities). A figure such as Coriolanus, who has resonance in Eliot's later poetry (the final section of *The Waste Land* and the 1930s' piece *Coriolan*) becomes merely an alternative to Sir Philip Sidney among 'other heroes of that kidney'; while in view of Eliot's subsequent reverence for Dante it comes as something of a shock to find that Piccarda de Donati from *Paradiso*, Canto III, whose words are integrated with the final lines of *Ash-Wednesday*, is coupled with Madame Blavatsky (the probable prototype for Madame Sosostris in *The Waste Land*) as an acceptable alternative to Pipit's company in heaven.

> I shall not want Pipit in Heaven:
> Madame Blavatsky will instruct me
> In the Seven Sacred Trances;
> Piccarda de Donati will conduct me.[40]

In Eliot's amusing but jaundiced catalogue in the central section of 'A Cooking Egg', history is abstracted into surfaces, and when Frank writes of the suppression of temporality which he regards as the premise of 'spatial' techniques, his views offer us some revealing clues as to Eliot's practice. Following the example of T. E. Hulme, he goes back to Worringer's *Abstraction and Empathy* to argue that, as Worringer posited, linear geometrical art suppresses the temporality, the element of 'depth', in three-dimensional naturalistic representation, so in the literary techniques of 'spatial form' an 'abstraction' of history occurs by which 'history becomes unhistorical: it is no longer seen as an objective, causal progression in time, with distinctly marked out differences between each period, but is sensed as a continuum in which distinctions between the past and the present are obliterated'.[41] While Frank's argument fails to convince as an aesthetic generalization, here he does touch on a salient aspect of Eliot's style in these quatrain poems, but in a manner which is almost the reverse of his intention. When he states that 'past and present are seen spatially, locked in a timeless unity which, while it may accentuate surface differences, eliminates any feeling of historical sequence by the very act of juxtaposition',[42] it can be suggested that it is indeed these 'surface differences' that Eliot accentuates, with the effect of 'eliminating any feeling of historical sequence'. However, the purpose is not to view history as a continuum, a 'timeless unity', but rather as a locus of dislocations and satiric disjunctions. This abstraction of history into 'surfaces' occurs in Eliot's quatrain poems not merely with reference to his caricatural portrayals, but also in his employment of literary references and allusions; taken from their original context, they often function in Eliot's poems as detached fragments, as surfaces in a literary mosaic. Thus, it can be agreed that Eliot's mode denies history as causal connection or sequence, with the sense of objective progression that would entail; but his aim, mediated through the particularity of his 'surfaces', is to posit a historical incoherence, and in doing so, paradoxically, time and history reassert themselves within the poem

through the friction of historical dislocations, and we are sent, in a reflexive movement, back to the manner of seeing of the poet.

In discussing Eliot's quatrain poems in the context of Gautier's 'sculptured'
verse, I have tried, through the concept of 'spatial form' to reveal basic similarities
in the aesthetic premises that motivate both poets. This is a corrective to analyses
that, content with acknowledging the obvious dissimilarities between Eliot's
quatrain poems and *Emaux et Camées*, suggest that the similarities are restricted to
'form', accepting without question a highly restricted definition of form (metre
and stanzaic pattern) without perceiving that 'form' can be a value-bearing instrument as effectively as that other circumscribed label, 'content'. With regard to
such highly wrought poems as Eliot's *Poems* of 1920 and *Hugh Selwyn Mauberley*,
any rigid distinction between the realms of 'form' and 'content' becomes
extremely problematic. We can suggest, as a working definition, that 'form',
beyond metre and stanzaic pattern, is the sphere of the implicit and connotational,
as manifested particularly in linguistic usage (tone), while that which is discursive,
overtly presented 'meaning' is 'content'. The role of form as a value-bearing
instrument through connotation becomes even more crucial in poetry of the kind
Pound and Eliot were producing, since that poetry is dedicated to the eschewing of
discursive commentary and the achievement of aesthetically autonomous, 'auto-
telic'[43] (Eliot's term) spatial effects.

Finally, and relatedly, it can be suggested that in following Hulme back to
Worringer's *Abstraction and Empathy*, Frank might have paid more attention to the
main thrust of Worringer's attack on Lipps's normative concept of empathy,
rather than concentrating exclusively on an intriguing, but finally untenable,
attempt to argue a formal convergence between modern literature and abstract art,
based on the latter's suppression of temporality, or three-dimensional 'depth'.
Here, Worringer calls into question the then pre-eminent aesthetic theorist's
belief that 'Aesthetic enjoyment is objectified self-enjoyment. To enjoy aesthetically means to enjoy myself in a sensuous object diverse from myself, to empathize
myself into it.'[44] In arguing against Lipps's belief that 'Only insofar as this
empathy exists, are forms beautiful',[45] Worringer posits the existence of a different set of psychological gratifications necessary to explain the appeal of abstract
art. As the concept of empathy can be applied both to the visual and literary arts, it
allows a more tenable, though admittedly less specific complex of analogies than
the particular idea of 'spatial form'. In suggesting that Eliot's modes in the
quatrain poems are anti-empathetic, we are led to consider the historical, cultural
and psychological factors that went to distinguish the writer from his potential
public, and made his aims different from the 'objectified self-enjoyment' Lipps saw
as the central purpose of art.

The two major issues that have emerged here: Eliot's employment of history, or
'tradition' and his employment of caricatural, satiric techniques – both fundamentally interrelate, especially once it is perceived that the apparent 'objectivity'
of the spatial-presentative modes of the quatrain poems remains at base no more

than a technique of treatment, a mode of objectification that is finally equivalent to an attitude taken towards the poem, its material or subject, and the potential reader. We will return to these issues later; in the next chapter we turn to *Hugh Selwyn Mauberley.*

5
Pound's *Hugh Selwyn Mauberley*

Poetry is a statement of overwhelming emotional values, all the rest is an affair of cuisine, or art.
On n'émeut que par la clarté. Stendhal is right in that clause.
He was right in his argument for prose, but poetry also aims at giving a feeling precisely evaluated.
Satire is the expression of disgust with false evaluations.
Pound, 'Breviora', *Little Review*, October 1918

i

As Pound's contribution to the joint poetic campaign employing Gautier's quatrains upon which he and Eliot decided in 1917, *Hugh Selwyn Mauberley*, first published by the Ovid Press in 1920, rounds out the major complex of historical themes dealt with thus far. Having offered some preliminary consideration of Eliot's use of the form it is necessary to give some attention to the instigator's contribution: the suite of poems that was his sole sustained deployment of the quatrain stanza and also his farewell to England and English literary culture. The critical and cultural premises upon which the adoption of the form was based can be seen to be poignantly exemplified in Pound's use of the strict quatrain to fashion his own leave-taking from the amateurish English attitudes to which he so vehemently objected. Thus, aside from its literary qualities, *Hugh Selwyn Mauberley* is Pound's final gesture as a Vorticist, an enemy within the English cultural status quo.

Up to this point, my main concern has been to provide the parameters for Eliot's satiric poems and claim that they can be seen in the context of social and literary tendencies in which Pound took a leader's role. *Hugh Selwyn Mauberley*, which, with the 'Homage to Sextus Propertius', is the culminating achievement of Pound's early poetry (the poetry which preceded his exclusive concentration on *The Cantos*) can be regarded as *prima facie* evidence to support such a treatment of Eliot's work. The first section of the *Mauberley* suite to the 'Envoi' is a predominantly satiric delineation of English literary culture; the second section, from 'Mauberley (1920)' to 'Medallion' is a depiction and implicit analysis of the stunted career of a minor poet, the eponymous Hugh Selwyn Mauberley, within, and finally outside that culture. Both Eliot and Pound employed the Gautier quatrain to produce satire that is to some degree an indictment of the 'vice and folly' they perceived within their contemporary situation: thus a challenging of the social and literary actualities in which they were working as poets; and the quatrain form, which Pound tells us was initially intended to be an implicit rebuttal of 'sloppy' *vers libre*, was used as the vehicle for more ambitious and wide ranging oppositional statements. However, once this important general point has been made, it is crucial to go on to take cognizance of the differences between Eliot's and Pound's use of the Gautier quatrain as a satiric medium. After a brief, preparatory differentiation between Pound's and Eliot's employment of 'tradition', the focus of this chapter will be upon the underlying intellectual and cultural logic of Pound's suite of poems, a discussion that follows and examines the two-part structure of *Hugh Selwyn Mauberley* in order to specify its intellectual infrastructure. It will be argued that this infrastructure can only be fully comprehended within the context of Pound's Vorticist poetics.

At first glance, Pound's poetic employment of 'tradition' within *Hugh Selwyn Mauberley* would seem to offer substantial similarities to Eliot's practice within the quatrain poems. In both poets we discern a dense, allusive verse texture, including the occasional interpolation of words and even lines from foreign texts, and the obtrusive references to source materials which are liable to baffle the reader with no prior knowledge of these sources. In fact, what we discern is the poetic exemplification of the wide, supra-national definition of 'tradition', which was fought for in the joint critical campaign conducted by Pound and Eliot during these years. However, in Pound's poem, unlike Eliot's quatrains, many of these difficulties tend to evaporate once we have acquired a knowledge of Pound's sources. It is not difficult to choose a short poem to illustrate this point, and demonstrate Pound's achievement of a local historical, referential coherence, which is itself coherent even when removed from the total context of the sequence.

It is probably most convenient to consider the entire poem 'Mauberley (1920)', which begins the second section of the sequence, a poem which offers the communication of some relatively clear meanings through the mediation of traditional referents, and which is also an important element in the sequence as a whole. (This poem has been used for a similar purpose in Donald Davie's *The Poet in the Imaginary Museum*.)[1] The point to be made is that successfully illustrated in John Espey's scrupulous study of the sequence: that, as he puts it, 'the traditional academic method of attack, with its full panoply of textual collation, identification of sources and historical method'[2] is effective as a means of discussing and analysing Pound's sequence. Any effective treatment of Eliot's poetry of this period must proceed from the initial realization that this traditional academic method is largely impotent in relation to Eliot's verse – which does not, of course, mean that it is not employed.

In 'Mauberley (1920)', the adapted epigraph from Ovid's *Metamorphoses*, which translates as 'his empty mouth bites the air', is a reference to Cephalus's dog Laelaps, who was turned to stone as he attempted to attack the monster sent to terrorize Thebes. The epigraph can be held in suspension until the final stanza of poem II, where the line is translated and employed directly to describe the consequences of Mauberley's sexual and emotional insentience:

> Mouths biting empty air,
> The still stone dogs,
> Caught in metamorphosis, were
> Left him as epilogues.[3]

The epigraph, here employed as an image of Mauberley's failure to achieve active and intense personal engagement, a failure which results in a state of petrified stasis, has ramifications in relation to Mauberley's literary career and aesthetic preferences which are introduced in the first poem. Mauberley is introduced to us as turning from the 'eau-forte/Par Jacquemart' to the severe art of the engraver of medallions, a mode suggested (ironically) by the coins bearing profligate Messalina's profile. Thus, Mauberley moves from the etching, a relatively expansive and inclusive medium, towards the analogy of the engraving, a severe, selective medium. The particular 'eau-forte/Par Jacquemart' that Pound seems to have had in mind is an etching of Théophile Gautier in three-quarter face, which was included as the frontispiece to an 1881 edition of *Emaux et Camées*. Here, Pound is employing a private reference, but his intention is clear: it is the etching technique that is relevant, not the hidden, almost sly reference to Gautier.

The next two stanzas amplify this initial choice. 'His true Penelope/Was Flaubert' – a reiteration from the first poem of the sequence, indicating that Mauberley has elected to go in Flaubert's direction in a search for the telling detail, the exact designation, *le mot juste*. This Flaubertian, prose tradition Pound saw as being introduced to English writing through the influence of Ford Madox Ford. However, as Pound was later to revalue his positive estimation of Ford's work by including him under the general designation of Impressionism (a passive, receptive literature, as opposed to an active intense vorticist art), so here, the Flaubertian impulse, while implicitly approved of as having no truck with diffuse, degenerate native literary practice, is seen as finally resulting in artistic sterility:

> Colourless
> Pier Francesca,
> Pisanello lacking the skill
> To forge Achaia.

Piero della Francesca was renowned as a colourist, and his pale muted tints are referred to in Reinach's *Apollo* as 'cold and impersonal'.[4] Thus, we can see Mauberley in the initial stages of his career as an inferior Francesca, master of form and colour, and then subsequently as an inferior Pisanello, the medallist, who did have the skill to 'forge Achaia', to create his own 'tradition'. Mauberley's art is thus described in derivative terms, in relation to two primary modes which he tries and fails in the literary medium to emulate.

Pound is thus mediating relatively clear intellectual meanings through his use of traditional referents. In contrast to Eliot's use of obscurity, which in a poem such as 'Mr. Eliot's Sunday Morning Service' seems an intrinsic aspect of the poem's aesthetic effect (designed at once to keep the reader at a guarded distance from the text and to connote the debasement of the present) Pound's use of the recondite is pedagogic, suggesting that if we learn about the sources they will form a coherent whole, a live tradition going back to the beginning of Western civilization. But it is to make a different and more ambitious claim for Pound's sequence if we propose that his use of source material demonstrates a clear and consistent reading of tradition (history and literary history), rather than being merely a coherent, occasional use of 'traditional' referents to underpin the skeletal narrative of Mauberley's career and explicate local obscurities in the text. This claim depends on what the phrase suggests, a *reading* of tradition, a selection and employment of literary material from an intellectually consistent standpoint. It can be argued that this coherence is achieved in *Hugh Selwyn Mauberley* from the beginning of the sequence, thus far before the 'Mauberley (1920)' that has been just discussed; and in the reading of tradition that is proposed the figure of Théophile Gautier assumes a presiding importance. Pound, of course, adopted Gautier's quatrain form; but Gautier's significance to Pound's sequence goes far beyond the limited area designated by such formal borrowing. For Eliot, the quatrain was a technical discipline, a suitable vehicle for the compressed conveyance of satiric and personal meanings. For Pound, it was a form that retained the authority of Gautier's employment of it, that was thus sanctioned by 'tradition', and could be adapted to suit contemporary needs. Analogous to the position Laforgue assumes in Eliot's early poetry, Gautier is virtually the tutelary deity of the sequence, and Pound mediates his historical perspective through the precedent of Gautier's intellectual development, as well as employing his stanzaic form.

At this point it is necessary to refer to what is arguably the most helpful and convincing overall reading of the structure of the sequence, that proposed by Kenner[5] and retained by Espey, which would see the first section of the sequence, from 'E. P. Ode Pour l'Élection de Son Sépulchre' to 'Envoi (1919)', as being predominantly 'Pound's section', and regards the second section from 'Mauberley (1920)' to 'Medallion' as being Pound's delineation of Mauberley's career as a minor poet in a hostile culture. (This Kenner–Espey reading is not incontestable: indeed it has been contested, most notably by Donald Davie. It is adopted without debate here because the literature surrounding this issue is an infinite regress of critical perspectives which it is no longer helpful to enter, and more pertinently, because none of the alternative readings seems to me to enhance our appreciation of the sequence, while nearly all detract from its coherence.)[6] Accepting this reading, it is notable that it is in this first section, 'Pound's', that the references to Gautier are concentrated; while he almost disappears as an active influence on the verse texture and sources of the fictive presentation of Mauberley's career (where

James and de Gourmont become the hidden influences) to reappear problematic-
ally in the title and modes of the final poem 'Medallion'.

The first section, therefore, in which a satiric portrayal of contemporary English
culture, a series of urbane poetic 'Blasts' is offered, is where Gautier makes his
presence felt – not least in a wry sophistication of tone which is not usual for
Pound – and where we will focus on Gautier's central position in Pound's critical
evaluation of contemporary culture. This initial analysis gives ideological
consistency to the entire sequence, and provides a thread to link the various topics
with which Pound subsequently deals in the first section of *Hugh Selwyn
Mauberley*. However, from the first Gautier's influence is subsumed and integrated
within the Vorticist aesthetic, which, as formed and interpreted by Pound, was an
aesthetic of cultural opposition: art and society were seen as inextricably but antag-
onistically linked. Thus, in the first poem of the sequence, 'E. P. Ode Pour
L'Élection de Son Sépulchre' (a false epitaph perhaps suggested by Twain's cable
to the Associated Press to complain that 'The report of my death was an exaggeration') the poet presented as an aesthetic craftsman and perfectionist who
strove 'to maintain ''the sublime''/In the old sense', is seen as being 'out of key
with his time'.

> Unaffected by 'the march of events',
> He passed from men's memory in *l'an trentuniesme*
> *De son eage*; the case presents
> No adjunct to the Muses' diadem.

Poem II, contrasting the demands of the age with the prerequisites for the production of good poetry, reflects back on Gautier's manifesto poem 'L'Art'. This is
seen most overtly in the conclusion:

> The 'age demanded' chiefly a mould in plaster,
> Made with no loss of time,
> A prose kinema, not, not assuredly, alabaster
> Or the 'sculpture' or rhyme.

But the fundamental reflection from Gautier depends on the first two stanzas
where the leitmotif of a degenerate post-war English culture is contrasted with 'an
Attic grace', a classical golden age against which the present is held in satiric disjunction.

> The age demanded an image
> Of its accelerated grimace,
> Something for the modern stage,
> Not, at any rate, an Attic grace;
>
> Not, not certainly, the obscure reveries
> Of the inward gaze;
> Better mendacities
> Than the classics in paraphrase!

Pound's contact with the Vorticist artists makes the terminology of these first two lines familiar. We recollect his judgement that Futurism, lacking the aesthetic stasis achieved by the Vorticist arts, was 'a sort of accelerated impressionism',[7] referring to Impressionism, he stated that, 'The logical end of impressionist art is the cinematograph.'[8] This condemnation is implicit in the body of Vorticist doctrine which Pound and Lewis developed and is part of their opposition to all art which interprets mimesis in restrictive realist terms. The 'classic' alternative to this debased status quo, introduced in a couple of pungently ironic negatives, immediately brings to mind *Emaux et Camées*, where, anticipating Parnassian attitudes, Gautier consciously, even self-consciously, turns away from 'the demands of the age' towards an attempt to achieve 'an Attic grace', an art conversant with Classical ideals of beauty, through the enduring 'sculpture of rhyme'. (The preface poem of *Emaux et Camées* has Gautier reflecting on the example of Goethe, ignoring the Napoleonic wars and writing *le Divan occidental* (sic), which suggests to Gautier that he too should ignore 'l'ouragan/Qui fouettait mes vitres fermées',[9] and write *Emaux et Camées*.) Finally, even what may appear to be an aesthetic contradiction, the wedding of 'the obscure reveries/Of the inward gaze' with the demands for a sculptural, presentative verse, becomes explicable in the context of the compromise Gautier makes between the Romantic basis of his art in reverie, and the desideratum of exact presentation proposed in the final stanza of 'L'Art': 'Sculpte, lime, cisèle;/Que ton rêve flottant/Se scelle/Dans le bloc résistant!'

Having established the dominant theme of pagan grace in contrast to contemporary degeneration in poem II, this theme is amplified in poem III, maintaining close reference to Gautier sources. The central proposition of the poem is contained in the second stanza:

> Christ follows Dionysus,
> Phallic and ambrosial
> Made way for macerations;
> Caliban casts out Ariel.

Here, we can adduce two direct sources: the poem 'Bûchers et tombeaux', discussed previously in relation to Eliot's 'Whispers of Immortality' and the preface and contents of *Mademoiselle de Maupin*,[10] where the theme of post-Christian ascetic maceration (a wasting away by fasting) is broached ironically and a nostalgic aestheticism, which itself celebrates the pagan celebration of beauty, is recommended in contrast to Christian asceticism and eschatology. The point here is that Pound's echoing of Gautier's reaction to his world in *Emaux et Camées* and *Mademoiselle de Maupin* is a referring back to the sources of nineteenth-century aestheticism, which Pound saw as emerging in England in the 1890s. In making this reference, Pound has engineered a bridge that leads logically and coherently to the discussion of pre-Raphaelitism in 'Yeux Glauques', and late nineteenth-century English aestheticism in ' "Siena Mi Fe'; Disfecemi Maremma" '. Pound regarded Gautier as the man who anticipated and surpassed the English aesthetes at the beginning of the century:

> Théophile Gautier is, I suppose, the next man who can write. Perfectly plain statements like his 'Carmen est maigre' should teach us a number of things. His early poems are many of them no further advanced than the Nineties. Or to put it more fairly the English Nineties got about as far as Gautier had got in 1830, and before he wrote 'L'Hippopotame'.[11]

In Pound's remarks on those poets of the 1890s that he valued, such as Dowson and Lionel Johnson, he habitually referred back to Gautier; as in the essay on Johnson, in which he praises the poet's lapidary 'hardness', and regards it as being a filiation of the Gautier tradition. 'One thinks that he has read and admired Gautier, or that at least, he has derived similar ambitions from some traditional source. One thinks that his poems are in short hard sentences.'[12]

The substance of the connection Pound makes between Gautier and the poets of the 1890s is contained in the paradigm of oppositional attitudes Pound perceived in Gautier's work, and which he elaborates upon in *Hugh Selwyn Mauberley*. As suggested, this oppositional model is based upon a contrast between a classical golden age and a debased present, which Pound updates historically and applies to post-war England with a diminution of Gautier's irony and a good deal of satiric hardening. Thus, rather than following Gautier in the attempt to attain a contemporary 'Attic grace' in despite of social actualities, Pound employs the ideology of Gautier's attitudes and reactions for a satiric attack on the present. This means that, rather than following English aestheticism in the claim that art has no direct social or moral utility, Pound lays claim to a didacticism based on a true art's oppositional status in contemporary cultural conditions, which he regards as inimical to the production of that art. Pound consistently emphasized what he saw as the social utility of good writing; as he puts it in the 1922 article on *Ulysses*, 'The "mot juste" is of public utility. I can't help it. I am not offering this fact as a sop to aesthetes who want all authors to be fundamentally useless. We are governed by words, the laws are graven in words, and literature is the sole means of keeping these words living and accurate.'[13] Maintaining the language meant for Pound maintaining it against the forces of degeneration he perceived at work in popular democratic journalistic culture. He felt with Gautier that, 'For our part, we like a great deal that art which is hieroglyphic and abrupt, where one does not feel at home; it is necessary to raise the crowd to the level of the work, and not to lower the work to the level of the crowd.'[14] However, Pound was willing to take Gautier's aesthete's dismissal of 'the crowd' a step further, and admit a reactionary and oppositional didacticism in a world in which the 'revelations' of poetry were, if not dismissed, hardly encouraged.

An oppositional didacticism meant satire; and this satiric hardening has its effect upon Pound's poetic employment of Gautier's formulae, and, in particular, his treatment of what in Gautier remains essentially a nostalgic Classicism. In *Emaux et Camées* Gautier's Classicism remains at the level of Parnassian sentiment; his

attempt to achieve an art conversant with Classical modes does not necessitate
much specific reference to the Classical literary past. In *Hugh Selwyn Mauberley*,
however, Pound's attempts to adapt Gautier's attitudes by giving them a tight
literary and historical underpinning, involving extensive reference to the classics,
and a far less ironic, more straightforward attempt at historical analysis than that
offered, say, in Gautier's 'Bûchers et tombeaux'. Take, for example, the central
two stanzas of poem III:

> All things are a flowing,
> Sage Heracleitus says;
> But a tawdry cheapness
> Shall outlast our days.

> Even the Christian beauty
> Defects – after Samothrace;
> We see τὸ καλόν
> Decreed in the market place.

Here, Pound seems to be referring to St Paul's visit to Samothrace, which made
the island, renowned for Dionysiac worship, the first to feel the influence of ascetic
Christianity. Paul, according to Pound, 'neither wrote good Greek nor represented the teaching of the original Christian'.[15] Such specific references serve to
give the 'sense' of a substantiated historical case, which is used to give depth and
ironic bite to the indictment of the present. It is, however, the sense rather than
the substance of a historical analysis that is given in the poem: we remain unsure
exactly how Paul's visit to Samothrace contaminated *Christian* beauty. But these
local ambiguities, or incoherencies, count for little beside the sureness of tone, the
ironic *brio* that sweeps us onwards, and commands our attention for a conclusion
which characterizes the present as having lost Classical grace, while combining a
degenerate Pauline Christianity with a popular democracy which was perhaps
degenerate from its inception.

> Faun's flesh is not to us,
> Nor the saint's vision.
> We have the press for wafer;
> Franchise for circumcision.

> All men, in law, are equals.
> Free of Pisistratus,
> We choose a knave or an eunuch
> To rule over us.

Here, Pound is willing to forgo his condemnation of circumcision as an 'antique
abracadabra'[16] in order to enforce his condemnation of popular democracy as a
debased participatory ritual. The insertion of the caveat, 'in law', in the first line
of the following stanza would seem to point ironically to a difference of opinion
with the Declaration of Independence, which has it as a 'self-evident' truth that

'all men are created equal'. Pound, perhaps, would not go so far. We are finally warned of what occurs when we are 'Free of Pisistratus'. Pisistratus, the benevolent Athenian tyrant, is known to have encouraged the rites of Dionysus, and hence may well have been influential in the establishment of the Greek drama. There is also a tradition, which Pound refers to, that Pisistratus was the first to collect and revise the Homeric poems.[17] The debased conclusion of contemporary conditions is expressed in the final stanza, where instead of Pindar's classical laurel, to be bestowed on 'god, man, or hero', all that the present can offer is 'a tin wreath'.

While it would be excessive to regard Pound's recommendation of Pisistratus in 1920 as indicating an anticipation of his subsequent political choices, this is not for any dearth of evidence that Pound regarded Mussolini as a latter-day Pisistratus, but because the extreme ironic compression of *Hugh Selwyn Mauberley* does not allow us to dwell upon particular references and use them for more than a description of the dominant political tendencies of Pound's poem. Thus, while it is apparent that a reactionary political case is being made, this opportunist, brilliant (the exact term) verse offers us no more than is necessary to focus attention upon its affective power. In employing specific historical references to give the impression of a substantiated argument to what in Gautier is a generalized theme (an awareness of, and attempt to reproduce Classical grace within a reduced present), one might almost say that Pound 'takes Gautier seriously'. A nostalgic Classicism, which was in Gautier, the aesthete, socially elitist, becomes with Pound, politically elitist, and a sense of the 'tawdry cheapness' of the present is integrated with suggestions as to why that present is reduced.

If we enquire into the precise nature of the connection which existed in Pound's mind between aesthetics and politics, and the place of Gautier in this nexus, we need look no further than Pound's August 1922, 'Paris Letter' in *The Dial*, which succinctly elucidates all these areas. Writing on a study of Flaubert's *Bouvard et Pécuchet* by Descharmes, Pound presents Flaubert as 'the tragedian of democracy, of modernity', and in a lengthy disquisition on Flaubert's historical situation brings Gautier into the discussion. The relevant passages deserve to be quoted in full in order to convey the characteristic flavour of Pound's prose style in this period.

> Civilization, as Flaubert had known it, appeared to be foundering; Gautier died, as Flaubert wrote, 'suffocated by modern stupidity', and Flaubert thinking of Gautier feels 'as if a tide of filth' were rising around him and submerging him. This tide of *immondices* must be considered as messy thought, general muddle. 'We pay for the long deceit in which we have lived, everything was false, false army, false politics, and false credit.' 'The present is abominable, and the future ferocious.' So run the phrases of his correspondence.
>
> And the old man's last stand against this tide is his 'dictionnaire des idées recues', his encyclopedia 'en farce'; his gargantuan collection of imbecilities,

of current phrases ('Bosseut is the eagle of Meaux') and his 'Album' of citations ('The Loire floods are due to the excesses of the Press, and the lack of
sabbath observance', Bishop of Metz, in his Mandements, Dec. 1846). Thus
Flaubert goes about making his immense diagnosis of the contemporary
average mind. And this average mind is our king, our tyrant, replacing
Oedipus and Agamemnon in our tragedy.

It is this human stupidity that elects the Wilsons and Ll. Georges and puts
power into the hands of the gun-makers, demanding that they blot out the
sunlight, that they crush out the individual and the perception of beauty.
This flabby blunt-wittedness is the tyrant.

Gautier, poor all his life, driven from one bit of hack work to another
(Mes colonnes sont alignées) reacts in his Olympian perfection:

> 'Le squelette était invisible
> Au temps heureux de l'Art païen;
> L'homme, sous la forme sensible,
> Content du beau, ne cherchait rien.'

and Flaubert who until his quixotic abandonment of his fortune had been
'able to keep out of it', Flaubert capable of his great engineering feat, reacts
in his huge labour of drainage and sanitation, beginning as Descharmes so
intelligently points out, 'when as a small child, he was already registering
the imbecile remarks of an old lady who had come on a visit to his father'.[18]

The satiric assault in the first section of *Mauberley* closely follows the ideas expressed in the August 1922, 'Paris Letter', where passing from the late nineteenth
to the twentieth century, he attacks the domination of the 'average mind', which,
empowered through the mechanisms of popular democracy, he regards as 'our
king, our tyrant, replacing Oedipus and Agamemnon in our tragedy.'

Pound's politics during the period of composition of *Hugh Selwyn Mauberley*
remain the projection of his 'red-blooded' aestheticism into a vehement elitism.
Unlike those Americans who saw the First World War as a conflict between the
Western democracies and the autocratic Central European monarchies, Pound had
expressed his disillusioned analysis in the second and final edition of *Blast*:
' "Blast" alone dared to present the actual discords of modern civilization,
DISCORDS only now too apparent in the open conflict between teutonic atavism
and unsatisfactory Democracy.'[19] For Pound, humanity is divided into first-,
second- and third-rate minds, and through popular democracy the third-rate
minds have the power, and persecute their betters. We may regard Pound's
attitudes as simplistic, but it is important to realize the apparent, affective logic of
Pound's indictment; for while Pound was involved in the ill-fated Vorticist
endeavour, he was also witnessing British jingoism at close quarters. Taking the
claims of Western democracy at face value, he regarded 1914–18 as a popular war,
and blamed those who had elected 'the Wilsons and Ll. Georges, and put power
into the hands of the gun-makers'. This line of argument is that followed in

Hugh Selwyn Mauberley, where in poem III a questioning of popular democracy leads us to the disaster of the Great War in poem IV, with more than an implied connection between the two.

Thus section IV, a perfectly cadenced adaptation of Bion's elegiac verses on the death of Adonis, is intellectually consistent within the context of Pound's close reference to the classics, although the subject to which Pound applies his 'syncopation from the Greek', the tragic waste of life in the Great War, is only formally consistent with Bion's verses in that both are elegies on the deaths of young men. Bion remains behind the text. ('The metre in *Mauberley* is Gautier and Bion's "Adonis"; or at least those are the two grafts I was trying to flavour it with. Syncopation from the Greek; and a general distaste for the slushiness of the post-Swinburne British line.')[20] However, the converse of this sense of intimacy with the classics, or more precisely, its corollary, is a sense of estrangement from, and hostility to, commercial, material, popular democratic social actualities: the rule of 'homo canis'. It is important to realize that poems IV and V relate to the three preceding poems almost as the conclusion of a proposition. Structurally, we are encouraged to see the disaster of 1914–18 as being explicable in terms of the condemnation of contemporary civilization we have already been given; and Pound enforces this sense of connection.

> Died some, pro patria,
>   non 'dulce' non 'et decor' . . .
> walking eye-deep in hell
> believing in old men's lies, then unbelieving
> came home, home to a lie,
> home to many deceits,
> home to old lies and new infamy;
> usury age-old and age-thick
> and liars in public places.

Here, what seems ostensibly to be the general contemporary 'poetic' explanation for the Great War, a betrayal of the young by the old – as evinced in much of the work of the Georgian war poets and given exemplary expression in Kipling's two-line poem 'Common Form' ('If any question why we died,/Tell them, because our fathers lied.')[21] – is given point and reference by its interconnection with the poems that precede it, while being given weight by the sense of a cultural diagnosis. In 1918 Pound had met Major C. H. Douglas, whose doctrine of social credit was to have an enormous effect on his subsequent ideas and political development. The doctrine of social credit is based on the argument that when money becomes a commodity controlled by the banking system it no longer reflects the needs, wealth or labour of the community. However, as is amply demonstrated in Pound's later pronouncements, an overtly populist doctrine swiftly opens itself to reactionary (precisely, fascist) inflections, when capitalist lending, usury, is located as the root of all evil, and usury is equated with Jewish financiers and then with the Jews in general. Here, however, the reference to 'usury age-old and age-thick' is neither obtrusive nor obsessive (as it was to become), but merely one term in a cumulative indictment in which aesthetic balance is maintained by a poignant and dominating sense of loss. Yet without an appreciation of the devastatingly negative cultural analysis of poems I to IV of *Hugh Selwyn Mauberley*, the savage and sweeping denunciation of poem V would seem unprepared for and intellectually and tonally excessive.

> There died a myriad,
> And of the best, among them,
> For an old bitch gone in the teeth,
> For a botched civilization,
>
> Charm, smiling at the good mouth,
> Quick eyes gone under earth's lid,
>
> For two gross of broken statues,
> For a few thousand battered books.

In the sustained force of this indictment we can trace the grounds for Pound's differentiation of his stance both from Gautier and the poets of the 1890s. Towards the end of his life, in the brash materialistic climate of the Second Empire, Gautier felt himself to have been abandoned by literary fashion, which was turning towards emergent realism and away from his exotic aesthete's preoccupations. As he put it, 'Singing for deaf women is a melancholy occupation.'[22] In the first poem of *Mauberley* Pound perhaps thought of Gautier in labelling himself, from a hostile perspective, as 'out of key with his time' and 'Unaffected by ''the march of events'' ', and may well have had Gautier in mind not only as 'the stylist' in retreat, of poem X (where the obvious model is Ford Madox Ford, who retired to Sussex and raised pigs after being wounded and gassed during service in the First World War), but also as another example of one who had suffered the fate of M. Verog (Gustave Plarr):

> M. Verog, out of step with the decade,
> Detached from his contemporaries,
> Neglected by the young,
> Because of these reveries.

Gautier thus becomes for Pound a precedent for those who, like Pound himself, are 'out of step' with their age, with explicit satiric criticism for those who make facile judgements of literary worth on the dictates of literary fashion. Gautier would 'react in his Olympian perfection', but in no sustained manner, and with no underlying analysis of his predicament; the poets of the 1890s, like Plarr, attempted to ignore it disdainfully by retreating into a world of reverie; Pound, following and extending the example of Flaubert, attacked.

In the first section of *Hugh Selwyn Mauberley* Gautier remains behind the surface of the verse, and in his role of originator and personal example is accepted and subsumed; while the post-Gautier pre-Raphaelites and 1890s' aesthetes are accorded acute, ironic critical attention in 'Yeux Glauques' (where the pre-Raphaelite ideal of female beauty refers us back textually to Gautier's 'Caerulei Oculi') and ' "Siena Mi Fe'; Disfecemi Maremma"'.' In both poems the implication is that, for all their commendable efforts to fight the levelling, materialist pressures of their periods, both groups, while illustrating England's maltreatment of her talented writers and artists, failed in the kind of vitality that fuels Pound's own satiric farewell to English culture. 'Yeux Glauques' is loosely based on the life of Elizabeth Siddall, the seamstress who modelled for Burne-Jones's painting 'Cophetua and the Beggar Maid' as well as other major pre-Raphaelite works, and who became the favourite model, mistress and eventual wife of Dante Gabriel Rossetti. Rossetti was unfaithful and Elizabeth Siddall was to end her life by suicide, a fate congruent with the tenor of Pound's poem where it is the woman's passivity and bewilderment in the face of her lover's infidelities which are used to embody the representative traits of the period. The effect is so pronounced that the stanzaic conjunction of

> Thin like brook-water,
> With a vacant gaze.
> The English Rubaiyat was still-born
> In those days

suggests not only the hostility of the social environment to the reception of Fitzgerald's Rubaiyat, but also, by semantic transference across the full stop, some critical perspective on the translation – which, in actuality, Pound greatly admired. In ' "Siena Mi Fe'; Disfecemi Maremma"',' the title's echo of Dante's hapless La Pia is significant, and M. Verog's reminiscences suggest the grounds on which Pound differentiated himself from post Gautier aestheticism. 'I am perhaps didactic . . . It is all rubbish to pretend that art isn't didactic. Only the aesthetes since 1880 have pretended the contrary, and they aren't a very sturdy lot.'[23] In itself, Pound's poem can be seen as an implicit contrast to the work of the poets of the 1890s. If we set the first stanza of one of Dowson's finest lyrics, 'Non sum qualis eram bonae sub regno Cynarae',

> Last night, ah, yesternight, betwixt her lips and mine
> There fell thy shadow, Cynara! thy breath was shed
> Upon my soul between the kisses and the wine;
> And I was desolate and sick of an old passion,
>   Yea, I was desolate and bowed my head:
> I have been faithful to thee, Cynara! in my fashion.[24]

against the extreme, ironic concision of Pound's one-line summation of Dowson's career, 'Dowson found harlots cheaper than hotels', then it is possible to appreciate the succinct, worldly focus of Pound's poem both as a mode of intellectual engagement and the eventual fruit of Ford's warnings against the 'curial' poetic diction of the 1890s. Dowson and Lionel Johnson barely survived the decade with which they are closely associated and they allowed themselves to become victims of Mammon and Empire; the *poète maudit* was not a role that Pound wished to play.

In succeeding poems, Pound turns from the detailing of the immediate literary past, to the depiction of a debased cultural present, in which all the negative elements that disabled the nineteenth century are accentuated with a reinforced commercial bias. 'Brennbaum' (probably Max Beerbohm, whom Pound mistakenly thinks of as a Jew) is a standard piece of anti-Semitic cultural suggestion hinting at the disguised, sterile presence of the 'hidden Jew' in England's cultural establishment; 'Mr. Nixon' (Arnold Bennett) deals with the disabling nexus between commercial journalism and literature; X details the ostracism dealt out to the literary 'stylist' who will not compromise his 'standards'; XI, with the desuetude of romantic traditions at the lower end of the social scale, when they are in the keeping of women who live in Ealing 'with the most bank-clerkly of Englishmen'; XII, with the distorted 'patronage' relation with women at the higher end of the social scale ('Lady Valentine' is probably meant to suggest Ottoline Morrell), who have no real interest in literature, except for its social and sexual uses. The 'Envoi', a fine, intentionally derivative lyric farewell to Anglo-Saxon attitudes provides Pound with an emphatic conclusion to the first section of *Hugh Selwyn Mauberley*, for it triumphantly exemplifies Pound's ability to achieve poetic integration within the English lyric tradition – at the point at which he is about to abandon English literary culture. Previously, the satiric portrayal of the status quo had culminated with a psychic visit to 'Fleet St. where/Dr. Johnson flourished', where the poem concludes dismissively,

> Beside this thoroughfare
> The sale of half-hose has
> Long since superseded the cultivation
> Of Pieran roses.

In conclusion, this reading of the first section of *Hugh Selwyn Mauberley* should suggest that Pound is offering a critical perspective on the work of Gautier as well as extending his 'tradition' in this, his one sustained employment of the Gautier quatrain. In *Ezra Pound's 'Mauberley'*, John Espey scrupulously and accurately cites numerous verbal borrowings and adaptations between the verse of *Emaux et Camées* and the first section of *Hugh Selwyn Mauberley* in order to substantiate his claim that there is a 'close parallel between the entire first section of *Mauberley* and the tone of Gautier's reaction to his own world as expressed in *Emaux et Camées*'.[25] Without questioning the value of Espey's research (upon which my own argument is reliant) it is possible to question the validity of this particular judgement. While the textual parallels cannot be denied, they are perhaps not as predominant as primary sources as a cumulative list makes them appear to be; but, more fundamentally, there is a great variance between the *tone* of *Emaux et Camées* and this first section of *Mauberley*, as a reading of Gautier's collection will demonstrate. *Emaux et Camées*, both in tone and content, is far more sentimental, lyric, resigned, and though it may appear a strange epithet, good-humoured, than the first section of *Mauberley*; it offers no attempt at serious social analysis. Pound politicizes Gautier's nostalgic classicism and cultural elitism, and thus goes one step beyond the premises of aestheticism towards a socially combative pose built upon those assumptions. This choice cannot but involve him in a different choice of 'tone', a different connotational intentionality, a different *écriture*. It is possible to make the same point in textual rather than conceptual terms. Only one quotation from Gautier can be found in *Hugh Selwyn Mauberley* and that is found at the beginning of poem XII where Pound has adapted Gautier's lines from 'Le Chateau du souvenir':

> Un jour louche et douteux se glisse
> Aux vitres du salon
> Où figurent, en haute lisse,
> Les aventures d'Apollon.
>
> Daphné, les hanches dans l'écorce,
> Étend toujours ses doigts touffus;
> Mais aux bras du dieu qui la force
> Elle s'éteint, spectre confus.[26]*

In Pound's poem, by the deft substitution of 'towards me' for 'toujours', Daphne becomes no longer a figure in a salon mural, but a representation both of the offering of the poet's laurel and, in a suggestion of the original myth, a sexual prize.

> 'Daphne with her thighs in bark
> 'Stretches towards me her leafy hands,' –
> Subjectively. In the stuffed-satin drawing-room
> I await The Lady Valentine's commands,
>
> Knowing my coat has never been
> Of precisely the fashion
> To stimulate, in her,
> A durable passion;

Here, the laconic use of one word, 'Subjectively' underlines the sudden shift from nostalgic, erotic reverie (itself suggested by the title of Gautier's poem) to a reduced, unidyllic actuality, in which the poet, no longer an Apollo, awaits 'The Lady Valentine's commands' aware that in this world of stuffed satin drawing-rooms 'fashion' glibly rhymes with 'passion'.

Thus, in Pound's only citation from Gautier we find a revealing poetic index of the historical distance between the two. This poetic shift is also reflected in a cultural and political development. In Pound, the historical dialectic of the 'alienated' post-Romantic poet has proceeded beyond the occasional social elitism of a Gautier or Baudelaire to harden into reactionary premises. In the first section of *Hugh Selwyn Mauberley* Pound deploys the arguments, via references that are accessible to

---

* A shady and doubtful day slides across the windows of the salon where figure, highly polished, the adventures of Apollo. Daphne, her thighs in bark, stretches out forever her leafy fingers; but in the arms of the god who takes her by force she fades away, an indistinct spectre.

the student, to make a particular historical, satiric indictment of contemporary English culture, in which, situating himself as the lonely bearer of minority values in a society to which he feels no allegiance, right-wing political attitudes become the comprehensible, but uncritical, response to what are perceived as the levelling tendencies of the 'average mind'. Since Pound was drawn to prescriptive cultural analyses, rather than to engage with the social credit doctrine of C. H. Douglas, an alternative perspective would have been to define late capitalism as a causal agent; and as William Chace points out, Pound did have a flirtation with Marxism in the 1920s.[27] But, as Chace indicates, Pound's entrepreneurial, individualistic cast of mind prevented his acceptance of a Marxist analysis. Pound never abandoned a fundamental, and sometimes naive empiricism, which in *Hugh Selwyn Mauberley* has the positive effect of giving the poetry its realistic flavour and sharp, localized engagement with cultural actualities, but which eventually reinforced his fixation with the 'luminous detail' and impeded the achievement of a balanced overall view.

Pound's individualism and 'red-blooded' oppositional aestheticism also provide the reason why, unlike Hulme, Eliot and Lewis, he was not really drawn to the authoritarian ideas of the *Action Française*. In *Time and Western Man* (1927), Lewis locates the residual romanticism in Pound's work in order to berate his erstwhile Vorticist associate from the standpoint of a Classicist orthodoxy, and states, in accordance with his earlier Vorticist doubts about Pound's status as a Modernist, that 'He has never loved anything living as he has loved the dead.'[28] In so far as this remark describes a standard attitude of the aesthetes, it can be seen to apply to *Hugh Selwyn Mauberley*, where in the 'Envoi', Pound concludes with what is an aesthete's profession of faith: 'Till change has broken down/All things save Beauty alone'. Not for nothing did Lewis in *Blasting and Bombardiering* relate Pound most closely to a previous American emigré in London: James McNeill Whistler, the meticulous aesthetic craftsman who was also the author of *The Gentle Art of Making Enemies*, a role in which Pound also sought to emulate the master.

ii

Up to this point, in discussing the first section of *Hugh Selwyn Mauberley*, we have been involved in analysing an oppositional survey of English literary culture; in the second section of *Mauberley* the eponymous protagonist of the suite emerges for our scrutiny and we are presented with a representative literary figure who exemplifies the failures of the writer within this society. Since Pound's intellectual bias has little in common with historical materialism his primary purpose is not to demonstrate how society maims the writer, but how a representative, indeed composite figure, fails to transcend his society. Mauberley's failures are not seen as symptoms of a disabling nexus between commerce and literature, not even the effects of vulgar democracy upon the achievement of a dedicated 'stylist', but personal failures to be ascribed to Mauberley the individual, who only becomes representative in that he exemplifies the failures of the aesthetes, the lack of 'sturdiness' to which Pound refers in the letter to his old professor Felix Schelling, and suggests in the first section of *Mauberley*. Society is an unsympathetic context for Mauberley's endeavours, but his failure is to be ascribed to roots other than the societal. Pound follows de Gourmont, the Symbolist and idealist, in regarding the individual and his perceptions as primary. However, like de Gourmont, in his essay 'The Roots of Idealism',[29] where he argues that since perception has its physiological base in the brain and body, idealism and 'materialism' are ultimately identical, Pound wishes to ground his analysis of Mauberley's failure at a level more basic than the conscious and voluntary. To do so, he employs his Vorticist distinction between the passive-receptive artist and the active-dynamic Vorticist artist, tracing that distinction back to a sexual base.

Despite the temptation, in relation to 'Mauberley (1920)', it would be a mistake to see Mauberley as a writer who can be equated with Gautier, except in so far as the artistic aspirations and modes which he prefers represent the final decadence of Gautier's aestheticism. The use of Gautieresque literary criteria to describe Mauberley's ambitions is probably evidence of no more than Pound's preoccupation with Gautier at this period, allowing us to see Mauberley as a reduced Gautier, working in purely visualist, pictorial modes. More pertinently, it is worth considering the implications of Mauberley's desire to work in a medium as severely selective as that of the medallion:

> Firmness,
> Not the full smile,
> His art, but an art
> In profile;

Here (particularly in the light of Mauberley's subsequent development) it is implied that this aesthetic detachment represents a disinclination to meet the world and others 'full-face', and with this, a consequent lack of awareness and engagement. It is also worth paying some attention to the sexual double-meaning contained in the previous description of Mauberley's literary ambitions:

> 'His true Penelope
> Was Flaubert,'
> And his tool
> The engraver's.

where the blatant and ironic sexual meaning is meant far more seriously than might immediately appear to be the case. Poem II describes Mauberley's failure in terms that, for all their local obscurity, make it clear that Mauberley's artistic sterility can be correlated with an emotional and sexual failure: both being refusals of active engagement resulting from failures of perception, and the temperamental hesitancy that underlies this failure of perception.

> −Given that is his 'fundamental passion,'
> This urge to convey the relation
> Of eye-lid and cheek-bone
> By verbal manifestation;

> To present the series
> Of curious heads in medallion –
>
> He had passed, inconscient, full gaze,
> The wide-banded irides
> And botticellian sprays implied
> In their diastasis;

If we insert the words 'All that' as a silent addition at the beginning of the line 'The wide-banded irides' to complete the sense of the line, it is clear that what is 'implied' by the diastasis of 'The wide-banded irides/And botticellian sprays' is, as in the dilation of the pupils, an invitation to active, sexual love. (Mauberley, with his inclination to view the face 'in profile' would remain crucially unaware of this.) The dashes that punctuate the central stanzas of the poem designate Mauberley's 'bewilderment' and ineffectual hesitancy, and more fundamentally, his inability to select, organize, and synthesize his perceptions, with the result that, like Prufrock before him, Mauberley fails 'to force the moment to its crisis':

> Which anaesthesis, noted a year late,
> And weighed, revealed his great affect,
> (Orchid), mandate
> Of Eros, a retrospect.

Eliot's poem is, of course, far less sexually explicit than is Pound's ('Orchid' here designates both the flower type, and through that the Greek etymological root, ὀϱκιζ,[30] meaning testicle); but the thematic echo of 'The Love Song of J. Alfred Prufrock' remains extremely significant. 'Prufrock' itself, a quintessential portrayal of failure of engagement, is a Jamesian poem; and it is worth recalling Pound's 1915 judgement on 'Prufrock' as a 'portrait of failure' to suggest that Pound had something very similar in mind for the relevant poems of *Hugh Selwyn Mauberley*. As in 'Prufrock', the Jamesian echoes in Pound's poem are intentional. In particular, the line 'He had moved amid her phantasmagoria', as Kenner has pointed out, relates to a remark of Strether's at the conclusion of *The Ambassadors*;[31] while the discreet, barely interconnected phrases, '. . . time for/arrangements –/Drifted on/To the final estrangement', recall related lines on the theme of time in 'Prufrock', both through verbal echoing and thematic reflection. These two facets of verbal mannerisms and thematic reflections, which make the relation between *Mauberley* and 'Prufrock' almost unavoidable, both lead us back to James; and we can suggest that Pound wishes not only to emulate 'Prufrock', but through the greater sexual explicitness of his poem to go beyond the Jamesian surface as it is employed in 'Prufrock', to locate these embodied hesitancies not merely in the James novel, but, as Espey diffidently suggests, in the ambiguous figure of Henry James himself.

I am not here implying that Mauberley is James (there is no single model for Mauberley), but that in Pound's articulation of literary, psychological and sexual levels in the second section of the sequence, the sexual level must be regarded as primary – as is manifested in what Espey terms, 'the final, sexual series on which "Mauberley" rests'.[32] Both psychological and literary levels are to be regarded as secondary manifestations which can be traced back to a fundamental sexual bias; or, in Mauberley's case, failure of bias. Thus, while Mauberley's literary ambitions cannot be compounded with Pound's view of James, whose subject he saw as the depiction of modern life in terms of 'velleities, atmospheres, timbres, nuances etc.',[33] James's calm disengagement from personal, emotional commitments for 'aesthetic' reasons could be aligned with that 'Olympian "apathein"/In the presence of selected perceptions' which Pound applies to Mauberley. In brief, sexual passivity underwrites artistic and intellectual passivity; while the rationale for these connections, and beyond of the intellectual infrastructure of the entire suite, can be traced back to Pound's Vorticist ideas.

With regard to

> Unable in the supervening blankness
> To sift TO AGATHON from the chaff
> Until he found his sieve . . .
> Ultimately his seismograph:

Pound had written in *The New Age* in 1915, 'The good artist is perhaps a good seismograph, but the difference between man and a machine is that man can in some degree "start his machinery going". He can, within limits, not only record but create.'[34] Thus, we can see Mauberley, as Pound tended to see James, and, more particularly, the Impressionist followers of Flaubert, as primarily a sensitive recipient of impressions, but incapable of that 'intensity, selection, and concentration'[35] that he discerned in the Vorticist artists. In the terms of the central antithesis in Pound's *Blast* 'Vortex', Mauberley is 'the TOY of circumstance . . . the plastic substance RECEIVING impressions', as opposed to the virile, active Vorticist artist, who he thinks of 'as directing a certain fluid force against circumstance, as CONCEIVING instead of merely observing and reflecting'.

At this date, for Pound, Rémy de Gourmont represented the contrasting Vorticist type in the literary arts. The pervasive flower-eye symbolism of poems II to IV derives from de Gourmont; and during this period Pound translated his *Physique de l'amour* as *The Natural Philosophy of Love* (1921),[36] through which Pound extended his sexually based Vorticist conceptions. To Pound, the figure of de Gourmont was the converse of James, as he makes clear from the inception of his *Little Review* article on de Gourmont, using each to contrast with the other through an extended series of comparisons. 'Where James is concerned with the social tone of his subjects, with their entourage, with their *superstes* of dogmatized "form", ethic, etc., Gourmont is concerned with their modality and resonance in emotion.'[37] While James is seen as a depictor and recorder of *moeurs contemporaines*, the social superficies of a particular period, de Gourmont is seen as concerned with 'permanent' personal emotion and its physiological base; and pertinently much of his mature writing deals with the interrelation between the sexual and the aesthetic spheres, which he refused to maintain as distinct. Gourmont's value for Pound was that he reinforced his belief in the physiognomic basis of aesthetic judgement. 'The emotions are equal before the aesthetic judgement. He does not grant the duality of body and soul, or at least suggests that this mediaeval duality is unsatisfactory; there is an interpenetration, an osmosis of body and soul, at least for hypothesis.'[38] (Pound saw this belief as exemplified in the troubadour poets, whose psychology, ideas, and writings he located as a 'love-cult'.) This has bearing on the distinction between de Gourmont and James, for, as Pound states, 'In contradistinction to, in wholly antipodal distinction from, Henry James, Gourmont was an artist of the nude,' and, 'Emotions to Henry James were more or less things that other people had and that one didn't go into; at any rate not in drawing rooms. The gods had not visited James, and the Muse, whom he so frequently mentions, appeared doubtless in corsage, the narrow waist, the sleeves puffed at the shoulders, à la mode 1890–2.' In contrast to this temporal, externalized registration of *moeurs contemporaines*, Pound sees de Gourmont's mode as atemporal, having a 'biological basis in instinct'; and states, 'He was an intelligence almost more than an artist; when he portrays, he is concerned with hardly more than the permanent human elements. His people are only by accident of any particular era.' In the *Little Review* piece de Gourmont is seen as the active, Vorticist artist; his is

> The conception of love, passion, emotion as an intellectual instigation; such as Propertius claims it; such as we find it declared in the King of Navarre's
>
> > 'De fine amor vient science et beauté';
>
> and constantly in the troubadours.

Pound allies himself with the Vorticist side of this dissociation, as against the James–Mauberley converse: 'the aesthetic receptivity of tactile and magnetic values, of the perception of beauty in these relationships'.[39]

It is the lack of this implicitly sexual, active Vorticist concentration that explains Mauberley's diffusion of intellect in poem III, 'The Age Demanded'.

> A pale gold, in the aforesaid pattern,
> The unexpected palms
> Destroying, certainly, the artist's urge,
> Left him delighted with the imaginary
> Audition of the phantasmal sea-surge,
>
> Incapable of the least utterance or composition,
> Emendation, conservation of the 'better tradition',
> Refinement of medium, elimination of superfluities,
> August attraction or concentration.

It is Mauberley's passivity that is emphasized here. In the first of these stanzas, 'The unexpected palms' destroy 'the artist's urge' because Mauberley is not 'directing a fluid force against circumstance' as does the Vorticist, but reacting to a stimulus, like a photographic plate, without modification, without 'conception'.

The second stanza enumerates the Vorticist qualities Mauberley lacks, without which he cannot emend or eliminate 'superfluities'. With this in mind the preceding stanzas become clearer.

> The coral isle, the lion-coloured sand
> Burst in upon the porcelain revery:
> Impetuous troubling
> Of his imagery.
>
> Mildness amid the neo-Nietzchean clatter,
> His sense of graduations,
> Quite out of place amid
> Resistance to current exacerbations,
>
> Invitation, mere invitation to perceptivity
> Gradually led him to the isolation
> Which these presents place
> Under a more tolerant, perhaps, examination.

Pound's attitude to Mauberley is tolerant (almost indulgent), but again Mauberley is presented as the tool of his environment: both his 'porcelain revery' and connoisseur's 'sense of graduations' are redundant in an environment of tropical extremes, and instead of active discrimination, he is left with 'invitation, mere invitation to perceptivity'. His response is not to seek to order or synthesize his perceptions, but to reduce perceptions to appearances and to ignore the social and political implications of art – in implicit opposition to Pound's achievement in *Hugh Selwyn Mauberley* itself:

> By constant elimination
> The manifest universe
> Yielded an armour
> Against utter consternation,

He is left therefore, 'In the presence of selected perceptions', without the ability to order or choose; leaving him finally

> Nothing, in brief, but maudlin confession,
> Irresponse to human aggression,
> Amid the precipitation, down-float
> Of insubstantial manna,
> Lifting the faint susurrus
> Of his subjective hosannah.

Mauberley's subsequent fate is described with Homeric irony in poem IV

> Coracle of Pacific voyages,
> The unforecasted beach;
> Then on an oar
> Read this:

> 'I was
> And I no more exist;
> Here drifted
> An hedonist.'

Here, not only the irony of the 'unforecasted beach' (like the previous 'unexpected palms') reinforces Mauberley's status as 'the TOY of circumstance', but this final condemnation is only fully coherent within the context provided by Pound's 'Vortex':

> Hedonism is the vacant place of a vortex, without force, deprived of past and future, the vortex of a still spool or cone.[40]

In poem IV, Mauberley's hedonism and intellectual dispersion are presented as 'deprived of past and future' in both psychological and literary senses. He is reduced to an undifferentiated and meaningless present,

> Scattered Moluccas
> Not knowing, day to day
> The first day's end, in the next noon;
> The placid water
> Unbroken by the Simoon;

and in Pound's 'Vortex' this hedonism is the converse to the conservation of the dynamic forces of 'tradition' in the present: 'All the past that is vital, all the past that is capable of living into the future, is pregnant in the vortex, NOW.'

With Pound's 'Vortex' in mind, it is difficult to consider 'Medallion' as 'Pound's poem', although it may well have been based on Pound's experience of listening to the singing of Raymonde Collignon, which was probably also the basis of 'Envoi'. Rather, it seems to be intended as a companion piece and, in its brittle visualist modes, obvious aesthetic contrast to the unabashed lyricism of the earlier poem. What is stressed in 'Medallion' is the transference of aesthetic criteria from the visual arts to the human: 'Luini in porcelain!'; 'Honey-red, closing the face-oval,'; 'The face-oval beneath the glaze,/Bright in its suave bounding-line . . .' This treatment of the human as an art-object is extended in the description of the hair as

> A basket-work of braids which seem as if they were
> Spun in King Minos' hall
> From metal, or intractable amber

where the 'metallic' terminology indicates lifelessness; while the pedantic citation of Reinach in

> The sleek head emerges
> From the gold-yellow frock
> As Anadyomene in the opening
> Pages of Reinach

is bathetic, and clinches the sense that as a live Venus the woman is not present, but only as a reminder of Reinach's *Apollo* and its reproduction of the head of Aphrodite by Praxiteles. All these elements parallel modes specifically ascribed to Mauberley's art in 'The Age Demanded', and, in particular, the second and fourth stanzas, where the use of 'glaze' to describe a 'porcelain' complexion is anticipated. More pertinently, aside from the question of ascription, if we wish for a criticism of such aesthetic attitudes, we find it in Pound's 'Vortex', where he criticizes all 'secondary applications': 'Elaboration, expression of second intensities, of dispersedness belong to the secondary sort of artist. Dispersed arts HAD a vortex.' Mauberley's 'Medallion' can be seen within the context of this criticism, as an imitation in words of what has already been done, and done better, by sculptors, painters and engravers.

In more contemporary terms, Mauberley can be seen to be condemned under the general designation of an Impressionist, a label which for Pound bore increasingly derogatory connotations as he absorbed, applied, and eventually disengaged himself from the aesthetic criteria of Ford Madox Ford, whose emphasis on *le mot juste* and exact presentation informs Pound's early Imagism, but whose influence waned as Pound searched for more dynamic Vorticist desiderata. In 1914 Pound stated 'The followers of Flaubert deal in exact presentation. They are often so intent on exact presentation that they neglect intensity, selection, and concentration. They . . . have been perhaps the most beneficent force in modern writing.'[41] By 1918, in the essay on 'Arnold Dolmetsch', fortified by four years of Vorticist effort, Pound's attitude to what he loosely terms Impressionism is clearer and more condemnatory. 'Impressionism had reduced us to such a dough-like state of passivity that we have ceased to like concentration. Or if it has not done it has at least set a fashion of passivity that has held since the romantic movement.'[42] Within the context of a discussion on music, the terms of this criticism are Vorticist, and related to those applied to Mauberley. It is interesting to see how Pound proceeds.

> That is the whole flaw of impressionist or 'emotional' music as opposed to pattern music. It is a drug . . . I do not mean that Bach is not emotional, but the early music starts with the mystery of pattern; if you like, with the vortex of pattern; with something that is, first of all, music, and which is capable of being, after that, many things. What I call emotional, or impressionist music, starts with being emotion or impression and then becomes only approximately music. It is, that is to say, something in the terms of something else.[43]

The above can be taken as a reflection on Mauberley's aesthetic modes, and those displayed in 'Medallion' in particular.

As a contrast to the 'female' receptivity characteristic of 'impressionism', Pound fully develops his own 'intuitive' theory of the intellect in a postscript to his translation of de Gourmont's *Physique de l'amour*, and in the course of doing so interestingly demonstrates the evolution of his vortex metaphor during the decade that ended with his abandonment of London literary culture. Before lending Lewis the term to christen his art movement, Pound had employed the word vortex to designate great cities, which were a confluence of energies, unlike America, which is 'like a province without a centre. London, to carry out the simile, is like Rome of the decadence, so far at least as letters are concerned, she is a main and vortex drawing strength from the peripheries.'[44] In the same year he wrote to William Carlos Williams that 'You may get something slogging away by yourself that you would miss in The Vortex – and that we miss.'[45] Pound's use of the term in his Vorticist aesthetics relates quite closely to this sense of a concentration of energies: 'The vortex is the point of maximum energy', though here the term is used as a polyvalent metaphor for the dynamic stasis of the Vorticist artwork. When attention is focused on the artist, however, the 'virile' employment of 'force' becomes Pound's main emphasis (Figure 12). In the 1914 *Egoist* article on Wyndham Lewis, Pound writes, 'From the beginning of the world there has been the traditional struggle, the struggle of Voltaire, of Stendhal, and of Flaubert, the struggle of driving the shaft of intelligence into the dull mass of mankind.'[46] This quotation can serve to introduce the final metamorphosis of the vortex metaphor. In the postscript to his translation of *Physique de l'amour*, published in 1921 – after *Mauberley* and Pound's final disillusionment with, and abandonment of London – he elaborates on his own theory of the brain, which he sees as 'in origin and development only a sort of great clot of genital fluid held in suspense or reserve', and goes on to say

> There are traces of it in the symbolism of phallic religions, man really the phallus or spermatozoid charging, head-on, the female chaos; integration of the male in the male organ. Even oneself has felt it, driving any new idea into the great passive vulva of London, a sensation analogous to the male feeling in copulation.[47]

This encapsulates Pound's retrospective sense of his own exasperated response to the London literary environment, but also leaves an impression, which I find not uncharacteristic of Pound's work as a whole, of a highly impressive intellectual mobility and range of understanding, suddenly and disconcertingly scaling down into a few simple, and in this case, crude ideas.

The previous discussion has tended to play down certain vexed critical issues in relation to *Hugh Selwyn Mauberley* (particularly those centred upon Pound's use of the persona) in favour of considering overall context and meaning, an area that criticism has neglected. This is not simply a choice of emphasis, for the issues that arise when attempts are made to extricate Pound's exact relation to the Mauberley persona are to some degree insoluble, not least because terms which are ostensibly applied to *Pound*, such as 'His true Penelope was Flaubert' in the first poem of the sequence, are subsequently applied to Mauberley (see 'Mauberley (1920)'). The previous discussion of 'Medallion', which is only intellectually coherent when regarded as 'Mauberley's poem', could have added that the brittle brilliance of this poem is not the least impressive achievement of the sequence, and this is not just because of Pound's investment in Gautier's aesthetics, but because Pound and the persona are not fully disengaged.

As an overall critical perspective this chapter has adopted Schneidau's position, by far the most coherent critical stance: 'a *persona* is not necessarily a character . . .' which 'suggests the simple truth that the speaker in a Pound poem, no matter what mask he wears, is always Pound himself . . . his method commits him so intensely to "what is being presented" that he could spend no more time on "building a character" than on novelistic accretion of detail'[48] However, Schneidau's conclusion that this 'makes us think rather of what ironic possibilities the words would have if viewed in shifting or flexible perspectives',[49] while critically acceptable, does not really resolve the issue of how far Pound's kaleidoscopic irony is intentional, and how far it manifests a lack of full intellectual coherence.

What is essentially the same issue can be approached from the perspective of two of Pound's own comments. In the important letter to Felix Schelling, Pound remarked of *Hugh Selwyn Mauberley*, '(Of course I'm no more Mauberley than Eliot is Prufrock. Mais passons.) Mauberley is a mere surface. Again, a study in form, an attempt to condense the James novel. Meliora speramus',[50] a remark that suggests aesthetic impersonality and detachment and contrasts interestingly with his comment while he was revising *The Waste Land*, where his suggestions conclude with the aside, 'Complimenti, you bitch. I am wracked by the seven jealousies, and cogitating an excuse for always exuding my deformative secretions in my own stuff, and never getting an outline. I go into nacre and objets d'art.'[51] Here Pound does not mention *Hugh Selwyn Mauberley* specifically, but at this date it is hard to know what other work he would be thinking of, and the admission of a lack of authorial disengagement throws the statement to Schelling into questionable relief. I will leave Pound himself with the last word, not to imply an ungenerous assessment of *Hugh Selwyn Mauberley*, but because his mention of 'the outline' usefully anticipates the concerns of the following chapter.

6
Satire and Reification: Eliot, Jonson and Lewis

Between Personality and Mankind it is always a question of dog and cat; they are diametrically opposed species. Self is the ancient race, the rest are the new one. Self is the race that lost. But Mankind still suspects Egotistical plots, and hunts Pretenders.

Wyndham Lewis, *The Enemy of the Stars.*

The purpose of the following chapter is to consider Eliot's employment of satiric modes in the *Poems* of 1920, and, in particular, his use of caricatural, spatial-presentative techniques. In this context, the work of Wyndham Lewis can be seen to be of particular relevance, for Lewis was an accomplished satirist working in Eliot's circle in the years 1914 to 1920, and comparison and contrast can uncover period emphases in both writers' employment of satiric techniques. However, in contrast to the relation between Pound and Eliot, one of active influence need not be asserted here. While Eliot would have been aware of Lewis's early work through *Blast*, the pieces he had written for the *Little Review*, and his novel *Tarr*,[1] which was published in 1918 (having been previously serialized by the *Egoist*, on which Eliot was employed as an assistant editor), there is no need to argue that Eliot's quatrain poems were directly affected by Lewis's writings. While it seems reasonable to suggest that Lewis's work provided oblique support for the satiric tendencies in Eliot's verse, and while Eliot expressed his admiration for Lewis in this period (and was to do so throughout his career), much of what both writers share is generic and historical, rather than the product of specific individual influence.

As the focus of this chapter is upon satire and satiric techniques, we will begin by considering a number of formulations in Eliot's 1919 'Ben Jonson' essay, which he concludes in characteristically wry and pertinent fashion, by suggesting that

Of all the dramatists of his time, Jonson is probably the one whom the present age would find the most sympathetic, if it knew him. There is a brutality, a lack of sentiment, a polished surface, a handling of large bold designs in brilliant colours, which ought to attract about three thousand people in London and elsewhere. At least, if we had a contemporary Shakespeare and a contemporary Jonson, it would be the Jonson who would arouse the enthusiasm of the intelligentsia![2]

The use of the visual metaphor, central to Eliot's judgement here, is representative of a particular strain in his criticism of this period. In the earlier 1919 essay on 'The Blank Verse of Marlowe' Eliot makes the judgement that Marlowe's verse, before he 'dyed swearing' was moving towards 'this intense and serious and indubitably great poetry, which, like some great painting and sculpture, attains its effects by something not unlike caricature',[3] taking as an example *The Jew of Malta*, which he considers is misunderstood.

> If one takes the *Jew of Malta* not as a tragedy, or as a 'tragedy of blood', but as a farce, the concluding act becomes intelligible; and if we attend with a careful ear to the versification, we find that Marlowe develops a tone to suit this farce, and even perhaps that this tone is his most powerful and mature tone. I say farce, but with the enfeebled humour of our times the word is a misnomer; it is the farce of the old English humour, the terribly serious, even savage comic humour, the humour which spent its last breath on the decadent genius of Dickens. It has nothing in common with J. M. Barrie, Captain Bairnsfather, or *Punch*. It is the humour of that very serious (but very different) play, *Volpone*.[4]

Eliot's essay on 'Ben Jonson' is an act of advocacy. He wishes to assert Jonson's contemporary relevance against what he wittily designates as a 'conspiracy of approval', which relegates Jonson to the status of the important and respected but unread. This Eliot sees as a function of neglect by poets, for not since Dryden has Jonson been looked to to provide 'the stirring of suggestion, the stimulus that a poet feels in his enjoyment of other poetry'. Because the poets have not looked to Jonson for creative stimulus, there has been no 'living criticism', but, Eliot asserts, 'there are possibilities for Jonson even now'.[5] Jonson's neglect, in comparison with his contemporaries Marlowe, Webster, Donne, Beaumont and Fletcher, Eliot explains by suggesting that he writes a different kind of poetry from these writers, one that involves different expectations. Eliot then makes his main point about Jonson's work, the rest of the essay being amplification, substantiation, and explanation. 'He is no less a poet than these men, but his poetry is of the surface. Poetry of the surface cannot be understood without study; for to deal with the surface of life, as Jonson dealt with it, is to deal so deliberately that we too must be deliberate, in order to understand.'[6] Shakespeare and the lesser writers have a different appeal, offering a more immediate gratification: 'they are suggestive, evocative, a phrase, a voice; they offer poetry in detail as well as in design', while, 'the polished veneer of Jonson reflects only the lazy reader's fatuity; unconscious does not respond to unconscious; no swarms of inarticulate feelings are aroused. The immediate appeal of Jonson is to the mind; his emotional tone is not in the single verse, but in the design of the whole.'[7]

Implicitly, Eliot is describing Jonson's qualities in spatial-pictorial terms; and, in distinguishing Jonson from his contemporaries, subtly predicating the non-empathetic nature of his art. In the terminology of *Einfühlung*, or empathy, as employed by Worringer, we could say that the reader or spectator of a Jonson play does not 'lose himself' in the action; he does not project his vitality into the aesthetic structure with which he is presented; 'identification' is prevented, and he remains a spectator, not subject to the 'self-alienation'[8] *Einfühlung* implies. In designating Jonson's poetry a 'poetry of the surface', Eliot is coming close to discussing Jonson's work in terms applicable to the abstractionist, Vorticist arts, which eschewed sentimental 'literary values' in favour of formal design.

In a crucial differentiation, Eliot distinguishes Jonson's satire from that of Swift or Molière: 'Jonson's drama is only incidentally satire, because it is only incidentally a criticism of the actual world.' Asserting that Jonson was more a 'creator' than a 'critic', Eliot contrasts Jonson's characterization – 'The characters of Jonson, of Shakespeare, perhaps of all the greatest drama, are drawn in positive and simple outlines' – with that of Flaubert's Frédéric Moreau in *L'Education sentimentale*.

> He is constructed partly by negative definition, built up by a great number of observations. We cannot isolate him from the environment in which we find him; it may be an environment which is or can be much universalized; nevertheless it, and the figure in it, consist of very many observed particular facts, the actual world. Without this world the figure dissolves. The ruling faculty is a critical perception, a commentary upon experienced feeling and sensation.[9]

This offers a suggestive analogy with the direction of Eliot's own poetic development: for this 'critical' mode by which 'we cannot isolate him [the character] from the environment in which we find him', accords far more with the Jamesian, impressionistic method Eliot pursued in the writing of 'The Love Song of J. Alfred Prufrock' than with the mode of the *Poems* of 1920, where the dominant poetic 'character', Sweeney, has 'the positive and simple outlines' of those characters in Jonsonian satire who exist relationally within the drama, rather than as a creation of 'observed particular facts, the actual world'. The visual analogy is implicit. Impressionism, in its aesthetic and literary manifestations, is held in contrast with styles that impose form and design.

To Eliot, Jonson's power resides in the vitality with which he imbues an overall dramatic design. This he sees not primarily as a commentary upon the actual world; hence it is not 'pure' satire according to Eliot's stringent definition: 'satire like Jonson's is great in the end not by hitting off its object, but by creating it; the satire is merely the means which leads to the aesthetic result, the impulse which projects a new world into a new orbit'. Of Jonsonian characterization, Eliot states,

> His characters are and remain, like Marlowe's, simplified characters; but the simplification does not consist in the dominance of a particular humour or

monomania. This is a very superficial account of it. The simplification consists largely in reduction of detail, in the seizing of aspects relevant to the
relief of an emotional impulse which remains the same for that character, in
making the character conform to a particular setting. This stripping is essential to the art, to which is also essential a flat distortion in the drawing; it is
an art of caricature, of great caricature, like Marlowe's.[10]

Finally, stating that, 'He did not get the third dimension, but he was not trying to
get it,' we can note that Eliot is at pains to acquit Jonson's work from the accusation that being an 'art of the surface' it must be, in a derogatory sense, 'superficial'.

We cannot call a man's work superficial when it is the creation of a world; a
man cannot be accused of dealing superficially with the world which he himself has created; the superficies *is* the world. Jonson's characters conform to
the logic of the emotions of their world. It is a world like Lobatchevsky's;
the worlds created by artists like Jonson are like systems of non-Euclidean
geometry.[11]

At this point we must beware of the danger of making mechanical ascriptions.
While Eliot's remarks on Ben Jonson can be applied, with some qualification, to
the early work of Wyndham Lewis, and those terms can also be referred, more
directly, to Eliot's own satiric quatrains, it is important to remember that such
terms and emphases can also be related back to satire as a literary genre. In Alvin
Kernan's account of Renaissance satire, *The Cankered Muse*, we can see many of
the elements that Eliot describes as being coherent within a traditional satiric
context, and Kernan can generalize confidently that 'The author of satire always
portrays the grotesque and distorted, and concentrates to an obsessive degree on
the flesh.'[12] However, a generic focus can effectively conceal historical distinctions. Here it is necessary to outline the central difference between Jonson and
Lewis, before applying Eliot's terms to Lewis's work. This difference can be comprehended by suggesting that while Jonson uses techniques of caricature and reification – here meant in its literal sense, as the translation of the animate to the
inanimate – for traditional satiric purposes, to contest prevalent vices and follies,
Lewis (and Eliot) wish, at least initially, to satirize the pervasive 'reification' of
modern life. The concept of reification, used here in general terms to indicate the
fragmentation and mechanization of social relations in post-industrial cultures, is
necessary to comprehend Eliot's renewed interest in Jonson and the salient aspects
of Lewis's work. Thus, while Eliot's remarks can be placed within a generic
literary context, the particularity of his emphases are a period phenomenon, and
can be most meaningfully related to his contemporary concerns, and, as a first
stage, to indicate period affinities to the work of Wyndham Lewis. When we
have considered Lewis's early fiction, the bearing of that fiction and Eliot's own
'Ben Jonson' essay upon his quatrain poems will be assessed.

Although Eliot was, of course, not thinking of Lewis when he wrote on Ben

Jonson, he was aware of a connection between the two. In the 1918 *Egoist* review of Lewis's first novel *Tarr*, Eliot states,

> Wit is public, it is in the object; humour (I am speaking only of *real* humour) is the instinctive attempt of a sensitive mind to protect beauty against ugliness; and to protect itself against stupidity. The older British humour is of this sort; in that great but decadent humorist, Dickens, and in some of his contemporaries it is on the way to the imbecilities of *Punch*. Mr. Lewis's humour is near to Dickens, but on the right side, for it is not too remote from Ben Jonson.[13]

In order to broach the relevance of the terms of Eliot's 'Jonson' essay to Lewis's writings it is convenient to take a theoretical standpoint and indicate Lewis's declared intentions. The most relevant document here is the essay 'Inferior Religions', which Lewis published in *The Little Review* in 1917 as a commentary upon his early stories, which were later revised and published in 1927 as *The Wild Body*.[14] Eliot wrote of this essay in the 'Tarr' review, ' "Inferior Religions" remains in my opinion, the most indubitable evidence of genius, the most powerful piece of imaginative thought, of anything Mr. Lewis has written.'[15]

We are presented with a helpful and not entirely fortuitous parallel with Eliot's 'Ben Jonson' essay almost as soon as we begin reading 'Inferior Religions'. Eliot, in his essay, with what is at this period a significant fondness for quasi-scientific metaphors and terminology, having specified that 'Jonson's characters conform to the logic of the emotions of their world' goes on to draw a parallel with mathematics. 'It is a world like Lobatchevsky's; the worlds created by artists like Jonson are like systems of non-Euclidean geometry. They are not fancy, because they have a logic of their own; and this logic illuminates the actual world, because it gives us a new point of view from which to inspect it.'[16] Subsequently, in the essay's conclusion, Eliot remarks that from Jonson 'we can derive not only instruction in non-Euclidean humanity; but enjoyment. We can even apply him, be aware of him as a part of our literary inheritance craving further expression.'[17]

Lewis, at the beginning of 'Inferior Religions', sets out to explain the original rationale of his stories of peasant life in Brittany and Spanish Galicia, and does so by indicating the degree of mechanical activity he perceived in the everyday occupational life of his characters: 'The fascinating imbecility of the creaking men-machines, that some little restaurant or fishing-boat works, was the original subject of these studies'[18] – to Lewis, it being the object that 'works' the men. Lewis continues by emphasizing the mechanical and intoxicating work rhythms imposed by these occupations.

> In the case of a fishing-boat the variety is so great, the scheme so complex, that it passes as open and untrammelled life. This subtle and wider mechanism merges for the spectator, in the general variety of Nature. Yet we have in most lives a spectacle as complete as a problem of Euclid. Moran, Bestre and Brobdingnag are essays in a new human mathematic. But they are

each simple shapes, little monuments of logic. I should like to compile a book of forty of these propositions, one deriving from and depending on the other (sic).[19]

This is a slight verbal parallel; but it is less trivial than it might appear to be. (That Eliot's geometry should be non-Euclidean, and Lewis's more staidly traditional is largely irrelevant; and would be so even had Eliot known much more about Lobatchevsky than his readers.) Eliot's perception of Jonson's satiric plays is of a self-bounding universe in which 'simplified' characters obey 'the logic of the emotions of their world', having no autonomous existence outside the dramatic design of which they are constituents. Lewis's rationale for his stories, seen here essentially as a satire on reification, could well provide the 'further expression' of Jonson's heritage that Eliot desired.

As indicated, Lewis sees his portrayals of peasant life as 'essays in a new human mathematics', but though he views such 'primitive' existences as mechanical, he does not wish his characters to be seen in stereotypic terms: 'When we say "types of humanity", we mean violent individualities, and nothing stereotyped.'[20] We are reminded here of Eliot's mention of the theory of humours in connection with Jonson, where he concedes that this theory has some relevance, particularly to Jonson's early work, but, 'The Humour, even at the beginning, is not a type, as in Marston's satire, but a simplified and somewhat distorted individual with a typical mania.'[21] Lewis, like Eliot, traces the genesis of grotesque but memorable comic characters back to the expressive needs of the artist.

> Sam Weller, Jingle, Malvolio, Bouvard and Pécuchet, the 'commissaire' in *Crime and Punishment*, do not live; they are congealed and frozen into logic, and an exuberant, hysterical truth. They transcend life and are complete cyphers, but they are monuments of dead imperfection. Their only reference is to themselves, and their only significance their egotism.
>
> The great intuitive figures of creation live with the universal egotism of the Poet. They are not picturesque and over palpable. They are supple with this rare impersonality; not stiff with a common egotism. The 'realists' of the Flaubert, Maupassant, and Tchekoff school are all satirists. 'Realism', understood as applied to them, implied either photography or satire.
>
> Satire, the great Heaven of Ideas, where you meet the Titans of red laughter, is just below Intuition, and Life charged with black Illusions.[22]

The parallels between Eliot's perception of Jonson and Lewis's fictional practice include less immediate analogies in overall narrative and structural design. To Eliot, Jonson's characters, being exemplars of a 'non-Euclidean humanity', have no existence outside the dramatic design of which they are constituent parts. Their existence is relational: 'Volpone's life . . . is bounded by the scene in which it is played'. The same, or similar, could be said of the characters in Lewis's short stories. Stating that 'They are only shadows of energy, not living beings. Their mechanism is a logical structure, and they are nothing but that', he sees them as fulfilling a mechanical ritual dance around the chosen fetish object, which may result in a violent dénouement when the fetish is human, but does not permit any gain in awareness or self-acknowledge or any character development. They exist without entelechy; they fit in with each other; sometimes come into violent collision with each other; but they do not act upon each other, or modify each other, except in brute physical terms. As Jonson's characters fulfil the logic of their dramatic co-existence, 'The artistic result of *Volpone* is not due to any effect that Volpone, Mosca, Corvino, Corbaccio, Voltore have upon each other, but simply to their combination into a whole',[23] so Lewis's characters are constituent elements in 'a spectacle as complete as a problem of Euclid', a ritualized, rhythmic dance pattern depending on the individual characters being not more than factors and variables, their combination making the narrative whole of a theorem in a 'new human mathematic'.

Thus, in both Jonson's and Lewis's work the complete work of art is the un-ravelling of the various permutations allowed by combining these human factors, and the working out of the inner logic of their confrontation to its necessary con-clusion or result. We can appreciate that an art of this type must be an 'art of the superficies', for characters with 'depth' or imaginative autonomy are not amen-able to this rigorous, quasi-mathematical, deterministic treatment. In other words, the element of individual volition must be all but eradicated from the drama or narrative, in order that the character be fully circumscribed by the scene in which he plays. In fictional practice this means the use of exteriorization tech-niques which proceed beyond reification to what can only be described as 'de-humanization' techniques.

Lewis's fictional practice, at least those aspects of it with which Eliot would have been familiar during the writing of his quatrain poems, is likely to appear less radical than its theoretical justification. While Jonson's caricatural concentration upon the grotesque externals of the human is aided by the nature of his medium (theatre being the most 'visible' of literary modes), Lewis's medium, psycho-logical narrative, is the most 'interior' of modes. In view of the restraints imposed by his medium, Lewis's overall narrative strategy is as significant as literary technique in attempting to achieve the exteriorized effects he desires.

However, two salient aspects of Lewis's narrative modes can be indicated, one, an obvious technique for achieving exteriorization, the other less so. The first is an obsessive concentration on the details of physical appearance, which includes clothing and mannerisms. Lewis's early stories abound with examples of a scrupu-lous attention to the material trappings of the human being, which serves a deeper purpose: it is not to familiarize us with the physical quality of the character, as it might be in Lawrence's writings, but to emphasize the materiality of the human. Lewis's tactic is to describe the human being as an object by employing a bizarre battery of tropes, analogies and similes that force the reader to view the human body as a structure divorced from any animating spirit. For example, in 'A Soldier of Humour', the anger of Monsieur de Valmore, the irascible French-American with whom Kerr-Orr, the Lewis figure, or puppet-master, has a prolonged skirmish, is described thus: 'His beard bristled round his drawling mouth, his thumbs sought his arm-pits, his varnished patterned shoes stood up erect and aggressive upon his heels.'[24] While as a painter Lewis can dehumanize the human by presenting it in rigid puppet shapes, or by assimilating the human form within an abstract composition (both techniques are demonstrated in the designs for *Timon of Athens*), in literary terms he attempts to achieve an analogous effect by concentrating, often microscopically, on surface physical detail. Thus, in 'Brotcotnaz', Julie, the battered wife is described in this way:

> The distillations of the breton orchard have almost subdued the obstinate yellow of jaundice, and Julie's face is a dull claret. In many tiny strongholds of eruptive red the more recent colour has entrenched itself. Her hair is very dark, parted in the middle, and tightly brushed down upon her head. Her eyebrows are for ever raised. She could not depress them, I suppose, any more, if she wanted to. A sort of scaly rigor fixes the wrinkles of the forehead into a seriated field of what is scarcely flesh, with the result that if she pulled her eyebrows down, they would fly up again the moment she released the muscles.[25]

While on one level apparently a defamiliarization technique, this impasto verbal style employing the vocabulary of the painter's palette is also meant to be a form of hallucinated realism. In 'A Soldier of Humour', Kerr-Orr, the Lewis persona, refers to such delight in 'stylistic anomalies' as a 'grotesque realism'.[26]

The second, less obvious aspect of Lewis's exteriorization techniques, can be illustrated by reference to Lewis's first novel, *Tarr*, in which a concentration upon the transcription of psychological states would seem to militate against exteriorized narrative. The method that Lewis adopts could be termed the 'exteriorization of interior psychology'. Early in the novel, Tarr, the Lewis figure, proposes to Butcher that if he is to conduct his affairs on a more rational basis, and disengage himself from his unwanted fiancée, Bertha, there is only one cure: 'All my mock matrimonial difficulties come from humour. I am going to gaze on Bertha inhumanly, and not humorously. Humour paralyses the sense for Reality . . .'[27] Tarr's statement, the rationale of his future conduct, provides an analogue to Lewis's narrative technique. This technique records the processes of consciousness, but from a severe, distanced authorial viewpoint, which, while reporting thoughts and emotions, simultaneously analyses them and presents them to the reader via an often grotesque series of figurative comparisons.

Unsurprisingly, it is in the 'Tarr' sections of the novel, where the authorial viewpoint is most closely identified with that of his showman, that this technique is most fully exemplified. For example, reporting Bertha's 'self-sacrificing' mental decision to let Tarr do as he wishes, Lewis presents this burlesque simile of her imagined state after Tarr's departure, after he has gone off with 'her heart'. 'She did not want it! She must indulge her mania for tasteful arrangement in future without this. Or rather what heart she had left would be rather like one of those salmon-coloured, corrugated gas office stoves, compared to a hearth with a fire of pine.'[28] A few passages further, when Tarr approaches Bertha to kiss her, and indulge his 'humane "indifference" ', she does not respond in the intended manner. 'She covered him, docilely, with her inertia. He was supposed to be performing a miracle of bringing the dead to life. Gone about too crudely, the willing mountebank, Death, had been offended. It is not thus that great spirits are prevailed upon to flee.' The technique is characteristic: a comic metaphor breeds a burlesque personification, and the immediate occasion for the tropes, a character's actions or emotions are almost lost sight of in a baroque accumulation of analogies. Emotions are structured, and frequently reified by concrete analogies, being almost detached from any personal psychic context, and then displayed as mental phenomena – in this case literally mental furniture – to be inspected by the reader. In contrast to the fictional practice of writers such as Lawrence or Virginia Woolf, Lewis's method is anti-mimetic, in that he employs tropes to reify and solidify the flux of consciousness into a progression of discontinuous states. Very little movement is necessary between Tarr's 'indifferent' standpoint and the author's point of view: the two perspectives generally coincide. When Bertha begins to cry, her tears having not been 'very far back in the wings' during the whole of this scene, Lewis does not need to qualify Tarr's reaction as he goes through the motions of comforting her:

'Oh! dis, Sorbet! Est-ce que tu m'aimes? M'aime-tu? Dis!'
'Yes, you know, Don't cry.'
A wail, like the buzzing on a comb covered with paper followed.

This anti-empathetic, 'inhuman', detached stance is held in common by the author and his hero, to whom Bertha's distraught 'female' possessiveness is akin to 'the sightless clammy charging of a bat'.[29]

Associated with such dislocating, externalizing procedures there are various narrative strategies to maintain satiric distance. For example, we are prevented from seeing Bertha as a totality; she is frequently seen as one aspect of her body, a material phenomenon. When Tarr first enters her room, 'He put his hand on her hip . . . and led her into the room.' When Bertha's thigh slips out of her dressing-gown, 'It looked dead, and connected with her like a ventriloquist's dummy with its master.' We are similarly distracted from becoming absorbed by the emotions of the protagonists by a pedantic, precise concentration on the details of physical movement and the topography of the room. 'She lay there like an animal, he thought, or someone mad, a lump of half-humanity. On one side of him Bertha lay quite motionless and silent, and on the other the little avenue was equally still.'[30]

Even from such a few examples, it is easy to perceive that Lewis's authorial stance, using the vehicle of an author-surrogate or persona, is one of icy detachment. Tarr, who in *Rude Assignment* Lewis admitted to be a 'caricatural self-portrait of sorts',[31] is the showman, or puppet-master of the eponymous novel, the controlling intelligence through which all authorial judgements are made. In 'A Soldier of Humour', Kerr-Orr is the Lewis figure, who defeats the French-American de Valmore in a series of grotesque confrontations, a battle or skirmish being the typical Lewis metaphor for the mechanics, and perhaps larger significance, of human relationships. In the revised 'A Soldier of Humour', Kerr-Orr is allowed a statement which is revealing of Lewis's authorial stance. 'I admit that I am disposed to forget that people are real – that they are, that is, not subjective patterns belonging specifically to me, in the course of this joke-life, which indeed has for its very principle a denial of the accepted actual.'[32] The significance of this authorial stance in relation to Eliot's work will be discussed subsequently.

In his review of *Tarr* in the *Egoist* of September 1918, in general terms Eliot brings the concern with exteriorized dehumanization techniques we have analysed in Lewis's early fiction into focus, and provides the basis for the connection we wish to make with Eliot's own work. Taking the 'critical commonplace' of the comparison between Lewis's *Tarr* and Dostoevsky's work (made by Pound among others) and subjecting it to critical scrutiny, Eliot states:

> In contrast to Dostoevsky, Mr. Lewis is impressively deliberate, frigid; his interest in his own personages is wholly intellectual. This is a peculiar intellectuality, not kin to Flaubert; and perhaps inhuman would be a better word than frigid. Intelligence, however, is only a part of Mr. Lewis's quality; it is united with a vigorous physical organism which interests itself directly in sensation for its own sake. The direct contact with the senses, perception of the world of immediate experience with its own scale of values, is like Dostoevsky, but there is always the suggestion of a purely intellectual curiosity in the senses which will disconcert many readers of the Russian novelist.[33]

In an October 1917 'Reflections on Contemporary Poetry' *Egoist* review, in discussing a volume of poetry by Jean de Bosschère (an admirer and associate of Pound's) Eliot uses terms that are similar to those in which he discusses Lewis, but particularly revealing in a poetic context. Comparing Harold Monro's empathetic poetry, which 'arrives at a degree of consistency in a charming flirtation with obscure, semi-philosophic sentiments', with that of de Bosschère, he states, 'With M. de Bosschère there are none of these sidelong glances; he is directly in front of his object; it occupies the fovea.' The current of this neo-Imagistic comparison to the advantage of de Bosschère is extended by contrasting two poems both dealing with 'the relationship between a man and his personal property'; but while Monro 'speaks characteristically in the first person; he states his theory bluntly and reflectively . . . His utensils are provided with adjectives which connect them with human emotions – "the gentle bed", "the old impetuous gas", "the independent pencil", "you my well trampled Boots". He reflects on a general situation; de Bosschère concentrates on a single instance.' Eliot continues by quoting de Bosschère to confute Monro's simple animistic conceits and offer a more acceptable non-empathetic practice:

Homere Mare

n'est pas un prophète ni un critique.
Chaque matin il met lui-même le feu dans l'âtre.
Tout le jour

Il est l'époux du feu,
L'aimé des flammes.

And here neither 'époux' nor 'aimé' have any sentimental associations . . .
There is no pretence in the poem of a quasi-human relationship . . . M. de
Bosschère never employs his thoughts and images in decorating ordinary
human sentiments.

Eliot draws two lessons from de Bosschère's practice (which from the examples
he gives does not seem to bear the weight of significance he attributes to it). First,
the virtue of the concrete and non-empathetic over the abstract and moralizing.
'M. de Bosschère is in fact almost a pure intellectual; leaving, as if disdainfully, our
emotions to form as they will around the situation which his brain has selected.
The important thing is not how we feel about it, but how it is. De Bosschère's
austerity is terrifying.' Then, as an anticipation of Eliot's commitment to a theory
of 'art emotions', derived from de Gourmont, and applied in 'Tradition and the
Individual Talent', he offers this formulation:

A poet like M. de Bosschère is an intellectual by his obstinate refusal to
adulterate his poetic emotions with human emotions. Instead of refining
ordinary human emotion (and I do not mean tepid human emotion, but
human however intense – in the crude living state) he aims direct at the
emotions of art. He thereby limits the number of his readers, and leaves the
majority groping for a clue which does not exist. The effect is sometimes an
intense frigidity which I find altogether admirable.[34]

The parallels between Eliot's comments on Lewis's 'inhuman' stance and de
Bosschère's 'frigidity' are apparent, and include a realization that such purely
'intellectual' interest is likely to baffle the public (with the covert appeal to
minority values that such critical judgements contain). The value of these comments on de Bosschère is not merely to show how prevalent non-empathetic
critical values were in Eliot's writings between 1917 and 1919 when he was
composing his satiric quatrains, but to indicate the areas in which Eliot perceived
that non-empathetic techniques could be given poetic application. He points out
the eschewal of Monro's first person; direct Imagist contact with the object; the
avoidance of the abstract and reflective; and continues by recommending de
Bosschère's refusal to adulterate his objects or situations with any sentimental or
quotidian 'emotional' associations. This last brings Eliot's comments beyond a
recommendation of Imagist disciplines towards an engagement with non-
empathetic modes.
    At this point it is necessary to demonstrate the relevance of the previous analysis
of Eliot's 'Ben Jonson' essay and Lewis's early fiction to Eliot's quatrain poems.
This can be achieved most effectively by offering a brief commentary on 'Sweeney
Erect', the first of the Sweeney poems, which can be seen to exhibit many of the
characteristics that have been discussed, but is cast in Eliot's presentative poetic
idiom.

> *And the trees about me,*
> *Let them be dry and leafless; let the rocks*
> *Groan with continual surges; and behind me*
> *Make all a desolation. Look, look wenches!*

Paint me a cavernous waste shore
    Cast in the unstilled Cyclades,
Paint me the bold anfractuous rocks
    Faced by the snarled and yelping seas.

Display me Aeolus above
    Reviewing the insurgent gales
Which tangle Ariadne's hair
    And swell with haste the perjured sails.[35]

As in 'Whispers of Immortality' the initial sections of the poem, in this case the epigraph and the first two stanzas, are used to create a satiric juxtaposition, and as in that poem the satiric contrast resides more in a tonal disjunction than in a simplistic contrast between an idealized past and a debased present. Sweeney's attitude to his epileptic companion in the brothel offers parallels with Theseus, who abandoned (the sleeping) Ariadne on Naxos; a parallel reinforced by the epigraph from Beaumont and Fletcher's *The Maid's Tragedy* where 'the wronged Aspatia'[36] abandoned by her lover, Amintor, sees herself as another Ariadne, and addressing her attendant women in the quoted words, tells them to use her as a model for Ariadne in a tapestry they are weaving.[37] Here, Eliot coolly combines, and perhaps distorts, two aspects of the legend of Theseus. His use of the epithet 'perjured' referring to Theseus's sails to suggest deceit when he abandons Ariadne is sanctioned by the conclusion of the legend, where returning victorious from Naxos he neglects to raise a white sail, a signal pre-arranged with his father, Aegeus, to denote success against the Minotaur. Aegeus, seeing the black sail, puts an end to his life. Allowing for this connection between the two faithless lovers, the tonal contrast inheres in the disjunction between the magniloquent language and leisurely rhythms of this section and the clipped, rhetorically constrained cameos that follow. As in 'Whispers of Immortality', the past may not be ethically preferable to the present, but it has rhetorical, linguistic amplitude, a grace of gesture, that invests it with a certain sombre dignity. The first and final lines of the second stanza extend themselves quantitatively through the use of opulent vowel sounds:

Display me Aeolus above
    Reviewing the insurgent gales
Which tangle Ariadne's hair
    And swell with haste the perjured sails.

which gives way to a jaunty, parodic vaudeville rhythm, in a sudden rhythmic contraction.

Morning stirs the feet and hands
    (Nausicaa and Polytheme)
Gesture of orang-outang
    Rises from the sheets in steam.

This third stanza establishes the dominant technique which is employed to present Sweeney and the woman: a concentration upon their material physicality rendered in terms of the body not as a totality but as parts, treating the human in divorce from any animating spirit as an aggregate of limbs and spasmodic movements. 'Morning stirs the feet and hands': awakening brings not consciousness but restless physical movements in isolated portions of the anatomy. This mode of treatment is to some extent underwritten by the woman's state: undergoing a fit of epilepsy (or hysteria) she can be seen as no more than a process of uncontrolled convulsive motions, while Sweeney (as is the mode with other quatrain poems) is presented as a genial-sinister brute. His significance is to be comprehended in terms of his limitations, his insentient physicality. He

> Tests the razor on his leg
>> Waiting until the shriek subsides.
> The epileptic on the bed
>> Curves backward, clutching at her sides.

Here, an implied connection between the woman's fit and Sweeney's actions (he is presumably only leaving her) seems to be enforced by the imagery of the previous stanzas, which are dominated by verbs of cutting and laceration: 'slitted below', 'gashed', 'jackknifes upward', 'clawing at the pillow slip'. Sweeney's blankness or sinister sang-froid seems to be accentuated when we realize that it is only in this, the eighth stanza, that a primary indication of individuality, the sex of his companion, has been dignified with a personal pronoun.

This is a technique of material rendition, an 'art of the surface', in the phrase that Eliot applied to Jonson. We are presented with portions of the anatomy as synecdoches for the human, and the intended satiric effect is created by the implication that these humans at least can be comprehended by their material attributes. It is worth noting how insistently throughout the poem Eliot reiterates parts of the body; even Doris, who brings 'sal volatile/And a glass of brandy neat', 'Enters padding on broad feet'. This stress on the visible and material operates as a mode of fragmentation, and, as has been suggested, dehumanization. Eliot's characters, much like those of Wyndham Lewis, are mechanisms, automata, puppets; and many of Lewis's comments on his own work, from 'Inferior Religions' and elsewhere in his writings, could be applied to this poem quite accurately. Despite the sharp impression of vitality conveyed by such part notations, we could state of Doris, Sweeney, and the epileptic woman, as Lewis does of his characters in what was to be *The Wild Body*:

> With their attendant objects or fetishes they live and have a regular food for vitality. They are not creations, but puppets. You can be exterior to them, and live their life as little, as the showman grasping from beneath and working about a Polichinelle. They are only shadows of energy, and not living beings. Their mechanism is a logical structure and they are nothing but that.[38]

Similarly, it would be possible to apply to Eliot's poem many of the perceptions and emphases of his 'Ben Jonson' essay. In particular, the lack of the 'third dimension' of depth which Eliot perceives in Jonson's satire, and its dramatic consequences, could be taken as a comment on 'Sweeney Erect'. Substituting 'Sweeney' for 'Volpone' we could say that 'Sweeney's life, on the other hand, is bounded by the scene in which it is played; in fact, the life is the life of the scene and is derivatively the life of Sweeney; the life of the character is inseparable from the life of the poem.'

One significant facet of this technique is to present us with a self-bounding universe. Sweeney's potential is defined by his realization in the poem; as in a Hogarthian low-life tableau, the superficies manifests its own signficance. A figure like Sweeney could be comprehended in Lewis's terms as a 'tyro', defined in 1921, in the magazine of that name, as 'An elementary person; an Elemental, in short . . . The action of a Tyro is necessarily very restricted; about that of a puppet worked with deft fingers, with a screaming voice underneath.'[39] Lewis's elementals (Figure 13), or tyros, were successors and relatives of the Breton peasants, the carapace of whom he describes with baroque, comic gusto in the stories collected in *The Wild Body*. Subsequently, in *Rude Assignment*, he described these characters as 'primitive creatures, immersed in life, as much as birds, or big, obsessed, sun-drunk insects'.[40] Being no more than puppets, machines, or insects, they were at any rate fit as 'elementals' for satiric portrayal as slightly sub-human. In 1921 Lewis drew portraits of a number of tyros, and in the introduction to the exhibition catalogue, defending his 'forbidding and harsh' creations, he comments, 'Swift did not develop in his satires the comeliness of Keats, nor did Hogarth aim at grace.'[41] These tyros are portrayed as creatures dominated by an immense, flashing grin.

> These immense novices brandish their appetites in their face, lay bare their teeth in a valedictory, inviting, or merely substantial laugh. A laugh, like a sneeze, exposes the nature of the individual with an unexpectedness that is perhaps a little unreal. This sunny commotion in the face, at the gate of the organism, brings to the surface all the burrowing and interior broods which the individual may harbour.[42]

Any one of these creatures could be allied with Sweeney, as a northern manifestation of what Lewis sees as primarily a 'Mediterranean' phenomenon; as, for example, in the opening stanza of 'Sweeney Among the Nightingales'.

> Apeneck Sweeney spreads his knees
> Letting his arms hang down to laugh
> The zebra stripes along his jaw
> Swelling to maculate giraffe.

Lewis's tyros and Eliot's Sweeney are not fit material for interiorized treatment, they are suitable only for presentation. Thus, in Lewis's stories the narrative is generally a narrative of action as it is in the two quatrain poems in which Eliot employed Sweeney most fully: 'Sweeney Erect' and 'Sweeney Among the Nightingales'. In these two poems an external, quasi-narrative depiction of events is offered from a rigorously detached standpoint. The 'dramatis personae' in 'Sweeney Among the Nightingales' are treated according to the techniques of material rendition employed in 'Sweeney Erect':

> The silent vertebrate in brown
> Contracts and concentrates, withdraws;
> Rachel *née* Rabinovitch
> Tears at the grapes with murderous paws;[43]

As in 'Sweeney Erect', in 'Sweeney Among the Nightingales' we are offered a scene for contemplation. The concision forced upon Eliot by the tetrameter line and quatrain stanza makes it difficult for him to achieve a clear delineation of the various actions that occur in 'Sweeney Among the Nightingales' (while the action in 'Sweeney Erect', where he has a limited number of characters, is reasonably clear). But though we may have some difficulty in distinguishing Sweeney from 'the silent man in mocha brown', who is presumably organizing his downfall, these methods of caricatural portrayal confer a vivid tangibility and sharp definition on Eliot's *tableau vivant*. A sudden, sharp focus of definition concentrating attention on an epithet describing appearance or action compensates for the obscurity and impenetrability of much of the 'manoeuvring' that the poem describes.

> She and the lady in the cape
> Are suspect, thought to be in league;
> Therefore the man with heavy eyes
> Declines the gambit, shows fatigue,
>
> Leaves the room and reappears
> Outside the window, leaning in,
> Branches of wisteria
> Circumscribe a golden grin;

The terms which Eliot used to describe Jonson's 'caricatural' art are relevant to this technique: 'simplification' and 'distortion' – the concentration on a single attribute which defines this 'art of the surface', the antithesis of the interior, empathetic mode which Lewis attempted to combat throughout his career.

In Lewis's terms, Sweeney could be a tyro, and Lewis would have regarded him as another 'elemental' around which he could exercise his satiric art. In Eliot's quatrain poems, however, he serves a different purpose: he is a caricatural representative of the entropy of the present, a reified consciousness, who need merely be invoked to establish a dominant tonality. Eliot's primary investment in the figure of Sweeney seems to be comprehended by his curt refutation of Emerson's earnest humanism in what is almost the central (parenthetic) stanza of 'Sweeney Erect':

> (The lengthening shadow of a man
>   Is history, said Emerson
> Who had not seen the silhouette
>   Of Sweeney straddled in the sun.)

In 'Mr. Eliot's Sunday Morning Service' he appears only once, as a counterweight to the vision of the spiritualized flesh of Christ, described according to an iconograph convention:

> But through the water pale and thin
> Still shine the unoffending feet
> And there above the painter set
> The Father and the Paraclete.

Sweeney appears at the end of the poem, the anchorman, a vision of unspiritualized flesh:

> Sweeney shifts from ham to ham
> Stirring the water in his bath.
> The masters of the subtle schools
> Are controversial, polymath.[44]

What unites the various incarnations of Sweeney in the quatrain poems (which must, of course, be taken as distinct from his subsequent appearance in 'Sweeney Agonistes') is this emphasis upon his brute physiognomy: 'broadbottomed', 'apeneck Sweeney', 'gesture of orang-outang'. This, when combined with his name, with Irish-American associations, and the obvious echo of Sweeney Todd, the 'demon barber' (and through him both crime and appetite) strongly establishes Sweeney as caricatural presence, which does not require or allow further elaboration. In Sweeney's case part of the satiric effect resides in the low life associations his name invokes, an effect accentuated by his schematic presence in such highly sophisticated, ultra-literary artefacts. Here Eliot can be seen to be following Lewis's advice in his *Blast* article 'The Exploitation of Vulgarity', where he suggests that 'Today the Artist's attention would be drawn . . . to anything particularly hideous or banal, as a thing not to be missed', while making explicit the implicit cultural assumptions behind Lewis's conviction that 'Our material of discord is to an unparalleled extent forcible and virulent.'[45] We can consider, for example, the precise effect of the word 'intimates' in

> Observing that hysteria
>   Might easily be misunderstood;
> Mrs. Turner intimates
>   It does the house no sort of good.

where the sophisticated term when set against the demotic transcription of Mrs. Turner's words creates a social nuance that serves to subtly differentiate the author (and his poem) from the milieu he is ostensibly describing.

Sweeney is precisely a name, a cypher, and one which need merely be deployed with suitable epithets to establish an affective tonality which oscillates between repulsion and fascination. For ultra-physical Sweeney, seen characteristically in a sordid, amorous situation (consider the obvious wordplay in the title 'Sweeney Erect'; 'nightingale' is one of the many Elizabethan-Jacobean synonyms for prostitute) is the converse of the highly self-aware, but emotionally ineffective Prufrock, a persona treated empathetically, using the interior monologue mode, and one who is closer to Eliot, the poet. Sweeney is repulsive by virtue of his brute insentience; but there is also a strong counter-current of fascination for the 'otherness' that such a simplified, two-dimensional presence represents. Certainly, a great deal of satiric friction is caused by his presence in poems which rely extensively on Eliot's employment of 'tradition', that sense of the significance of the literary past which his presence categorically negates. Unlike Prufrock or Gerontion, he is not the aggregate of a disembodied intellectual awareness, a consciousness barred from action; he is a monumental, caricatural presence, to be appreciated only through the superficies, in what he physically *is* and what he *does*.

It is now necessary to offer some qualifications and discriminations, particularly between Lewis's fictional practice and Eliot's poetic method in the quatrain poems. This can be achieved most efficiently by returning briefly to Eliot's 'Ben Jonson' essay. Eliot is here very concerned to qualify the term 'satire' when applied to Jonson's work.

> Jonson's drama is only incidentally satire, because it is only incidentally a criticism upon the actual world. It is not satire in the way in which the work of Swift or the work of Molière may be called satire: that is, it does not find its source in any precise emotional attitude or precise intellectual criticism of the actual world. It is satire perhaps as the work of Rabelais is satire; certainly not more so.[46]

The distinction is crucial; for while Eliot admits that Jonson's language does not have the evocative depth, the 'third dimension' of his contemporaries – 'Their words have often a network of tentacular roots reaching down to the deepest terrors and desires. Jonson's most certainly have not' – and that Jonson's characters also lack the other 'third dimension' of imaginative autonomy which is possessed by Shakespeare's characters – 'they have no life outside the theatrical existence in which they appear'[47] – he also wishes to assert that there is a power and vitality in Jonson's work, which depends on 'unity of inspiration', and renders his 'surface', or superficies, 'solid' (as opposed to the 'hollow' work of Beaumont and Fletcher), and animates his characters with the mode of vitality possessed by the characters of Rabelais, or some of the comic characters of Dickens.

Comparing Jonson with Shakespeare, Eliot offers an argument which would explain these differences with reference to the creative personality of the writer: 'The creation of a work of art, we will say the creation of a character in a drama, consists in the process of transfusion of the personality, or in a deeper sense, the life, of the author into the character.' While Shakespeare's characters demonstrate the working of a more complex, supple, susceptible temperament, and exemplify 'a greater range of emotion, and emotion deeper and more obscure', his great characters, such as Falstaff, satisfy 'deeper, but not necessarily stronger or more intense' feelings than those of Jonson. Shakespeare's world is larger; but Jonson's world is not merely to be regarded as a lesser world in magnitude: it is complete in itself, and differs in kind. 'His type of personality found its relief in something falling under the category of burlesque or farce – though when you are dealing with a *unique* world, like his, these terms fail to appease the desire for definition.'[48]

The discriminations Eliot offers here can be applied to his own work: Eliot's quatrain poems are only incidentally satire because the 'reference to the actual world' is tenuous, as it is in Jonson; and, as indicated in a previous chapter, our engagement with the scenes that Eliot portrays inevitably returns us, in a reflexive movement, back to the poet's own mode of seeing; 'the "satire" is merely a medium for the essential emotion'. When Eliot remarks of Jonson's characters, 'The Humour, even at the beginning, is not a type, as in Marston's satire, but a simplified and somewhat distorted individual with a typical mania',[49] the implied qualification of the 'realism' of Jonson's characters has its bearing on Eliot's own miniature gallery of 'individuals', and also serves to make us consider the priority of the 'lyric' impetus, as in Jonson's case, 'the process of transfusion of the personality, or, in a deeper sense, the life, of the author into the character'. Thus, in general terms, we can qualify the accuracy of the term 'satire' when applied to Eliot's work, in a manner similar to that in which *he* qualifies it with respect to Jonson. Eliot was well aware of the limitation of the designation 'satire' when applied to the quatrain poems. In 1920, after the publication of *Ara Vos Prec*, he wrote to his brother, 'Some of the new poems, the Sweeney ones, especially *Among the Nightingales* and *Burbank*, are intensely serious, and I think that those two are among the best that I have ever done. But even here I am considered by the ordinary newspaper critic as a wit or satirist, and in America I suppose I shall be thought merely disgusting.'[50]

We cannot say quite the same of Lewis's fiction. Lewis was a satirist by métier, and he was concerned to defend the 'realism' of his literary techniques. With regard to Eliot's poetic methods, the question of the 'interior consciousness' of say, Sweeney, is irrelevant; this is not the case in Lewis's narratives. In 'Inferior Religions', having established a characteristic Cartesian dualism between mind and body, he states that his stories deal with the visible and external, *res extensa* rather than *res cogitans*, exemplifying an 'objective Play-World corresponding to our social consciousness, as opposed to our solitude . . .' He is thus aware of the partiality of his chosen mode of treatment, and states that he does not deal with the 'travail within'. 'Were you the female of Moran (the first Innkeeper) and beneath the counterpane with him, you would be just below the surface of life, in touch with a nasty and tragic organism. The first indications of the proximity of the real soul would be apparent.' Rather, Lewis claims to deal with the material and social carapace, 'our legitimate and liveried masquerade': 'In this objective Play-World, corresponding to our social consciousness as opposed to our solitude, no final issue is decided.' It is the travail of 'interior consciousness' that creates 'the original and intense grotesqueness' of the social and material mask; but that consciousness is barred from the fiction, and 'if he comes at all it must be as he is, the skeleton or bogey of True Life, stuck over with corruptions and vices. He may have a certain "succès d'hysterie".'[51]

It seems impossible to avoid the implication that rather than suggesting, as Eliot does of Jonson, that although this is a world of superficies, it is not superficial, for 'the superficies *is* the world', in reality Lewis's superficies is hollow, for he suppresses or ignores interior consciousness – in contrast to Jonson's or Eliot's own literary practice. Similarly, we find in Lewis's deployment of authorial personae (Kerr-Orr in 'A Soldier of Humour', or Tarr, in the eponymous novel) that they too are schematized presences, lacking or denied interior complexity in the interests of defined presentation. As Kerr-Orr states, 'I realize, similarly, the uncivilized nature of my laughter . . . It sprawls into everything. It has become my life. The result is that I am *never* serious about anything. I simply cannot help converting everything into burlesque patterns.'[52] The congruence of this stance with that of the author helps prevent that reflexive movement back to an evasive, ironic, but distinct authorial consciousness which occurs when reading Eliot's quatrains, and also accounts for the different impression created by each writer's techniques. Here, Lewis's statement implies what seems to be exemplified in his literary development: that a fictional practice which began in the early *Wild Body* sketches (1909–10) as a satire upon mechanical reification, has swiftly (in the writing of 'A Soldier of Humour' and 'Inferior Religions', both published in 1917) become an exploration of, and identification with, those modes of reification, from which the author cannot achieve true critical detachment. In Eliot's case we feel we are dealing with 'projections' created by the poet's emotional and intellectual preoccupations and concerns; in Lewis's case, often we feel we are witnessing a strategic means of coping with experience.

The consequence of Lewis's stance, which was more or less maintained throughout his career, was that he failed to achieve any sense of real personal interaction in his fiction: his characters '*fit in* with each other', they do not '*act upon* one another', except by brute physical violence (to employ the phrases Eliot applies to Jonson). We can trace this stance back to personal, psychological roots. In *Rude Assignment* Lewis admits that while collecting material for what were to be *The Wild Body* stories, 'I remained, beyond the usual period, congealed in a kind of cryptic immaturity. In my social relations the contacts remained, for long, primitive. I recognized dimly the obstruction: was conscious of gaucherie, of wooden responses . . . It resulted in experience with no natural outlet in conversation collecting in a molten column within.'[53] The vocabulary of 'obstruction' and 'wooden responses' suggests that Lewis's early personal isolation can be seen as engendering a commitment to modes of reification which he never fully superseded either in life or in fiction. These modes can be regarded as a self-protective psychological tactic, a paranoiac reflex which permitted him to avoid dealing with the full humanity of individuals by means of an aggressive objectification.

These themes can be traced back to Lewis's prototype Vorticist drama, *The Enemy of the Stars*. Here, Arghol, the Lewis figure, is subject to a destructive dualism between Self and Other; the purity of his solitude is contaminated by social and personal interaction with his mournful disciple, Hanp. However, within this dualism there is a contrary and pre-existentialist implication which depends on

Lewis's Cartesian awareness of the gulf between the interior solitude and isolation of personal consciousness, and the material 'wild body' and its attendant social roles and assumptions (by which 'self' becomes 'other'). In a central retrospective section, Arghol relives an incident in his student years in which he pretended not to be himself in order to confront and confute the bland social assumptions of his friends:

> This man would never see anyone but Arghol he knew. – Yet he on his side saw a man, directly beneath his friend, imprisoned, with intolerable need for recognition.
>
> Arghol, that the baffling requirements of society had made, imprudent parasite of his solitude, had foregathered too long with men, and borne his name too variously, to be superseded.[54]

It is possible to sense the contrary dictates of the 'need for recognition' and the impulse towards solitude behind much of Lewis's work. He concludes 'Inferior Religions' with the suggestion that 'we should live a little more in small communities'; but previously even his expression of the utopian impulse of his art, 'Beauty is an icy douche of ease and happiness at something suggesting perfect conditions for an organism',[55] seems to imply a reference back to the individual artist. In the post-war period, when aggressively trapped in self-elected isolation and increasingly committed to modes of self-division and self-reification, Lewis, the rebarbative literary satirist, produced a visual art in which a fineness of linear definition and planes of lustrous metallic coloration work to create a sense of haunting and haunted solitude and purity.[56]

The previous remarks are obliquely relevant to Eliot's presentative stance in the *Poems* of 1920; but as Eliot was a writer who could both achieve and imply a greater range of intellectual and affective response than Lewis, we can discern the historical reference of Eliot's employment of Lewis's techniques. These tendencies are also manifested in Eliot's critical writings of this period, and in particular, in what can be described as his 'theory of art emotions'. This distinction, demonstrated in the de Bosschère *Egoist* review, where Eliot praises the poet for his 'obstinate refusal to adulterate his poetic emotions with human emotions', can be discerned in many of the pieces collected in *The Sacred Wood*, and in particular, 'The Perfect Critic' and 'Tradition and the Individual Talent'. This distinction between 'ordinary human emotions' and the 'emotions of art' is one that he drew, as he drew so much in his early criticism, from Rémy de Gourmont; one of Pound's enthusiasms, which he certainly communicated to Eliot between 1914 and 1918.

In 'The Perfect Critic' piece in *The Sacred Wood*, Eliot, after praising de Gourmont as the critic closest to his ideal, goes on to state that 'The end of the enjoyment of poetry is a pure contemplation from which all the accidents of personal emotion are removed . . .'[57] This statement is paralleled in many places in de Gourmont's writings, with a similar distinction drawn, as in the de Bosschère review, between the 'intellectual' interest in literature, and the 'sentimental – unenlightened'. In the essay 'Success and the Idea of Beauty',[58] de Gourmont, writing in the context of a Symbolist denunciation of any utilitarian or moral claims being laid on literature, states, 'The representatives of the aesthetic caste also judge a work of art by the emotion they experience, but this emotion is of a very special order: it is *aesthetic emotion.*' This category of 'aesthetic emotion' de Gourmont sees as excluding 'all utilitarian, moralizing, social works', or works of too overtly erotic a nature (although de Gourmont regards all art as proceeding from re-routed sexual impulses).

> Art, therefore, is what arouses a pure emotion, that is to say, without vibrations outside a limited group of cells. It is what conduces neither to virtue, nor to patriotism, nor to debauchery, nor to peace or war, nor to laughter or tears, nor to anything that is not art itself. Art is impassive, and as an old Italian has said of love, *non piange né ride.*[59]

In relation to this category of 'aesthetic emotion', Eliot's tendency is to suggest a more austere, anti-empathetic version of the concept than de Gourmont's idea necessitates. The contrast can be appreciated in 'Tradition and the Individual Talent', where Eliot introduces the notion of 'art emotions' to reinforce his theory of the impersonality of the artist. De Gourmont is throughout his critical writings committed to a subjectivist stance, and is far more willing than Eliot to admit personality and emotion into the literary work, provided they are expressed in an original and sensory 'concrete' manner. This contrast, perhaps more apparent than essential, can be traced back to each writer's period concerns. De Gourmont stressed 'aesthetic emotion' to relieve literature of the burden of utilitarian, didactic claims (a central Symbolist concern), while Eliot was writing against the self-expressive and sentimental late Romantic that both he and Pound condemned. The result, in Eliot's case, is the construction of a theory which overtly forbids personal expression in literature as well as empathetic, emotive readings. Here we can discern that the concept of aesthetic emotion, derived from de Gourmont, is combined with the hostility to the Romantic 'cult of personality' evinced by the French Classicist thinkers of the emergent *Action Française*; and interestingly in a piece written for Lewis's own magazine *The Tyro* (1921), Eliot uses Lewis's 'enemy' publication to commend Baudelaire's concern with morality, and express a criticism of Rousseau, the supposed originator of the Romantic cult of personality, in a statement which could be taken directly from any of the French authoritarian thinkers: 'Romanticism endeavoured to form another Morals – Rousseau, Byron, Goethe, Poe were moralists. But they have not sufficient coherence; not only was the foundation of Rousseau rotten, his structure was chaotic and inconsistent.'[60]

However, Eliot's emphasis on 'impersonality' and 'art emotions' does cause various problems once it is recognized that this Symbolist campaign is taking place within what is still a fundamentally Romantic aesthetic. De Gourmont's claim, in *Le Problème du style*,[61] that Flaubert cannot be in a true sense 'impersonal' has substance, not just because 'style is the man', but because the post-Romantic writer or poet does not have access to a Classical structure of authority by which he can mediate the personal accent of his verse through the expression of a wider social consensus; he can at best, as in Eliot's later verse, express the authority that he himself has consciously adopted. This allows us to view Eliot's statement in 'Tradition and the Individual Talent', that 'The emotion of art is impersonal' from a number of perspectives. As a statement of the autonomy of the literary medium we can accede to its implicit premise that the poem, a literary artefact, is different in kind from any idea or sentiment which may have preceded it in the author's mind, and, as an aesthetic representation, different in whatever 'quality' of emotion it may convey. However, Eliot's bias towards seeing the literary medium as therefore 'impersonal' and non-communicatory, must be regarded as an oblique, strategic defence of his own poetic practice.

This means, in the terms of Eliot's quatrain poems, that he elects a dehumanized presentation of Sweeney; but while the technique is overtly 'impersonal' and presentative, the decision to adopt this mode of treatment is not, and once deployed it carries an affective charge which is none the less obvious for remaining implicit. The choice of treatment, be it 'detached', 'lyrical' or 'engaged' carries its own implicit values. Thus, when Eliot in 'Sweeney Among the Nightingales' describes one of the undifferentiated conspirators as 'the silent vertebrate in brown', the technique of exteriorized, physiognomic description reveals an austere, fastidious, though caricatural orientation to experience, by which the materiality of the human receives satiric emphasis and that emphasis promotes non-humanist premises.

Such dehumanizing techniques can be seen as serving both a psychological and socio-political function, and it is the interrelation between these two terms that allows us to qualify the term 'satire' as a generic description capable of explaining the similarities between Lewis's early work and Eliot's *Poems* of 1920. We are here dealing with 'satiric modernism', in which in a modern awareness of social fragmentation and reification, psychological strategies, and socio-political biases interreact and elide, and the term 'dehumanization' takes on a precise period inflection, as a mode of literary treatment that proceeds by purposively denying interior consciousness. This covers the similarities between Lewis's work and Eliot's quatrains; the differences, as indicated previously, are that the term satire is in the last resort inadequate to comprehend the precise effect of Eliot's quatrains, which send us back to the poet in a way that Lewis's harsh satiric delineations do not. We should leave the final word to Eliot, who in 'Tradition and the Individual Talent' states, with the finest of his early irony that, 'Poetry is not a turning loose of emotion, but an escape from personality. But, of course, only those who have personality and emotions know what it means to want to escape from these things.'[62] Perhaps at this date Eliot believed that 'tradition' might provide him with an avenue of escape.

7
Eliot and Tradition

'The inclusion of expression in the general appeasement is the innermost principle of musical pretence. It is all up with it. The claim to consider the general harmonically contained in the particular contradicts itself. It is all up with the once blindingly valid conventions, which guaranteed the freedom of play.'

I: 'A man could know that and recognize freedom above and beyond all critique. He could heighten the play, by playing with forms out of which, as he well knew, life has disappeared.'

He: 'I know, I know. Parody. It might be fun, if it were not so melancholy in its aristocratic nihilism. Would you promise yourself much pleasure and profit from such tricks?

I (retort angrily): 'No.'

Mann, *Dr Faustus*

i Practice

The most economical way of approaching the issues to be discussed in this chapter is to empirically consider an instance of Eliot's poetic employment of 'tradition'. Tradition is here understood as the literature of the past, without suggesting that sense of 'orthodoxy', which from the first is implicit and throughout the 1920s becomes increasingly explicit in Eliot's critical use of the term. The example chosen, the epigraph to 'Burbank with a Baedeker: Bleistein with a Cigar', has the advantage of raising questions about Eliot's employment of the epigraph convention as well as his orientation towards tradition.

The epigraph convention can be regarded as a perfect example of what Barthes would term a 'literary sign': a hieratic sign designating the literary institution, and the writer's attitude towards it. As Barthes puts it in *Writing Degree Zero*, 'it is possible . . . to trace a history of literary expression which is neither that of a particular language, nor that of the various styles, but simply that of the Signs of Literature, and we can expect that this purely formal history may manifest, in its far from obscure way, a link with the deeper levels of History'.[1] The modern writer's attitude towards such literary signs helps us to designate his choice of *écriture*, his 'linguistic morality'.

1 Roger Fry 'Textile: Amenophis'
(1913–14)

2 Umberto Boccioni 'Unique Forms
of Continuity in Space' (1913)

3 Georges Braque 'Clarinet and Bottle of Rum on a Mantlepiece' (1911) © ADAGP, Paris/DACS, London 1988

4 Jacob Epstein, torso in metal from 'The Rock Drill' (1913–1916)

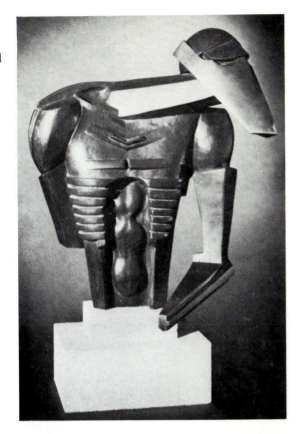

5 C. R. W. Nevinson 'Marching Men' (1916)

6 Edward Wadsworth
'Abstract Composition' (1915)
© Edward Wadsworth 1988,
all rights reserved DACS.

7 P. Wyndham Lewis 'Before
Antwerp', cover design of
Blast(2), 1915

8 P. Wyndham Lewis 'The Crowd' (1914–1915) © Estate of Mrs G. A. Wyndham Lewis. By permission

9 P. Wyndham Lewis 'Alcibiades' design from the *Timon of Athens* series (1912)

1

BLESS ENGLAND !

BLESS ENGLAND

FOR ITS SHIPS

which switchback on Blue, Green and Red SEAS all around the PINK EARTH-BALL,

BIG BETS ON EACH.

BLESS ALL SEAFARERS.

THEY exchange not one LAND for another, but one ELEMENT for ANOTHER. The MORE against the LESS ABSTRACT.

———————

BLESS the vast planetary abstraction of the OCEAN.

———————

BLESS THE ARABS OF THE ATLANTIC.

THIS ISLAND MUST BE CONTRASTED WITH THE BLEAK WAVES.

———————

10 Specimen page from *Blast*(1), 1914

11 Henri Gaudier-Brzeska 'Red Stone Dancer' (1913)

12 P. Wyndham Lewis 'The Vorticist'
(1912).
Subsequently given this title, possibly by
its former owner, Edward Wadsworth

13 P. Wyndham Lewis 'Mr. Wyndham
Lewis as a Tyro' (1920–1921)

Now every form is also a Value, which is why there is room, between a language and a style, for another formal reality: writing. Within any literary form, there is a general choice of tone, of ethos, if you like, and this is precisely where the writer shows himself clearly as an individual because this is where he commits himself . . . A language and a style are objects; a mode of writing is a function: it is the relationship between creation and society, the literary language transformed by its social finality, form considered as a human intention and thus linked to the great crises of History.[2]

It is impossible to effectively discuss Eliot's poetic employment of tradition without broaching the area of what Anglo-American criticism would descriptively term 'style' or 'tone', and Barthes, more conceptually, écriture. Choice of écriture manifests itself through connotation; as Barthes states in Elements of Semiology, 'a system of connotation is a system of which the plane of expression is itself constituted by a system of signification',[3] and most of the phenomena dealt with in this chapter are connotative rather than denotative. The epigraph to 'Burbank with a Baedeker: Bleistein with a Cigar' can provide us with a route into an area that Anglo-American criticism has often failed to engage with.

> Tra-la-la-la-la-la-laire – nil nisi divinum stabile est; caetera fumus – the gondola stopped, the old palace was there, how charming its grey and pink – goats and monkeys, with such hair too! – so the countess passed on until she came through the little park, where Niobe presented her with a cabinet, and so departed.[4]

Having negotiated the cryptic title of the poem, the reader is confronted with a montage of quotations, conjoined, yet discretely separated by hyphens, to form a composite artificial quotation, which possesses in its own right a surreal aesthetic coherence. The epigraph can be seen as being akin to a riddle, for we discover that all but the final quotation occur in works associated with Venice (either as location or subject). This, however, the reader is only likely to realize after background reading or research; the aesthetic signifiers have almost no apparent connection with the elusive, laterally induced signified, 'Venice'. In swift succession we are presented with the opening from a Gautier poem, 'Sur les Lagunes' – the only direct citation from Gautier in Eliot's poetry; a Latin inscription within a painting by Mantegna located in Venice; a line from a pastiche quotation referring to Henry James's short story The Aspern Papers, given in Ford Madox Ford's Henry James, A Critical Study (1913); a phrase from Othello, yoked together with a phrase from the final stanza of Browning's 'A Toccata of Galuppi's' (Galuppi was an eighteenth-century Venetian composer); and finally the stage directions that close a courtly masque by John Marston.

Scholarly research into the original literary context of each constituent quotation reveals elements that have thematic relevance to the main body of the poem. Browning's poem deals with the analogies between spiritual, physical and cultural decay, and Othello's ejaculation refers to sexual corruption; both themes are conjoined in Eliot's poem, as they are conjoined in this artificial quotation. Yet, by yoking the two phrases together Eliot has created an almost Dadaist literary effect: the exclamation 'with such hair too!' seems to refer back to the 'goats and monkeys', suggesting that by effecting this artificial conjunction Eliot has metamorphosed, if not subverted, his quotations. Connections made between the individual quotations and the poem that follows have to remain conjectural rather than necessary. The original sources do not form a homogeneous canon, and though it is difficult to decide where the critical search for significance becomes no more than that, it is not so difficult to discern when this has happened. Viewing the epigraph as a whole it is not easy to specify the sense in which Eliot is aligning himself with 'tradition'. An overt awareness of the literary past can obscure the reality that here tradition is no longer a public domain which is at least potentially available to the layman, but rather an eclectic collation of references from Eliot's private reading which includes a Latin inscription in a painting by Mantegna that the poet viewed within a private house on the Grand Canal.

The dimension which is left out of scholarly readings of the poems based upon research into the original context of allusions or quotations, such as Grover Smith's *T. S. Eliot's Poetry and Plays*, or a useful compilation of source material such as Southam's *Student's Guide to The Selected Poems of T. S. Eliot*,[5] is one that is crucial to any discussion of a literary effect such as this epigraph: the question of its impact on and reception by the reader and his immediate response (to be understood both in terms of the likely response of Eliot's contemporary public, and anyone's, now historically mediated, first reading of Eliot's poem). It is apparent that the epigraph cannot be held to serve a direct elucidatory purpose, nor does it present us with a traditional orthodoxy, a stable literary referent, which can help us to assess the main body of the poem. Eliot has created a montage of quotations which by its inordinate length, within the formal limitation of its position as the epigraph to a relatively short series of quatrains, achieves a transition from quantitative to qualitative distinction. It stands as an autonomous artefact, an anticipation of the themes and methods of the poem which almost functions as a surreal short story placed at its threshold.

If the epigraph does not serve an explanatory purpose, what purpose does it serve? A neo-Classical poet's use of allusion or quotation is, in the widest sense, explanatory, while also serving to refer the reader back to a traditional orthodoxy; reference to a traditional text sanctions the meanings contained in the new poem. Latin culture was the common possession of the educated public, and this allowed poets such as Marvell, Milton, Dryden and Pope to rely on a shared body of textual reference. As R. A. Brower demonstrates in detail in *Alexander Pope: The Poetry of Allusion*,[6] allusion, for a poet such as Pope, was not merely a matter of localized textual reflection, but needed to be viewed in a larger context of stylistic reference to the meanings, ethos, and literary 'manner' of Classical and more recent predecessors. Thus, Pope's 'Essay on Criticism' and 'Essay on Man' are not merely indebted to Horace's poems, or even his 'style', but are compositions in, as Pope divined it, 'the true Horatian mode'.[7] In this context we can consider the genre of the 'Imitation', initiated by Rochester's 'An Allusion to Horace, The Tenth Satyr of the First Book',[8] and continued by Pope in his 'Imitations of Horace'.[9] This mode, while not being strictly translation, relied on a close knowledge in the reader of the Latin original, while interpolating and developing thematic variations 'in the manner' of the original, but devoted to more contemporary concerns. Thus, Brower can write of the first of the 'Imitations', 'Taken as a whole, the poem is a "realization" of the poet's life as Pope sees it through the image of Horace.'[10]

This intellectual coherence and consistency cannot be asserted for Eliot's employment of allusion in the epigraph, or the main text, of 'Burbank'. Eliot's declared intention in the deployment of so many allusions in the writing of 'Burbank with a Baedeker: Bleistein with a Cigar' is of some relevance: he said that, following the example of James's *The Aspern Papers*, he wished 'to make a place real not descriptively but by something happening there'.[11] The accumulation of literary references serves a subsidiary aspect of this aim by revealing Venice as the situation or focus of literary and artistic achievement through a number of historic periods. The epigraph is intended, perhaps, to add an element of stratification, of geological literary depth to Eliot's poem. But from the reader's perspective, this intention, if accepted, must remain largely at the level of intention. Eliot's collage does not communicate a 'depth' of reference, but rather remains a collocation of fragments which have no necessary commerce with the past, or even their own literary contexts. Once we have grasped that each constituent quotation (except the last) refers to Venice, their interrelation must be regarded as opportunist rather than essential.

When stating that the purpose of the epigraph to 'Burbank' is not elucidatory, we imply that one important element in the epigraph's aesthetic effect cannot be dissociated from its very impenetrability: that effect is to leave the reader disoriented, outside the poem, unable to use the epigraph to naturalize the poem's concerns by reference to his own concerns and experience and thus, unable to make the empathetic leap which constitutes *Einfühlung*, to project his own vitality into the text. This use of the literary past, seen in microcosm in the 'Burbank' epigraph, to maintain distance between the reader and the text, allows us to apprehend the important point that here the literary past (tradition) does not mediate between poet and audience; this lack of mediation can be seen as a function of the disjunctive relationship between the quotations employed in Eliot's epigraph and the original contexts from which they have been rent. If in contrast we compare Pope's directive use of (altered) lines from Virgil's Sixth *Eclogue* which are followed by an imitation by Dryden as the epigraph to 'Windsor Forest', we can see that there the poet intends both the pastoral resonance and reference to Virgil. An imitation of the closing lines of Virgil's *Georgics* ends 'Windsor Forest', and Brower comments, 'The allusion – youthfully ostentatious – implies that *Windsor Forest* is the poet's georgic phase, perhaps with the added suggestion that an *Aeneid* is coming next.'[12] In contrast, the bias of Eliot's mode is entirely towards the aesthetic effect of the fragment in its new context; we are not gestured back to the source, as a sanction or authority for whatever meaning the fragment may contain. The meaning, if meaning there be, is largely irrelevant to the primary aesthetic effect of disjunction, the very strangeness of the fragment in its new literary context.

Once we have accepted that the overall bias of Eliot's development from 'Prufrock' to *The Waste Land* was from communicatory and empathetic to spatial and non-empathetic form, it is easier to perceive that an epigraph such as this could be deployed not to facilitate the reader's understanding of the main text, but for an almost antithetical purpose: to emphasize that the poem, even down to its epigraph, is a consciously created artefact, and one in which the reader must not expect to be presented with an easily assimilable 'message', but rather must work to get to grips with any meanings *the poem* may proffer. Such a deployment of a cacophony of many voices at the beginning of the poem militates against any assumption that the poem is a communicatory vehicle in which the poet, with one voice, discourses with his audience, 'a man speaking to men',[13] as Wordsworth put it, in terms of the expressive aesthetic of the 'Preface of 1802'. The alternative, which Eliot elects, is to view the epigraph as a construct drawing attention to its own artificiality, while the poet has absented himself, and is not overtly implicated by his work.

We would not wish to extend this line of thought to claim that here, Eliot, like Stephen's exaggerated version of the Flaubertian artist in *A Portrait* dwells 'within or behind or above his handiwork, refined out of existence, indifferent, paring his fingernails',[14] for one can perceive that this epigraph, almost by virtue of the impassivity with which it is presented, is, in intention, if not quite a joke, certainly somewhat tongue in cheek. Its very length, sandwiched as it is between a puzzling title and a not over-long series of quatrains, gives it a certain parodic prominence, by which as a linguistic gesture it draws attention to itself and flaunts its deviance from the usual modes of epigraph employment. This deadpan disjunction from formal conventions (an implicitly ruptural relation with traditional modes) is reinforced by the content, where an 'Alice in Wonderland' atmosphere is created at the inception, by Gautier's 'Tra-la-la-la-la-la-laire', and also at the end of the epigraph, by the unlocated specificity of the closing directions of Marston's masque.

This implicitly parodic employment of the epigraph convention cannot be dissociated from the way Eliot had employed the epigraph in his previous poetry. The epigraph to 'The Love Song of J. Alfred Prufrock',[15] giving Guido de Montefeltro's unrestrained but mistaken words from Dante's *Inferno*, must be regarded as ironic in the context of Prufrock's urbane, burlesque, although not unserious, confession of his dilemma. (Guido, although speaking from within a prison of flames, believes that his interlocutor, Dante, is one of the damned and thus unable to return to earth and recount his villainy; while the innocuous Prufrock is unable to find the right words to formulate his sense of unease and dislocation.) Thus, whatever parallels we may perceive between Guido and Prufrock, we must be equally aware of the dissimilarities and ironic dissonances between the situation of Dante's self-assertive character and Eliot's hapless persona who is condemned to a mundane, secular hell of afternoon tea parties. (This is apart from the issues conjured up by giving a lengthy epigraph in Dante's mediaeval Italian.) We are here dealing with a mode of poetic 'dandyism' on Eliot's part: the use of the epigraph for parodic prominence and ironic contrast, as well as thematic parallelism with the poem that follows.

Yet, if the use of the epigraph is not straightforwardly explanatory even in Eliot's early poetry, the employment of arcane and often impenetrable epigraphs is not quite given the formal prominence which is attained in the quatrain poems. In fact, the epigraphs presented with Eliot's *Poems* of 1920 in *Collected Poems* are significantly pruned down from their original luxuriance in *Ara Vos Prec*, where 'The Hippopotamus' is given a lengthy Latin epigraph from St Ignatius's epistle to the Trallians, and 'Sweeney Among the Nightingales' carries a supplementary epigraph from the anonymous *Raigne of King Edward the Third*: a capitalized 'WHY SHOULD I SPEAK OF THE NIGHTINGALE? THE NIGHTINGALE SINGS OF ADULTEROUS WRONG' (an epigraph that can be seen as anticipating the Philomel motif in *The Waste Land*). It is as if in the interim between the publication of *Prufrock and Other Observations* (1917) and *Ara Vos Prec* (1920) Eliot had become aware of the potential of a parodic employment of the epigraph and literary reference in general, which remains only latent in his early poetry. In English poetry the use of epigraphs is unusual; the density and prominence they attain in Eliot's work is unprecedented. It is, however, possible that it was Tristan Corbière, who was fond of deploying burlesque epigraphs in his poetry, who suggested the *dandysme* of this mode to Eliot. For example, the poem 'Epitaphe' carries half a page of parodic prose as its epigraph; while 'Ça?' has as an epigraph the single word 'What? . . .' which is attributed to Shakespeare.[16]

At this point, it is necessary to widen the discussion to take cognizance not only of Eliot's relatively more obtrusive employment of the epigraph in the *Poems* of 1920, but also of the vast increase, the qualitative as well as quantitative difference in the density of allusions to and quotations from the literary past in *Ara Vos Prec* and *The Waste Land* when compared to those poems contained in *Prufrock and Other Observations*, of which the use of epigraphs is merely one aspect. Returning to 'Burbank with a Baedeker: Bleistein with a Cigar', the method of the epigraph can be related to the method of the main text.

> A lustreless protrusive eye
>   Stares from the protozoic slime
> At a perspective of Canaletto.
>   The smoky candle end of time
>
> Declines. On the Rialto once.
>   The rats are underneath the piles.
> The Jew is underneath the lot.
>   Money in furs. The boatman smiles,

Short staccato sentences, which are denied syntactic connection, retard the linear impetus of the poetic narrative and by accumulating details and references ('On the

Rialto' is a phrase used by Shylock in *The Merchant of Venice*) build up a composite perspective, a montage analogous to that of the epigraph. It is as though the main text, in echoing the method of the epigraph, seeks to replicate that quality of overt objectivity and detachment. This impression of apparent 'impersonality' is also sustained by the rhythm of these lines – the periods and heavy stresses create an abrupt, jerky movement which phonetically gives the impression that the text, like the epigraph, is proceeding as a linguistic mosaic.

The skeletal narrative developed in the poem offers a vision of contemporary reality as both chaotic and corrupt. Burbank, presumably the earnest and ingenuous American tourist (he has a Baedeker; Bleistein a phallic-plutocratic cigar) arrives in Venice, 'Descending at a small hotel' (a phrase applied to Strether in *The Ambassadors*), and begins a liaison with Princess Volupine, a representative as her name implies, of the decadent Venetian aristocracy. There is a parodic reference here to a Tennyson lyric, 'The Sisters', which concerns a revenge on an earl for his seduction of one of the sisters – 'They were together, and she fell;/Therefore revenge became me well' – which becomes in Eliot's hands a reference to Burbank's sexual 'fall' (anticipated associationally by his 'descent') at the end of the first stanza: 'They were together, and he fell.' The deft parodic reference will be lost for the reader unacquainted with Tennyson, for the line is not tonally distinguished to alert the reader to the allusion. This is not a danger in the next two, somewhat incoherent stanzas, which use ironic references to Shakespeare's 'Phoenix and the Turtle', Marston's *Antonio and Mellida*, and *Antony and Cleopatra* to designate the illicit sexual liaison, in which it is ironically implied that Burbank (who is associated with Antony) has become a sexual failure: 'the God Hercules/Had left him, that had loved him well'. Bleistein then makes his appearance. He is a figure associated with Burbank in the title of the poem, another American tourist, but racially and culturally distinct:

> But this or such was Bleistein's way:
>   A saggy bending of the knees
> And elbows, with the palms turned out,
>   Chicago Semite Viennese.

The descriptive method of these lines can be aligned with those exteriorized, non-empathetic techniques discussed in the previous chapter: that method of 'essential reduction', closely allied to the pictorial art of caricature, which Eliot comments upon in his 'Ben Jonson' essay. ('We cannot call a man's work superficial when it is the creation of a world . . . the superficies *is* the world.') The world created in 'Burbank with a Baedeker: Bleistein with a Cigar' is created with a disenchanted satiric gaze that employs the caricatural concentration upon physical appearance which has been seen to be a primary weapon in Eliot's arsenal of literary techniques. The final line of this stanza functions as a verbal triptych: the two trisyllables, 'Chicago' and 'Viennese', with their very different cultural associations, enclose the evenly weighted spondee 'Semite' – foregrounding this term as Bleistein's fundamental identity.

Bleistein is a representative Semite – in a malicious pun, 'Money in furs' – and an anticipation of Sir Ferdinand Klein, Burbank's titled successor for Princess Volupine's favours. Burbank is finally left outside to his disenchanted musings.

> Princess Volupine extends
>   A meagre, blue nailed, phthisic hand
> To climb the waterstair. Lights, lights,
>   She entertains Sir Ferdinand

> Klein. Who clipped the lion's wings
>   And flea'd his rump and pared his claws?
> Thought Burbank, meditating on
>   Time's ruins, and the seven laws.

The rudimentary narrative is clear enough in its general figural intentionality: it portrays a vitiated and corrupt (physically, sexually and morally) European aristocracy seduced by Semitic wealth and ostentation, while Burbank, the American abroad, not innocent, but the next best thing, ineffective, is left outside to his disillusioned meditation on the decline of Venice (Europe). Here, we must note that the overt impersonality of the quasi-narrative framework, and Eliot's use of caricatural, externalized techniques is only overt. Burbank's jaundiced perspective in the final stanza is one that is condoned by the entire poem. There is no first person in the poem, but Eliot deploys effects that arouse strong affective currents (as cultural stereotypes tend to), and while it is true that 'the Jew' functions in Eliot's early poetry almost as a synecdoche for debased commercialism, Eliot also offers the bare bones of an anti-Semitic cultural diagnosis within the confines of his 'sculptured' quatrains: 'The rats are underneath the piles./The Jew is underneath the lot.' But finally, and with some hesitation, I feel that the rhetorical, caricatural effects of the poem and Eliot's necessary distance from the figure of Burbank work to imply simultaneous levels of authorial investment and disengagement, suggesting that the poem is as much the achievement of an 'objective correlative' as it is an embodiment of securely held cultural convictions and antagonisms.

To my mind, the most valuable commentary on the manner in which social and cultural meanings are mediated in Eliot's poetry of this period is Gabriel Pearson's essay, 'T. S. Eliot: an American use of symbolism',[17] in which Pearson suggests how language and poetic form can themselves achieve gestural meanings, implicitly condemning and exacting retribution from those cast as cultural villains. Pearson's readings of various lines from 'Burbank' and 'Gerontion' relate to (but do not depend on) his realization that Eliot's orientation to the present and to the literary tradition is one of disinheritedness. 'Eliot's world is itself constructed as a huge, sounding memory in search of a contemporary identity to attach itself to. Such a condition arises when the present has lost its meaning. It represents an acute crisis of disinheritedness.'[18] Subsequently, he states,

> My argument is that in Eliot's case there is an unusual isolation of, and concentration on, language as direct enactment of social attitudes. Poetry has

traditionally mediated social existence through conventions, genres, myths, symbols. For Eliot, this mediation has largely collapsed. Eliot is reputed a peculiarly learned and literary poet, and this is true. It is true also that a good deal of raw personal and social emotion is fed back into the action of the language; this need not involve contradiction. Traditional forms no longer compose an inherited order. Rather, they become themselves manifestations of despair and anxiety, because no longer credited and sanctioned. Hence the ultimate unfruitfulness of reading these poems as reworkings of traditional modes. These have become themselves objects of historical attention within a universe of relative values. They lie exposed on the surface of history like withered roots. When the poet self-consciously uses them and discriminates among them, he can no longer derive nutriment from them. Instead, he has to feed them out of the substance of his own life. From this derives the highly personal impersonality of much modern art, and the inevitably ironic use of tradition.[19]

Pearson is accurate in this, the acute central judgement of the essay, and almost alone in being so, since the vast majority of critical exegetes fail to break with the orthodoxies that derive from Eliot's own critical statements, such as 'Tradition and Individual Talent'. When applied to his own work (as Eliot undoubtedly intended them to be) these constitute an implicit strategic defence which arrogates the category of 'tradition' to a literary practice, which at least before 1927, can only be regarded as 'traditional' in the limited sense that it displays an overt, obtrusive awareness of the literary past. The displacement of Eliot's early poetry in relation to available genres results in a lack of formal mediation in the poem, of social attitudes between poet and audience; the consequence, which Pearson analyses, is verbal enactment of social attitudes and social animus. However, this enactment is controlled and distanced by formal and rhetorical modes, making the cultural intentionality Pearson observes more difficult to define than he indicates. An example can be cited, both for its intrinsic interest and for the issues to which it gives rise. Quoting these lines from 'Gerontion',

> My house is a decayed house,
> And the Jew squats on the window-sill, the owner,
> Spawned in some estaminet of Antwerp,
> Blistered in Brussels, patched and peeled in London.

Pearson comments,

> One notices that 'my house' quickly becomes someone else's, 'the owner's'. We are alerted to submerged paradox by 'And'. What is a Jew doing owning *my* house? is the implied question. The Jew 'squats' (an undoubted filament to 'merds' here), is 'spawned', 'blistered', 'patched' and 'peeled' in a swift aggressive flurry of strong verbs. One can scarcely avoid an impression of inflicted retaliations. Here is the 'Jew' placarded, as owner, on an appositional sill, being spattered, degraded and mutilated. Like a veritable Elder of Zion he is made to exemplify the squalor he is accused of causing.

Yet the attack is at the same time deftly distanced. The indefiniteness of 'some' is furthered by the allusive knowingness of 'estaminet'. The reader finds himself divided between levels of aggression and disdain which may turn out to be an attack on him.[20]

We can concede that something of what Pearson describes does happen in these lines, but the effect is not so straightforward or univalent as Pearson suggests. Like the grotesque portrayal of 'the Jew', 'the aggressive flurry of strong verbs' in these lines is, in its linguistic context, rhetorically excessive (which works to destabilize the obvious cultural intentionality), while the verbs themselves, by culminating in 'patched and peeled' would seem in their final impersonality to apply to the house itself, as representative of all 'houses of decay'[21] rather than a human agency. In their textual context, these lines read as an extension of Gerontion's violent and futile rhetoric of inaction ('Bitten by flies, fought'), at least as much as they suggest Pearson's meanings.

However, Pearson's readings are extremely valuable because they suggest the instability of the mediation of social attitudes between poet and audience at this stage of Eliot's development, and lead to complex issues as regards the social intentionality of Eliot's employment of 'tradition'. Social values are, of course, mediated between poet and audience in *Ara Vos Prec*, but in poems such as 'Burbank' and 'Gerontion' this mediation depends for its effect on an overt impersonality which allows the language to enact such gestures of condemnation and social retaliation in a way seemingly unmotivated by the poet. In *Ara Vos Prec* and *The Waste Land*, this distancing or deferment (far more accurate terms than impersonality) is very much involved in, almost a function of, Eliot's employment of the literary past, 'tradition', which becomes a source of parodic references, ironic contrasts, quotation and close allusion; a storehouse of isolated fragments of verbal intensity. All these functions are integrally involved in the construction of a metalanguage of cryptic notations which achieves an unstable mediation between poet and audience without the poet being directly implicated.

One example, which can serve for many, occurs in the passage on 'the hyacinth girl' in 'The Burial of the Dead' section of *The Waste Land*. Here, Eliot's lines are framed by two contrary implications taken from the libretto of Wagner's *Tristan und Isolde*. The first citation, itself a light and hopeful lyric from early in the opera translates approximately as, 'The wind blows freshly/Towards the homeland/My Irish child,/Where are you lingering?'; the second, from the conclusion of the opera, gives the look-out's words as the dying Tristan waits in vain for his beloved, Isolde: 'The sea is desolate and empty.' Here, however, the line is far more effective without translation, – '*Oed' und leer das Meer*' – phonetically the sound values of the line can be described as empty if not ugly – and the line functions as a shard of verbal expression suggesting a shift to failure and sterility after the indeterminate plenitude of the previous lines.

But as this 'impersonality' is not achieved through a consistent use of formal mediation (genre) or the referring of the text back to a coherent canon of literary

precedents (tradition), what we find by the *Poems* of 1920, and in the context of
Eliot and Pound's aggressive cultural politics, is that this achievement of distance
can simultaneously be employed as an urbane 'impersonal' means of making a gesture of exclusion, complicity, or even attack, at the reader. Connotationally this
implies that the reader is not outside the satiric, or simply aggressive, scope of the
poem. In this connection, it is worth considering the development of Eliot's
employment of personal pronouns. In the early poems, such as 'Prufrock' and
'Portrait of a Lady', Eliot had used personal pronouns to implicate the reader in
the action of the poem and draw him/her within the orbit of a shared body of
social values: 'Let us go then, you and I, . . .' ('Prufrock'), or in the first verse-
paragraph of 'Portrait of a Lady', 'We have been, let us say, to hear the latest
Pole/Transmit the Preludes, through his hair and finger-tips.' In both cases, the
address is to the reader *and* a shadowy interlocutor, who at this point in the poem
(and entirely through 'Prufrock') has little definition. In the early poetry the instability of Eliot's use of pronouns suggests a complicity between persona and reader,
and while this remains true of the quatrain poems, 'Gerontion' and *The Waste
Land*, Eliot's practice has significantly become more ironic, edged and threatening. It can be suggested of the vehement line that follows the clotted meditation
on history in 'Gerontion' as a sudden reintroduction of the spiritual/religious
dimension – 'The tiger springs in the new year. Us he devours', – that failing a
definite interlocutor at this point, the reader cannot and should not take the
heavily accented 'Us' as excluding himself (though here, as with Pearson's readings, we must guard against a univalent interpretation of the line).

With regard to Eliot's employment of the epigraph, perhaps the most
intriguing example of parodic instability implying an attitude taken to the reader,
is the epigraph to 'Ode', a poem published in *Ara Vos Prec*, and subsequently
excised, one might almost say exorcised, from Eliot's *oeuvre*. The poem itself, an
arid and over-allusive exploration of the themes of sexual guilt and failure, com-
prises of three stanzas, each of which begins with a single word: the first 'Tired',
the second 'Tortured', the third 'Tortuous' – a word which aptly describes the
entire poem, except for the second stanza, where we read:

> Tortured,
> When the bridegroom smoothed his hair
> There was blood upon the bed.
> Morning was already late.
> Children singing in the orchard
> (Io Hymen, Hymenaee)
> Succuba eviscerate.[22]

Here, despite the third person treatment and the rudimentary framework of allusions (especially to Catullus), we, and the poet, are too near places of painful,
private emotion. The janiform balance of disguise and revelation which constitutes
Eliot's employment of 'tradition' is heavily biased towards the latter term, with a
consequent loss of aesthetic distance.

This can help us understand Eliot's choice of, and manipulation of, his epigraph, which is taken from *Coriolanus*, Act IV, scene v: 'To you particularly, and to all the Volscians/Great hurt and mischief.' This epigraph is excerpted from the speech where Coriolanus, having bitterly assumed his forced exile, reveals his identity to Aufidius, leader of the Volsces and offers his 'revengeful services' against Rome.

> AUFIDIUS   I know thee not. Thy name!
> CORIOLANUS My name is Caius Marcius, who hath done
>   To thee particularly, and to all the Volsces,
>   Great hurt and mischief; therefore witness may
>   My surname, Coriolanus.

It is apparent from the original context that Eliot has radically subverted the meaning of his reference, with the effect that the epigraph reads as an implicit attack on the reader, gesturing him away from this allusive but personal poem, even before he begins reading it.

These examples and analyses have local applicability, but I think the line of inquiry they suggest allows a more fruitful approach than that of orthodox exegesis when discussing a poem such as 'Mr. Eliot's Sunday Morning Service', which in its entirety excludes the reader through the ironic employment of recondite allusions and orotund, wilfully elaborate circumlocutions. Here the most pertinent statement that can be made about the poem is the most obvious and superficial: that we have difficulty in understanding it. To ignore this, or to presume that Eliot was not aware of it, is not only to ignore a primary element in the poem's aesthetic effect, it is also to close a whole avenue of intellectual debate. Like Pearson, I find it difficult to comprehend the methodological premises of a critic such as Grover Smith, who having devoted many lines to an involved, meticulous, but not overly convincing interpretation of the poem, referring individual lines back to their sources, then disposes of the poem in a single line: 'Unhappily, the poem is obscure, precious, and bombastic.'[23] Grover Smith is correct; but his correctness is curiously beside the point, for the poem is intentionally obscure, precious and bombastic, and announces it in the one word first line – Polyphiloprogenitive – which achieves the syllable count of the Gautier tetrameter. 'Mr. Eliot's Sunday Morning Service' is an arch, satiric smile directed at 'The sapient sutlers of the Lord', but perhaps that smile wanders sardonically over Eliot's own congregation of readers. By delivering a one line evaluative condemnation after a two page exegesis Grover Smith seems to presume that Eliot was trying to write a different poem, one that was not 'obscure, precious, and bombastic', but instead wrote 'Mr. Eliot's Sunday Morning Service'.

What 'Mr. Eliot's Sunday Morning Service' does is to render inapposite any immediate response by the reader. A bewildered and impatient dismissal of the poem merely points to the reader's ignorance, and connotationally aligns him with the imperturbable Sweeney; while the well meaning attempt at scrupulous

and informed exegesis has the even crueller function of potentially aligning the
interpreter and reader with impotent Origen, who castrated himself for his
spiritual health, and is said to have produced six thousand books and endless
biblical commentaries. As Piers Gray comments in the course of a related discussion, 'It is a curious effect of the poem that it breeds exactly the form of exegesis
which it satirizes.'[24] Exactly. But this effect seems less curious when we realize
that this exegesis is a necessary function of the formal modes of the text and must
be seen as part of its satiric intention. I would argue that 'Mr. Eliot's Sunday
Morning Service' is perhaps the most formally perfect of the quatrain poems,
because here Eliot's subject matter, treatment, use of rhetorical modes and connotational meanings are held in a fine alignment (as they are not, for example, in
the conclusion of 'Whispers of Immortality'). The poem itself, far clearer in its
overall figural and intellectual emphases than most critical readings would make it
seem, can be regarded as a recasting and extension of the themes of 'The Hippopotamus', in which, unlike the quasi-dramatic development of the earlier poem,
Eliot employs static juxtapositions and frictions in line with the formal economy
of a montage technique.

The first section of the poem plays on the irony of the incarnate Logos ('In the
beginning was the Word') entering historical time and becoming the occasion for
a babble/Babel of words: sterile and contradictory theological commentaries,
schisms and controversies, characterized by the efforts of 'enervate Origen'. The
final stanza of the first section rounds out the ironies thus far by reminding us that
through Christ the Word became flesh:

> But through the water pale and thin
> Still shine the unoffending feet
> And there above the painter set
> The Father and the Paraclete.

– a perfect equilibrium of the physical and the spiritual that reflects ironically back
on Origen, and becomes the central affective emphasis of the poem.

In the second section, 'the sable presbyters' are seen as descendants of Origen
and multipliers of theological controversy; their attempt to engender a 'spiritual'
awakening through guilt ('The avenue of penitence') being largely irrelevant to
the more pressing sexual needs of the 'red and pustular' young. In the penultimate
stanza, a wry parallel to the priests is offered by the bees, who also perform the
'Blest office of the epicene' (of either sex or sexless) in carrying pollen between the
staminate (male) and pistillate (female), but achieve a more successful fertilization
of their horticultural 'flock'. The final vision of Sweeney 'Stirring the water in his
bath', is a laconic and emphatic vision of insentient physicality, that serves to contrast a debased present with the spiritualized flesh of Christ; while this 'stirring of
the waters' serves to render *any* textual commentary (biblical or critical) that
ignores the Spirit in favour of the Letter, ultimately redundant.

Thus, 'Mr. Eliot's Sunday Morning Service' deals with, and to some extent
plays with, serious themes at the same time as it guardedly keeps the reader at a

distance. But in regarding anti-empathetic desiderata as one aspect of Eliot's con-temporary employment of 'tradition', it is also necessary to beware of unitary readings of the literary text, which is polysemous, as is Eliot's employment of tradition. The phenomena that have been discussed thus far fall within Barthes's concept of *écriture*: the alignment of history with form, by which values are evinced by the choice of a mode of writing which itself implies an orientation taken towards the chosen literary institution, and thus obliquely towards the audi-ence. The quality of unstable mediation between 'public' and 'private' in Eliot's poetry of this period calls to mind Eliot's remarks on Kipling's 'public' poetry in 'Kipling Redivivus' (*Athenaeum*, May 1919), where he concludes a brilliant and unlikely parallel between Kipling's rhetoric and Swinburne's with the wry obser-vation that, 'It is wrong, of course, of Mr. Kipling to address a large audience; but it is a better thing than to address a small one. The only better thing is to address the one hypothetical Intelligent Man who does not exist and who is the audience of the artist.'[25] Recollecting another poet, the obscure dedication to whose *Sonnets* has prompted ceaseless scholarly dispute, it might be suggested that if this 'one hypothetical Intelligent Man' did exist, he might be no other than Mr Eliot Himself. Certainly, Eliot's laconic conclusion offers a revealing insight into that quality of highly personal 'impersonality' which characterizes his poetry of this period.

Eliot's extreme, disenchanted vision of the present, of contemporary realities, in 'Mr. Eliot's Sunday Morning Service', 'Burbank' (or other quatrain poems, 'Gerontion' and *The Waste Land*) is one that necessarily has the effect of calling the past, including the literary past – 'tradition' – into question. As Hannah Arendt puts it in the introduction to her selection of Walter Benjamin's essays, *Illumina-tions*, 'Insofar as the past has been transmitted as tradition, it possesses authority; insofar as authority presents itself historically, it becomes tradition.'[26] Evidently, Eliot's poetry of this period (in fact all his poetry between 1914 and his reception into the Anglican Church in 1927) enacts a failure of tradition, seen both as literary tradition and social custom: for either tradition has lost its authority over corrupt contemporary realities, or tradition is itself, in some sense, flawed, corrupt (as Eliot tended to regard the central current of post-Romantic English poetry, that poetry of the 'inner voice' which denied the principle of authority outside the individual). Whether we accept either or both of these premises – a failed tradition or one that is flawed – the dilemma becomes that of orientating oneself to a past that displays multiplicity and richness of detail, without the internal coherence and authority that can link it constructively with the present. It is here that the work of Walter Benjamin can help us to an understanding of Eliot. Benjamin was Eliot's contemporary, and much that is exemplified in Eliot's poetry is articulated in Ben-jamin's criticism.

Beginning with a sense that a crucial break in tradition had occurred in his life-time, a belief voiced in central essays such as that on 'Karl Kraus'[27] or 'The Work of Art in the Age of Mechanical Reproduction',[28] Benjamin realized that he had to elaborate new modes of dealing with the past. To this end, he proposed that rather than being transmissible the past had now become citable and that this citability could be used to disturb the complacency of the present: 'Quotations in my work are like robbers by the roadside who make an armed attack and relieve an idler of his convictions.'[29] Thus the modern function of quotations can be seen as an act of aggression against the present: quotation wrenches lines from their original context and places them as foreign bodies in an alien structure; their effect is 'not the strength to preserve but to cleanse, to tear out of context, to destroy'.[30] Quotations, in this context, become not elucidatory material, but 'thought fragments' which interrupt the narrative in which they are presented, and at the same time concentrate within themselves the 'otherness' of the original text from which they have been transferred.

The applicability of this to Eliot's poetry is immediate. Writing on the use of foreign language in *The Waste Land*, Michael Edwards remarks, 'But their profoundest significance is surely the most superficial: that they *are* written out in other languages (Eliot could have translated them as a neo-classical poet would have done)./Reading the work, we encounter lines we don't understand, and that is the point. The text is impenetrable.'[31] Edwards is right; but this insight has more than local applicability to the use of foreign languages. When we come across obscure literary references, lines that have been adapted to serve the poet's ends, or, as in *The Waste Land*, the collation of radically disparate source material, ranging from Wagner to Frazer's anthropology to Sanskrit, the result is disorientation and impenetrability. A neo-Classical poet (Milton in 'Lycidas' or Pope in 'Windsor Forest'), would not only have translated his quotations, he would have endeavoured to restrict his sources to a consistent range of material which in theory at least, would be shared and respected by the poet and his educated public (the individual poet counterpointing his gifts against a traditional frame of reference). But in Eliot's early verse, culminating in *The Waste Land*, tradition has undergone a metamorphosis into fragments, which (intentionally) do not intellectually mediate between the poet and his audience. In its ostensible striving for the authority and tangibility of 'tradition' and its evident failure to achieve this end, Eliot's early poetry seems, almost purposely, to enact an abortive Classicism.

We can demonstrate and scrutinize some possible uses of impenetrability by looking at the final lines of 'The Burial of the Dead' section of *The Waste Land*, which culminates in the exclamation:

> 'O keep the Dog far hence, that's friend to men,
> 'Or with his nails he'll dig it up again!
> 'You! hypocrite lecteur! – mon semblable, – mon frère!'[32]

Dealing with this section from 'Madame Sosostris' onwards, Hugh Kenner constructs a stimulating but eccentric series of parallels with 'Sweeney Agonistes' which leads him to read the whole of this section retrospectively in terms of its final resolution: what he calls 'a sinister dialogue about a corpse in the garden'.[33] Here, as often in Kenner's criticism, a brilliant empathetic reading becomes tendentious, and by developing a mass of detail, ends by totally obscuring questions of overall strategy. Of all modern poems, *The Waste Land* most resists such generalized interpretation. When we reach the lines 'Then I saw one I knew, and stopped him crying: "Stetson!/You who were with me in the ships at Mylae!" ', the correlation of a modern surname with a battle in the Punic Wars alerts us to the fact that the poet is employing what could be termed 'intentional incoherence'. So likewise in the following lines (which are not, as Kenner believes, 'a dialogue' but a series of abrupt interrogations) no knowledge of literary antecedents can finally clarify an effect which functions through displacement and disjunction, stirring echoes rather than providing meanings. Thus, the corpse in the garden can revive memories of Blake's 'A Poison Tree' without relating directly to the poem; a dirge in Webster's *The White Devil* – 'But keep the wolf far thence that's foe to men,/For with his nails he'll dig them up again'[34] – is coolly subverted to provide the more mundane, and in context more sinister, 'O keep the Dog far hence, that's friend to men'. The final line, taken from Baudelaire's 'Au Lecteur' is explicated by Kenner by reference to the seventh stanza of that poem, which asserts that we would all be murderers had we the courage. Within the context of Eliot's poem it is just as relevant (or irrelevant) to refer to the stanza which this line concludes, which deals with the fantasies of violence prompted by *tedium vitae*. What we need to grasp is the impact of the line within Eliot's structure. Here it serves a purpose similar to that it has in Baudelaire's original poem: it is a direct accusation *and* an assertion of kinship, which destroys the complacency with which the reader can distance himself from the writer's concerns. However, in Eliot's poem the rhetorical effect is concentrated and magnified. The previous lines function as a series of opaque references to an act that has been guiltily concealed: Baudelaire's line then compounds the effect, by at once claiming the reader's complicity and drawing him within the obscurity of the poet's concerns, yet at the same time alienating him through its obvious 'foreign' derivation and the sinister obscurity of those concerns.

I would argue that to comprehend the full literary achievement of these lines it is necessary to read them in their historical specificity: as an uncanny (*unheimlich*, in Freud's precise contemporary usage; his essay on 'The Uncanny' was published in 1919) evocation of the spectral atmosphere of post-war London, in which the guilt, shock, and primarily, incomprehension of a traumatized society is manifested and translated through a sequence of historical, cultural and psychic dislocations. As Paul Fussell writes, 'the Great War was more ironic than any before or since. It was a hideous embarrassment to the prevailing Meliorist myth which had dominated the public consciousness for a century. It reversed the idea of Progress',[35] and in accord with this wholesale inversion of cultural expectations Eliot's passage can be seen to mediate some of this sense of guilt, estrangement and absurdity. In the lines 'Stetson!/You who were with me in the ships at Mylae!', Eliot's citation of a battle in the Punic Wars indicates, with other examples that can be cited from his poetry, that this choice of a Trade War as an historical parallel is not fortuitous; and relatedly, that Eliot, the banker's, contemporary understanding of the causes of the First World War was unusually sophisticated. Thus,

I would argue that Kenner – writing in 1960, and admittedly without the benefit of the greater historical distance that is available at the present – fails to engage with the dominant historical *and* literary meanings of Eliot's text. The section is, after all, entitled 'The Burial of the Dead'.

If we follow Benjamin's insights into the disturbing metamorphosis tradition seemed to have undergone in the early twentieth century, we find many remarks that have direct relevance to Eliot's poetry; but perhaps no general analysis is more relevant than Benjamin's considerations on, and exemplification of, the role of the collector. To Benjamin, the collector, while ostensibly working to preserve the past is, in fact, undermining tradition. If tradition is seen as a systematizing force which preserves that which remains relevant, separates the orthodox from the heretical, and discards the merely interesting, then the collector, with his criterion of 'authenticity' works against classifiability and systematization, and thus against tradition so defined. When Benjamin became a collector of quotations, juxtapos-ing 'thought fragments' from the past against newspaper reports of present day realities, he desired not to claim the affinity of the past with the present, but to deny it, to assert an irreparable distance. He wished to confute empathetic analysis, the implication that the past has immanent meaning to guide the present.[36]

In Eliot's poetry we can observe a similar process. The obligatory truths of tradi-tion which have their place within a meaningful schema have been replaced by the collector's criteria: the authentic, significant and interesting. The material that Eliot deploys will always be relevant to the concerns of the poem, but criticism dis-torts in trying to make it in any univalent, 'traditional' sense, explanatory. Indeed, the work itself often constitutes a critique on all conventional modes of explanatory purpose and seeks to appropriate for itself the maximum of potential meanings. This can be seen, in almost paradigmatic fashion, in the epigraph to a later poem, 'Marina' (1930),[37] where the epigraph from Seneca's *Hercules Furens*, quoting Hercules's words as he returns to sanity, having in his madness killed his wife and children, would seem to entirely contradict the implied reference to Shakespeare's joyful recognition scene in *Pericles*, which seems intended by entitling the poem 'Marina', the name of Pericles's daughter. Eliot, however, was thinking in generic terms, and wrote, 'I intend a crisscross between Pericles finding alive, and Hercules finding dead – the two extremes of the recognition scene'.[38]

But, in Eliot, as in Benjamin, though tradition is subverted into 'fragments', quotations and literary references transposed to their new environment assert that it is precisely because the past is alien that its weight can be brought to bear on the pres-ent. Much critical debate has been expended upon the question of whether Eliot, particularly in the Sweeney poems, is making crude comparisons between the past and the present, to the advantage of the past. One school stresses the parallels, in terms of content, that this traditional material has with the contemporary scene that Eliot depicts; the other stresses the contrast implicit, say, in juxtaposing Sweeney with Agamemnon, a hero of antiquity. But both schools effectively obscure the issue by equating tradition with coherence. In the Sweeney poems, the past is at once related by thematic contiguity with the present, yet radically disjunctive, being all that a debased present cannot assimilate nor understand. It provides a weight of alien experience.

The quatrain poems function effectively as satires, but through their formal modes. In dealing with the past Eliot employs a dignified, magniloquent, though often somewhat tongue in cheek rhetorical expansiveness which he explicitly denies 'apeneck Sweeney' or Grishkin who 'has a maisonette'. In a highly problematic poem like 'Sweeney Among the Nightingales', while the plot against Agamemnon relates dynamically to the plot against Sweeney, the formal dignity of the language applied to Agamemnon's death in the final stanza is not applied to Sweeney:

> The host with someone indistinct
> Converses at the door apart,
> The nightingales are singing near
> The Convent of the Sacred Heart,
>
> And sang within the bloody wood
> When Agamemnon cried aloud
> And let their liquid siftings fall
> To stain the stiff dishonoured shroud.

Among his overwhelmingly negative comments on Eliot's early poetry (in which he accuses Eliot's work of having 'an exaggerated plainness that has the effect of novelty'), W. B. Yeats, a devoted practitioner of high literary style, singled out this conclusion for special commendation in his *Oxford Book of Modern Verse* (1892–1935), commenting, 'I think of him as a satirist rather than poet. Only once does the early work speak in the great manner.'[39] But Yeats seems to miss the point here, for the rhetorical effects of these stanzas are more complex than is immediately apparent. In particular, the phrase 'liquid siftings', which would seem in its narrative context to be a euphonious poeticism for birdsong is, with great aplomb, hijacked to become a euphonious euphemism for bird droppings. One central implication seems to be that the high literary style can provide a means to rhetorically dignify intrinsically sordid matters. Agamemnon's death was sordid; but the ritual of Aeschylean tragedy invested it with a breadth of gesture and cultic significance that Eliot refuses to provide for the quasi-rituals of contemporary violence. Thus, the past is made to reflect ironically on the present, without the implication that the past was ethically preferable or *per se* more coherent.

Only once in the poems employing Gautier's quatrains does Eliot depart from the quatrain structure, and that is at the conclusion to 'A Cooking Egg', where, in a detached ironic exclamation, Eliot uses an irrecoverable past (a personal, lyric, childhood, as well as historical past) for satiric contrast with a vitiated present.

> But where is the penny world I bought
>   To eat with Pipit behind the screen?
> The red-eyed scavengers are creeping
>   From Kentish Town and Golder's Green;
>
> Where are the eagles and the trumpets?

> Buried beneath some snow-deep Alps.
> Over buttered scones and crumpets
> Weeping, weeping multitudes
> Droop in a hundred A.B.C.'s.[40]

Here, even 'the eagles and the trumpets' of the *ubi sunt* tradition (themselves lightly ironized, for the 'snow-deep Alps' seem to suggest Hannibal, and thus an innocent, childhood version of heroism) are parodically tarnished by their rhymed association with the 'scones and crumpets' of Pipit's contemporary existence. The point in Eliot's work of this period is not that of an idealization of the past, but that the past and 'tradition' cannot be excluded from the contamination of a reduced and disenchanted present.

ii Theory

The previous argument would suggest that Eliot's specific employment of the literary past, 'tradition', in his verse relates only tangentially to his employment of 'tradition' as a critical category in his prose writings of this period. To conclude this chapter, it is necessary to consider Eliot's critical understanding of tradition, and the ambiguities implicit in his use of the term. This can be introduced by a sequence of quotations.

> 'Originality', when it is most actual, is often sheer lineage, is often a close-ness of grain. The innovator most damned for eccentricity, is often most centrally in the track or orbit of tradition, and his detractors are merely ignorant. The artist is in sane equilibrium, indifferent utterly to oldness or newness, so the thing be apposite to his want.[41]

> We dwell with satisfaction upon the poet's difference from his predecessors, especially his immediate predecessors; we endeavour to find something that can be isolated in order to be enjoyed. Whereas if we approach a poet without this prejudice we shall often find that not only the best, but the most individual parts of his work may be those in which the dead poets, his ancestors, assert their immortality most vigorously. And I do not mean the impressionable period of adolescence, but the period of full maturity.[42]

> I take it that the phrase 'break with tradition' is currently used to mean 'desert the more obvious imbecilities of one's elders'; at least, it has had that meaning in the periodical mouth for some years. Only the careful and critical mind will seek to know how much tradition inhered in the immediate elders.[43]

> In an ideal state of society one might imagine the good New growing natur-ally out of the good old, without the need for polemic and theory; this would be a society with a living tradition. In a sluggish society, as actual societies are, tradition is ever lapsing into superstition, and the violent stimulus of novelty is required.[44]

The first quotation is from Pound's 'Irony, Laforgue, and Some Satire' (1917); the second from Eliot's 'Tradition and the Individual Talent' (1919); the third from Pound's 'Notes on Elizabethan Classicists' (1917); and the fourth from Eliot's 'Reflections on *Vers Libre*' (1917).

Eliot's critical use of the term 'tradition' within the period 1917 to 1922 can be aligned with Pound's use of the term and both, when appraised within a historical perspective, are using the term with polemic intent. When Eliot began his first period of sustained critical labour as assistant editor of *The Egoist* between 1917 and 1919 he was embarking on what can be seen as a critical campaign in association with Pound, who had a large measure of control on *The Little Review*, their shared objectives being the promotion of certain writers (Henry James, Rémy de Gourmont, Wyndham Lewis, and Joyce, together with lesser figures), the denigration of others (for example, the Georgian poets), and a general opposition to what they perceived as the inertia and insularity of the English literary and artistic scene. Eliot's distinctive contribution was to take the issue of 'tradition', which was first formulated by Pound in relation to the Vorticist artists, and give it both consistent expression and various suggestive emphases in a sequence of reviews and occasional essays which include, but are not dominated by, 'Tradition and the Individual Talent'.

That an American avant-garde poet should arrogate and aggrandize the category of 'tradition', an emotive term closely aligned to 'orthodoxy' was, as can be appreciated in retrospect, an extremely effective stroke of literary politics; and Eliot himself, in a retrospective consideration of his critical work made late in his life, the essay 'To Criticize the Critic', is explicit about the polemic bias of his early criticism.

> in my earlier criticism, both in my *general affirmations about poetry* and in writing about authors that had influenced me, I was implicitly defending the kind of poetry that I and my friends wrote. This gives my essays a kind of urgency, the warmth of appeal of the advocate, which my later, more detached and I hope more judicious essays cannot claim. I was in reaction, not only against Georgian poetry, but against Georgian criticism; I was writing in a context which the reader of today has either forgotten, or has never experienced [author's emphasis].[45]

We can adopt his further suggestion that in order to appreciate the criticism of a past age, his own as well as Johnson's *Lives of the Poets*, we need to see the author in a historical context, even if exact appreciation of historical relations is difficult to achieve: 'But if any part of it does have this timeless value, then we shall appreciate the value all the more precisely if we attempt to put ourselves at the point of view of the writer and his first readers.'[46]

At least two salient aspects of the polemic intent behind Eliot's use of the term 'tradition' need to be indicated. Pound was aware, even before his Vorticist involvement, that it was necessary to have a wider definition of literary and artistic traditions than that provided by English post-Romanticism if his own work was to be accommodated; as early as 1910 in the 'Praefatio ad lectorem electum' of *The Spirit of Romance*, he wrote, 'All ages are contemporaneous . . . This is especially true of literature, where the real time is independent of the apparent . . . What we need is a literary scholarship which will weigh Theocritus and Yeats with one balance';[47] this, nine years before Eliot's charge in the pages of *The Egoist* that 'contemporary poetry is deficient in tradition'.[48] Contemporary criticism tended to reserve consideration for the major English literary figures, accepted without question the achievement of the nineteenth-century English poets, displayed a vestigial awareness of the Classical poets and almost no awareness of developments across the Channel. In this climate of 'provinciality', to use Pound's favourite term, the sources of his own, and subsequently Eliot's work, were effectively unknown to the English public. In an essay on 'The Tradition' of 1913, Pound states,

> The tradition is a beauty which we preserve and not a set of fetters to bind us. This tradition did not begin in A.D. 1870, nor in 1776, nor in 1632, nor in 1564. It did not begin even with Chaucer. The two great lyric traditions which most concern us are that of the Melic poets and that of Provence. From the first arose practically all the poetry of the 'ancient world', from the second practically all that of the modern.[49]

The assumption is that the poet who wishes to learn about his craft will inform himself about this 'tradition'. Eliot, in 'Tradition and the Individual Talent' writes (characteristically) in more general terms about the knowledge required by the poet 'who would continue to be a poet beyond his twenty-fifth year', and states in relation to the 'historical sense' that it 'must be obtained by great labour' and that it

> involves a perception, not only of the pastness of the past, but of its presence; the historical sense compels a man to write not merely with his own generation in his bones, but with a feeling that the whole of the literature of Europe from Homer and within it the whole of the literature of his own country has a simultaneous existence and composes a simultaneous order.[50]

It is apparent that in Eliot, as in Pound, a 'non-provincial', which in practical terms means non-native, definition of the literary tradition is being recommended, and one that demands 'professionalism' of the poet. However, the central emphasis of both writers' statements is upon the contemporaneity of the tradition as opposed to its pastness, and in this we can perceive an implicit defence of their own avant-garde literary practice: for this stress implies not only reverence for a 'live tradition', but also the claim in Pound's remark that, 'The innovator most damned for eccentricity, is often most centrally in the track or orbit of tradition, and his detractors are merely ignorant.' Thus we find the consciousness of the elect, an assumed confidence which reflects more than just the warmth of the partisan, in many of Eliot's remarks in the *Egoist* during this period; as, for example, when he comments in 'Observations' (May 1918) that,

> England puts her Great Writers away securely in a Safe Deposit Vault, and curls to sleep like Fafner. There they go rotten; for if our predecessors cannot

teach us to write better than themselves, they will surely teach us to write worse; because we have never learned to criticize Keats, Shelley, and Wordsworth (poets of assured though modest merit), Keats, Shelley, and Wordsworth punish us from their graves with the annual scourge of the Georgian anthology.[51]

This emphasis on 'tradition' in Eliot's early critical writings has the simultaneous effect of underwriting the obtrusive employment of literary references and allusions in both his and Pound's poetry of the period; and this in tacit contrast to the contemporary practice of the Georgian poets which was labelled 'deficient in tradition'. As Eliot wrote in the *Egoist*, 'The serious writer of verse must be prepared to cross himself with the best verse of other languages and the best prose of all languages. In Georgian poetry there is almost no crossing visible; it is inbred. It has developed a technique and a set of emotions all of its own.'[52] However, from a more sympathetic perspective Georgian poetry can be seen as being a valid continuation of the Romantic tradition of English verse, employing a predominantly expressive aesthetic and achieving an accessible discourse between poet and reader. Eliot himself, in his *Egoist* criticism, makes the connection between the Georgian poets and Wordsworth, but does so in order to condemn the Georgians as epigones of a tradition he sees as exhausted at its inception. In 'Reflections on Contemporary Poetry' (September 1917), he states, 'In the Georgian poets we observe the same attitude (to the "object" of the poem as in Wordsworth). The emotion is derived from the object, and such emotions must either be vague (as in Wordsworth) or if more definite, pleasing.' He concludes, after a review that damns with faint praise: 'Only in something harder can great passion be expressed; the vague is a more dangerous path for poetry than the arid.'[53]

The central point to be made is not that of a comparison between the achievement of those poets associated with the Georgian movement with that of the Imagists – though if the names of the war poets who were associated with the Georgian movement (Wilfred Owen, Isaac Rosenberg, Robert Graves, Edward Thomas) are mentioned it is hard to see that achievement as being less than impressive – but to emphasize that literature deals with a *plurality* of traditions and that the Georgian poets can be regarded as legitimate inheritors of a particular line of English verse, derived from their Romantic predecessors, modified to suit their contemporary needs. Aligning the Georgians within the Romantic tradition is not a particularly problematic exercise; fitting the poetry of Eliot or Pound within any available tradition of native verse is. Moreover, although both Eliot and Pound employ the term 'tradition' in the singular, the traditions they refer to in practice are radically different: indeed, their only real point of contact was their enthusiasm for nineteenth-century French poetry (but radically different French poetry, for Pound did not share Eliot's high valuation of the Symbolist poets), an admiration for Dante and a rejection of Milton. If we consider Eliot's critical use of the term 'traditional' bearing this in mind, the polemical advantages of his arrogation of the word become clear. Not only does he widen the terms of the definition of 'tradition' beyond that of the native, national traditions, to take in 'the whole of the literature of Europe from Homer', thus accomplishing a breadth of reference to take in his, and most of Pound's poetic practice; but by instituting such a *singular* definition of tradition (as opposed to plurality) he retains the sense of tradition in its social intentionality, indicating an obligatory practice, based upon custom or usage, and connoting order and authority: a sense of 'predisposed continuity',[54] to use Raymond Williams's phrase.

It will be apparent that this view of Eliot's critical employment of the term 'tradition' does not easily align itself with what has been said concerning his poetic employment of the literary past: the polemic aspect of his critical work provides a crucial difference in bias. However, if Eliot's poetic practice does not encompass the order and authority which he implies are inseparable from his concept of tradition, this does not mean he is dissembling in his criticism, but rather that his concept of tradition is, in fact, far more complex and ambiguous than it would appear when reduced to its various polemical guises; and that the poetic practice is, as would be expected, even more complex than the criticism; and that Eliot has not (yet) managed to achieve a relation to the literary past in which authority and tradition are equivalent. In other words, in the criticism we find a temperamental, intellectual and cultural bias towards the alignment of 'tradition' with authority that Eliot cannot yet accomplish in his poetry.

The first of these points requires some amplification. To recognize the complexity of Eliot's concept of tradition it is necessary to realize that its genealogy goes back to his paper on 'The Interpretation of Primitive Ritual', given in Josiah Royce's seminar at Harvard in 1913 and develops through his researches in the philosophy of F. H. Bradley, to find its quintessential (though problematic) formulation in 'Tradition and the Individual Talent', published as a two part article in the *Egoist* of 1919.[55] In indicating this genealogy I wish to suggest that the particularities and peculiarities of Eliot's concept of tradition need to be understood from within the complex of his previous intellectual concerns, and, above all, the difficulty he experienced in transcending a Bradleyan subjectivism towards a belief in the intellectual bases of a common world.

Here it is necessary to give a schematic summary of the relevant aspects of Eliot's intellectual development. In 'The Interpretation of Primitive Ritual' Eliot had questioned the objectivity of sociological 'facts' in explaining the modes of collective, ritual behaviour. As he put it many years later, in the introduction to his mother's poem *Savonarola*,

> The role played by interpretation has often been neglected in the theory of knowledge. Even Kant, devoting a lifetime to the pursuit of categories, fixed only on those he believed, rightly or wrongly to be permanent, and overlooked or neglected the fact that these are only the most stable of a vast system of categories in perpetual change. Some years ago, in a paper on *The Interpretation of Primitive Ritual*, I made an humble attempt to show that in many cases no interpretation of a rite could explain its origin. For the meaning of the series of acts is to the performers themselves an interpretation; the

same ritual remaining practically unchanged may assume different meanings for different generations of performers; and the rite may even have originated before 'meaning' meant anything at all.[56]

This questioning of positivist 'objectivity' in the human sciences (directed against Durkheim's sociology) led naturally into Eliot's interest in the sceptical idealism of F. H. Bradley, whose philosophy, to Eliot, had the advantage of being founded not upon would-be scientific suppositions, but derived its premises from the immediate data of consciousness as presented to individual 'finite centres'; and thus attempted the logical construction of a system from what can be known through 'experience'. However, as Eliot argued through, and foundered upon, in his doctoral thesis, *Experience and the Objects of Knowledge in the Philosophy of F. H. Bradley*,[57] Bradley's painstaking discriminations lead at most to the necessary hypothesis (rather than logical conclusion) both of a common world and a transcendent Absolute in which the perceptions of the individual 'finite centre' have place and meaning. Eliot explored these fundamental problems in the chapter of his thesis entitled 'Solipsism',[58] where he tackles the central issue of 'how do we yoke our divers worlds to draw together? how can we issue from the circle described about each point of view?',[59] but the most he can eventually offer is

the world is a construction out of finite centres. Any particular datum can be certain only with regard to what is built upon it, not in itself: and every experience contains the knowledge of its own self-transcendence. Every experience is a paradox in that it means to be absolute, and yet is relative; in that it somehow always goes beyond itself and yet never escapes itself . . . There is an ideal identity which persists between experiences and rectifies our judgements; and it is this identity, together with the transcendence, which gives us degrees of truth.[60]

Here, Eliot's contorted formulation masks rather than makes explicit a rejection of the Bradleyan Absolute (of which he wrote in a *Monist* article of October 1916 that 'Pretending to be something that makes finite centres cohere, it turns out to be merely the assertion that they do'),[61] in favour of a perception of 'truth', and by extension, a common world, as being fundamentally *relational*: as depending on a correlation of multiple points of view, none of which singly can be taken as authoritative, but which when taken together (as an 'ideal identity') allow us to speak, albeit provisionally, of reality. Thus, through his study of Bradley, Eliot had not really argued himself out of subjectivism, but rather reached a compromise position which retained the existential integrity of 'immediate experience' as presented to isolated finite centres ('All significant truths are private truths'), but which also entailed the rejection of the central metaphysical tenet of Bradley's system. At this point (and, we may suggest, having reached an intellectual *impasse*), Eliot sent his thesis to Harvard where it was accepted by the philosophy department in June 1916; but he decided not to return to America for the *viva voce* exam, thus effectively abandoning his doctorate and academic career in philosophy.

In the interim, Eliot's interests had shifted – in retrospect, decisively – towards London and poetry; though to some extent he continued to wrestle with the same complex of issues in both his poetic practice and theory, where I think it can be readily appreciated that the concept of the world as relational, as 'a construction out of finite centres', anticipates crucial emphases in Eliot's later modernist and formalist definition of 'tradition'. What we find in examining the concept of tradition is that Eliot is again trying to posit a common world (tradition), transcending and validating the 'individual talent', but from the basis of an intellectual subjectivism that does not necessarily contain the *principle* of such self-transcendence. In other words, Eliot's stance is fundamentally subjectivist, but he is straining against the personal and intellectual isolation this entails and seeking a refuge in 'tradition'. However, 'tradition' is not the necessary consequence of either Eliot's poetic practice or its conceptual premises; nothing but time itself – which can only arguably be equated with 'tradition' – can sort the central from the eccentric.

We can particularize these issues by scrutinizing a famous key passage from 'Tradition and the Individual Talent' where Eliot offers a stimulating analogy for the relation between the new literary work and 'tradition'. Eliot, writing that the new writer must be valued in relation to his predecessors, states,

> I mean this as a principle of aesthetic, not merely historical, criticism. The necessity that he shall conform, that he shall cohere, is not one-sided; what happens when a new work of art is created is something that happens simultaneously to all the works of art which preceded it. The existing monuments form an ideal order among themselves, which is modified by the introduction of the new (the really new) work of art among them. The existing order is complete before the new work arrives; for order to persist after the supervention of novelty, the *whole* existing order must be, if ever so slightly, altered; and so the relations, proportions, values of each work of art towards the whole are readjusted; and this is conformity between the old and the new. Whoever has approved this idea of order, of the form of European, of English literature, will not find it preposterous that the past should be altered by the present as much as the present is directed by the past. And the poet who is aware of this will be aware of great difficulties and responsibilities.[62]

Here we are offered a suggestive paradigm for the relation between the new work of art and tradition. The tradition is seen as relational rather than fixed, and involved in a continual process of dialectical becoming. As each novel and valuable work of art alters the sensibility with which the reader perceives the art of the past, 'tradition' is changed and revalued in relation to the new work. Eliot's idea is significantly close to that of Borges, in his essay 'Kafka and his Precursors',[63] where he argues that Kafka's *oeuvre* elects its own predecessors and creates its own 'tradition', for it brings into retrospective prominence aspects of the work of previous writers, such as Dickens, which we label as 'Kafkaesque', but which would never have been seen in these terms had Kafka not written. It can be seen that this distinctly Modernist conception of tradition is not fundamentally normative. It would seem to allow for a new work of art to be a parodic reversal of 'traditional' modes, as Eliot's poetry of this period comes significantly close to being. The problem omitted from this definition is that which Barthes fixes on unerringly in his discussion of Flaubert in *Writing Degree Zero*: what happens when the forms and conventions the writer receives from tradition are no longer in accord with his contemporary experience?[64] As Michael Edwards comments in his essay *Eliot/Language*, 'All Eliot's poetry is *displaced* with respect to a genre without necessarily being parody.'[65] With this issue in mind, it can be seen that Eliot's crucial ambiguity when designating a new work of art as 'the new (the really new) work', his refusal of a more precise definition constitutes a significant absence.

Yet, at the same time, Eliot is at pains not to abandon the terms that connote a normative concept of tradition – particularly the term 'conformity', as in 'this is conformity between the old and new', which follows his modernist definition of tradition. To employ the term 'conformity' in this context is to give it a very problematic usage, difficult to align with the usual dictionary definition, 'form according to a pattern, make similar to', implying that sense of tradition as precedent which Eliot would seem to have denied. He also reiterates the term 'order', gradually shifting from the sense of the word 'order' as 'sequence' to imply the value-laden 'order' as 'authority', as in 'Whoever has approved this idea of order, of the form of European, of English literature' where the absence of an article speaks volumes. It is apparent that in employing these normative terms in relation to what is essentially a non-normative concept of tradition, Eliot is hedging his bets; but here, it is not just polemic advantages that are at stake.

The substance of Eliot's sense of the 'traditional' in literature is given in the first line of the next paragraph which follows, where he states, 'And the poet who is aware of this will be aware of great difficulties and responsibilities. In a peculiar sense he will be aware also that he must inevitably be judged by the standards of the past.'[66] Thus, we must understand Eliot's sense of the traditional in morally obligative terms that denote a qualitative conformity to a literary past which is greater than the individual artist. In 'The Function of Criticism' (1923) this is amplified: the tradition is that to which the individual artist 'owes allegiance, a devotion to which he must surrender and sacrifice himself in order to earn and to obtain his unique position'.[67] This Eliot, following Middleton Murry's terms, defines as a Catholic and Classicist doctrine, a doctrine of 'spiritual authority outside the individual', for, as he wishes to assert, 'men cannot get on without giving allegiance to something outside themselves'.[68] This is in opposition to the rival doctrine of the Protestant-Nonconformist 'inner voice'. Nearly all Eliot's critical judgements (in this period and subsequently) arise from this opposition. Hence, for example, his Classicist enthusiasm for Dante or the metaphysical poets, and his rejection of the Protestant-prophetic line of English poetry – Spenser, Milton, and the Romantic poets – *in toto*.

Eliot's position in the later essay makes explicit that bias towards a normative concept of tradition which could be perceived in the less polemical and self-confident 'Tradition and the Individual Talent', and by this date (significantly, after the completion of *The Waste Land*) Eliot's criticism has decisively aligned itself with the Hulmian equation of tradition, order and authority. However, beyond such polemical and cultural goals Eliot's desire that the literary tradition should constitute a 'spiritual authority outside the individual', with the sense of community that this implies, bespeaks a real need in Eliot as man and poet: a desire to align his poetic practice with 'tradition' as both precedent and authority, which one can see his poetic development to this point as striving towards but radically failing to accomplish. In the period 1914 to 1922 this desire remains as aspiration rather than actuality, but there are good grounds for arguing that with the publication of *Ash-Wednesday* (1930) – Eliot's conversion to the Anglican Church having occurred in 1927 – some crucial aspects of this desired alignment between Eliot's poetic practice and 'tradition' were achieved. The penultimate chapter of this book will discuss *Ash-Wednesday* and 'tradition'; but before doing so we must see how Eliot handles these issues in 'Gerontion' and *The Waste Land*.

8
'Gerontion' and
The Waste Land

If the initial impulse behind the quatrain poems was formal (as Eliot put it, 'the form gave the impetus to the content'), a similar initial technical stimulus cannot be predicated for either 'Gerontion' or *The Waste Land*. While the quatrain poems can fruitfully be discussed in the context of Eliot's association with Pound and the bias towards the exteriorized, societal poetry which Pound encouraged, in adopting the more expansive, self-determined formal modes of these two poems Eliot permitted himself to explore themes and preoccupations which could not be contained within the stringent form of the tetrameter quatrain – nor perhaps within the confines of his immediate association with Pound. 'Gerontion' was written in May to June 1919, in all probability after the last of the quatrain poems and during the period in which he reviewed *The Education of Henry Adams*,[1] while the bulk of *The Waste Land*, the 'long poem I have had on my mind for a long time . . .'[2] of which he wrote to his mother at the end of 1919, was written in 1921 and revised by Pound early in 1922; but fragments in the unrevised manuscript have been dated back to 1914.[3]

Until Pound dissuaded him, Eliot wished to publish 'Gerontion' as a prelude to the revised *Waste Land*.[4] The two poems can be examined together, for they conclude the phase of Eliot's close co-operation with Pound (who had left England in 1920) and through Pound's revision of the *Waste Land* manuscripts mark the intellectual culmination of their association; while at the same time their distinctive emphases indicate some of the possible constraints of that association. In considering *The Waste Land* some reference will be made to the original drafts of that poem, published in the facsimile edition, and to the effect of Pound's editorial revisions on the final structure of the work, thus completing our detailed consideration of Pound's influence upon Eliot's poetic development.

i 'Gerontion'

But it is fallen nature which bears the imprint of the progression of history.
Walter Benjamin, *The Origin of German Tragic Drama*

The distance in chronological time between the completion of 'The Love Song of

J. Alfred Prufrock' in 1911–12 and 'Gerontion' in 1919 is less than nine years. This short span takes us from T. S. Eliot as a talented and precocious Harvard student, an amateur poet inclining towards an academic career in philosophy, to Eliot as a married man, settled in London, working at Lloyds Bank, and an enigmatic rising star in the English literary firmament. It takes us from a world before the cataclysm of the Great War to a world after the unsatisfactory peace treaties of Versailles, signed within 'a wilderness of mirrors', in which the violent political turbulence of Central Europe seemed to mock the hopes of those who had believed that the previous conflict had been 'a war to end war'. It seems necessary to remind ourselves that this span of time is approximately eight years, for the distance between 'Prufrock' and 'Gerontion' cannot be measured solely by the dates of a calendar: it is a distance between two worlds, worlds that are related to each other but without the ease that a term like 'development' would imply.

The relationship of 'Gerontion' to the genre of dramatic monologue, within which 'Prufrock' can be relatively straightforwardly sited, is one of unease, reversal and dislocation. In place of the wry collocation of 'Love Song' with the ponderous, burlesque but distinctly individual 'J. Alfred Prufrock', the title 'Gerontion' offers us no more than a type: a transliteration of the Greek for little old man, which is then subtly undercut by the epigraph from *Measure for Measure*: 'Thou hast neither youth nor age/But as it were an after dinner sleep/Dreaming of both', by which even Gerontion's old age seems to be given metaphoric status. Then, as we read our way into the main text our unease gathers force as we begin to realize that the present of this fragmented monologue is one in which things seem almost purposively not to cohere. None of the co-ordinates of 'Gerontion' – the speaker, his world, the past, nor the present his voice inhabits – has any referential substance. The deictics of the poem, the demonstrative elements of grammar, do not locate us in a knowable environment: the house, with its profiteer landlord, who 'squats on the window-sill' is not created with any tangibility; indeed phrases which grammatically apply to the owner, such as 'patched and peeled in London' would seem equally to apply to the house in so far as it stands for all 'houses of decay',[5] and at the end of the poem (but implicitly throughout) we are invited to see the house as little more than a metaphor for Gerontion's mind, thus compounding the confusion of mental and physical environment. What we are left with is a voice, a voice that merely designates a putative zone of consciousness, which from the first is constructed by reiterated negatives.

> I was neither at the hot gates
> Nor fought in the warm rain
> Nor knee deep in the salt marsh, heaving a cutlass,
> Bitten by flies, fought.[6]

Gerontion defines himself by what he has not done, by the violent, heroic action and participation he has not achieved. The only activity he achieves is verbal: the vehemence of imagined action in the fractured spondees above, and other linguistic acts like the explosive whirling 'In fractured atoms . . . Beyond the circuit of the shuddering Bear' that speculatively awaits 'De Bailhache, Fresca, Mrs. Cammel' which, despite (or perhaps as a consequence of) their apparent assertiveness, read as fundamentally gestural and ineffective. Words in 'Gerontion' become physical agents through the deployment of semantic ambiguity, rhythm and cadence; they are used to suggest accusation and culpability, and finally even seem to exact retribution, as though in compensation for the speaker's declared inaction. However, they remain incapable of transcending that inaction. (A similar investment in verbal 'vitality', deployed for related ends, can be found in the increasingly vestigial physical presences of Beckett's *Trilogy*.)[7]

'Gerontion' differs from Eliot's previous and relatively conventional dramatic monologues by dissolving the material environment and with it the speaker's precise social identity. (The house is unlocated, but through its owner connotationally sited in a mercantile, Free Trade capital: Antwerp, Brussels or London. But what then is the goat doing, coughing 'at night in the field overhead'? To what except this implicitly constellated 'field' do we attach the list of associated properties: 'Rocks, moss, stonecrop, iron, merds', with its strangely neutralized final syllable?) Unlike the Laforguian and Jamesian Prufrock, Gerontion, merely 'an old man,/A dull head among windy spaces', has hardly any personality or social identity; the poem cannot be viewed as Pound viewed 'The Love Song of J. Alfred Prufrock' as 'a portrait-satire on futility'. Indeed, any individuality the speaker may be said to create for himself in the first section of the poem dissipates swiftly, and more and more drastically, as we approach the middle passage of pastiche Jacobean blank verse: the meditation on History. In this meditation, history, the secular and temporal, is presented in the terms of the Jacobean revenge drama as a cunning courtesan; the emotion applied to this abstract substantive being akin to the charnel-house eroticism of the passage from *The Revenger's Tragedy* which contains the lines which so preoccupied Eliot: 'Are lordships sold to maintain ladyships/For the poor benefit of a bewildering minute?'[8] In Eliot's lines history is seen as a sexual force, a harlot who 'deceives with whispering ambitions,/Guides us by vanities'; her 'gifts' are inapposite and ambivalent, and her effects (her 'issue') are those of perversity and moral inversion:

> Think
> Neither fear nor courage saves us. Unnatural vices
> Are fathered by our heroism. Virtues
> Are forced upon us by our impudent crimes.
> These tears are shaken from the wrathbearing tree.

As in the final lines of 'The Burial of the Dead', behind this passage we feel the traumatic effects of the First World War, and, in particular, the dislocating and absurd inflection it gave to normal, established historical relations of cause and effect, thus undermining the stability and integrity of such moral categories as 'heroism'. But in Eliot's lines it is impossible to specify exactly how these effects are attributable to 'History'. Though the 'contrived corridors/And issues' may suggest the Polish Corridor contrived at Versailles, the language of the poem eschews referential engagement in favour of the abstract categories of moralism (virtues, vices, vanities, heroism, etc.) in order to suggest an atmosphere of moral and sexual corruption which refers us back to the whispering galleries of Jacobean revenge drama. The resulting opacity of Eliot's lines is not inapposite: our confusion in reading the metaphor mirrors the 'supple confusions' of the force Eliot wishes to convey (not portray), and we are left with a linguistically claustrophobic impression of the incoherence of history and the moral ambivalence of secular ambition which represents Gerontion's viewpoint only to the extent that we feel Gerontion to be the organizing consciousness at this stage of the poem.

While it may appear superficially that this employment of blank verse offers a formal alignment with the literary tradition, in line with Eliot's admiration for Renaissance drama, it is easy to perceive that we are dealing here with a self-conscious parody or pastiche, and one that systematically exploits bombastic vices of style derived from Seneca: a diffuse 'verbalism' to which Eliot believed the Elizabethan and Jacobean theatres were inclined. If in its hyperconscious critical manipulation of Jacobean blank verse 'Gerontion' is an artful exploitation of, rather than integration with, that literary tradition, the same can be said of the poem's relation to the nineteenth-century tradition of dramatic monologue. The sudden eruption of an almost anonymous Jacobean mode ruptures the expectation of that tradition that the form will be deployed to 'create a character', as for example, in Tennyson's 'Ulysses' or Browning's 'My Last Duchess'. We could attempt to naturalize these lines by suggesting, as Eliot does of Hamlet, that Gerontion 'is dominated by an emotion which is inexpressible, because it is in *excess* of the facts as they appear',[9] thus endorsing the rhetorical luxuriance of the passage, the preponderance of the signifiers to the signified 'history'; but the impersonal historical particularity of the Jacobean idiom blocks any such attempt at 'dramatic' integration.

What connection 'Gerontion' does have with Jacobean blank verse is self-consciously critical: not only stylistically (as in Kenner's suggestion that the poem is a means of purging the language of Elizabethan metaphoric diffuseness), but also conceptually, for one developing aspect of Eliot's view of the Elizabethan drama in this period is that it is an 'impure' sensationalist drama, lacking in conventions, and, partly because of its Senecan roots, without true moral import. This position is argued at length, with respect to Webster, Tourneur, Middleton, and Chapman, in the 1924 essay 'Four Elizabethan Dramatists',[10] the entire conclusion of which is relevant to 'Gerontion'. Emphasizing the inadequacy of the Senecan 'philosophy of life' of the Elizabethans, which Eliot elsewhere views as a sterile, posturing, self-dramatizing 'stoicism', he concludes

> Even the philosophic basis, the general attitude towards life of the Elizabethans, is one of anarchism, of dissolution, of decay. It is in fact exactly parallel and indeed one and the same thing with their artistic greediness,

their desire for every sort of effect together, their unwillingness to accept any limitation and abide by it. The Elizabethans are in fact a part of the movement of progress or deterioration which has culminated in Sir Arthur Pinero and the present regiment of Europe.

The case of John Webster, and in particular *The Duchess of Malfi*, will provide an interesting example of a very great literary and dramatic genius directed towards chaos.[11]

Given this critical perspective (which, it should be said, contemporary criticism would challenge)[12] it is fitting that Eliot should have employed Jacobean blank verse to characterize the anarchic, dissolute force of 'History', which is seen as being as secular as Senecan stoicism, and as temporal as the allure of the courtesan. If in historical terms the Great War seems to stand behind 'Geronion' and underwrite its claustrophobic pessimism (as a violent reversal of the shaken but hitherto dominant liberal-humanist belief in social progress and perfectibility), two contemporary literary works seem to stand as the dominant sources behind the text. The first is Joyce's *Ulysses* – in which significant verbal and thematic reflections can be found between the opening 'Telemachiad' section and Eliot's poem – but to which 'Geronion's' most important debt is speculative: that Eliot obliquely derived, or at least was encouraged to undertake, his own experiment in the deployment and relativization of poetic styles and idioms (Biblical, Jacobean, satiric and colloquial, etc.) by the innovatory, radical deployment and ironization of literary styles to be found in Joyce's text. (Since *Ulysses* will be given some attention in the latter part of this chapter it need not be considered in further detail here.) The second is the autobiography, *The Education of Henry Adams*,[13] a source which has been frequently acknowledged, and about which Eliot wrote one of the finest of his early book reviews, 'A Sceptical Patrician' (*Athenaeum*, May 1919), in the period in which he is most likely to have written 'Geronion'.

From *The Education* Eliot adapted the 'dogwood and chestnut, flowering judas' of 'depraved May', taking up Adams's suggestion that 'No European spring had shown him the same mixture of delicate grace and passionate depravity that marked the Maryland May'.[14] The citation is worth a moment's thought, for here the method of the poem is revealed in almost paradigmatic fashion. Adams had written 'Here and there a Negro log cabin alone disturbed the dogwood and the judas tree', and it is possible that in adapting the passage to suit his purpose, Eliot, rather than having a Wordsworthian relation of intimacy with nature, might not have been able to recognize the flora that he cites. The text is literature created from literature: an echo-chamber of resonances situated in a paralysed and intransitive present. Yet I think that Eliot's ambition is not to be a structuralist *avant la lettre*, making a point about the intransitive nature of *all* writing (an intransitive verb is one that doesn't govern a direct object, and Barthes used the formula ' "To write": an intransitive verb' as a means of representing the formal self-referentiality of all writing, and conversely its inability to act on or transform the world),[15] but rather to posit historical, cultural and psychological dilemmas which are focused through the shadowy figure of Gerontion. At this point, in looking behind the poem to its formative influences and sources, I will be less concerned with possible textual attributions than an attempt to shed light on the formal logic that informs its distinctive contrasts, emphases, and discords.

Henry Adams, the 'disinherited' Boston patrician, directionless in the industrial late nineteenth century, and nostalgically yearning for the eighteenth century, when, as Eliot put it in a letter to Herbert Read of 1928 (referring to himself), 'the U.S.A. . . . was a family extension',[16] has an obvious relevance to Eliot's own social position and intellectual and cultural background. It seems clear that in analysing the New England temperament and its failings as manifested in Adams's career, Eliot is to some extent analysing himself in his review, 'A Sceptical Patrician', at least in so far as he still regards himself as subject to 'the Boston doubt: a scepticism which it is difficult to explain to those who are not born to it. This scepticism is a product, or a cause, or a concomitant of Unitarianism; it is not destructive, but it is dissolvent.'[17] Adams's eager search for education, for unifying theories and principles, and in particular a means of reconciling his own discipline, history, with developments in contemporary science, led nowhere: 'Wherever this man stepped, the ground did not simply give way, it flew into particles; towards the end of his life he came across the speculations of Poincaré, and science disappeared entirely.'[18] Eliot sees Adams's failure as a consequence of his unsensuous susceptibility to 'all the suggestions which dampen enthusiasm and dispel conviction'; 'a great many things interested him; but he could believe in nothing'.

In *The Education* Adams provides Eliot with a model of personal and cultural ineffectuality that was too close to his own background for comfort; and in 'Gerontion' Eliot takes upon himself, and as it were distils the essence of such ineffectuality in order to exorcise it (a process similar to that undergone in 'Burbank with a Baedeker: Bleistein with a Cigar', where Burbank has at least a tangential relation to Eliot). The verbal explosion to 'fractured atoms' that awaits the denizens of the cosmopolitan milieu at the conclusion of 'Gerontion' owes something to Eliot's perception of Adams's intellectual development ('Wherever this man stepped, the ground did not simply give way, it flew into particles . . .'), an analogy itself suggested by 'The Grammar of Science' chapter, in which Adams finds his search for a unifying theory of history shattered by Poincaré's speculations and the kinetic theory of gas: 'The kinetic theory of gas is an assertion of ultimate chaos. In plain words, Chaos was the law of nature; Order was the dream of man.'[19] At the end of this chapter Adams offers a grim admission of failure that may well have inspired Eliot's employment of the epigraph from *Measure for Measure*.

Every fabulist has told how the human mind has always struggled like a frightened bird to escape the chaos which caged it; how – appearing suddenly and inexplicably out of some unknown and unimaginable void; passing half its known life in the mental chaos of sleep; victim even when awake to its own ill-adjustment, to disease, to age, to external suggestion, to nature's compulsion; doubting its sensations, and, in the last resort, trusting only to instruments and averages – after sixty or seventy years of growing astonishment, the mind wakes to find itself looking blankly into the void of death.[20]

Because of its relation to Eliot's cultural background, *The Education* can tell us something about the poet's relation to the structural and perceptual modes of 'Geronion' both as comparison and contrast. The most important contrast is Eliot's reaction against the shared religious background of Unitarianism, evinced in 'A Sceptical Patrician' as well as 'Geronion'. Adams's remarks upon 'the disappearance of religion', by which 'The children reached manhood without knowing religion, and with the certainty that dogma, metaphysics, and abstract philosophy were not worth knowing'[21] provide a necessary context for Eliot's intellectual and religious development. As Adams puts it, 'Even the mild discipline of the Unitarian Church was so irksome that they all threw it off at the first possible moment, and never afterwards entered a church', and it was against this very mildness, and 'the Boston doubt' with which he associated it, that Eliot was to react both intellectually and poetically, and eventually, doctrinally.

'Geronion' is not a religious poem in the sense of offering us any securely held religious certainty or commitment – it explicitly does not do that – but it does present us with a world seen as being in desperate need of eschatological renewal, and in terms antithetical to Unitarianism's mild deism.

The two central passages on profane degeneracy, the inverted rituals of the cosmopolitan aesthetes, which significantly lead into the evocation of the illusions of secular history, are both virtually framed by a broken statement, almost an injunction:

> Signs are taken for wonders. 'We would see a sign!'
> The word within a word, unable to speak a word,
> Swaddled with darkness. In the juvescence of the year
> Came Christ the tiger

After the portrayal of, and meditation upon, profane degeneracy the injunction is closed:

> The tiger springs in the new year. Us he devours.

This initially hesitant (as in the fleeting reference to Lancelot Andrewes's 1618 'Nativity Sermon',[22] which was to emerge in *Ash-Wednesday* as the doctrinal focus of Eliot's later poetry and poetics), yet eventually vehement reference to the idea of spiritual retribution (the presentation of Christ as a Blakean tiger) provides a structural dissonance, an extra 'vertical' dimension to the poem that has weight beyond the brief space allotted to its presentation. The only positive, unsullied gesture the poem can afford is towards the idea of the Incarnation and judgement; but this shadowing forth of the metaphysical remains gestural: the abrupt introduction of a dimension disjunctive with the temporal and profane, which cannot be maintained as the true locus of an alternative to societal corruption.

In 'Gerontion' the gesture towards the spiritual and metaphysical is employed to literally frame, contain and underwrite the attack on secular history and cosmopolitan profanity. Christ answered 'An evil and adulterous generation seeketh after a sign' to the unbelieving Pharisees who asked him to perform a miracle with the words 'Master, we would see a sign from thee' (*Matthew* xii, 38, 39), and the hell of cosmopolitan culture is presented in terms of inverted ritual in the lines that follow the initial reference to 'Christ the tiger'.

> In depraved May, dogwood and chestnut, flowering judas,
> To be eaten, to be divided, to be drunk
> Among whispers; by Mr. Silvero
> With caressing hands, at Limoges
> Who walked all night in the next room;
> By Hakagawa, bowing among the Titians;
> By Madame de Tornquist, in the dark room
> Shifting the candles; Fraülein von Kulp
> Who turned in the hall, one hand on the door.

Here, a scenario which can be approximately located as that of a cosmopolitan hotel late at night is used to suggest a parody of the Eucharist, a black Mass, conducted by profane aesthetes. The burden of condemnation is, as in other passages, carried as much by phonetic and rhythmic effects as by direct suggestion. Thus, the caressive sibilants of 'Mr. Silvero' endorse the sinister activity of his 'caressing hands', while the gulping gutturals of 'Fraülein von Kulp' indicate phonetically that whatever she is doing in the hallway, she is up to no good. By using such techniques, Eliot, as in the earlier quatrain poems, can achieve condemnation without descending to an uncouth and aesthetically inept statement of intent. Such employment of Jonsonian, 'humorous' naming serves to imply that these individuals have no particular significance beyond the rudimentary identity of the names they bear. These are, as in the quatrains, caricatural techniques that concentrate upon the superficies: here a name rather than a physiognomy, to limit and condemn. (In comparison, one can consider the obvious connotational message in the specification 'Rachel *née* Rabinovitch', who 'Tears at the grapes with murderous paws' in 'Sweeney among the Nightingales'.) Ultimately such techniques depend for their effectiveness upon a common core of cultural understanding between the poet and reader: the method being one of cultural suggestion, a playing, however lightly, upon the receptive chords of social (and racial) prejudice.

To understand this presentation of cosmopolitan culture as a black mass, and the other modes of social animus manifested in the poem, we can again turn to *The Education*, but this time as comparison rather than contrast. We can accurately locate the basis of Eliot's hostility to cosmopolitanism and his anti-Semitism, which is relevant to this particular poem at least, in a process of social and cultural displacement which Adams sees himself as having undergone.

His world was dead. Not a Polish Jew fresh from Warsaw or Cracow –
not a furtive Yacoob or Ysaac still reeking from the Ghetto, snarling a

weird Yiddish to the officers of the customs – but had a keener instinct, an intenser energy, and a freer hand than he – American of Americans, with Heaven knew how many Puritans and Patriots behind him, and an education that had cost a civil war . . . The defeat was not due to him, nor yet to any superiority of his rivals. He had been unfairly forced out of the track, and must get back into it as best he could.[23]

The sense of resentment, bordering on incoherence, manifested in this passage is revealing. Here, a rejection of the commercial bourgeoisie, and beyond this, of the rapid capitalist industrialization and immigration of the late nineteenth century, which brought in 'alien' cultural groups, is condensed and displaced into a rejection of, and hostility towards, 'the Jew'. Adams's Freudian trope makes the occasional, but consistent anti-Semitic references in Eliot's early work, and his general hostility to cosmopolitanism, far more comprehensible, if no more appealing, by its precise social and historical context; and can help us to place his later notorious remarks in *After Strange Gods* (1934) on the undesirability of 'any large number of free-thinking Jews' to any 'homogeneous' unified culture.[24]

This can help us understand the manner in which Geronion articulates himself between an unavailable, significantly ironized, 'heroic' past and a contaminated present in which his only consolation is to negotiate a resentful and retaliatory response to these processes of cultural and personal marginalization. However, the modes of apprehension 'Geronion' embodies and employs – and it is, in the related usage, an apprehensive poem – are not those of Henry Adams, nor, except tangentially, those of Eliot himself, unless we wish to claim far too close a relation between the poet and the defeatist persona he presents. As the poem develops after the meditation upon History Eliot narrows the scope of the verse towards an exploration of personal and emotional desiccation in which the immediate reference is to the central scene in *The Revenger's Tragedy* (Act III, scene V), in which Vindice addresses the skull of his long-deceased beloved as a parable of worldly vanity. ('Look you, brother,/I have not fashioned this only for show/And useless property', *Revenger's Tragedy*, 11.98–100; 'I have not made this show purposelessly/And it is not by any concitation/Of the backward devils. 'Geronion'.) However, while the rhetorical and affective modes of the relevant passages are very closely aligned ('Does the silk-worm expend her yellow labours/For thee? For thee does she undo herself?'; 'What will the spider do,/Suspend its operations, will the weevil/Delay?') the significant difference remains that in 'Geronion' it is Geronion himself, addressing a shadowy interlocutor, who is his own *memento mori*.

During this period Eliot had become interested in the sermon as 'a form of literary art',[25] and we discover that Geronion's loss of 'sight, smell, hearing, taste and touch' can be referred to Newman's sermon on 'Divine Calls', quoted in *Apologia pro Vita Sua*: 'Let us beg and pray Him day by day to reveal Himself to our souls more fully, to quicken our senses, to give us sight and hearing, taste and touch of the world to come.'[26] However, the complete absence of Newman's positive teleology drastically subverts the reference, which is applied negatively to personal relations, and reveals not only, or even primarily, Gerontion's lack of a 'divine call', but that the emphasis in any discussion of Eliot's poem must fall on asceticism rather than religion: for the major dynamic element is a revulsion from and against the present which encourages the appearance of whatever is farthest removed from it. This suggests that Eliot's employment of the rhetorical modes of the Jacobean drama at the conclusion of 'Gerontion' needs to be comprehended within his negative perspective on the use made of Senecan stoicism by the Renaissance dramatists. In 'Seneca in Elizabethan Translation' (1927), Eliot commented, 'The ethic of Seneca is a matter of postures. The posture which gives the greatest opportunity for effect, hence for the Senecan morality, is the posture of dying: death gives his characters the opportunity for their most sententious aphorisms – a hint which the Elizabethan dramatists were only too ready to follow.'[27] Eliot's use of Jacobean modes in 'Gerontion' is consistently critical and can be related to his comments on Othello's closing speech in 'Shakespeare and the Stoicism of Seneca' (1927), where he remarks that, 'What Othello seems to me to be doing in making this speech is *cheering himself up* . . . Othello succeeds in turning himself into a pathetic figure, by adopting an *aesthetic* rather than a moral attitude, dramatizing himself against his environment. He takes in the spectator, but the human motive is primarily to take in himself.'[28]

Although the poem consistently places Gerontion's attitudes, and suggests little sense of doctrinal commitment or certainty, the metaphysical functions within the poem at the level of spiritual, linguistic and affective 'gesture'. As in 'Mr. Eliot's Sunday Morning Service', written not long before 'Gerontion', where we find that the 'unoffending feet' of Christ serve as a locus of stillness and purity to be set equally against the historically shifting doctrines of the theologians, the sterility of the epicene clergy, and Sweeney's magnanimous shifting hams; in 'Gerontion', 'The word within a word, unable to speak a word,/Swaddled with darkness', is a still centre of value to be set against the mobile dispersion in 'fractured atoms' that awaits the inhabitants of the cosmopolitan milieu. In Eliot's poetry as a whole the secular and temporal cannot contain or account for the sacred: it is that against which the societal is judged as inadequate. The sacred can, however, contain and place the secular – even if only in negative terms – as we find once the doctrinal commitment is made, in *Ash-Wednesday*. Here we find the fundamental structural contrast of 'Gerontion' compactly recast and made explicit in the lines which begin section V: '. . . the unstilled world still whirled/About the centre of the Silent Word.'

Here, though, it is necessary to guard against the temptation of reading Eliot's later poetry into his early work. There is an obvious danger, particularly for readers who sympathize with Eliot's eventual doctrinal choices, of regarding the early poetry as in some way a preparation or prelude to the committed poetry of *Ash-Wednesday* and *Four Quartets*, whereas the early poetry depends for an appreciation of its individuality upon a realization of its very lack of commitment. We retrospectively limit the options Eliot had available to him before 1927 by regarding his religious commitment as inevitable. In 'Gerontion', after the mobile dispersion of 'De Bailhache, Fresca, Mrs. Cammel' is enacted as the linguistic climax of a poem, imbued and obsessed with febrile sexual puns and metaphors, the text does not so much conclude as entropically run down:

> Gull against the wind, in the windy
> straits
> Of Belle Isle, or running on the Horn.
> White feathers in the snow, the Gulf claims,
> And an old man driven by the Trades
> To a sleepy corner.
> Tenants of the house,
> Thoughts of a dry brain in a dry season.

Here, a gestural process of resistance ('Gull against the wind') is swiftly overcome by 'the Gulf': death in the guise of sexual extinction, which 'claims' Gerontion, whose marginality to history, or purposive action, is seen explicitly, if metaphorically, in terms of a process of cultural decline and commercial (implicitly intellectual) displacement: 'an old man driven by the Trades/To a sleepy corner.' As in the reference to the Punic Wars in 'The Burial of the Dead', trade winds here implicate trade wars; and the final lines read both as an assertion of sterility – 'Thoughts of a dry brain in a dry season', and a laconic disavowal of the previous text, for which as 'Tenants of the house' Gerontion would presumably be justified in disclaiming responsibility.

In conclusion, it can be suggested that 'Gerontion' demonstrates that Eliot's view of literary history, 'tradition', cannot be excluded from, or remain unimplicated in his negative vision of 'history' proper. In 'Gerontion', Eliot explored his sense of the impact of historical incoherence on the individual by constructing a substanceless persona, who is less a 'character' than a consciousness disbarred from action; an echo chamber sounding with distorted and contorted resonances from the literary past. As previously mentioned, until Pound dissuaded him Eliot had wished to publish 'Gerontion' as a prelude to the revised *Waste Land*, and in the latter poem, it will be argued, Eliot attempted through the use of a 'mythical method', which relates to Joyce's method in *Ulysses*, to overcome the sterile fragmentation that constitutes 'Gerontion': the persona and the poem. We will now turn to the intellectual drama of *The Waste Land*, the culmination of Eliot's early poetic development.

ii *The Waste Land*

> Why then, I'll fit you; say no more
> When I was young, I gave my mind
> And plied myself to fruitless poetry;
> Which though it profit the professor naught,
> Yet it is passing pleasing to the world.
>
> Kydd, *The Spanish Tragedy*

Although 'Gerontion' is displaced in relation to its genre, dramatic monologue, the voice of the poem is still that of a single individual (in Bradleyan terms, a 'finite centre'; in Jamesian terms, a 'point of view'), and so does not constitute the 'order and form', the impersonal objectivity that Eliot regarded as a pre-requisite for a desired Classical art. These terms are taken from Eliot's article, '*Ulysses*, Order, and Myth', published in *The Dial* in November 1923, which has been accurately located as a retrospective acknowledgement of the relation between Joyce's 'epic' narrative and Eliot's own, recently published, *Waste Land*. In the following pages I wish to consider the meanings of *The Waste Land* through a complex of issues relating to its form, issues which can be introduced through a comparison and differentiation between Eliot's and Joyce's use of a 'mythical method'. Eliot proposes this term in defence of *Ulysses* and as an implicit rebuke to Richard Aldington, who writing before the work was completed, had 'treated Mr. Joyce as a prophet of chaos; and wailed at the flood of Dadaism which his prescient eye saw bursting forth at the tap of the magician's rod'. Aldington had not only accused Joyce of a 'libel on humanity' (not an accusation that in any way impresses Eliot) but had gone so far as to refer to Mr Joyce's 'great *undisciplined* talent'.[29] It is this irresponsible use of the adjective that calls forth Eliot's magisterial strictures.

Eliot bases his defence on Joyce's use of the *Odyssey* as a formal device, and writes in terms that immediately suggest the relation between Joyce's work and *The Waste Land*.

> In using the myth, in manipulating a continuous parallel between con-temporaneity and antiquity, Mr. Joyce is pursuing a method which others must pursue after him. They will not be imitators, any more than the scien-tist who uses the discoveries of an Einstein in pursuing his own, independent, further investigations. It is simply a way of controlling, of ordering, of giving a shape and a significance to the immense panorama of futility and anarchy which is contemporary history. It is a method already adumbrated by Mr. Yeats, and of the need for which I believe Mr. Yeats to have been the first contemporary to be conscious. It is a method for which the horoscope is auspicious. Psychology (such as it is, and whether our reac-tion to it be comic or serious), ethnology, and *The Golden Bough* have concurred to make possible what was impossible even a few years ago. Instead of narrative method, we may now use the mythical method.[30]

Eliot is writing here in very general terms, and terms that can be seen to apply at least as much to his own recently completed poem as to Joyce's *Ulysses*. At this point, therefore, I would like to make a number of analytic distinctions which Eliot is understandably not concerned to make, and which he blurs by his description of the method of *Ulysses* as 'the parallel to the *Odyssey* and the use of appropriate styles and symbols to each division'. It is stretching definitions to consider Homer's *Odyssey* to be a myth rather than a legend; and, *pace* Eliot, Joyce's method is not truly a 'mythical method' but rather a narrative method. In David Lodge's suc-cinct formulation, this is a structural (not merely decorative) metaphor, in that it exerts control over the development of the narrative. Once Bloom has been cast as Odysseus, Stephen as Telemachus and Molly as Penelope, then the story must end with Bloom and Stephen united (however briefly and casually) with Bloom returned (however ingloriously) to his wife (however unfaithful she has been in his absence).[31]

Thus, to employ structuralist terminology, the linear, diachronic narrative structure is controlled 'by the parallel to the *Odyssey*', and can at least formally be distinguished from Joyce's synchronic literary method of counterpointing antiquity and the present: the 'use of appropriate styles and symbols to each division'.

I would like to retain this division and apply it to *The Waste Land* as a distinction between the five part linear *structure* of the poem and the stylistic *method* of each section. The most important point to be made is that the narrative structure of *The Waste Land* lacks the sustained formal parallelism we can posit between the *Odyssey* and *Ulysses*. If we turn to Jessie Weston's *From Ritual to Romance*,[32] which Eliot's 'Notes' indicate as, and subsequent criticism has looked to for the source of such a formal relationship, we will be largely disappointed. The story of the Fisher King, wounded or rendered impotent by the Dolorous Stroke, upon whose restoration to health the renewal of the Waste Land depends, requires that there be a narrative distinction between the Fisher King and the Quester whose task it is to cure him. In Eliot's poem we are forced to posit a unity of identity between the two, and therefore do not find the mode of sustained and elaborate formal parallelism which characterizes *Ulysses*, and which in relation to *The Waste Land* would require a formal correspondence between Eliot's text and the succession of episodes (such as the meeting with the Loathly Damsel) upon which the development of the Grail quest depends. Eliot has used Weston's book as a storehouse of motifs and symbols, some, such as the motif of the dying god, reaching back to the animist rituals and fertility cults Eliot would be familiar with through his student reading of Fraser's *Golden Bough*, some connecting through the Romance of the Grail quest forward to Wagner's late nineteenth-century drama-opera.

In his 'Notes', Eliot indicates that 'the plan and a good deal of the incidental symbolism of the poem were suggested by Miss Jessie L. Weston's book on the Grail legend'; but here I think we need to interpret 'plan' as meaning 'situation'. While I do not think the poem requires this interpretation, we can, if we wish, locate a crucial emotional 'wounding' around the incident in the hyacinth garden (in the original drafts of the poem the incident is alluded to in the arid 'dialogue' of 'A Game of Chess')[33] or, if the verse itself refutes such an unambiguous reading, more precisely a moment of self-surrender and plenitude, which, framed by the contrary implications of the lines from Wagner's *Tristan und Isolde*, is followed and surrounded by decisive failure and sterility. This can be held to underlie subsequent references to the Fisher King and the Waste Land itself; the use of particular, usually fertility cult motifs; and what, for now without further definition, can be referred to as the structure of the quest, the attempt to cure the sterility of the Waste Land, which is, however, an unspecific structure in that it seems to culminate in an interdenominational search for metaphysical salvation. Thus, when Eliot alludes to 'From Ritual to Romance; chapter on the Fisher King' as his citation to the lines near the close of the poem:

> I sat upon the shore
> Fishing, with the arid plains behind me

his use of Weston's text seems more playful and approximate than his interpreters would often seem to desire.

But if The Waste Land does not display the mode of narrative parallelism which can be discerned in Ulysses, what formal modes underlie the five part structure of the poem and generate the diachronic movement of the quest narrative? Here it is useful to examine the original manuscripts of the poem and consider the overall effect of Pound's revisions, since in these drafts Eliot's implicit structural emphases can be discerned more clearly than in the revised poem, published in 1922.

The initial impression we gather from even a cursory examination of the Facsimile edition of The Waste Land is that the work Eliot submitted to Pound's editorial talents in November 1921 was a far more extensive and uncompromisingly satirical document than the published poem. The shift of emphasis from the meditative early fragments (which can be dated back to 1914, and seem to provide the basis for the spiritual quest element in the completed poem) to the societal and satiric bias of the first three sections is comprehensible within the context of Eliot's years of joint endeavour with Pound on the depiction of moeurs contemporaines. The original title Eliot appended to the first two sections of the poem, and which was possibly intended to apply to the whole, was 'He Do the Police in Different Voices',[34] a reference to Sloppy's talents as a newspaper reader in Dickens's Our Mutual Friend, and by extension, a reference to the anecdotal reportage technique Dickens experimented with in this his final, uncompleted and sombre novel in order to give an impersonal panoramic view of London society. Relatedly, up to the 'Death by Water' section, Eliot seems to offer a far more extensive and inclusive cultural survey than that retained in the published poem.

In the first three sections of the poem the entire passages that Pound successfully encouraged Eliot to excise were, first, the initial half of 'The Burial of the Dead', a narrative of a sordid, Boston night out, spoken by one of the participants – a passage that was intended to establish a tonal contrast to set the gravity of 'April is the cruellest month' in powerful contradistinction, and second, the lengthy first section of 'The Fire Sermon', giving a Popian pastiche based on The Rape of the Lock, presenting the trivial and corrupt world of Fresca, a London demi-mondaine, who has come up in the world (significantly this is one of the names that is 'whirled . . . in fractured atoms' at the conclusion of 'Gerontion'). Eliot was to write that Pound 'induced me to destroy what I thought an excellent set of couplets; for, said he, ''Pope has done this so well you cannot do it better'' ';[35] here criticism cannot but validate Pound's judgement. The 'Fresca' passages are marred by an unpleasant misogyny ('For varying forms, one definition's right;/Unreal emotions, and real appetite.'),[36] which removes Eliot's authorial investment from Pope's more urbane and balanced presentation of Belinda. It is, however, interesting to see Eliot attempting a view of the trivialization and misuse of literature which can be related in conception (though not execution) to Pound's portrayals in *Hugh Selwyn Mauberley* (for example, 'Lady Valentine').

> She scribbles verse of such a gloomy tone
> That cautious critics say, her style is quite her own,
> Not quite an adult, and still less a child,
> By fate misbred, by flattering friends beguiled,
> Fresca's arrived (the Muses Nine declare)
> To be a sort of can-can salonnière.[37]

Finally, also in 'The Fire Sermon', Eliot was encouraged to excise a brief, Baude-lairean lyric apostrophization of 'London', the tenor of which is conveyed by the refrain, 'London, your people is bound upon the wheel!' (here, I think, a reference to Samsara, the Buddhist wheel of endless becoming rather than the wheel of fortune). Pound, perhaps missing the reference, scribbled the brief but pungent critical comment 'B *ll* s' in the margin of this section.

   Then, going beyond the first three societal sections, the entire initial section of 'Death by Water' was cut, in which Eliot had presented a Ulyssean voyage of ulti-mately shipwrecked New England fishermen, to retain only the brief coda on 'Phlebas the Phoenician', itself adapted from 'Dans le Restaurant'. That this sec-tion was intended to offer a purificatory contrast to the preceding anatomization of social sterility and degeneracy is evinced by the respect with which Eliot introduces his sailors:

> The sailor, attentive to the chart or to the sheets,
> A concentrated will against the tempest and the tide,
> Retains, even ashore, in public bars or streets
> Something inhuman, clean and dignified.[38]

The change of tone between this Ulyssean voyage and the preceding sections is emphatic. In this first stanza, Eliot associates the 'inhuman' with the 'clean and dignified'; an association that relates to the sailor's daily traffic with the elements, but which is also revelatory of the bias of Eliot's perceptions and an emphasis that Hulme would certainly have comprehended. Eliot was undoubtedly dispirited by the cuts he was encouraged to make in 'Death by Water', to the extent that he suggested to Pound that the 'Phlebas' coda should go too, thus eradicating the entire section. (A suggestion of which Pound did not approve.) We can, however, appreciate Eliot's implicit point that the coda makes little sense without its con-text. After the somewhat stiff introductory quatrains (to which Pound appended the comment 'Bad – but cant attack until I get typescript'), the narrative, spoken by one of the sailors, is precise and evocative while perhaps being too obviously a 'literary construction' to ring true. Eliot has attempted to stir echoes of Dante's Ulysses canto (*Inferno*, xxvi), Homer, and Coleridge's 'Ancyent Marinere' without losing the dramatic particularity that he commends in Dante's Ulysses as against Tennyson's: 'Dante is telling a story. Tennyson is only stating an elegiac mood.'[39] Here, setting aside the issue of the quality of the verse, there are some grounds for arguing that Eliot wanted, and the poem might have benefited from, a more gradual structural and thematic transition from the societal and satiric first three sections to 'What the Thunder Said'. Structurally, 'Death by Water' enacts a narration that concludes with a death by drowning, while the coda hints at a process of metamorphosis, thus gesturing, however obliquely, towards the 'spiritual death and rebirth' of the traditional religious schema after the 'cauldron of unholy loves' figured in 'The Fire Sermon'.

'What the Thunder Said', written by Eliot in Lausanne in late 1921 while he was recovering from what today would be termed a nervous breakdown, was written with extreme facility (a phenomenon Eliot commented upon in the 1931 essay on 'The *Pensées* of Pascal'),[40] and soon after the poem's publication, in 1923, he not only considered that it contained the only 'good lines' in *The Waste Land*, but also that it was 'the only part that justifies the whole, at all'.[41] Part of this judgement was perhaps due to the fact that this section passed through Pound's censorship without question (he writes on the holograph manuscript 'O.K. from here *I think*'); but more fundamentally it is in this section that the asocial, meditative spiritual quest element emerges as the focus of the verse, and Eliot is able to speak most directly, and (in relative terms) personally.

In his recension of the *Waste Land* manuscripts Pound's effect on the texture of the verse is confined almost entirely to the first three sections (and in particular, 'The Fire Sermon') where apart from these excisions he also offered revisions and critical comments, which, through his feel for *le mot juste*, not only helped improve the verse (as, for example, in the substitution of 'demotic' for 'abominable' in 'Mr. Eugenides . . . Asked me in demotic French/To luncheon at the Cannon Street Hotel/Followed by a weekend at the Metropole'),[42] but also helped curb Eliot's tendency towards the overt expression of social and personal animosity. Thus, Pound helped Eliot to make the Augustan quatrains of the central passage of 'The Fire Sermon', 'What Tiresias *sees*', the sexual encounter between the young man and the typist, the sustained and powerful poetic achievement that they are. Here, Pound's revisions are thick in the margin, it being a question of at once tightening and shortening the verse, and removing the traces of the poet's animosity. Two examples will suffice. In the published poem the lines, 'Bestows one final patronizing kiss/And gropes his way finding the stairs unlit . . .' ends in these dots, and the verse breaks off before giving the woman's automatic reactions now she is alone. In the manuscript this couplet is completed with the lines, 'And at the corner where the stable is,/Delays only to urinate and spit', to which Pound comments, 'Probably over the mark.' Secondly, the lines in the published poem that enact a collapsed quatrain, 'I, Tiresias, old man with wrinkled dugs/Perceived the scene, and foretold the rest −/I too awaited the expected guest', are a complete quatrain in the manuscript by the inclusion between the second and third lines of 'Knowing the manner of these crawling bugs', of which Pound commented 'Too easy'.[43] It is clear that Eliot did not originally intend the faint aura of sympathy that seems to hang around the woman in the published version. The overall effect of the excisions and revisions suggested by Pound, and in the main agreed to and furthered by Eliot, was to reduce the elements of overt authorial investment and social specificity in the unrevised poem. (The quatrains originally contained, for example, a cursory and somewhat derisive reference to Nevinson, the Futurist painter, who became a subject for Vorticist derision when he continued to espouse Marinetti's doctrines after they were fashionable.)

A detached examination of the excisions and revisions made in *The Waste Land* manuscripts leads to the conclusion that while these changes do not radically alter the relative weighting between the societal, satiric element in Eliot's poem and the meditative spiritual quest element, they do tend to obscure the clarity of the contrast between the two differing emphases. At least structurally we can speak of these elements in disjunction, for the first three sections of the manuscript, as in the published poem, concentrate upon a negative depiction of the secular world, seen in terms of the temporal city, in which I centres on the poverty of social relationships and pastimes; II on the sterility of personal relationships; and III on the corruption of sexual relationships; 'The Fire Sermon' being the central section, for Eliot's tendency, in the quatrain poems and elsewhere, was to embody corruption in sexual terms. Significantly, in 'The Fire Sermon' we find a single line interpolated before the Tiresias episode: 'Not here, O Glaucon, but in another world.'[44] This is a reference to the relevant section of Plato's *Republic* which inspired the ideal of the *Civitas Dei*, the 'City of God', as expounded by St Augustine in the work of that title, as opposed to the actuality of the secular, temporal city and its corruption. The final two sections move outside the city, and develop through the idea of voyage (IV), or pilgrimage (V), the spiritual quest element. The revisions, while they reduce the extensiveness and much of the unmediated hostility of the societal sections (in fact making them less overtly satiric in intention), also, and perhaps more crucially, reduce the element of contrast provided by IV and V by the complete excision of the 'Death by Water' narrative, leaving this section noticeably slight and under-weighted compared to the other four sections of the poem. The result is that the quest element, seen in terms of desert pilgrimage in 'What the Thunder Said' is relatively sudden in its emergence and less thematically prepared for than if more of IV had been retained.

But in the revised poem as in the manuscripts, the five part structure of *The Waste Land* enacts the theme of the quest in terms of the contrasting emphases of each section. This generates a development by which we move beyond the societal and corrupt to a 'purificatory' fourth section, and beyond, to an individual and personal quest outside society which has as its implicit goal some mode of metaphysical insight. Here, as Lyndall Gordon suggests, Eliot is following 'the traditional schema of the exemplary life', but in terms which replace the unified self of spiritual autobiography with a set of discrete structural emphases, which are close enough to that schema to invoke it, without necessitating allegorical readings and recourses. Gordon goes too far in suggesting both straightforward allegory and concealed confessional statement, so that when she writes, 'In the lives Eliot invokes – Dante, Christ, the grail knight, Ezekiel – there is always a dark period of trial, whether in a desert, a slough of despond, or a hell, followed by initiation, conversion or the divine light itself',[45] the terms are far too diffuse to relate to the particularity of a text which interprets and exploits this schema rather than merely replicating it. This traditional quest pattern does, however, underlie the narrative structure and development of *The Waste Land*, allowing us to return to the question of its stylistic method.

At this point we should recall the initial, hermeneutic distinction made between narrative structure and stylistic method, terms which it was suggested Eliot conflates under the general designation of 'mythical method' in his discussion of *Ulysses*. In '*Ulysses*, Order, and Myth', Eliot questions the status of *Ulysses* as a novel, 'if you call it an epic it will not matter', suggesting that 'the novel is a form which will no longer serve . . . because the novel, instead of being a form, was simply the expression of an age which had not sufficiently lost all form to feel the need for something stricter'.[46] But, as regards his desire for such formal stringency, Eliot is not only thinking of the manner in which the metonymic, linear movement of what is apparently a 'realist' narrative is underpinned and ironized by the structural, Ulyssean metaphor, but also of Joyce's deployment of a plurality of 'appropriate styles and symbols to each division'. This is made clear in a comment made in the *Nouvelle Revue Française* of December 1922.

> My opinion is that *Ulysses* is not so much a work which opens a new epoch as the enormous outcome of a completed epoch. With this book Joyce achieves a singular result, singularly distinguished, and perhaps unique in literature: that distinction consists in not having a style at all, – and not having one, not in a negative sense, but much to the contrary in a very positive sense.[47]

Here, Eliot is implying that the multiplicity of relativized and ironized literary styles Joyce deploys in *Ulysses*, ranging, for example, from the parodic use of the modes of newspaper reportage in 'Aeolus', to a mélange of modes dominated by mock Irish epic in 'Cyclops' (where the monster is the nationalistic Citizen) results in a work that can be regarded as radically styleless, in that formal experimentation in which style begins to determine the treatment of content (rather than vice versa) serves to reveal all literary styles as contingent, if not arbitrary. However, it is not fundamentally the proliferation and relativization of literary styles in *Ulysses* that attracts Eliot's commendation, but the lack of a single, adequate authorial style, which to Eliot argues for a radical detachment or 'impersonality' which he would see as a move towards the desired objectivity of a Classical art. From a different perspective though, it could be suggested that in *Ulysses* Joyce is *playing* with styles and ideologies and that his intentions are fundamentally ludic, serving not only to reveal the relative and arbitrary nature of all cultural forms, but also their possible integration in, and through, the virtuosity of the writer. I think that one amusing analogy to Joyce's use of style/s in *Ulysses* is provided by the anecdote Ellmann gives of Joyce framing a picture of Cork (the place) in cork (the wood)[48] – thus, a tongue in cheek playing with modes of representation, forms and media, which has the potentially disturbing effect of revealing the contingency of these forms and their lack of intrinsic relation. But for Eliot, believing that 'the parallel with the *Odyssey*' provides a principle of purely formal coherence, Joyce's 'stylelessness' argues for the impersonality of a 'mythical method'; a bias that must obviously be seen from within the context of his own recently completed poem.

The intellectual conjuncture Eliot wishes to make between 'myth' and 'formal coherence' refers us to *The Waste Land*, but can also be traced back through the development of his own intellectual interests to the paper on 'The Origin of Primitive Ritual' given at Harvard in 1913, which it has been suggested exercised a formative influence on his concept of tradition. Here, Eliot had argued an insight into the formal, internal coherence of mythic ritual and the inaccessibility of its meanings to any point of view from outside the ritual itself ('the meaning of the series of acts is to the performers themselves an interpretation')[49] that at the time of giving the paper he used to question the positivistic, interpretative method of Durkheim. During the period of the composition of *The Waste Land*, Eliot seems to have returned, more as an extension than as an alternative, to his original sense of myth and ritual as offering a model of formal cohesion both theoretically and in the literary practice of the poem. This is meant in the initial and primary sense of Eliot's retrospective (and significantly ironized) suggestion in '*Ulysses*, Order, and Myth' that anthropology, as in Weston or Frazer's *Golden Bough*, may provide the intellectual basis for a literary method (as, relatedly, in Eliot's interest in Sanskrit as an Ur language underlying European linguistic models and developments); but also in a less specific sense by which 'primitive ritual' can be seen as informing the perceptual and literary modes of the poet. At the conclusion of his review of Lewis's *Tarr* Eliot had written,

> the artist, I believe, is more *primitive*, as well as more civilized, than his contemporaries, his experience is deeper than civilization, and he only uses the phenomena of civilization in expressing it. Primitive instincts and the acquired habits of ages are confounded in the ordinary man. In the work of Mr. Lewis we recognize the thought of the modern and the energy of the cave-man.[50]

In 'The Metaphysical Poets' (1921), again opposing the artist to the ordinary man, Eliot had argued his contemporary belief in the detachment of the poet and his ability to act as a 'catalyst', amalgamating disparate areas of experience, '. . . the ordinary man's experience is chaotic, irregular, fragmentary. The ordinary man falls in love, or reads Spinoza, and these experiences have nothing to do with each other, or with the noise of the typewriter or the smell of cooking; in the mind of the poet these experiences are always forming new wholes';[51] while in 'Tradition and the Individual Talent' Eliot had reminded the would-be poet

> that art never improves, but that the material of art is never quite the same
> . . . the mind of Europe – the mind of his own country – a mind which he

learns in time to be much more important than his own private mind – is a mind which changes, and that this change is a development which abandons nothing *en route*, which does not superannuate either Shakespeare, or Homer, or the rock drawings of the Magdalenian draughtsmen.[52]

This sense of the active forming of 'new wholes' by the artist in relation to a tradition that changes, dialectically becomes, rather than improves, and the possible integration of that awareness in the present, allows the suggestion that such a 'primitive' quality as expressed in the poem will manifest itself through a 'defamiliarized' treatment of material, including literary material, to form 'new wholes': a practice of tradition (the Grail romances) reaching back, as in Weston's book, to anthropological, primitive, mythic roots. (During this period Eliot had been interested in, and impressed by, Stravinsky's *Rite of Spring*.) But the poem itself can also be seen as being akin to ritual in that it seeks to constitute and enact an impersonal, collective meaning, which as myth (or tradition) has intrinsic cohesion, and is to some extent hermetic, closed to external interpretation. Thus, within the drama of Eliot's intellectual development, the poem itself becomes the focus of an attempt to transcend the potential for solipsism that Eliot deduced from the isolation of the Bradleyan 'finite centre'.

However, tradition and myth are not equivalent, and problems will arise if the critic attempts to make them so. The stylistic problem that Eliot faced is that, unlike in *Ulysses* where Joyce's parallel of Bloom's peregrinations with the episodes of Odysseus's voyage allows a sequence of 'appropriate', if generally ironic, 'styles and symbols to each division', in *The Waste Land* Eliot is not basing his narrative structure upon the distinct episodes of the Grail legends, and therefore cannot rely on such narrative parallels for stylistic cohesion. Therefore, while these issues need to be discussed in relation to the text, before doing so we need to be a little more specific about the manner in which *The Waste Land* could stylistically be said to constitute a 'mythical method'. Here, Franco Moretti's illuminating comments on the analogies between Levi-Strauss's anthropological insights in *The Savage Mind* and Eliot's 'mythical method' provide a stimulating sociological overview on this aspect of the poem and a framework for further critical debate.[53]

Moretti bases his argument on the evidence provided by structural anthropology for the formal cohesion of myth. 'It seems worthwhile to specify the semantic peculiarity of myth in its ability to attest that between different orders (for example, the cosmic order, the cultural, zoological, meteorological, social . . .) there is a precise isomorphism . . . Each myth . . . must be considered as a veritable *intercode* destined to permit a reciprocal convertibility between the different levels.'[54] Moretti specifies Levi-Strauss's conviction, anticipated by the precocious Eliot, that 'Savage thought does not distinguish the moment of observation and that of interpretation' and sees Eliot's central intention as an attempt to 'heal the split between factual judgements and value-judgements' through the deployment of a 'mythical method', an intercode, that, with inordinate ambition, aims to be 'a way of controlling, of ordering, of giving a shape and significance to the immense panorama of futility and anarchy which is contemporary history'.[55] History and myth are therefore seen in diametrical opposition (while the analogy between myth as permitting a structural intercode and Joyce's use of the *Odyssey* in *Ulysses* is apparent).

The most immediate way we can discern this method at work in the poem is through its treatment of literary references, which Moretti perceptively allies with Levi-Strauss's observations on mythical 'bricolage': 'Mythical thought, that "bricoleur", builds up structures by fitting together events, or rather the remains of events . . . fossilized evidence of the history of an individual or society.'[56] Relating this to Eliot's 'two-sided' use of literary references, by which the reference is a 'fragment' in relation to its original literary context but a 'function' in relation to Eliot's text, Moretti comments

> *The Waste Land*'s construction therefore involves the reader in two simultaneous evaluations: on one hand, it makes history seem an accumulation of debris, a centrifugal and unintelligible process; on the other hand, it presents mythic structure as a point of suspension and reorganization of this endless fugue. Sense of history and faith in myth appear as inversely proportioned criteria for evaluation: the more senseless and directionless the past appears, the more will the eternal present of the myth be able to absorb every signifying capacity within itself. '. . . (I)t is always earlier ends', observes Levi-Strauss, 'which are called upon to play the part of means: the signified changes into the signifying. . .'[57]

At this point, we must demonstrate and analyse this effect in the poem itself. After the introductory passage of 'The Fire Sermon', where Eliot counterpoints the purity of Spenser's 'Prothalamion' against the squalor of the present day Thames, from line 187 a shadowy narrator is found 'fishing in the dull canal . . . Musing upon the king my brother's wreck/And on the king my father's death before him'.[58] The immediate reference to the Fisher King seems to include an oblique gesture towards fertility rituals by which the image of the drowned god would be taken out from the water to symbolize resurrection (spring); while in literary terms *The Tempest* is evoked, in which Ferdinand is discovered in Act I, scene ii,

> Sitting on a bank,
> Weeping again the King my father's wrack,
> This music crept by me upon the waters,
> Allaying both their fury and my passion
> With its sweet air . . .
>
> (ll. 392–6)

The music is Ariel's beautiful song, which provides an anticipation of the theme of restoration in the play through the idea of metamorphosis:

> Full fathom five thy father lies;
>   Of his bones are coral made;
> Those are pearls that were his eyes:

> Nothing of him that does fade,
> But doth suffer a sea-change
> Into something rich and strange.
> Sea-nymphs hourly ring his knell:
>
> > Burthen: Ding-dong.

Here, the literary context indicates that Eliot is dealing with the theme of resurrection or restoration in both sets of references: fertility rituals providing a basis for Shakespeare's romance theme, by which in the recognition scene that concludes the play, Ferdinand's father, Alonso, is reunited with his son. In Eliot's poem, however, no indication of (seasonal) resurrection or affective restoration is given:

> White bodies naked on the low damp ground
> And bones cast in a little low dry garret,
> Rattled by the rat's foot only, year to year.
> But at my back from time to time I hear
> The sound of horns and motors, which shall bring
> Sweeney to Mrs. Porter in the spring.
> O the moon shone bright on Mrs. Porter
> And on her daughter
> They wash their feet in soda water
> *Et O ces voix d'enfants, chantant dans la coupole!*

The first lines gain from an implicit contrast with Ariel's song: for no 'sea-change', metamorphosis or resurrection, occurs to the narrator's dry bones – this difference positing the gulf at this juncture between *The Tempest* and Eliot's text. The next lines refer to and parody, both Marvell's *carpe diem* poem, 'To His Coy Mistress' and *The Parliament of Bees*, a Renaissance play by John Day, which provides Sweeney's contemporary 'horns and motors' with a wonderfully wry heritage:

> 'When of the sudden, listening, you shall hear,
> A noise of horns and hunting, which shall bring
> Actaeon to Diana in the spring,
> Where all shall see her naked skin. . .'[59]

Actaeon (and relatedly, Eliot's burlesque version, the waiter in 'Dans le Restaurant') was turned into a stag and hunted to death as a punishment for seeing Diana, the goddess of chastity, bathing. Perhaps a similar fate awaits Sweeney, who is to make a spring visit to Mrs Porter, the madame of 'Sweeney Erect'. Mrs Porter was 'a legendary brothel-keeper in Cairo',[60] and Southam in his *Student's Guide* seems somewhat disingenuous in suggesting Eliot's ignorance both of this, and the other, obscene versions of the Australian camp-fire ballad. The final line of this passage is a quote from Verlaine's sonnet 'Parzifal' ('And O those children's voices, singing in the dome'), and functions as a reference to Wagner's opera as well as the relevant aspect of the Grail legend, where as Southam writes 'the choir of children sings at the ceremony of the foot-washing which precedes the restoration of the wounded Anfortas (the Fisher King) by the knight Parzifal and the lifting of the curse from the waste land.'[61]

While these lines achieve a mode of intellectual integration based on a reference back to fertility ritual which we can align within the terms of a 'mythical method' ('the signified changes into the signifying'), stylistically they derive their effect from sharp poetic and cultural disharmonies, enforced and emphasized by rhythmic contrast. The uneasy, parodic familiarity of 'But at my back from time to time I hear' dissolves into the grotesque assertiveness of the ballad rhythms, which are then held in disjunctive relation to Verlaine's line, where linguistic removal helps counterpoint the 'voix d'enfants' against the sordid events that precedes them. (The effect is an exact parallel to that employed in the second stanza of the excised poem 'Ode', where the interjection 'Children singing in the orchard', counterpoints by its intimation of innocence, the sterility of the events that surround it.)[62] These disharmonies serve to deprive the literary tradition of any sense of linear development or intrinsic coherence, and imply that this tradition exists in the present as a pot-pourri of subverted fragments, metamorphosed into 'something rich and strange' within the confines of Eliot's poem. These effects of formal dislocation are reinforced by the collation of culturally disparate source materials, which rather than being integrated into the verse texture of the poem, are allowed to co-exist in a state of dynamic disharmony, like exhibits in a grotesque *musée imaginaire*[63] of stylistic possibilities.

Thus, in so far as 'myth' can be held to function in Eliot's poem, it works by destabilizing not only history but literary history – tradition. This would confirm rather than conflict with Moretti's thesis, which I think is strongly persuasive as regards the intellectual aetiology of *The Waste Land* and Eliot's cultural and stylistic intentions. But the central critical issue remains largely unanswered: for despite Eliot's constant reference to a background of fertility ritual in the analysed lines, in textual terms Eliot's effects depend upon formal literary conjunctions, by which facts and values are not truly united, but values are generated implicitly, say, by the choice of Verlaine's line, which counterpoints the innocence of children 'singing in the dome' against the sordidness of Sweeney and Mrs Porter. Are we therefore dealing with a structural principle, a 'mythical method', or an artful deployment of non-discursive, presentative techniques? The question relates to more than just a choice of terminology, for it engages with the fundamental formal issues of *The Waste Land*: the riddle behind Eliot's enigmatic sphinx.

We, like the poem's first readers, are more inclined to see *The Waste Land* as an embodiment of, rather than an alternative to, cultural fragmentation. As the poem concludes it is difficult to see its central achievement as being that of transmuting both private experience and history into a larger mythic coherence. We can regard this as a necessary effect of the heterogeneity of, and disparity between, the various materials and systems of belief (pre-Christian animism; Christian asceticism; the pre-Buddhist, Brahminic *Upanishads*; and the Buddha's 'Fire Sermon') that Eliot gestures towards at the conclusion of the text; but more fundamentally we can see this fragmentation as the necessary function of a fissure within Eliot's employment of the 'mythical method' itself: a formal contradiction. Moretti elects the former, ideological alternative, and from the first tends to avoid the issue by not focusing in sufficiently specific terms on the myth of the Fisher King, which he assumes rather than demonstrates to be at work in the poem. Subsequently, he concedes that in comparison to the rigid combinatory logic of primitive myth, *The Waste Land*, written in a vastly different cultural situation and with an enormous diversity of cultural codes, was doomed to approximation.

> his undertaking could only emerge as some sort of compromise between the demands of the mythic *structure* and its constituent *materials*. *The Waste Land*'s irony – what little there is – consists precisely in recognizing that the purity of the mythic project can never be fully realized. Only to a certain extent do things tally in *The Waste Land*: all connections are questionable, all homologies transmute into analogies.[64]

Moretti's comments are reasonable as regards 'the mythic project' but approximate with regard to the poem itself, which requires that attention be shifted from the conceptual category of myth to the manner in which the mythic project is to be realized: that is Eliot's literary practice of Symbolism.

It is possible to engage with these issues by considering Moretti's comments on Madame Sosostris's fortune-telling, which he justifiably locates as central to the poem's formal method. 'On the fortune-teller's table, the ideal of a cyclical history takes on exemplary form. Characters, situations, developments find themselves existing in a configuration dominated by *simultaneity*: one card under another, or next to another.'[65] This spatial mode (a means of 'reversing the temporal flow into spatial terms'), as exemplified by the Tarot pack, Moretti regards as integral to, and emblematic of the poem's formal method, commenting,

> The fact that, in *The Waste Land* this aspiration is revealed through a charlatan's empty words must not mislead: in spite of the surface irony, as Cleanth Brooks has observed with great precision: '. . . all the central symbols of the poem head up here . . . and the "fortune-telling", which is taken ironically by a twentieth-century audience, becomes *true* as the poem develops . . .' When all is said, in *The Waste Land* superstition comes true.[66]

But does it? If we examine the passage itself, it is apparent that effect and intention are pulling apart – but within themselves, not just in relation to each other. The overall effect (and implicit intention) of the passage is satiric, and can be related forwards to Eliot's dry comments on those who 'describe the horoscope, haruspicate or scry . . .' in section V of 'The Dry Salvages' in *Four Quartets*. Madame Sosostris, whose probable prototype was the theosophist Madame Blavatsky, with whom Yeats was associated, is indeed a charlatan with 'a wicked pack of cards'; but equally, and more troublingly in terms of the forthcoming text, the general literary intention to deploy the central symbols of the poem, is also achieved through the clairvoyante's 'empty' words. Here, Cleanth Brooks's

New Critical terminology of 'surface irony' is inadequate to get to grips with what is happening in the poem, and leads to his and Moretti's partial and apologetic conclusion that here 'true' Mysteries are dispensed by Madame Sosostris, albeit in debased circumstances: 'superstition comes true'. But if we refer to the original drafts of the poem, we discover that Eliot had interpolated a single line, 'I John saw these things, and heard them',[67] from the beatific vision that concludes the Revelation of St John the Divine, between the line 'I see crowds of people, walking round in a ring' and Madame Sosostris's concluding 'Thank you', suggesting by this atemporal counterpointing with the apocalyptic Book of Revelations that a satiric and spiritual judgement on such secular, societal superstitions was integral to Eliot's intentions. Here, therefore, the issues must be grounded at the level of formal method.

Eliot's use of symbolism in this passage and elsewhere in the poem needs to be placed within the history of Symbolist poetics reaching back to Baudelaire, and in particular referred to his notion of *correspondances*, of which Walter Benjamin comments,

> the *correspondances* record a concept of experience which includes ritual elements. Only by appropriating these elements was Baudelaire able to fathom the full meaning of the breakdown which he, a modern man, was witnessing. . . . What Baudelaire meant by *correspondances* may be described as an experience which seeks to establish itself in crisis-proof form. If it transcends this realm, it presents itself as the beautiful. In the beautiful the ritual value of art appears.[68]

At this point in his career Eliot was closer to Baudelaire than to any contemporary poet, and Benjamin's insights deserve to be read *in toto* for the oblique light they shed on Eliot's work; but here it is only necessary to indicate the genealogy of this concept, which as Benjamin suggests came to Baudelaire as 'the common property of the mystics; Baudelaire encountered them in Fourier's writings'.[69]

In the development of Symbolist poetics there can be seen to be a tension between overlapping and not entirely compatible definitions of 'the symbol': the first, which is dominant in practice if not in theory, is the symbol as a material 'objective correlative' for an emotion and/or idea in the mind of the poet; the second, associated with what is often termed as transcendental Symbolism, regards the symbol, as exemplified in the poem, as intimating the existence of an ideal realm to which the material only relates on the level of 'correspondences'. This vein of philosophic idealism reaches back through the mystic Swedenborg and can be traced back to Plato. In Baudelaire's poetry the *correspondances* offer hints of an ideal world of essences, often seen as lost in the past, but evoked in the present through symbolism and hypnotic, incantatory verse rhythms. The appeal is to the completeness of a lost ritual, a wholeness of experience; as Benjamin remarks, 'The *correspondances* are the data of remembrance – not historical data, but data of prehistory.'[70]

The distance between Baudelaire, who stood at the threshold of Symbolist poetics, and Eliot, who wrote *The Waste Land* at a point of historical culmination and crisis (the next major English poet to emerge, in the late 1920s, was the non-Symbolist W. H. Auden) can be measured by Eliot's relatively arbitrary and sceptical deployment of symbolism in this passage. While the mythic project itself attests to the temperamental and intellectual affinities between Eliot and Baudelaire, any intimation of the ideal seems to be embodied more in the excised line from St John of the Cross than in Madame Sosostris's mysteries, which in their poetic situation are far more defined and limited than Baudelaire's *correspondances*. By the excision of the line from St John Eliot has, as it were, closed the door on the transcendent; and failing any underlying system of meanings, Madame Sosostris's Tarot symbols are precisely 'literary' symbols, which are presented and formally validated in the course of the poem, having been sharply ironized and undercut in their initial presentation. Here, irony, even in its 'unstable' variations (terms which comprehend most of the effects in *Ulysses*) is a term that is inadequate to describe an effect which – given that the satiric and realist level undermines the metaphoric and symbolic – goes beyond irony into inherent methodological contradiction. To express the same more theoretically in the structural terminology developed by Jakobson and employed by Lodge, the *metonymic*, realist level of the text, which proceeds by contiguity, is simultaneous with, and contradicts the *metaphoric*, Symbolist level of the text in all its subsequent transformations.

The resulting structural ambivalence of Eliot's text causes a formal uneasiness which we can articulate around the question of the literal or purely literary status of Eliot's symbols and mythic motifs. But the text itself, as Moretti suggests, attempting to 'order' history through the simultaneity of a 'mythical method' does not allow us to choose either option. We are obliged at once to discredit the symbols as arbitrary ('Here is the man with three staves, and here the Wheel') in line with the sceptical intelligence which led Eliot to comment coolly in his Notes, 'I am not familiar with the exact constitution of the Tarot pack of cards, from which I have obviously departed to suit my own convenience . . .',[71] and yet to endorse them by a 'willing suspension of disbelief' as the text legitimates them in its metaphoric development. Here, the most pertinent comparison is with the work of W. B. Yeats, who was able to negotiate the accusation that his use of the 'system' embodied in *A Vision* was no more than the exploitation of a 'creative fiction' by his wholehearted commitment to a subjectivist Romantic aesthetic. Eliot, however, was deeply suspicious of subjectivism.

The same fundamental issue recurs in relation to Eliot's 'Note' on Tiresias:

> Tiresias, although a mere spectator and not indeed a 'character', is yet the most important personage in the poem, uniting all the rest. Just as the one-eyed merchant seller of currants, melts into the Phoenician sailor, and the latter is not wholly distinct from Ferdinand Prince of Naples, so all the women are one woman, and the two sexes meet in Tiresias.[72]

Once again, the diachronic 'realist' movement of the text and the diversity of its 'characters' are sacrificed to symbolic, metaphoric equivalences, and again a formal unease is manifested as we are asked to cancel one element in what seems, and what it seems should be, an intrinsically contradictory response. Stephen Spender comments revealingly on how, in the 1920s, undergraduates received the poem as, like Proust's *Sodom and Gomorrah*, Broch's *Sleepwalkers* and Spengler's *Decline of the West*, reflecting contemporary cultural and political realities: '. . . *The Waste Land* was exciting in the first place because it was concerned with a life we felt to be real. It carried the equipment of the world beyond the screen, a landscape across which armies and refugees moved.'[73] The unease is apparent when Spender notes the reluctance to comply with the reading suggested by Eliot, by which the Phoenician sailor is 'a symbol to be equated with other symbols'. 'The fact that this section of the poem is a translation of an earlier poem of Eliot's, written in French, confirms the suspicion that the linking-up is an arbitrary cinematic effect like a "fade-in". We saw the Phoenician Sailor as the Phoenician Sailor.'[74] The congruence of Eliot's poem with the culturally pessimistic texts Spender mentions above serves to indicate the profound contemporary resonance of *The Waste Land*; while Eliot himself seems to court this historical focus by his citation from Hesse's *Blick ins Chaos* ('Already half of Europe, already at least half of Europe, [is] on the way to Chaos . . .') as a commentary upon the 'hooded hordes' of 'What the Thunder Said'.[75] Of course, Spender's remarks do not resolve an irresolvable issue, but they do suggest the fundamental structural tensions within the method of the poem.

Thus, rather than seeing the text as exhibiting the formal unity of a 'mythical method' we have a text that is fissured at its base. The problems that result, which remain latent throughout the first four sections (partly because, as was indicated, the overall presentative effect of the text was accentuated by Pound's editing) surface unambiguously in the concluding section. Symbolism, as a literary creed, presumes a basis in mysticism and leans towards philosophic idealism in suggesting an immaterial world of ideas and *correspondances*; Eliot's realistic, sceptical and satiric impulses undercut this 'irrational' basis and set up tensions which eventually fragment the surface of the poem. In 'What the Thunder Said', it is crucial that a shadowy protagonist, who can be discerned as an implicit presence in the preceding sections (particularly 'The Fire Sermon') to some degree emerges for our scrutiny. Although this protagonist remains austerely depersonalized, almost entirely denied the definition of a first person pronoun, and projected solely in terms of solitary pilgrimage and consequent visionary experience, the emergence of a protagonist in itself renews and engages with the problems centred upon the limitation of individual perception in relation to a text that wishes to totalize its meanings in line with a 'mythical method'. If we attend to the linguistic, formal surface of Eliot's text (rather than the sequence of references that can be used to naturalize its meanings) what we find is a poem that in its concluding passages increasingly interrogates and ironizes its own method and meanings.

If we follow the poem from 'Who is the third who walks always beside you?' (line 359), we can trace these issues as they develop, and also discern Eliot's ambiguous gestures towards their resolution. Initially no strain is evinced: the 'third' could be Christ on the journey to Emmaus, or an experience of the explorers on one of Shackleton's expeditions – it does not matter which, the implications are compatible, and we have been prepared by the paratactic formal modes of the preceding lines for visionary experience. The quester, or voice, moves beyond the temporal Cities of the Plain ('Jerusalem Athens Alexandria/Vienna London') which are succinctly and dismissively designated 'Unreal'. The following passage, based on one of the earliest lyric fragments contained in the manuscripts of the poem, introduces an hallucinatory heightening of perception, reminiscent of the details in a canvas by Hieronymus Bosch, leading to what we would expect to be the climax, but which turns out to be the anti-climax of 'the empty chapel, only the wind's home'. We can, if we wish, align the chapel with the Chapel Perilous of the Grail legends, which could to some degree authorize the lack of response; but here the analogies with the Grail legends seem too tenuous to permit a convincing integration. Rather, as the chapel is presented as both empty and sterile ('Dry bones can harm no one') it seems as valid to suggest that failing the intervention of a personal, providential deity, Eliot reverts to what in Western terms is a less culturally specific renunciatory conclusion based on some lines in the Sanskrit *Upanishads*, which he had studied while at Harvard in 1912. But while the renunciatory aspect of Buddhism is central to Eliot's investment in these lines, it should be remembered that he had studied Buddhism for a year at Harvard, and his interest at this point of his development was, as indicated by the central section of the poem, 'The Fire Sermon', more than simply academic.

The 'freeing of the waters', an important motif in the fertility rites underlying the Grail legends, is first adumbrated, 'Then a damp gust/Bringing rain'; but the rain has not yet arrived when the thunder 'speaks' in single terms, 'DA', interpreted as the three injunctions of the *Upanishads* which Eliot renders as 'Give, sympathize, control'. However, the response these injunctions elicit from the voice of the poem is crucially negative, both in terms of an admission of failure to comply with the modes of being enjoined by the thunder, and, by implication, subtly subversive of the impersonalizing formal ambitions of the previous text.

'*Datta*: what have we given?' – the injunction becomes an interrogation – and elicits an admission of the 'awful daring of a moment's surrender/Which an age of prudence can never retract', where the sense of almost involuntary self-surrender is implicitly sexual, and contrary to the sustained compassionate giving suggested by the Sanskrit command. The central command '*Dayadhvam*' – sympathize – elicits an assertion of the prison of the self, which as a reality of isolation runs counter to the sympathy demanded by the thunder:

> *Dayadhvam*: I have heard the key
> Turn in the door once and turn once only
> We think of the key, each in his prison
> Thinking of the key, each confirms a prison
> Only at nightfall, aethereal rumours
> Revive for a moment a broken Coriolanus

If we attend to the allusions Eliot employs, the 'self' is first associated with Dante's Ugolino, who 'heard the key/Turn in the door once' when he was locked into the tower in which he and his sons and grandsons starved to death, and then with Coriolanus, the unconquerable patrician general, who wished to behave 'As if a man were author of himself/And knew no other kin' (V. iii. ll. 36–7). Both characters are instances of deluded selfhood: Ugolino in his hatred, Coriolanus in his pride; but here beyond refusing separation from these exempla, the hesitant voice of the poem actually seems to work to naturalize and universalize its meanings. As in the previous lines, we move from the limited and personal, 'I have heard the key', to the generalized and impersonal 'each confirms a prison/Only at nightfall'. It seems almost as if the text itself refuses recuperation and ironization through its allusions, and here more than ever we have the sense of a private response straining within and almost subverting the mediation of 'tradition'. Then, in what is one of the most significant citations given in Eliot's 'Notes', he quotes Bradley from *Appearance and Reality*; a citation which is not required by the verse but which gains in significance from a knowledge of Eliot's intellectual development:

> My external sensations are no less private to my self than are my thoughts or my feelings. In either case my experience falls within my own circle, a circle closed on the outside; and, with all its elements alike, every sphere is opaque to the others which surround it . . . In brief, regarded as an existence which appears in a soul, the whole world for each soul is peculiar and private to that soul.[76]

'Perhaps this is only a statement of a usual idealistic position, but never has it been put in a form so extreme',[77] Eliot had remarked of the same passage in an article on 'Leibniz's Monads and Bradley's Finite Centres' in *The Monist* of October 1916 – and yet it is this extreme formulation that Eliot chose to deploy in the poem of 1922. As Eliot's concept of tradition had developed out of Bradley and as a means of transcending the potential for solipsism Eliot perceived as inherent in Bradley's epistemology, this citation from Bradley on the intrinsic isolation of the private self reads as an austere counterpoint to the aspiration towards impersonality implicit both in the concept of tradition and relatedly the formal pursuit of a 'mythical method'. Accepting that we cannot elide the voice of the poem with the voice of the poet, at this point it seems we are emphatically and movingly returned to hermetic subjectivity, the windowless monad of the private self, while the citation from Bradley leaves us in some doubt whether it is possible even with 'sympathy' to transcend this reality of isolation. This austere emphasis is extended through the final injunction: '*Damyata*' – control – which in the original implies self-control. Here, through the use of reiterated conditionals it is used to suggest a relationship which failed to reach fruition; and in the final lines, where 'your heart', like the boat, is seen as 'beating obedient/To controlling hands', it is difficult to avoid the semantic presence of an authoritarian implication, which it would be interesting to know how far the poet intended or was aware of.

Thus, at this, the intellectual and affective culmination of the poem we are given three overwhelmingly negative responses to the sequence of renunciatory commands. Thematically, we can integrate this episode with the Grail schema by arguing that rather than, at the culmination of the quest failing to put the right questions, the voice of Eliot's poem, as quester, gives the wrong responses, in the sense of admitting a failure to comply with the modes recommended by the thunder. This would be a suitably laconic reversal of the Grail pattern, which could endorse the failure of the quest and the continuance of the waste land. However, it is difficult to eradicate the impression of a personal, private response being mediated through what seems an implicitly distanced relation to the sources and the 'objectifying' techniques that, as references, they embody. This private response seems to strain within, and as a mode of sceptical disengagement, to destabilize and put in question the impersonalizing 'mythic' techniques and ambitions of the previous text, which here seem to function precisely as modes of 'recuperation'.

At this point, in the manuscripts and the published poem, the text fractures. In the original manuscript, what seems implicit in the finished poem is made explicit: that a 'dialogue' breaks off ('I left without you') and the concluding verse paragraph seems to resume by gesturing us back, however uncertainly, to the solitary lyric self, 'I sat upon the shore/Fishing, with the arid plain behind me . . .' The reference to the Fisher King oscillates between uncertainty and playfulness (but the rain promised by the approach of the thunder has not remained if ever it arrived); the 'arid plain' has been traversed, it is 'behind me' (but the only resolution, failing any sense of collectivity, seems to pertain to the private self): 'Shall I at least set my lands in order?' – where the stress seems to fall on the private and personal 'my', and reads almost as a version of 'tending one's own garden'. The concluding collocation of fragments seems at once a recapitulation and extension of the 'method' of the poem and at the same time a retrospective critique. It is unnecessary to provide a detailed critique of each constituent line to discern that this cryptic mosaic of references enacts the formal dilemma of Eliot's text. Are they functions in a new discourse which attains unity through a 'mythical method' or a collection of largely private references, of which Eliot's 'own' line provides the explicit and devastating criticism: 'These fragments I have shored against my ruins'? Are we, in other words gestured back to the closed, private self, as against the transcendence of the 'individual talent' in 'tradition'?

In his essay on 'Andrew Marvell' (1921), Eliot defined the quality of Marvell's wit as an 'alliance of levity and seriousness (by which the seriousness is intensified)',[78] a description which applies well to the conclusion of his own poem, where the children's rhyme 'London bridge is falling down' is used to intimate the collapse of the temporal city before we move to the gravity of the subsequent references, which gesture towards the state of purgatorial remorse and the possibility of spiritual renewal. The following, central reference is a line from Gerald de Nerval's sonnet 'El Desdichado' ('The Disinherited'), the opening stanza of which runs:

Je suis le ténébreux, – le veuf, – l'inconsolé,
Le prince d'Aquitaine à la tour abolie:

Ma seule étoile est morte, – et mon luth constellé
Porte le soleil noir de la Mélancholie.[79]*

De Nerval's sonnet was important to the development of transcendental symbolism, and here the poet presents himself as the disinherited prince of Aquitaine, heir to the 'tour abolie', the ruined or suppressed tradition of the troubadour poets. Eliot's own line, 'These fragments I have shored against my ruins', both concentrates and extends the issues. Do we move beyond the self in the poet's practice of 'tradition', or is that tradition itself largely self-created, a 'tour abolie', an aspiration that dignifies a deployment of literary referents that function as cryptic notations to the poet's private concerns, while as 'fragments' having no necessary commerce with their original literary contexts or the poet's personal 'ruins' against which they are merely 'shored'?

Eliot leaves the issues open. The subsequent, concluding line, yoking together two distinct references to Kydd's *The Spanish Tragedy* suggests levels of meaning and concealment in the previous text that Eliot, as Hieronymo, will not, or cannot, reveal to his audience. The sub-title of the play is *Hieronymo is Mad Againe*, and in the central scenes Hieronymo has been driven to madness by desire for justice and revenge on the murderers of his son, Horatio. But at the point where he agrees to supply a court entertainment in the quoted words 'Why then Ile fit you', he is merely feigning mad; for his play, made up from bits of verse in 'sundry languages' is to be made the occasion for the assassination of the murderers of his son. Balthazar, who is to be killed, demurs 'But this will be mere confusion,/And hardly shall we all be understood', but Hieronymo, with grim proleptic irony assures him that 'the conclusion/Shall prove the invention and all was good . . .' (Act IV, scene i, ll. 180–4). At the dénouement of the play, having executed his revenge and explained in detail its circumstances and purpose to the court, Hieronymo bites out his tongue rather than 'reveal/The thing which I have vowed inviolate' (Act IV, scene iv, ll. 187–8). This action has always remained a critical puzzle, since ostensibly Hieronymo has nothing left to explain. Here Catherine Belsey offers the intriguing suggestion that the only real question left unanswered is whether Hieronymo's revenge has any metaphysical sanction: 'He bites out his tongue to conceal what the subject of humanism is compelled to banish from its knowledge and therefore from its utterance, the absent legitimation of its own actions.'[80] Noting Eliot's gift for the profoundly appropriate literary reference, the conclusion of *The Spanish Tragedy* can be seen to offer a sequence of ironic parallels with the conclusion of Eliot's poem, in which in formal terms he too could be seen to mimic 'an antic disposition': almost wilfully drawing attention to the personal and private application of his impersonalizing literary techniques. The reiteration of the injunction 'Datta. Dayadhvam. Damyata.' enjoins modes of renunciation that are inscribed rather than complied with or confirmed in the text; and the concluding words 'Shantih shantih shantih', glossed by Eliot in his Notes as 'a formal

---

* I am the shadow, – the widower, – the unconsoled, the Aquitanian prince with the ruined tower: my only star is dead, – and my constellated lute carries the black sun of Melancholy.

ending to an Upanishad. ''The Peace which passeth understanding'' is our equivalent to this word' seem ironically appropriate as the strictly formal conclusion to a set of unconcluded formal issues. We remain unsure, among the Babel-like tumult of competing idioms that conclude Eliot's text, how far these words suggest 'The Peace which passeth understanding', how far a state of personal and cultural exhaustion.

Thus, both as 'myth' and 'tradition' the text must be seen as enacting (and in this sense of enactment going beyond) its own failure to transcend the private, personal bases of post-Romantic art. This inability to transcend Romantic subjectivity seems intrinsic to the formal modes of the concluding lines, where by foregrounding we are almost forcibly made aware of techniques that bestow an effect of impersonality on what are, in the final passages of the poem, implicitly personal and private perceptions. So, rather than a timeless, spatial impersonality, suitable to a 'mythical method', or an integration of the self within the tradition, we are left with a poem that returns us to a personal but ironically mediated lyricism. This, however, is not an argument for the aesthetic failure of the work, but rather a testimony to the scale of its ambitions. Unarguably the poem succeeds as literature; and here it should be stressed that it is precisely those structural contradictions (rather than ironies and ambiguities) which ensure its continuing challenge, and which need to be looked to for the site of further fruitful readings. Efforts to read *The Waste Land* as a unified text operate an intellectual closure on this most fractured and fragmentary of Symbolist poems. In terms of the central line of Anglo-American criticism, that represented by Cleanth Brooks's New Critical insights, this effort can be seen as an attempt to promote what John Feteke terms a 'telos of harmonic integration'[81] in the face of disintegrative social and historical realities.

Finally, I think these issues need to be referred back to the inherent, and eventually explicit tensions and potential fissures within Symbolist aesthetics and literary practice. Here, it is only possible to indicate the area within which such a debate would occur by posing the question whether Eliot's literary practice in *The Waste Land* is more meaningfully seen as being Symbolist (whatever definition is given) or as being fundamentally allegoric. Perhaps indeed Symbolism itself, dominated as it is by modes of association, notional *correspondances*, and personal 'objective correlatives', is allegoric, in the sense that failing a Classical mode of authority it is doomed to mediate a private idea and/or emotion of the poet. The mode I wish to suggest, that of allegories of loss and remembrance can be epitomized by some lines from Baudelaire's 'Le Cygne' ('The Swan') in which referring to the rebuilding of the Louvre, he writes:

> Paris change! mais rien dans ma mélancolie
> N'a bougé! palais neufs, échafaudages, blocs,
> Vieux faubourgs, tout pour moi devient allégorie,
> Et mes chers souvenirs sont plus lourds que des rocs,[82]*

---

* Paris is changing! but nothing in my melancholy has shifted! new palaces, scaffoldings, blocks of stone, old suburbs − everything becomes allegory for me, and my treasured memories are heavier than rocks.

In the concluding chapter of *The Origin of German Tragic Drama* (originally entitled *Ursprung des deutschen Trauerspiels*), Walter Benjamin remarks that 'Allegories are, in the realm of thoughts, what ruins are in the realm of things.'[83] Here, the critic's elegant and profound axiom has a bearing on his own literary practice, in which he, like Eliot, deployed literary 'fragments' in meaningful dialectical relations, as well as providing a potentially interesting complex of perspectives on the *Trauerspiel* of Eliot's great poem.

The Waste Land can be seen as both the aesthetic triumph and decisive intellectual *impasse* of Eliot's early development. If the 'mythical method' seemed to suggest a means 'of controlling, of ordering, of giving a shape and a significance to the immense panorama of futility and anarchy which is contemporary history', then any such belief in a literary 'ordering' seems to be cruelly disappointed at the end of the poem. Therefore, in so far as *The Waste Land* serves as an example of the heroic phase of early Modernism, a product of the belief that a capitalized Art could transcend what Lewis termed 'the subjectivity of the majority',[84] it belongs with the related Modernist achievements of the other 'Men of 1914' and indicates both the scale of their ambitions and the historic partiality of their understanding of their position. It is no accident that Eliot's early period culminated and concluded with the publication of *The Waste Land* in 1922, and that his next major poetry, *Ash-Wednesday*, published some eight years subsequently, was in conservative Symbolist modes which are formally and ideologically distinct from those of his period of co-operation with Pound. Henceforth, Eliot was to look to other means than that of a 'mythical method' to integrate the 'individual talent' and 'tradition'; which requires us to look to *Ash-Wednesday* and the place assumed in that poem by the figure of Dante.

9
Dante and *Ash-Wednesday*

'– nil nisi divinum stabile est; caetera fumus –', epigraph to 'Burbank with a Baedeker: Bleistein with a Cigar'

Eliot wrote in his 1929 'Dante' essay, 'The majority of poems one outgrows and outlives, as one outgrows and outlives the majority of human passions: Dante's is one of those which one can only just hope to grow up to at the end of life.'[1] In the following chapter I will examine the manner in which rather than having a fixed significance for Eliot, his interest in, and reliance upon the *Commedia* evolved in accordance with the development of his own intellectual commitments and poetic aims. The chronological leap from *The Waste Land* (1922) to *Ash-Wednesday* (1930) takes us beyond Eliot's entry into the Anglican Church in 1927, and allows us to examine the effect of this decision upon his poetry, and, in particular, the alignment between 'the individual talent' and 'tradition' it helped him to achieve.

In a talk given in 1950, 'What Dante means to Me', Eliot made a statement which is relevant to his use of Dantean allusion up to and including *The Waste Land*: 'I have borrowed lines from him, in the attempt to reproduce, or rather to arouse in the reader's mind the memory of some Dantesque scene, and thus to establish a relationship between the mediaeval inferno and modern life.'[2] This parallel between the mediaeval inferno and modern urban life deserves further consideration. On a fairly superficial level, but one that cannot be discounted, this is employing literary tradition to impose a tendentious analogy: using the literary past to condemn a debased present. This function is demonstrated, if obliquely, as early as 'The Love Song of J. Alfred Prufrock', where the epigraph giving Guido de Montefeltro's words from his eternally fixed condition in Hell establishes an undertow of high seriousness that works within Prufrock's burlesque testimony of his own condition, and allows the reader to realize that he too is 'fixed' and damned. But in the satiric *Poems* of 1920 and *The Waste Land* this analogy is strengthened until it attains the status of an equation. Such a condemnation of contemporary urban civilization is implicit within the first major allusion to Dante we meet in *The Waste Land*.

> Unreal city,
> Under the brown fog of a winter dawn,
> A crowd flowed over London Bridge, so many,
> I had not thought death had undone so many.
> Sighs, short and infrequent, were exhaled,
> And each man fixed his eyes before his feet.[3]

Here, as Eliot's 'Notes' inform us, two brief sections from Cantos III and IV of the *Inferno* are run together to construct an artificial quotation in which the workers of the City of London are equated with Dante's 'Neutrals' and the souls in Limbo, who are excluded from the punishment of Hell proper.

The fact that the quotation is artificial, an imposed reference at the beginning of a passage which employs intentional incongruities (the city crowds are, of course, not literally 'dead'), opens up the second, more interesting aspect of Eliot's use of Dante prior to *Ash-Wednesday*: his exploitation of literary tradition to induce an effect of formal dislocation in his verse. This too has its social implications, in that, as previously suggested, the explosion of the literary past into shards of obtrusive 'voices' and discontinuous fragments implies a radical failure of 'tradition' to contribute meaning and coherence to the present. Towards the conclusion of 'The Fire Sermon' Eliot's second major allusion to Dante can be used to demonstrate such techniques of formal dislocation. After the deceptively slight lyric 'The river sweats/Oil and tar', a voice emerges:

> 'Trams and dusty trees.
> Highbury bore me. Richmond and Kew
> Undid me. By Richmond I raised my knees
> Supine on the floor of a narrow canoe.'

> 'My feet are at Moorgate, and my heart
> Under my feet. After the event
> He wept. He promised "a new start."
> I made no comment. What should I resent?'[4]

These lines adapt La Pia's brief and poignant testimony in Canto V of the *Purgatorio*: 'ricorditi di me che son la Pia/Siena mi fe; disfecemi Maremma . . .'[5]* to construct a painful vignette of sexual exploitation. (All we know of La Pia is that she was supposed to have been imprisoned by her husband in the Maremma and murdered in order that he might remarry.) Eliot has noted the striking phrase, and has superbly adapted Dante's device of using place as a substitute for events: the curt, unexpressive precision of the place-names underlines the confused, arbitrary nature of the seduction he records. Moreover, the tone of the unnamed speaker in Eliot's monologue, passive and unresentful, 'My people humble people who expect/Nothing', is consistent with La Pia's resigned tone in the *Purgatorio*. This creative adaptation is successful despite the fact that Eliot's lines do not relate

---

* 'do you remember me, who am La Pia. Siena gave me birth; Maremma death . . .'

themselves directly and overtly to their source. Rather, Eliot is exploiting a literary echo, an exploitation that works well because the implicit formal discontinuity reinforces the sense of experiential disjunction which characterizes the speaker's testimony:

> 'On Margate Sands.
> I can connect
> Nothing with nothing.

Even the punctuation, where the period is largely supererogatory, drives home this lack of connection.

A central aspect of Eliot's early interest in, and use of Dante, is implicit in this particular allusion: Dante's dramatic presentation of the essence of character through speech patterns. In the 1929 'Dante' essay Eliot states that he was 'first convinced' of Dante's quality by certain intensely dramatic episodes in the *Inferno*, including those of Brunetto Latini, Ulysses, Bertrand de Born and Ugolino; and he describes the experience of a first reading of the *Inferno* in these terms: 'Proceeding through the *Inferno* on a first reading, we get a succession of phantasmagoric but clear images, of images which are coherent, in that each reinforces the last; of individuals made memorable by a perfect phrase'.[6] Howarth, in his *Notes on Some Figures Behind T. S. Eliot* informs us that an initial direct immersion in the verse was the usual method of approaching Dante during Eliot's period at Harvard,[7] and this would tend to give a formative impression, at least of the *Inferno*, as a sequence of powerful, vivid monologues. This aspect of the *Commedia* must have immediately appealed to Eliot, with his interest in the dramatic monologue, and developing interest in poetic drama. Indeed, in relation to the method of *The Waste Land*, with its *mélange* of evanescent voices, it seems apparent that even though this method was not drawn directly from Dante, it was the dramatic element in Dante's work which Eliot was most aware of, and responsive to, in the immediate post-war period. The initial drafts of *The Waste Land* contain far more dramatic variation than the published version; and it is worth recollecting, in particular, the lengthy monologue narrative which begins the 'Death by Water' section, a passage which Eliot admitted was 'rather inspired' by the Ulysses Canto. In the 'Dante' essay, it is the dramatic element in the Ulysses episode that Eliot particularly commends as against Tennyson's poem: 'The story of Ulysses, as told by Dante, reads like a straightforward piece of romance, a well-told seaman's yarn; Tennyson's Ulysses is primarily a very self-conscious poet.'[8]

The final reference to the *Commedia* to be found in *The Waste Land* can be used to epitomize Eliot's formal employment of the literary past at this stage in his development. In the cacophony of voices with which the poem concludes, Eliot inserts the line which follows Arnaut Daniel's injunction to Dante to remember his purgatorial suffering: 'Poi s'ascose nel foco che gli affina' – 'Then he dived back into the fire that refines them'. Inserted between a children's rhyme, which is used to intimate the collapse of the temporal city, and a line from an anonymous Latin poem, the 'Pervigilium Veneris', which translates as 'When shall I be as the swallow', Dante's line, taken from an episode which preoccupied Eliot, points towards a complex of associations centred upon the idea of 'turning' and purgatorial remorse, which were only to be fully explicated and explored with the distant publication of *Ash-Wednesday*. Here, the line retains little immediate sense of its original context and functions aesthetically as a cryptic private notation. It is a detached, free-floating shard of meaning, which we presume has great personal significance for the poet, but remains as only one idiom among the mosaic of fragments that jostle together at the conclusion of *The Waste Land*.

As the Arnaut Daniel motif in Eliot's early and middle period is as significant as, and almost a counterpart to, the complex of associations centred around the experience of 'the bewildering minute' (from the lines in *The Revenger's Tragedy*) it requires some critical attention. Eliot had been fascinated by the relevant passage in the *Purgatorio* from an early date (Gordon informs us that 'Poi s'ascose nel foco che gli affina' was to have been the original epigraph to 'Prufrock'),[9] and the manner in which Eliot's treatment of the motif develops between the publication of *The Waste Land* and *Ash-Wednesday* can illuminate formal differences in Eliot's later poetry. The passage itself is to be found at the conclusion of Canto XXVI, in which, on the highest terrace of Purgatory, Dante meets the penitents of lust, before he himself passes through the flames that surround and guard Eden, where, after parting with Virgil, he will be led to Beatrice. This particular Canto continues and rounds out Dante's investigation of his own art, by having Dante meet, at this climactic point, Guido Guinicelli, the Bolognese poet who was a crucial formative influence on Dante's love poetry, and upon the 'dolce stil novo' (sweet new style) referred to by Bonagiunta in Canto XXIV, of which Dante and Cavalcanti were the most notable practitioners. However, on hearing Dante's warm praise Guinicelli points out Arnaut Daniel, the Provençal poet, as a 'miglior fabbro del parlar materno' ('better craftsman of the mother tongue'), a compliment used by Eliot to praise Pound in the epigraph dedication of *The Waste Land*. Dante approaches the still unnamed poet and enquires courteously as to his identity, whereupon Daniel responds in his native Provençal.

> 'Tan m'abellis vostre cortes deman,
> qu'ieu no me puese ni voill a vos cobrire.
> Ieu sui Arnaut, que plor e vau cantan;
> consiros vei la passada folor,
> e vie jausen lo joi qu'esper, denan.
> Ara vos prec, per acquella valor
> que vos guida al som de l'escalina,
> sovenha vos a temps de ma dolor!'
> Poi s'ascose nel foco che li affina.[10]*

---

* 'So much does your courteous question please me that I neither can nor would conceal myself from you. I am Arnaut, who weep and sing as I go. I see with grief past follies and see, rejoicing, the day I hope for before me. Now I beg of you, by the goodness that guides you to the summit of the stairway, to take thought in due time for my pain.' Then he hid himself in the fire that refines them. [translated Sinclair]

Here private experience and the public practice of poetry are linked in a representation that has explicit pertinence for Dante, who is 'purged' by the fire in the next Canto, and also for the modern poet, whose fleeting reference to the passage at the close of *The Waste Land* has significance almost in inverse proportion to its brevity. Before citing them in *The Waste Land*, Eliot had used these lines to provide the title of his 1919 collection of quatrain poems, *Ara Vos Prec* (misspelt as *Ara Vus Prec* because Eliot's edition of Dante misspelt the Provençal), and they are directly employed in an interesting quatrain lyric 'Exequy', which Eliot had originally intended to publish with *The Waste Land*. (In late January 1922, Pound 'succesfully urged Eliot' to drop the three closing lyrics of the Lausanne draft, 'Song', 'Dirge' and 'Exequy' – all three of which can be examined in the facsimile edition of *The Waste Land*.)[11]

In 'Exequy', the speaker, represented as a Don Juan, a successful sexual hedonist, imagines himself as becoming after his death 'a local deity of love'; but when one 'more violent, more profound' than his vacuous neophytes comes to his 'suburban tomb' and falls

> Self-immolating on the mound
> Just at the crisis, he shall hear
> A breathless chuckle underground
> SOVEGNA VOS A(L) TEMPS DE MON DOLOR
> Consiros vei la passada folor.*

Both formally and tonally, this poem belongs with the more successful quatrain poems: a tense balance is struck between the satiric, cynical introductory stanzas, and the mordant, disturbing grimness of the conclusion, creating an impression which owes as much to Edgar Allan Poe as to Dante's purgatorial remorse. Such devices of ironic distancing (the poem cannot be read as personal statement, and it foregrounds its own derivativeness and self-conscious use of melodrama) present us with a formal contrast both with the manner in which these lines are employed in *The Waste Land* – where Eliot seems to wish to evoke rather than explain the motif – and with the manner in which these lines are employed in section IV of *Ash-Wednesday*, where the brief invocation of Daniel's words generates a fresh sequence of nuances in Eliot's poem.

But at this point, rather than going directly to the relevant lines in *Ash-Wednesday*, it is necessary to consider the formal development of Eliot's poetry from a less particularized textual focus. The question of Eliot's relation to Dante reflects on the wider issue of the poet's relation to 'tradition', and requires an attempt to describe and define the aesthetic modes of the later poem, which in practice means that Eliot's debt to Dante in *Ash-Wednesday* must be approached through a discussion of his employment of, and reliance upon, the liturgy and sacred texts in general. The second section of this chapter is based on the premise that the modes of formal dislocation Eliot employs in *The Waste Land*, which involve using the

---

* 'Be mindful in due time of my pain.' 'In thought I see my past madness.'

literary tradition as a set of private references largely inaccessible to the layman, no longer operate within the decorous poetry of *Ash-Wednesday*. In place of the compendious and seemingly eclectic source material that can be brought to bear on *The Waste Land*, the source material of *Ash-Wednesday*, in accord with Eliot's religious commitment, is far more consistent and restricted, being mainly biblical and liturgical references; Dante, and in particular, the *Purgatorio*; a few lines from Cavalcanti; and Ash-Wednesday sermons by Lancelot Andrewes. However, while this relatively narrow range of sources does help give the poem a greater degree of structural coherence and implies a narrowed zone of interests, the material is still recondite, and cannot account for the formal effect of the verse, which while giving a sense of aesthetic lucidity seems at least as resistant to fixed interpretation as is *The Waste Land*.

One statement of Eliot's seems particularly helpful in approaching *Ash-Wednesday*. In a 1933 lecture in which he mentions Beethoven's late quartets, Eliot commented that he aimed

> to write poetry which should be essentially poetry, with nothing poetic about it, poetry standing naked in its bare bones, or poetry so transparent that we should not see the poetry, but that which we are meant to see through the poetry, poetry so transparent that in reading it we are intent on what the poem *points at*, and not on the poetry, this seems to be the thing to try for. To get *beyond poetry* as Beethoven, in his later works, strove to get *beyond music*.[12]

This statement is relevant to the translucent first section of *Ash-Wednesday*, which adapts Cavalcanti's 'Ballata', 'Perch'io non spero di tornar giammai'. If we compare the way Eliot employs Cavalcanti as a source with the use of source material in *The Waste Land*, certain definite, but hard to define, differences become apparent. In place of a procedure which subverts, by parody, or by the 'hijacking' of untranslated lines which are placed in an alien context, we begin with a lyric which could be subtitled 'variations on a theme by Cavalcanti'. A literal translation of the first line of Cavalcanti's 'Ballata' would run 'Since I do not hope to return ever'. Eliot has kept as close as possible to the exquisite cadence of the Italian, and impregnated the meaning with the implications of some lines from Lancelot Andrewes's Ash Wednesday sermon 1602. 'What then, shall I continually "fall" and never "rise"? "turn away" and not once "turn again"? Shall my rebellions be "perpetual"? . . . Shall these swallows fly over me and put me in mind of my "return", and shall I not heed them?'[13]

At this point we can return to the collocation of fragments that concludes *The Waste Land* and see that Eliot's use of the line from the 'Pervigilium Veneris', 'Quando fiam uti chelidon' ('When shall I be as the swallow') in juxtaposition to the Arnaut Daniel motif effects a conjuncture between the idea of the swallows' migratory return and purgatorial remorse – as in Andrewes's sermon. Then, turning back to *Ash-Wednesday*, we can see that the cadence and word pattern of Cavalcanti's line has been abstracted from its context – Calvalcanti is in perpetual exile from his lady, but his 'Ballata' has no spiritual dimension beyond the pain of separation from 'la donna mia' – and that by translating 'tornar' as 'turn' the meaning has been generalized, as in the Ash-Wednesday sermon, to accommodate a religious dimension. Eliot develops his variations:

> Because I do not hope to turn again
> Because I do not hope
> Because I do not hope to turn
> Desiring this man's gift and that man's scope ˙
> I no longer strive to strive towards such things
> (Why should the aged eagle stretch its wings?)
> Why should I mourn
> The vanished power of the usual reign?[14]

In contrast with the method of *The Waste Land*, Eliot's line functions independently of its source: it exists autonomously in a new formal context. In place of a mode in which the literary past is brought into the present as a collocation of unassimilated fragments, we have a reintegration in the poet's sensibility, which generates a series of fresh meanings. The stately balanced iambic rhythm of 'Because I do not hope to turn again', its logical structure, reminiscent of the first term in a scholastic syllogism, is exploited, as in the first three lines, to generate a sequence of nuances. Then, in the following stanza, the line is slightly altered to begin a new series of meanings: 'Because I do not hope to know again . . .'

Because the formal structure avoids fixity of meaning a valid interpretation of these lines would require line by line, word by word attention in order to approach the subtleties of nuance Eliot achieves in this opening section. Even in this first stanza lines seem to develop more according to the logic of the musical phrase than according to some precise personal or social reference. Internal rhymes and repetitions and strong end rhymes maintain an impression of formal coherence, while the absence of punctuation and an approach towards liturgical paratactic modes generates a fluidity of meaning. This fluidity is reinforced by a generalized vocabulary; when Eliot introduces the striking phrase 'Because I know I shall not know/The one veritable transitory power', the phrase is more resonant than precise, indicating more a zone of experience than the conditions by which that experience may be brought about. Similarly, the problematic third stanza will not allow a fixed interpretation. Are the 'blessed face' and 'the voice', which are renounced, to be equated with the Beatrice-like mediator of the second section? Or is this a predominantly secular experience, like the one with the girl in the hyacinth garden in *The Waste Land*? Do the final lines of the stanza, 'Consequently I rejoice, having to construct something/Upon which to rejoice' indicate a true acceptance 'that things are as they are', or do they indicate an essentially solipsistic resolve – or both? Contrary implications overlap, but they are not mutually exclusive. The achievement of this formal mode is that, as meanings cannot be tied to precise referents, they can co-exist in a state of fruitful tension. But the overall tendency of the verse remains clear: at once a prayer for self-acceptance, acceptance of the external conditions of life, and forgiveness for previous sins – a prayer that carries within itself an awareness of the danger of self-delusion and solipsism.

If we contrast this method of employing source material, with the first allusion to Dante in *The Waste Land* ('A crowd flowed over London bridge'), it is apparent that the literary past is no longer being employed to 'establish a relationship between the mediaeval inferno and modern life', to enforce a social message by exploiting a literary analogy. Both the literary and the social concerns of *Ash-Wednesday* are subsumed within the spiritual, and this leads to a new set of formal relations. If we somewhat arbitrarily distinguish three stages in the development of Eliot's poetic 'impersonality', the first would accord with the dry, laconic distancing of personal emotions, as in 'Portrait of a Lady' or 'Prufrock' – the mode Eliot derived from Laforgue. The second, concurrent with the *Poems* of 1920 and *The Waste Land*, exteriorizes emotions by presenting sharp visual, caricatural images, and mediates personal emotion, as in *The Waste Land*, through an objectified structure of literary references. The third mode of impersonality, that of *Ash-Wednesday*, at first does not seem to warrant the term; the 'I' of the first section of the poem is omnipresent and surely extremely personal? However, this 'I' is absorbed in a poetic mode which is close to the act of prayer; thus, subsumed in what Austin would term a 'performative' function. It is at once extremely personal but also common to all human beings: a person divested of the social particularities of personality. Thus, in relation to *Ash-Wednesday* we must redefine 'impersonality' to accord with a removal from the substantiality of the temporal world in which the person has place and definition by such idiosyncrasies as speech patterns, and a move towards an interior, common realm of spiritual realities.

As a corollary, we can also sense the striving towards humility involved in prayer, which includes a placing in perspective, a sizing up of such social and personal idiosyncrasies. Some lines in section II of *Ash-Wednesday*,

> As I am forgotten
> And would be forgotten, so would I forget
> Thus devoted, concentrated in purpose

succinctly convey the impression of prayer as created by the entire poem, and emphasize this aspiration towards self-forgetfulness. It is in this context that Eliot's employment of biblical, and particularly liturgical references, in *Ash-Wednesday* becomes significant. While Eliot's employment of biblical references may initially seem eclectic (for example, the references to Elijah in section I; Kings; Jeremiah; Ecclesiastes; and Ezekiel in section II of the poem) we can eventually discern principles of coherence and consistency which refer such citations back to meanings taken from, or relevant to Anglo-Catholic or Roman Catholic ritual appointed for the first day of Lent. In particular, the elusive, parable-like section II of the poem (originally given the title 'Salutation' as an oblique reference to Dante's greeting by Beatrice in section III of *La Vita Nuova*) is dominated by references to Ezekiel and particularly the 'dry bones' chapter (xxxvii), which is also important to 'The Burial of the Dead' section of *The Waste Land*: 'And he said unto me, Son of man, can these bones live? And I answered, O Lord GOD, thou knowest.' (xxxvii, 3.) If we so wish we can stop with the biblical citations, but it is possible to attach the meanings of the relevant lines of *Ash-Wednesday* to the Anglican Service of Commination ('to be used on the First Day of Lent'), where Psalm 51 is employed, the 'Miserere mei, Deus', which contain the lines:

> Thou shalt purge me with hyssop, and I shall be clean: thou shalt wash me and I shall be whiter than snow.
> Thou shalt make me hear of joy and gladness: that the bones which thou hast broken may rejoice.

Eliot's scheme of allusions make it apparent that 'Salutation' weds the theme of the Lady (Beatrice or Mary) an intercessor for grace, with the biblical and allegoric figure of the 'dry bones' as a representation of spiritual aridity and dispersal.

In less specific and more structural terms, the Epistle for Ash Wednesday from Joel, chapter ii, containing verses 12 and 13, 'Therefore also now, saith the LORD, turn ye *even* to me with all your heart, and with fasting, and with weeping, and with mourning . . .'(12), are, together with the 1619 Ash Wednesday sermon of Lancelot Andrewes, preached upon these lines, an extremely important source not only of the meanings of sections I, III, and VI of the poem, but also, as explored in the commentary of Lancelot Andrewes, a precedent for the turning, circling, spiral movement of the entire poem. Playing upon all the possible applications of the participle 'turning', Andrewes says

> *Repentance* it selfe is nothing els, but *redire ad principia*, a kind of circling; to *returne* to Him by *repentance*, from *whom*, by sinne, we have turned away. And much after a *circle* is this *text*: beginns with the word *turne*, and *returnes* about to the same word againe. Which *circle* consists (to use the *Prophet's* owne word) of *two turnings*; (for, twise he repeats this word); which two must needs be two different motions. 1. One, is to be done with the *whole heart*: 2. The other with it *broken* and *rent*: So as, one and the same it cannot be.[15]

The second sentence of Andrewes's paragraph is a precise reflection of the cyclical text of Eliot's poem, which passes from 'Because I do not hope to turn again' to 'Although I do not hope to turn again' in the final section, having enumerated and explored the consequences and implications of the initial spiritual condition. The formal congruence between Andrewes's text and Eliot's poem is so exact as to make it unlikely that Eliot did not consciously bear this passage in mind as a structural model; while Andrewes's sermon deserves a complete reading in relation to the poem's meanings.

Finally, within the individual sections of *Ash-Wednesday* we can discern that towards the conclusion of each section Eliot tends to broaden the meanings and concerns of the verse away from any purely personal application by the employment of liturgical formulae. For example, at the close of section I, Eliot quotes from the end of the Roman Catholic Hail Mary: 'Pray for us sinners now and at the hour of our death/Pray for us now and at the hour of our death'; at the end of section III, fragments from Matthew viii, 8, as employed by Eliot, are compatible with the use of the line, 'Lord, I am not worthy that thou shoulds't come under my roof . . .' by the priest before the taking of the sacrament; and in section VI, the entire poem concludes with the single line 'And let my cry come unto thee', the response of the congregation to the priest's 'O Lord, hear my prayer', in the Roman Catholic Mass. The overall impression created by such usages is that of a movement *within each section* away from the personal and private towards a common realm of spiritual realities as embodied and exemplified in the tradition of the liturgy. This is seen most clearly in the first example, where Eliot's citation of the line 'Pray for us sinners now and at the hour of our death', is within the context of Eliot's development an emphatic gesture of belonging to a tradition and reality which is larger than the individual.

It is at this point that Dante's *Commedia* takes on a renewed significance for Eliot. As we saw in the examination of *The Waste Land*, the fragmentation of the literary tradition involves a disenchanted, disoriented view of society: a sense that 'tradition' has no authority over a debased present and cannot give it coherence. The removal of Eliot's attention from the conditions of social and material existence, the temporal world, to a certain extent negates this tension, and allows a reintegration with 'tradition' as exemplified by the greatest of spiritual autobiographies, Dante's *Commedia*. This reintegration cannot, of course, be based on Dante's extraordinary, personal synthesis of mediaeval cosmology (the details of which even his son Iacopo found it impossible to fully comprehend). It is a literary and spiritual reintegration, based not upon Dante's external cosmological scheme, but upon a reference to, indeed even reliance on, certain motifs of that scheme, such as the female 'mediator', and spiral purgatorial ascent, which are used to strengthen by precedent and association the texture of Eliot's own verse.

If we examine section III, originally given the title 'Som de L'Escalina', after Arnaut Daniel's words to Dante, certain salient features of this reintegration become apparent. After the arcane, elusive, parable-like technique of section II, 'Salutation', our immediate reaction to section III is that it marks a return to a more apprehensible, substantive mode. However, this impression of quasi-realism is a function of the formal properties of the verse: the regular rhythms, which become euphonious in the third stanza, are strengthened by strong, repetitious rhymes (there are eleven uses, including assonances, of the 'stair' rhyme, and 'stair' itself is used five times), all of which contrives an auditory effect which mimes the regular spiral progress of the poet. Similarly, the visual quality of the images in the second and third stanzas produce a sense of clarity and definition:

> And beyond the hawthorn blossom and a pasture scene
> The broadbacked figure drest in blue and green
> Enchanted the maytime with an antique flute.

This is a pastoral scene, in other words less an image from the objective world than an appeal to our knowledge of certain iconographic conventions, from which we can supply a suitably static visual image, such as an illustration from a missal. It is in such 'clear visual images' that Eliot locates one of the main advantages of Dante's allegoric method; this he sees as a consequence of Dante's 'living in an age when men still saw visions'. 'We have nothing but dreams, and we have forgotten that seeing visions – a practice now relegated to the aberrant and uneducated – was once a more significant, interesting, and disciplined kind of dreaming. We take it for granted that our dreams spring from below: possibly the quality of our dreams suffers in consequence.'[16] (Throughout the 1929 essay Eliot is at pains to defend the 'concreteness' of Dante's art against a readership which he assumes will have an inbuilt Coleridgean prejudice against allegory.) It is probable that Eliot is striving for a similar effect here, a method that will assimilate worldly experience, and then objectify that experience symbolically, in such 'clear visual images'. These images, not being realistic 'notations' for objects in the material world, retain no sense of material particularity, and thus attain to that condition of transparence that Eliot desired for his poetry: 'that in reading it we are intent on what the poetry *points at* and not on the poetry'. Eliot's withdrawal from the temporal world likewise involves a withdrawal from the attempt to catch the localized idioms of real speech, which can be seen as a move towards the 'universality' he commends in Dante.

> The Italian language, and especially the Italian language in Dante's age, gains much from being the product of universal Latin. There is something much more *local* about the languages in which Shakespeare and Racine had to express themselves.[17]

But once these aspirations have been noted it remains to be said that Eliot's religious commitment underwrites a choice of poetic development that Dante, to his advantage, was not presented with. After his period of co-operation with Pound in the societal depiction of *moeurs contemporaines*, Eliot seems to withdraw into his own verbal universe the autonomy of which is always in question, for periodically he attempts to escape through, as in section V of *Ash-Wednesday*, statements of belief rather than satiric presentations of the temporal world. In this Eliot is a long way from Dante. Studies such as those of Auerbach and Singleton have alerted us to the dynamic principles of figural reading that work within Dante's allegory, by which the historic personage can retain his temporal individuality and still exemplify spiritual realities.[18] In accordance with the four levels of mediaeval allegory outlined in Dante's famous letter to Can Grande della Scala (the literal, moral, allegoric and anagogic) Dante's allegory functions as a continuum, and seemingly divergent levels of signification interrelate harmoniously.[19] If we return to section III of *Ash-Wednesday* we see that Eliot's method is not truly allegoric, certainly not in Dante's sense, nor even in the reduced terms of an allegory like *The Pilgrim's Progress*; rather, it is a Symbolist mode. There is no definite moral or spiritual system on which *Ash-Wednesday* is based, though Eliot refers to such systems (such as the negative mysticism of St John of the Cross) implicitly; he is evoking spiritual states of being by exploiting the associative power of words, and in doing so he is building an ideal universe that owes as much to Mallarmé as it does to Dante.

An aspect of the associative power of words is the ability to invoke literary precedents, and we can feel the exemplar of purgatorial ascent in Dante's *Purgatorio* strengthening the texture of 'Som de L'Escalina'. This enables us to read a complex allegoric tradition summoning up a powerful nexus of emotions into Eliot's elusive symbolist structure. (These emotions are centred around the painful, arduous experiences of self-questioning and contrition.) However, we cannot compound Dante's 'external' scheme, involving a definite visionary topography, with what we find in Eliot, which is an almost arbitrary simulation of an allegory of ascent. There is no particular reason why Eliot should have a certain experience 'At the first turning of the second stair', and, indeed, it is worth considering that his purgatorial ascent involves the help of a banister. Eliot's verse conforms more with the concept of a dramatic recreation and re-assessment of past experience which is then cast into an allegoric guise. This is consonant with the cyclic structure of the poem and makes an obvious contrast with Dante's scheme, which involves a sense of real movement and physical progress. Moreover, there is nothing in Dante that reminds us overtly of the still active temptations of the natural, sensory world, as symbolized by the 'broadbacked figure'. Eliot, here, seems to wish to indicate the precarious nature of his ascent, which involves the continual danger of delusion and relapse – the possibility of succumbing to 'the love of created beings'[20] in the extremely significant words from St John of the Cross which Eliot cited as one of the epigraphs to *Sweeney Agonistes*. In comparison, Dante's ascent seems both orderly and predetermined; it is only when we meet Beatrice that we have a sense of dramatic unpredictability. However, the enumeration of such differences does not fundamentally alter the fact that by invoking the echo of the *Purgatorio*, Eliot's voice, while remaining his own, has invoked a powerful literary and religious tradition, and gains strength thereby.

This serves to indicate that Eliot's interest in Dante has shifted away from the dramatic aspects of the *Commedia*, the manner in which real speech can encapsulate a spiritual state, and is now centred more firmly on the spiritual realities Dante sought to describe. This leads to a more generalized reliance on some of the motifs of the *Commedia*, among which the theme of the Lady as intercessor between the poet and grace is particularly important. At this point it is possible to complete the analysis of the Arnaut Daniel motif by examining the extraordinary syntactic *tour de force* that begins section IV of the poem, in which certain elements of this reorientation are apparent. Here, we find an extended clause that begins by seeming to be an interrogative until one reaches the words 'Sovegna vos', 'be mindful', at which point one returns to the beginning of the sequence to discover that although the lines cannot be tied to any definite referent, they could articulate as a relative clause to those two abrupt words from Arnaut Daniel's injunction to Dante.

> 'Vos' – You – 'Who walked between the violet and the violet
> Who walked between

> The various ranks of varied green . . .
> Sovegna vos' – 'a temps de ma dolor'
> Be mindful in due time of my pain.

Here we will attempt a somewhat tendentious piece of interpretative analysis, according to which the poet, undergoing his purgatorial penance, pleads for the attention, perhaps mediation of the Lady, who is already in a state of grace, 'In blue of larkspur, blue of Mary's colour'. However, this would be tendentious, precisely because we cannot tie these lines to a specific referent; they exist free of specificity, evoking a dream landscape, 'the time between sleep and waking'. All we can say is that the words 'Sovegna vos' invoke the Arnaut Daniel motif and references to the 'silent sister' invoke a complex of emotions, some of which are centred on the figure of Beatrice. This seamless wedding of the Arnaut Daniel motif with that of the female intercessor serves to indicate the new mode of poetic integration Eliot achieves in *Ash-Wednesday*: in contrast to the method of *The Waste Land*, the *Commedia* is evoked rather than cited.

But it could, I think, be cogently argued, by a critic who was not enamoured of Eliot's use of symbolism, that he is here relying too strongly on this analogy with Beatrice, for his figure has no independent definition either in this section or in section II, 'Salutation' and she seems to merge with the figure of the Virgin Mary in section VI. With reference to the 'silent sister', it is important that, unlike Beatrice, she remains silent. Within the context of Eliot's poetic development this aligns here with a sequence of related guilt motifs running through 'Song' (published as 'Song to the Opherian' in 1921), 'Eyes that last I saw in tears', published in 1924, and the major exemplification of the theme, 'The Hollow Men' of 1925. In these poems a use of 'eye' symbolism is used to locate a radical failure of communication with a figure who is given no specificity. However, a complex of guilt and remorse is triggered in the speaker, who locates himself in 'death's dream kingdom', and seeks to evade the 'Eyes I dare not meet in dreams'.[21] Caught between the figure of Beatrice and Eliot's private experience, it is perhaps unsurprising that the female mediator of *Ash-Wednesday* remains an evanescent presence.

Eliot's debt to Dante in *Ash-Wednesday* cannot be confined to the exploitation of Dantean motifs, and the use of the *Commedia* as a literary parallel on which to base his own poem; it is possible to speculate that there is a degree of personal identification with the Italian poet. Here, there is no 'evidence' to rely on, except intuitive understanding of Eliot's personality and the characteristic concerns of his poetry. There does, however, seem to be one point in *Ash-Wednesday* at which Eliot seems to invoke Dante the man, rather than Dante the poet.

At the close of section IV we find a certain merging of the poet's private concerns into a wider area of discussion, centring upon the relation between poetry and faith, and how both relate to a secular, materialist civilization. Technically Eliot achieves the transition by playing on the creative ambiguity of a phrase like 'redeem the time', which can refer both to a re-assessment and consolidation of the poet's private experience, or can have a wider, public application, as in St Paul's Epistles: 'See then that ye walk circumspectly, not as fools, but as wise, Redeeming the time because the days are evil' (Ephesians v, 15, 16). At the end of the section these concerns are consolidated.

> Redeem the time, redeem the dream
> The token of the word unheard, unspoken
>
> Till the wind shake a thousand whispers from the yew
>
> And after this our exile[22]

The final phrase adapts a line from the Roman Catholic prayer to the Virgin Mary, which is said at the end of the mass: 'and after this our exile show unto us the blessed fruit of thy womb, Jesus'. Eliot's use of this phrase demonstrates not the mode of subversion that operates in *The Waste Land*, but rather the genesis of a new meaning that yet retains a tangential relation to its source (as in the first section 'Perch'io non Spero'). The state of exile to which Eliot alludes cannot be simply equated with Dante's exile, which was a physical banishment from Florence. Rather, when we read the opening lines of section V, which plays upon the relation between the word, as a symbol for poetry, and the Word made flesh, the Incarnation, we realize that Eliot is concerned to some extent with the status of poetry, particularly religious poetry, in a materialistic society. But might we not consider that Eliot regarded his position as a 'believing' poet in a secular society, as being in some way analogous in a spiritual, private sense, to Dante's position, when in exile he berated the inhabitants of his beloved city for taking up ungodly ways?

Throughout section V Eliot implies that the poetic word and the Word cannot be fully effective in this civilization: 'Where shall the word be found, where will the word/Resound? Not here, there is not enough silence . . .', and the section develops into the poet asking if the 'veiled sister' will pray 'for those who walk in darkness'. Yet, interspersed between the verse-paragraphs there is a one line interjection:

> O my people, what have I done unto thee.

which is truncated at the end of the section to 'O my people'. A standard work, such as Southam's *Student's Guide* refers us to the biblical source in Micah:

> The Lord cries to the people, reproaching them for their departure from the ways of virtue and faith. These words have been taken into the liturgy of the Church. In the Roman Catholic mass for Good Friday, the day of the crucifixion, these words are part of the Reproaches, a liturgy in which Christ on the cross speaks to the people: 'O my people, what have I done unto thee' Or in what have I grieved thee? Because I brought thee out of the land of Egypt, thou hast prepared a cross for thy Saviour.[23]

This is accurate, and helpful as far as it goes, but seems curiously irrelevant when assessing the poetry. It is rather more helpful to learn in Barbi's *Life of Dante* that during the initial stages of Dante's exile, he wrote 'not only to individual members of the government, but also to the people. Among these letters is a very extended one which begins "Popule mee, quid feci tibi?" '[24] The two sources are, of course, reconcilable, and it would be surprising if Eliot's interest in Dante did not extend to discovering such information. Perhaps it is not too fanciful to see Eliot as invoking the words of Dante directly at this point in the poem, an invocation that suits well with the themes with which he is dealing. Certainly, at this stage of his career Eliot could speak of Dante, as Dante spoke of Virgil in the *Inferno*: 'Tu se' lo mio maestro e'l mio autore'.[25]

What has become of the satiric impulse which informs Eliot's earlier poetry? As we commented previously, in 'Gerontion' and *The Waste Land* the atemporal, spiritual dimension structurally counterpoints the temporal, satiric elements, but without, at that stage of Eliot's career, being able to offer an authoritative alternative to a display of illiberal social attitudes. Eliot's religious commitment had more effect on his poetry than on his politics, so what we find in *Ash-Wednesday* is that the satiric impulse is not so much eradicated as displaced: instead of being 'foregrounded' it is contained by the religious dimension and appears under a radically different guise. In section V of *Ash-Wednesday* the opening lines play on the doctrine of the Logos, employing as a primary source Lancelot Andrewes's Nativity sermon of 1618,[26] which Eliot had used previously in 'Gerontion', and attempt through incantatory modes to achieve a juncture between Symbolist poetics and the mystery of Incarnation, the wordless child as the Word of God, 'The Word without a word . . .' This introduction is weak and teeters close to doggerel, but it does serve to establish a tension between 'the Word' (capitalized or uncapitalized) and 'the world', which is used to launch an attack on society in which the particularized, 'local' modes of Eliot's previous satire are abandoned for the generalized, sententious tones of the homiletic sermon (or, more unkindly, the Salvation Army hymn):

> Where shall the word be found, where will the word
> Resound? Not here, there is not enough silence
> Not on the sea or on the islands, not
> On the mainland, in the desert or the rain land,
> For those who walk in darkness
> Both in the day time and in the night time
> The right time and the right place are not here
> No place of grace for those who avoid the face
> No time to rejoice for those who walk among noise and
>   deny the voice

The heavy reliance on facile internal rhymes is an index of Eliot's uncertainty with this mode. The doctrinal religious base of *Ash-Wednesday* provides the parameters for Eliot's attack on society; but within the bounds of Symbolist aesthetics, with which Eliot had unambiguously re-aligned himself after his period of cooperation with Pound, there is no excuse for such refined pontificating. As Pearson comments,

'Symbolism offered no way of confronting and mediating the social reality that created it. Inherently, it transforms experience into verbal metaphysic, an autonomous universe as against the autonomisms of society.'[27] However, while Eliot is not happy in this mode, he is unwilling, both temperamentally and intellectually, to fashion a poetry which will not manifest an element of social and cultural disaffection. In containing the 'public' satiric impulse within the bounds of a 'private' religious commitment Eliot brings about a withdrawal from that powerful oppositional engagement with social realities which fuelled the dynamic tensions of his quatrain poems and inaugurates a mode of poetic moralizing that comes dangerously close to sanctimonious smugness. This is an infrequent lapse in *Ash-Wednesday*; but its ultimate fruit was to be the poverty of *The Rock*.

Ash-Wednesday is a crucial poem in Eliot's development, for the Symbolist formal modes employed in *Ash-Wednesday* differ in detail, but not principle, from the modes of *Four Quartets*, and conclusions reached with reference to *Ash-Wednesday* can, in general terms, be applied to the later poem. It can be seen that in *Ash-Wednesday* Eliot achieves the Hulmian equation of authority and tradition that he implied in his earlier critical writing, but was unable to achieve in his poetic practice. The concept of sacred texts allows him this juncture between tradition (seen in neutral terms as the literary past) and the disordered present, and the *Commedia* and Dante stand behind Eliot's text as literary precedent and personal exemplar. But in moving beyond the societal towards more interiorized Symbolist modes, Eliot cannot achieve the kind of creative adaptation he achieved in relation to the poetry of Jules Laforgue. This means in practice that Dante is not so much absorbed as evoked; *Ash-Wednesday* refers itself back to the *Commedia*, it does not integrate itself with it. Once this is perceived it is apparent that Eliot is not so much 'working within' Dante's tradition as exploiting it from the associational premises of a Symbolist aesthetic.

Textually, the consequences are at once positive and negative. In formal terms, the result is a mode of linguistic integration which cannot be predicated for the earlier poetry. If we consider the conclusion of the poem, and the concluding reference to Dante's *Commedia*, it is apparent that here specific textual reference is integrated, almost seamlessly, into the poetic texture of the verse:

> Blessed sister, holy mother, spirit of the fountain, spirit of the
> garden,
> Suffer us not to mock ourselves with falsehood
> Teach us to care and not to care
> Teach us to sit still
> Even among these rocks,
> Our peace in His will
> And even among these rocks
> Sister, mother
> And spirit of the river, spirit of the sea,
> Suffer me not to be separated
>
> And let my cry come unto Thee.

Here, Piccarda's words from *Paradiso*, Canto III, 'Our peace is His will, His will is our peace. It is that sea towards which moves all that it creates and all that nature makes' (see, in contrast, the sixth stanza of 'A Cooking Egg'), is woven in with phrases from the Roman Catholic liturgy and its hymns: for example, the line 'Suffer me not to be separated from thee' which figures in the 'Soul of Christ' hymn. The final effect is that of lines which belong to Eliot, and are subordinated to Eliot's meanings, but those very meanings are consistent within, and refer themselves back to, a traditional body of doctrine and verbal response, thus achieving a mode of formal integration that helps create that enigmatic transparency that Eliot desired for his later poetry.

These gains, however, entail the loss of that highly personal 'impersonality' that fuelled the tension of Eliot's early poetry and its ambiguous engagement with social and cultural realities. In this, Eliot's development can be seen as proceeding in the opposite direction to W. B. Yeats, who, partly due to the influence of Pound, worked his way out of Symbolism towards a more engaged, oppositional poetry. With the publication of *Ash-Wednesday* Eliot's poetry seems definitively to lose its sharp, antagonistic connection with the cultural present, and consequently to shrink in scale and ambition. Both the satiric and the unmediated personal impulse are now contained (doctrinally if not aesthetically) within the religious dimension, and in place of a poetry that asks difficult questions, we have a poetry that – from a hostile perspective – can be seen as offering inadequate answers. This, to some degree, is how Eliot's friend and early associate Conrad Aiken viewed what he termed Eliot's 'tragic metamorphosis' in his memoir *Ushant*. Aiken sees Eliot as retreating from his 'brilliantly analytic and destructive thesis at Harvard . . . as if that magnificent vision, into the apparent chaos which blazed and swarmed and roared beyond the neat walls of Eden, was one he found insupportable'. Henceforth, he sees Eliot as finding himself

> at Canterbury, after the pilgrimage of pilgrimages, in the very presence of the Ichtos itself. That the achievement was unique and astounding, and attended, too, by rainbows of creative splendour, there could be no doubt. Indeed, it was in the nature of a miracle, a transformation. But was it not to have been, also, a surrender, and perhaps the saddest known to D. in his life?[28]

Aiken's remarks need not be endorsed; they are certainly coloured by some envy of his more successful, and often acerbic friend. But surveying the trajectory of Eliot's development, it is difficult not to feel nostalgia and admiration for the innovative poet of the earlier work, who in freeing his poetry from the tyranny of a single discourse seems so fully to have heeded Stein's advice and judgement on the young Lord Jim, 'In the destructive element immerse'.

10
Conclusion

> – History, Stephen said, is a nightmare from which I am trying to awake.
> From the playfield the boys raised a shout. A whirring whistle: goal. What
> if that nightmare gave you a back kick?
>
> Joyce, *Ulysses*

To recapitulate briefly: the previous chapters of this study should have substantiated my initial premise that Pound and Eliot were working in close co-operation between 1914 and 1922, with Eliot to some extent under Pound's tutelage. *Hugh Selwyn Mauberley*, as Pound's disillusioned farewell to English literary culture – he moved to Paris in late 1920 – signalled the cessation of this close co-operation, which from Eliot's standpoint both terminated and culminated in Pound's revision of the manuscripts of *The Waste Land*. The years 1920–22 mark the end of a clearly defined phase in each poet's development. In Eliot's case, the division is perhaps even clearer than in Pound's, who continued work begun previously on what were to become *The Cantos*, while in Eliot's poetic production there was a substantial hiatus after 1922. If we except 'The Hollow Men' (1925), his next completed major poetry was produced some eight years later with Ash-Wednesday (1930) and in poetic modes that are formally distinct from those of his period of co-operation with Pound.

In retrospect it can be seen that in terms of literary groupings and cultural politics, a process of reorientation was taking place in the post-war period immediately before and after Pound's departure, with Eliot gradually moving from the maverick Pound alliance ('group' is perhaps too strong a term to describe those individuals who were associated with the Vorticist endeavour, or who had a personal allegiance to Pound) towards what was to become increasingly throughout the 1920s the dominant centre of English literary culture: the Bloomsbury group. Eliot had had an entrée into Bloomsbury since his arrival in England through his friendship with Bertrand Russell, who had met and been impressed by Eliot while the latter was still a Harvard graduate student in philosophy. Eliot's subsequent contacts with Clive Bell, Roger Fry, and above all, the Woolfs, were to lead to the publication by the Hogarth Press of *Poems* in 1919 (seven of Eliot's recent poems including the verse in French and four of the early quatrain poems), an important gesture of faith in Eliot's poetic talent which was to lead to the publication by the Hogarth Press of *The Waste Land* in 1922. The Bloomsbury group had been among the first to appreciate the originality of *Prufrock and Other Observations*; but this belief in Eliot's abilities did not extend to feeling fully at ease in his company.

Lytton Strachey, a central Bloomsbury figure with whom Eliot had little rapport, but who often set the tone in their evaluation of outsiders, described Eliot in a letter to Dora Carrington as 'rather ill and rather American; altogether not quite gay enough for my taste. But by no means to be sniffed at.'[1] Clive Bell describes the general reaction: 'To us at any rate this mixture, genius, in its rarest form, combined with studied primness of manner and speech, seemed deliciously comic. Virginia was a born and infectious mocker.'[2] However, Virginia Woolf was eventually able to breach Eliot's defensive stiffness and air of excessive erudition to discover a more vulnerable and sympathetic individual than she first suspected. But it would be an exaggeration to say that Eliot ever reached terms of intimacy with any of his Bloomsbury literary sponsors. Mutual respect was perhaps the most that was achieved. (Herbert Read, in his 1966 memoir of Eliot, wrote that 'The obituary of Virginia which he wrote for *The Criterion* shocked us all by its chilly detachment.')[3] Eliot's attitude to such native social and literary groupings was one of detached interest. He was interested in making personal friends and literary allies, but remained aware that his background as an 'American who wasn't an American',[4] prevented any true incorporation in these indigenous social and cultural alliances. In fact, this implicit detachment was one of the sources of Eliot's expertise and effectiveness in cultural politics. He did not regard his associations as mutually exclusive, and thus, unlike Pound, was able to think of the business of making friends as distinct from the business of making enemies.

In the years following the war, his developing rapport with the Bloomsbury group did not preclude an association with the Sitwell 'Wheels' group. Strachey describes a 'very sad and seedy' Eliot reading at a Sitwell dinner in 1921, and wonders 'why does Eliot have truck with such coagulations. I fear it indicates that there's something seriously wrong with him.'[5] In fact, by maintaining contact with the Sitwells, socially even more Establishment than the Bloomsburies, and conducting amicable, if distant relations with Harold Monro and his review *Poetry and Drama* (Monro's Poetry Bookshop was the centre for Georgian poetry, with which Eliot appeared to be at odds more in retrospect, by his own declaration and by his association with Pound, than was perhaps apparent at the time), Eliot achieved the distinction of having a measure of acceptance in each of what Herbert Read describes as the three post-war 'centres of intellectual ferment in London'.[6] This could be seen as a searching for literary identity in Pound's absence, but it is more pertinent to see it as a crucial element in Eliot's meteoric rise to public acceptance and eminence as both poet and critic in the period 1914 to 1922. Conrad Aiken, an early Harvard associate of Eliot's, recollected his surprise on visiting post-war London and finding Eliot 'so rootedly established, both socially and in the "politics" (as it were) of literature . . . as to have achieved what Emily

Dickinson had called "overtakelessness": he had built the splendid ramparts round that rare new domain of his, and behind them he had become all but invisible, all but intangible'.[7]

This process was consolidated by the foundation of *The Criterion* in 1922–3, of which Eliot assumed the editorship. Read writes, 'From that year Eliot was our undisputed leader. I imply the formation of a party, of a "new front", and that was indeed the intention, as the "commentaries" of "The Criterion" soon made clear.'[8] In the first of these commentaries (April 1924), Eliot used the publication of Hulme's *Speculations* to make his first explicit political statement by announcing his belief in a 'new attitude of mind, which should be the twentieth-century mind, if the twentieth century is to have a mind of its own',[9] and though, as Read makes clear, Eliot did not necessarily expect contributors to *The Criterion* to agree with him, they were expected to have 'an impersonal loyalty to some faith not antagonistic to my own'.[10] The role of *The Criterion* (and, in historic context, one might more unkindly suggest, its lack of a role), is not within the purview of this study, except in so far as it marks Eliot's full independence from Pound and the formation of a group which owed allegiance to Eliot himself. As Read states, 'The group that rallied round him was unique in that it never questioned his leadership – but there were two that held back: Richard Aldington, who had developed an intense jealousy of Eliot, and Wyndham Lewis, who, though pressed by Eliot to collaborate, preferred as always to cut his own lonely and aggressive swathe.'[11]

Thus, by the mid-1920s, ten years after his arrival in England, Eliot had effected a transfer, his ties with Pound being loosened, from an anti-Establishment, almost anti-English cultural alliance to a rapprochement with the centres of native literary culture, within which Eliot himself was rapidly becoming a central figure. This is not to suggest disloyalty to Pound on Eliot's part. Indeed, he was scrupulously loyal to all his old associates, and stood by Pound and Lewis, by any standards difficult individuals, throughout the vicissitudes of their careers. It would be fairer to reiterate that Eliot's loyalty to persons and ideas did not extend to literary groupings; and while Eliot was to disagree increasingly with Pound over the years, particularly over their antithetical evaluations of Christianity, he never failed to express his gratitude to and respect for the older writer. Eliot's post-war rapport with the centres of English literary culture was a move towards associating himself with everything that Pound and Lewis most disliked. Pound, not quite understanding that Eliot's assimilation was voluntary, was to write to Lewis from Paris, designating Eliot's associates as an 'arseblarsted (sic) lot', and urging him to 'get Eliot out of England somehow'.[12] Both Pound and Lewis, who were to retain their original peripheral, oppositional status (the latter fighting a bitter and paranoiac battle with the Bloomsbury group throughout the late 1920s and 1930s which had its roots in the Omega dispute of 1913) were in future to evince a certain bewilderment at the ease with which their erstwhile 'rebel' associate had integrated himself with the English literary Establishment.

Once Eliot had moved into a different cultural orbit, it becomes easier to perceive the degree to which his position between 1914 and 1920, as part of the

non-English Vorticist alliance centred on Pound, underwrote the satiric and oppositional bias of his early literary production. Pound had taken it upon himself to
become the enormously energetic entrepreneur of early Modernism, discovering,
propagandizing and seeking to co-ordinate the activities of 'the Men of 1914' as
well as other, lesser figures. Of this period alliance of the talented and unappreci-
ated (which includes Joyce as a peripheral figure who was never fully associated
with its cultural politics) only Wyndham Lewis was a satirist by *métier*. In both
Pound's and Eliot's cases, satire was a period concern, closely bound up with their
elected position as a disaffected minority calling for the maintenance of standards,
not exclusively literary, within what they saw as a debased political, social and
literary culture. The stance of opposition requires active and talented support if it
is not to become solipsistic aggression, and in the period with which we are dealing Eliot and Pound in particular provided that support for each other. Subsequently, geographical dispersion tended to accentuate the differences in aims and
strategies of all four figures.[13]

The case of James Joyce deserves further comment. While Joyce had eagerly
accepted Pound's proselytization of his work, and other more immediate forms of
assistance, while living penuriously in Trieste, he was never at one with the cultural and political tendencies of the other 'Men of 1914', although initially they
seem not to have fully appreciated this. Eliot's immediate interest and admiration
was centred on the technical resources displayed in Joyce's pursuit of a 'mythical
method' in *Ulysses*, but there is little to indicate that he disagreed with the central
critical thrust of Pound's early assessment of *Ulysses (The Dial*, May 1922), where
Pound wrote, 'To begin with matters outside dispute I should say that Joyce has
taken up the art of writing where Flaubert left it.' Seeing Joyce as a satirist of the
clichés of popular democracy ('Messrs Bouvard and Pécuchet are the basis of democracy; Bloom also is the basis of democracy'), Pound asserts,

> He has presented Ireland under British domination, a picture so veridic that
> a ninth rate coward like Shaw (Geo. B.) dare not even look it in the face. By
> extension he has presented the whole occident under the domination of
> capital. The details of the street map are local but Leopold Bloom (né Virag)
> is ubiquitous. His spouse Geo-Tellus the earth symbol is the soil from
> whence the intelligence strives to leap, and to which it subsides *in saeculum
> saeculorum*. As Molly she is a coarse-grained bitch, not a whore, an adultress,
> il y en a.[14]

It is impossible not to wonder what Joyce made of this; more importantly, this
general perspective initiates rather than follows what was to be a tendency towards
seeing *Ulysses* as a satiric work. As Ellmann informs us,

> The saturnine *A Portrait of the Artist* led critics to suppose that Joyce was
> castigating modern society in *Ulysses* with Swiftian rigor; Bloom became a
> slightly depraved nonentity, his wife a wholly depraved whore. Joyce's
> emphasis in conversation on his literary means led to an unwarranted belief

in the book's anti-humanist indifference. Another view had it that Joyce's criticism of society was fundamentally Catholic and that the Hound of Heaven was harrying him back into the fold. The fact which Larbaud had clarified in comparing Joyce to Rabelais, that *Ulysses* was a *comédie humaine*, was less often pursued.[15]

The critical issue would tend to resolve itself around the modes of irony we predicate for *Ulysses*. In his study of the novel, *The Classical Temper*,[16] S. L. Goldberg demonstrates at length, in reply to Kenner in *Dublin's Joyce*,[17] that the irony of the novel is filtered *through* the perspective of the main characters, and in particular Bloom, and that this irony when applied to those characters is tolerant and compassionate rather than satiric and harsh. Joyce had commented to Budgen that Bloom was 'all-round' in two senses: 'I see him from all sides, and therefore he is all-round in the sense of your sculptor's figure. But he is a complete man as well – a good man.' In subsequent conversation he emphasized to Suter and Budgen that Ulysses was not a God, for he had all the defects of the ordinary man; but he was kindly. For Suter's benefit he would distinguish in German: 'Ulysses was not "gut" but "gemütig" (decent). Bloom is the same. If he does something mean or ignoble, he knows it and says "I have been a perfect pig".'[18] Ironically, it seems that Joyce intended Bloom to be the epitome of that 'eclectic, tolerant and democratic mind' which Eliot, in his own reactionary tendencies, condemned.

However, in *Ulysses* stylistic virtuosity always threatens to undermine and destabilize the integrity of the book's humanist intentions, thus allowing more troubled and negative assessments of the text and making it more than comprehensible that Pound and Eliot should have read the novel in accordance with their own critical and cultural biases. There is an inherent and finally irreconcilable tension in the history of late nineteenth-century literary aesthetics between Symbolism itself – the work as art, as verbal icon and/or as 'objective correlative' for the consciousness of the author – and the demands of representational realism; a tension and divide that Flaubert, who wrote the purple prose epic *Salammbô* as well as *Madame Bovary*, *L'Éducation sentimentale* and *Bouvard et Pécuchet*, both represents and straddles. The urge to proclaim art as a superior reality is dominant, as when Flaubert writes, 'there are no noble subjects or ignoble subjects; from the standpoint of pure Art one might almost establish the axiom that there is no such thing as subject, style in itself being an absolute manner of seeing things.'[19] Joyce can be seen as moving from the deadpan (Flaubertian) realism of *Dubliners* through to the marvellous but precarious synthesis of *Ulysses* and then to the hermetic symbolism of *Finnegan's Wake*, in which he employs Vico's eternally recurrent cycles of history as an intellectual support to the endless circularity of his narrative. Joyce's inherent bias is, in the context of his literary development, only made manifest when he shocked his brother Stanislaus, who wished to discuss (Italian) fascism, with the impatient retort, 'Don't talk to me about politics, I'm only interested in style.'[20]

Finnegan's Wake, however, belongs to a world in which the paths of the four 'Men of 1914' had long since diverged. Returning to the issue of Pound's influence upon Eliot, and in particular the encouragement he gave to Eliot in the depiction of *moeurs contemporaines*, it is easy to fall into restrictive evaluations. Pound's *Hugh Selwyn Mauberley* is arguably his finest achievement – to my mind his least flawed – while Eliot's *Poems* of 1920 have generally rather embarrassed critics, and, compared to other of his poems, have received scant recognition. The tendency, as in Grover Smith, is to condemn Pound's influence on Eliot, and to regard him as pushing Eliot towards modes which were suitable for Pound himself, but not for the younger poet. Thus, Smith states,

> From 1917 to 1919 he based his technique more on Gautier than on anyone else. Pound having disastrously encouraged him to study Gautier's *Émaux et Camées*, he set to work being amusing. The future, when it thinks of Pound and Eliot, will not overlook certain paradoxes. Pound, the finest contemporary critic of texture in poetry, seems to have exerted an adverse influence on Eliot's work.[21]

While it is true that Eliot's period of co-operation with Pound marks a deflection away from the primary Symbolist tendencies of his verse, as manifested in 'Prufrock' or *Ash-Wednesday*, it would be a mistake to assess Pound's influence in such limited terms.

If Pound's influence is seen in a wider sense, as underwriting the satiric elements in Eliot's work of the period, that influence cannot be restricted to the *Poems* of 1920, but must be extended to all Eliot's work of the period: the Oxford poems, 'Gerontion', and *The Waste Land*. With regard to this last poem, because of his role in the revision of the manuscript, it is extremely difficult to disengage Pound's critical suggestions, and their effects, from the shape assumed by the final work. In one of his letters to Eliot, suggesting and cajoling him towards the final form of *The Waste Land*, Pound concludes with two pieces of doggerel, the first of which runs:

SAGE HOMME

These are the poems of Eliot
By the Uranian Muse begot;
A Man their Mother was,
A Muse their Sire.

How did the printed Infancies result
From Nuptials thus doubly difficult?

If you must needs enquire
Know diligent Reader
That on each Occasion
Ezra performed the caesarean Operation.[22]

Here, it is important to realize that Pound's self-congratulatory comment applies not only to *The Waste Land*, but also to Eliot's earlier poems, including the quatrains. Virtually from the date of his renewed poetic production in 1914 Eliot forwarded his work to Pound for revision and critical comment; thus, if we wish to assess thoroughly Pound's influence on Eliot in the period 1914 to 1922, we have to consider all of the poems Eliot wrote in this period. When Wyndham Lewis writes in 1948, 'Gerontion (1920) is a close relative of Prufrock, certain matters filtered through an aged mask in both cases, but Gerontion technically is "school of Ezra"',[23] the judgement itself might serve to obscure the differences between the two poets, but the general critical perspective is worth considering.

Thus, surveying the full sweep of Eliot's poetic development it can be seen that the poems in which Pound's influence on Eliot must be taken into account – the Oxford poems, the Poems of 1920, and The Waste Land – are central to any assessment of Eliot's poetic achievement; they are, in fact, the central block upon which that achievement was built. In the context of the total shape of Eliot's poetic the poetry of Ash-Wednesday and Four Quartets 'depends' upon this earlier poetry as the antithesis to a thesis. This means that rather than being a peripheral issue, Pound's influence on Eliot is central and so integrated to the shape of Eliot's poetic development that there are no grounds for speculating on what might have been the shape of that development without Pound; or, indeed, whether there might have been a development at all after the perhaps to remain unpublished early triumphs of 'Prufrock' and 'Portrait of a Lady'. In view of this, judgements on the 'advisability' of Pound recommending Eliot to write quatrains à la Gautier is restrictive and futile; it is more interesting to consider the effects and ramifications of their co-operation.

Pound's influence on Eliot is not confined to his poetry, and he saw himself as having been instrumental in forming the critical stance Eliot adopted in 1916–17. In 1925 Pound commented in a letter that he was to some extent to blame for the 'extreme caution' of Eliot's criticism: 'I pointed out to him in the beginning there was no use of two of us butting a stone wall; that he wd. never be as hefty a battering ram as I was, nor as explosive as Lewis, and that he'd better try a more oceanic and fluid method of sapping the foundations.'[24] Kenner, typically, gives a more colourful account.

> Mr. Pound has recalled an occasion, perhaps around 1916, when Eliot 'was about to commit a rash act.' He had written several pages of untrammelled shillelagh-swinging, and brought them round to 5 Holland Place Chambers for scrutiny. The response was prophetic: 'That's not your style at all. You le me throw the bricks through the front window. You go in at the back door and take out the swag'.[25]

While it is likely that Pound exaggerated his influence in this area (a shillelagh would never be a weapon natural to the student of F. H. Bradley), the assumption of common aims behind Pound's statement allows for a large area of shared critical and oppositional assumptions. This was to change. Eliot, in October 1923, wrote to Quinn on the difficulties of receiving Pound's idiosyncratic contributions to the recently launched Criterion, and commented that 'I have to keep an attitude of discipleship to him (as indeed I ought)',[26] though it is apparent that by this date the disciple felt constrained by the master. There is an amusing exchange in the correspondence columns of *The Athenaeum* in October 1919, over Eliot's review of Pound's *Quia Pauper Amavi*, which anticipates some of their subsequent critical differences. Eliot's review had been scrupulously, perhaps over-scrupulously, appreciative. In it he regarded Pound as an exponent of the 'historical method', and commented, 'As the present is no more than the present existence, the present significance, of the entire past, Mr. Pound proceeds by acquiring the entire past; and when the entire past is acquired, the constituents fall into place and the present is revealed'[27] – a comment that seems bound to elicit the retort that the 'entire past' is a great deal to acquire. Pound, with some justification, regarded Eliot's review as insufficiently enthusiastic. Commenting on 'the enormous weight of granite laurels wherewith the immortal author of "Sweeney among the Nightingales" has so generously loaded my superstructure,' he wonders whether Eliot 'has or has not found my "Homage to Propertius" enjoyable', and protests against 'the *universitaire* tendency, before noted in T. S. E.'s article on *Hamlet*, where, as in his later note, he seems to regard literature not as something in itself enjoyable, having tang, gusto, aroma; but rather as something which, possibly because of a non-conformist conscience, one *ought* to enjoy because it is literature (infamous doctrine).'[28] The jibe at Eliot's Puritan background was a sharp one, and Eliot retorted with dry dignity; but this was to be a continuing element in Pound's subsequent rejection of Eliot's later critical writings. In 1925 he commented 'He is now respected by the Times Lit Sup but his criticisms no longer arouse my interest.'[29]

In the period of Eliot's co-operation with Pound, as well as the immense poetic achievement of these years he produced *The Sacred Wood* (1920), a work which has proved to be the most influential book of Anglo-American criticism published in the early twentieth century. But *The Sacred Wood* is only the tip of the iceberg of Eliot's critical achievement during these years. As a literary reviewer, Eliot from the first seems to have realized that the review essay was capable of being employed as a literary form in its own right, and one which could afford him a space to test out critical perspectives and definitions in response to particular texts. Between the years 1916 to 1922, in a sustained feat of inspired improvisation, Eliot created *ex nihilo* his own literary 'tradition', and in fluid, non-dogmatic terms established the critical perspectives within which he wished his own poetry to be sited and judged. The relative anonymity Eliot enjoyed during his oppositional alliance with Pound seems to underwrite the critical bravura of many of these pieces; a quality which borders on performance and, occasionally on persiflage. (The uninformed reader of 'Euripides and Professor Murray' would be hard put to realize that the author of this devastatingly ironic piece of destructive criticism was anything other than an enormously accomplished Classical scholar; but, as Ackroyd informs us, Eliot at around this date had some difficulty remembering the Greek alphabet.)[30] Certainly, there can be little doubt that Eliot himself courted the reputation for learning of which he complained to Virginia Woolf in February 1921. 'We walked back along the Strand. "The critics say I am learned & cold" he said.

''I am neither.'' As he said this, I think coldness at least must be a sore point with him.'[31]

The reading of those review essays Eliot wished to include in *The Sacred Wood* is still an exhilarating experience. In the initial, extended 'Perfect' and 'Imperfect Critics' sections (in which, significantly, Rémy de Gourmont, one of Pound's great enthusiasms, is chosen as the modern type of 'the perfect critic'), Eliot establishes a set of defined but flexible critical criteria which allow the essays to be read as a sequence – an act which was important in establishing his role as a critical authority. However, there are uncollected review essays of this period, such as 'A Sceptical Patrician' and 'Kipling Redivivus',[32] which are as fine as those reprinted in *A Sacred Wood* or *Selected Essays*, and just as important in relation to Eliot's poetry. The extent, range and quality of Eliot's contributions to periodicals in 1919 is extraordinary; critically and poetically this was an *annus mirabilis*. By comparison with these eight years of sustained creative achievement, in which Eliot achieved more than most poets and critics could dream of achieving in a lifetime, the eight years following 1922 seem relatively sparse: not just as regards the quantity of Eliot's work, but also as regards its critical bravado and cultural significance. Here, it is apparent that with Pound's departure from England, and Eliot's gradual integration with the centres of English literary culture (crucially consolidated by the establishment of *The Criterion* in 1922–3) the strategic freedom of the peripheral position which Eliot had previously enjoyed was lost. Eliot had thrived on the dramatic possibilities of his marginal position; there were to be no more amusing fake letters enshrined in the correspondence columns of *The Egoist*, nor artful deconstructions of the tone and premises of *Times Literary Supplement* reviewing once Eliot had emerged from anonymity to take on the role of critical, and eventually cultural, magus.

The atmosphere and flavour of the marginal position Eliot had previously enjoyed with Pound is interestingly captured by a two part prose fragment, 'Eeldrop and Appleplex' which Eliot wrote for the *Little Review* in 1917. In this brief narrative, which Eliot probably wrote as a 'filler', we are introduced to two characters, Eeldrop and Appleplex (the names being reminiscent of Eliot and Pound, and, more distantly, Bouvard and Pécuchet), who have rented two small rooms in 'a disreputable part of town', away from their ordinary domestic environments: 'There are evil neighbourhoods of noise and evil neighbourhoods of silence, and Eeldrop and Appleplex preferred the latter, as being the more evil.' Their purpose in meeting occasionally in this strange environment is to escape 'the too well pigeon-holed, too taken-for-granted, too highly systematized areas, and – in the language of those whom they sought to avoid – they wished ''to apprehend the human soul in its concrete individuality''.' The two characters bear more than a passing resemblance to Eliot and Pound. 'It may be added that Eeldrop was a sceptic with a taste for mysticism, and Appleplex a materialist with a leaning towards scepticism; that Eeldrop was learned in theology, and that Appleplex studied the physical and biological sciences', and we are also informed that Eeldrop is 'in private life, a bank clerk'. From their position of marginality and anonymity (Appleplex has compiled files which 'contained the documents for his "Survey of Contemporary Society"') the two are detached connoisseurs and analysts of urban phenomena.

> It was a shady street, its windows were heavily curtained; and over it hung the cloud of a respectability which has something to conceal. Yet it had the advantage of more riotous neighbourhoods near by, and Eeldrop and Appleplex commanded from their windows the entrance of a police station across the way. This alone possessed an irresistible appeal in their eyes. From time to time the silence of the street was broken; whenever a malefactor was apprehended, a wave of excitement curled into the street and broke upon the doors of the police station. Then the inhabitants of the street would linger in dressing-gowns, upon their doorsteps: then alien visitors would linger in the street, in caps; long after the centre of misery had been engulphed in his cell. Then Eeldrop and Appleplex would break off their discourse, and rush out to mingle with the mob.[33]

The stance which Eliot records in 'Eeldrop and Appleplex' can be related to Eliot's earlier poetry and *The Waste Land* as a whole, in which we find these lines in a deleted passage.

> Some minds, aberrant from the normal equipoise
> (~~London, your people is bound upon the wheel!~~)
> Record the motions of these pavement toys
> And trace the cryptogram that may be curled
> Within these faint perceptions of the noise,
> Of the movement, and the lights![34]

Mediated through the influence of Baudelaire (and in particular the prose poem 'Le Joujou du pauvre'), the premise is that of a social marginality and intellectual detachment which regards such urban experience as providing 'cryptograms', not to be approved of, or even classified, but meditated upon, and, where possible, elucidated. That the initial drafts of *The Waste Land* contain a more panoramic survey of contemporary society than that retained in the published poem, and that the dramatic elements of the poem ('He Do the Police in Different Voices') are less perceptible, is, in this context, significant. In 'Eeldrop and Appleplex', Eeldrop is at pains to emphasize his perception of the irreducibility of individual experience. 'Men are only allowed to be happy or miserable in classes. In Gopsum Street a man murders his mistress. The important fact is that for the man the act is eternal, and that for the brief space he has to live, he is already dead. He is already in a different world from ours. He has crossed the frontier.'[35]

This comment can be related directly to the central situation of 'Sweeney Agonistes', the jazz age drama Eliot had planned to come after *The Waste Land* and the only real successor to the informing impulses and modes of Eliot's early poetry. Here, in the two fragments we have of this 'Aristophanic Melodrama'[36] (which utilizes Cornford's *The Origin of Attic Comedy* in the manner in which *The*

Waste Land uses *From Ritual to Romance* and *The Golden Bough*) Eliot employs 'characters' from his earlier verse to construct a situation in which one figure, Sweeney, has an awareness denied to the other characters, and (perhaps) shared by the audience, and also the knowledge of a crime which he may or may not have perpetrated ('I knew a man once did a girl in/Any man might do a girl in'), which puts him with the Gopsum Street murderer, 'beyond the frontier'. It is a pity that Eliot did not persist in attempting to solve the structural difficulties of his plan (described in *The Use of Poetry*),[37] for this work was the last in which Eliot engaged directly with colloquial idioms in the manner of his early work, and despite its lack of potential for dramatic development the work has a rhythmic and linguistic vitality that is often lacking in Eliot's later drama.

A reading of the 'Eeldrop and Appleplex' fragments can contribute to an understanding of the Pound-Eliot collaboration and Eliot's peripheral oppositional stance during this period; but there is much evidence to suggest that Pound's understanding of Eliot's temperament, and perception of the aims of his poetry was less than definitive. While Pound could perceive the 'sceptic' in Eeldrop/Eliot, he was less fully aware of the 'taste for mysticism' in his associate. While one of the central intentions of this study has been to place Eliot's work of this period within the context of 'the Men of 1914', whose defining feature was their distance from native English culture, that work cannot be comprehended as being predominantly satiric in intent, yet this would seem to be the manner in which Pound tended to perceive it. In the second piece of doggerel Pound wrote in the 1921 letter this seems clearly manifested:

> Cauls and grave clothes he brings
> Fortune's outrageous stings,
> About which odour clings,
>   Of putrefaction,
> Bleichstein's dank rotting clothes
> Affects the dainty nose,
> He speaks of common woes
>   Deploring action.
>
> He writes of A.B.C.s
> And flaxseed poultices,
> Observing fate's hard decrees
>   Sans satisfaction;
> Breeding of animals,
> Humans and cannibals,
> But above all else of smells
>   Without attraction
>
> Vates cum fistula[38]

However, as discussed in the chapter on Eliot's employment of satiric techniques, the modes of social engagement manifested in Eliot's early poetry tend to refer us back to the peculiar angle of vision of the poet, a quality of acute, anguished apprehension, rather than giving the impression of securely held social and political antagonisms.

To achieve a balanced assessment of the social intentionality of Eliot's early poetry it is important to realize that cultural displacement is the premise upon which Eliot's career was built, and that a vertiginous insecurity underwrites the extreme sensitivity of the early work as well as the later yearning towards orthodoxy. In Herbert Read's 1966 memoir of Eliot (to my mind the most revealing personal testimony we have) a letter is quoted which makes Eliot's dilemma explicit.

> 'Some day,' he wrote to me on St. George's day, 1928 (his own inscription), 'I want to write an essay about the point of view of an American who wasn't an American because he was born in the South and went to school in New England as a small boy with a nigger drawl, but who wasn't a southerner in the South because his people were northerners in a border state and looked down on all southerners and Virginians, and who so was never anything anywhere and who therefore felt himself to be more a Frenchman than an American and more an Englishman than a Frenchman and yet felt that the U.S.A. up to a hundred years ago was a family extension. It is almost too difficult for H. J. who for that matter wasn't an American at all, in that sense.'[39]

The surprising comment on 'H. J.' (Henry James) can be explicated by Spender's further citations from the May 1935 letter.

> Rather astonishingly he pronounces that 'James wasn't an American' because, although he had an acute sense of contemporary America, he had 'no American sense of the Past.' Eliot adds about his own America, that '*our* America came to an end in 1829, when Andrew Jackson was elected president', and he qualifies what he has said about James by adding that James had unconsciously '*acquired*, though not inherited, something of the American tradition. He was not a descendant of the witch-hangers'.[40]

While something similar might be said of Eliot's own sense of English cultural traditions and sense of the past, more personally we can sense an implicit reference to the first American Eliot who was town clerk for Beverley, Massachusetts in 1690, and of whom Savage's *Genealogical Dictionary* (1860) writes, 'He was of the juries, says tradit. wh. tried the witches, and had great mental affliction on that acc. for the residue of his life.'[41] Taking these two letters in the context of the previous discussion of 'Gerontion', we can discern that Eliot's repudiation of democratic, mass society was intimately linked with what was perceived as the loss of a world: 'the U.S.A. up to a hundred years ago was a family extension'. Eliot reacts and retaliates by an attack on those forces ('Chicago Semite Viennese') which he, as Adams before him, perceives as having displaced him. 'Reaction' is the correct term, for Eliot's social assumptions as evinced in the poetry have more the quality of defensive psychological reflexes than a coherent attempt to come to terms with the early twentieth century; and it is this quality of almost visceral response that Pound pinpoints in the second piece of doggerel in the *Waste Land* letter.

By 1927, after the General Strike of the previous year, Eliot is writing under the rubric of 'The Latest Muscovite Menace' in *The Criterion* (June 1927) to describe a no more threatening practice than community singing at Cup Finals and Test Matches, of which he inquires 'whether it has really taken hold of the British Massenmensch?' There is some irony here, but not of the kind one might expect, and Eliot continues with a not unserious sequence of speculations.

> We are already accustomed to seeing, from time to time, immense numbers of men and women voting all together, without using their reason and without inquiry; so perhaps we have no right to complain of the same masses singing all together, without much sense of tune or knowledge of music; we may presently see them praying and shouting hallelujahs all together, without much theology or knowledge of what they are praying about. We cannot explain it. But it should at present be suspect: it is very likely hostile to Art . . .[42]

Eliot's high cultural critique is by now explicit; but the arch-parodist has become eminently parodiable, and the effect is compounded when we suspect that Eliot himself realizes this and is to an extent playing up to it. Thus, when Eliot comes to enunciate his intellectual and political position in 1928, in his declaration in the preface to *For Lancelot Andrewes* that he is 'classicist in literature, royalist in politics, and anglo-catholic in religion',[43] we note firstly that this is close to a rendering into English terms of a description of Maurras in the *Nouvelle Revue Française* of 1913, as 'classique, catholique, monarchique';[44] but we can further discern that this declaration is not designed to accord with the realities of English life in the twentieth century, and that, in a deeper sense this is part of Eliot's purpose.

Looking well beyond the period with which I have been concerned, in a 1948 *Festschrift*, Wyndham Lewis begins his article on Eliot's 'Early London Environment' by commenting with some asperity on the dramatic contrast of his also having been asked to write on another old friend, Ezra Pound, with whom his memories of Eliot were inextricably linked: 'For one of these friends is confined in a criminal asylum in America; but the other is among us here, a rarely honoured member of his profession, dwelling in the bland atmosphere of critical approbation.'[45] Lewis's exasperation seems to be prompted partly by his awareness of his own diminished reputation and circumstances. If the latter part of Joyce's life, long before his death in Zurich in 1941, offers the spectacle of an extreme, albeit celebrated self-absorption, both Pound's and Lewis's attempts at active political engagement were to have more or less disastrous consequences for both individuals, while Eliot was the only one of 'the Men of 1914' to survive into the latter half of the twentieth century with his career and reputation intact.

However, if Lewis's comment suggests that we should adopt wider perspectives than those of public success, it is perhaps possible for us to adopt wider perspectives than those of Lewis himself; and then it is hard to avoid the conclusion that Eliot as well as the other 'Men of 1914' was to some degree the victim of the history they all disdained, combated, ignored or sought to mould to their purposes. Certainly, by the end of his writing career, in the late 1950s, with the definitive emergence and consolidation of mass cultural forms, the high cultural critique that Eliot had sought through the 1920s and 1930s and beyond to defend, was in the process of being superseded by an alien cultural configuration, and one that represented all that Eliot found inimical. He would probably have appreciated and acceded to Lewis's wry prediction made in *Blasting and Bombardiering* in 1937, that 'by the end of this century the movement to which, historically, I belong will be as remote as predynastic Egyptian statuary', though the analogy with its suggestion of a hieratic stiffness has perhaps its own unintended truth. Similarly, Lewis's phrase 'the Men of 1914' functions beyond historical description to effect a metaphoric conjunction with the idea of a 'virile', warlike deployment of intellectual force, and here again, while time has enhanced the historic resonance of the phrase, it has also served to accentuate and interrogate the implicit, unthinking chauvinism of Lewis's assumptions.

In our final impression of Eliot, both as man and poet, the quality of his developing political reaction needs to be both specified and analysed; but in the period with which I have been concerned, that which culminates with the publication of *The Waste Land*, both the poetry and criticism has a strategic mobility that suggests an implicit resistance to the making of mutually exclusive commitments or choices. It has been my argument that *The Waste Land* marks a crucial watershed in Eliot's poetic and intellectual development. Despite the enormous success of the poem; for the poet who had sought to order cultural realities through the deployment of a 'mythical method', the failure of this ambition marked the gradual relinquishment of his belief in the intellectual and ideological self-sufficiency of Art; a militant aestheticism which had linked him with the other 'Men of 1914'. Henceforth, Eliot's intellectual interests and ambitions narrowed towards commitments that in the context of his earlier work are rearguard, defensive and reactionary; and consequently the poetry itself seems to narrow in scope and ambition. His initially fluid and ambivalent concept of tradition hardens into a sense of orthodoxy; the culturally adventurous anthropological method employed in *The Waste Land* becomes a thing of the past as Eliot narrows his commitments towards a Eurocentric Classicism; and in 1927, a high Anglican commitment is made which contains and endorses a radical Conservatism that often seems to function as a refusal of the cultural present.

If *The Waste Land* is taken as the culmination of the early phase of Eliot's development, the distinctive achievement of that poem is not its 'impersonality', but rather the manner in which a discourse is created which eschews the limiting particularity of personal statement through an idiosyncratic reliance on 'tradition' and yet which remains capable of movingly implicating the poet within what is said. As in Eliot's citation of some lines from Dante's *Purgatorio* as the epigraph dedication of *Prufrock and Other Observations* to Jean Verdenal, a friend who had been killed in the Dardanelles, the emotive force is magnified rather than diminished by being rendered in a voice other than that of the poet. Thus, when in the introductory passage of 'The Fire Sermon', contrasting the squalor of the present day Thames with the purity of Spenser's 'Prothalamion', we come upon the interpolated line 'By the waters of Leman I sat down and wept . . .' we note the reference to Psalm cxxxvii: 'By the rivers of Babylon, there we sat down, yea, we wept, when we remembered Zion . . .'; we also perhaps note the relevance to 'The Fire Sermon' of the Middle English meaning of 'leman' as lover or paramour; and finally we note that Lake Leman is the French name for Lake Geneva, close to Lausanne where Eliot continued work on *The Waste Land* in 1921, while recuperating from the breakdown he had suffered earlier in that year. All these meanings coalesce in the line; but finally it is the almost concealed autobiographical implication that fuses the disparate meanings to create a poignant and memorable emotional power.

Notes and References

For ease of reference, when an article originally published in a journal has been republished in a book, the reference in these notes is to the republished text. The original context has been indicated in the main text of the study.

All editions are published in London unless otherwise stated.

Introduction

1 Ezra Pound, 'Harold Monro', *Criterion* (July 1932), p. 590.
2 T. S. Eliot, 'Tradition and the Individual Talent', *Selected Essays* (Faber, 1976), p. 15.
3 P. Wyndham Lewis, *Blasting and Bombardiering* (Calder, 1982), p. 292.
4 Ibid., p. 294.
5 Ibid., p. 250.
6 Ibid., p. 256.
7 Ibid., p. 15, p. 250.
8 T. S. Eliot, 'Observations', *Egoist* (May 1918), p. 69.
9 Lewis, *Blasting and Bombardiering*, p. 253
10 Ibid., p. 258.
11 Ibid., p. 257.
12 Ibid., p. 254.
13 J.-P. Sartre, *Qu'est-ce que la littérature?* (first published 1948; Paris, Gallimard, 1976), p. 90.
14 Ibid., p. 116.
15 Ibid., p. 130.
16 Roland Barthes, *Writing Degree Zero* (first published 1953; Cape, 1967), p. 19.
17 Ibid., pp. 66–7.
18 Sartre, *Qu'est-ce que la littérature?* p. 18.
19 R. Williams, *Marxism and Literature* (Oxford, OUP, 1977), p. 202.
20 Barthes, *Writing Degree Zero*, pp. 54–5.
21 Ibid., pp. 56–7.
22 Ibid., p. 48.

23 F. Jameson, *Marxism and Form* (Princeton NJ, Princeton University Press, 1974) pp. 34–5.

24 T. Adorno, 'Commitment', *New Left Review*, Nos 87–8 (September–December 1974), p. 86.

25 A. G. Lehmann, *The Symbolist Aesthetic in France (1885–1895)* (Oxford, Basil Blackwell, 1968).

26 Ibid., p. 14.

27 A. Symons, *The Symbolist Movement in Literature* (first published 1899; Constable, 1908).

28 G. Graff, *Literature Against Itself* (Chicago, Chicago University Press, 1979).

29 F. Lentricchia, *After the New Criticism* (Athlone Press, 1980).

Chapter 1

1 See R. Cork, Introduction to *Vorticism and Its Allies* (Arts Council of Great Britain, 1974), p. 7.

2 Ibid., p. 8.

3 Ibid., p. 12.

4 T. E. Hulme, *Speculations*, ed. H. Read (Kegan Paul, 1924), p. 94.

5 Ibid., p. 104.

6 Lewis, *Blasting and Bombardiering*, p. 36.

7 Cork, Introduction to *Vorticism*, p. 22.

8 *BLAST: Review of the Great English Vortex* Nos 1, 2 (Santa Barbara, Black Sparrow Press, 1981). Originally published 1914–15 in London. *Blast* (2), p. 33.

9 Hulme, *Speculations*, pp. 8–9.

10 T. S. Eliot, 'A Commentary', *Criterion* (April 1924), p. 231.

11 In 'A Commentary', *Criterion* (January 1926), Eliot links together Georges Sorel, Charles Maurras, Julien Benda, T. E. Hulme, Jacques Maritain and Irving Babbitt.

12 T. S. Eliot, 'Oxford University Extension Lectures. Syllabus of a Course of Six Lectures on Modern French Literature by T. Stearns Eliot . . . 1916'. Reprinted in facsimile in A. D. Moody, *Thomas Stearns Eliot, Poet* (Cambridge, Cambridge University Press, 1979), pp. 42–9. The original is substantially unpaginated and therefore subsequent references are to the pagination in Moody. For a full investigation of the relation between Eliot and Hulme, see R. Schuchard, 'Eliot and Hulme in 1916: Towards a Revaluation of Eliot's Critical and Spiritual Development', *PMLA* (October 1973), pp. 1083–94.

13 Schuchard, 'Eliot and Hulme in 1916', p. 1085.

14 An example of the critical confusion which has resulted from this refusal to consider Eliot's early ideological choices can be found in Frank Kermode's introduction to Eliot's *Selected Prose* (Faber, 1975), where he states, 'The main influences on his work at this time were Ezra Pound (and through him Rémy de Gourmont and Henry James) and Irving Babbitt, who at Harvard introduced Eliot to the philosophy of Humanism, and whose traditionalist doctrines were reinforced, a little later, by the ideas of T. E. Hulme and Charles Maurras' (pp. 11–12). It was, of course, the doctrines of Maurras and Hulme that led Eliot to reject Babbitt's 'humanism' while retaining his anti-democratic elitism.

15 Eliot subsequently declared himself to have been a Bergsonian while writing 'The Love Song of J. Alfred Prufrock', and one can discern both the traces of Bergson's

notion of the *durée*, 'real', lived time (as opposed to abstract chronological measure) and his concern with the ambiguous but potentially positive role of memory in that poem (and also 'Rhapsody on a Windy Night'). The reaction against Bergson was swift – in Eliot's case and more generally. He was attacked in Julien Benda's *Le Bergsonisme ou une philosophie de la mobilité* (1912) for his irrationalist bias and unmediated treatment of the self, which through his emphasis on the *élan vital* (life force) was held to suppress the philosophic and personal implications of life's gloomy prognosis (death), and relatedly seemed to have no necessary connection with the historical past or the social and institutional world. It was, in brief, a Romantic time-philosophy; and it is interesting to note that Lewis, whose theory of comedy was highly influenced by Bergson's *Le Rire* (1900) showed no compunction about awarding Bergson a BLAST in the periodical of that name.

16 E. Weber, *Action Française* (Stanford, Stanford University Press, 1962), p. 9.
17 Hulme, *Speculations*, p. 47.
18 E. Nolte, *Three Faces of Fascism: Action Française; Italian Fascism; National Socialism*, translated L. Vennevitz (Weidenfeld, 1965), p. 74.
19 Eliot, 'Extension Lectures', p. 43.
20 Hulme, *Speculations*, p. 47.
21 Ibid., p. 48.
22 Ibid., p. 50.
23 Ibid., p. 61.
24 Ibid., p. 117.
25 Ibid.
26 Ibid., p. 114.
27 Ibid., p. 115.
28 Eliot, 'Extension Lectures', p. 47.
29 Hulme, *Speculations*, p. 115.
30 Eliot, 'Extension Lectures', p. 44.
31 F. Kermode, *Romantic Image* (Fontana, 1976).
32 Ibid., p. 139.
33 M. Roberts, *T. E. Hulme* (Faber, 1938), p. 163.
34 P. Lasserre, *Le Romanticisme française* (Paris, Société du Mercure de France, 1907), p. 537.
35 James Joyce, *Stephen Hero* (Cape, 1956), p. 83.
36 W. Worringer, *Abstraction and Empathy: A Contribution to the Psychology of Style* (first published 1908; Routledge, 1953).
37 Hulme, *Speculations*, p. 106.
38 Ibid., p. 108.
39 Ibid., p. 106.
40 R. Cork, *Vorticism and Abstract Art in the First Machine Age*, 2 vols (Fraser, 1976).
41 R. Ellmann, 'Two Faces of Edward', *Edwardians and Late Victorians*, ed. R. Ellmann (New York, Columbia University Press, 1960), pp. 186–7.
42 Wyndham Lewis, *Tarr* (Calder and Boyars, 1968), p. 280.
43 D. H. Lawrence, *The Letters of D. H. Lawrence; vol. II, June 1913–October 1916*, ed. G. Zytaruk, J. Boulton (Cambridge, Cambridge University Press, 1981), pp. 182–3.
44 G. Dangerfield, *The Strange Death of Liberal England* (first published 1935; Granada, 1970). In this study the historian chooses three areas: the Tory rebellion over Ulster,

the Suffragette movement and the rise of organized labour to argue the abrupt collapse of the Victorian Liberal consensus in the years 1910 to 1914.

45 Lewis, *Blasting and Bombardiering*, pp. 100–104.

46 Ibid., p. 103.

47 *Blast* (1), p. 129.

48 Ibid., pp. 134–5.

49 Ibid., unpaginated.

50 In *Der Einzige und sein Eigentum* (1844) (translated as *The Ego and Its Own*), Max Stirner, the former young Hegelian, went beyond Feuerbach in proposing the disposal of any transcendent or metaphysical value in favour of the development of the anti-social self. To Feuerbach's altruistic humanism Stirner retorted, 'The self-willed egoist is necessarily a criminal, and his life is necessarily crime.' Stirner's egoism, which anticipates elements in Nietzsche's philosophy, was an intellectual nine days wonder, but in the early years of this century his work underwent a brief renaissance, and he was the guiding spirit behind the renaming of the *New Freewoman* as the *Egoist* in 1914. He was, I think, an important influence on Lewis's early work; and in a central retrospective section of his Vorticist drama *The Enemy of the Stars*, Arghol, Lewis's persona or 'showman' mentions Stirner's book as 'One of the seven arrows in his martyr mind' before flinging the book out of the window – a significant clue which allows us to suggest Stirner as a source for Arghol's elitist and anti-humanist statements. For Stirner's relation to early Modernism, see M. H. Levenson, *A Genealogy of Modernism* (Cambridge, Cambridge University Press, 1984), pp. 63–7.

51 *Blast* (1), p. 33.

52 Ibid., pp. 30–1.

53 Ibid., unpaginated.

54 Ibid., p. 17.

55 H. Kenner, *The Invisible Poet: T. S. Eliot* (Methuen, 1965), p. 83.

56 P. Wyndham Lewis, 'The Code of a Herdsman', *Little Review* (July 1917), p. 3.

57 *Blast* (1), p. 141.

58 Ibid., p. 145.

59 Ibid., p. 154.

60 Ibid., p. 135.

61 J. Ortega y Gasset, *The Dehumanization of Art and Other Essays* (Princeton, Princeton University Press, 1968).

62 E. Pound, *Gaudier-Brzeska: A Memoir* (first published 1916; Marvell Press, 1960), p. 93.

63 E. Pound, 'D'Artagnan Twenty Years After', *Criterion* (July 1937) pp. 606–608.

64 Lewis, *Blasting and Bombardiering*, p. 36.

65 *Blast* (1), p. 149.

66 P. Wyndham Lewis in *T. S. Eliot: A Symposium from Conrad Aiken (et al)*, compiled by R. March and Tambimuttu (Editions Poetry, 1948), pp. 25–6.

67 E. Pound, *The Letters 1907–41*, ed. D. D. Paige (Faber, 1961), p. 48.

68 E. Pound, 'Wyndham Lewis', *Egoist* (15 June 1914), p. 233.

69 E. Pound, 'The Bourgeois', *Egoist* (2 February 1914), p. 53.

70 See N. Stock, *The Life of Ezra Pound* (Harmondsworth, Penguin Books, 1974), p. 197.

71 All quotes E. Pound, 'The New Sculpture', *Egoist* (16 February 1914), pp. 67–8.

72 *Blast* (1), p. 45.
73 R. Aldington, 'BLAST', *Egoist* (15 July 1914), p. 273.
74 *Blast* (2), pp. 85–6.
75 Ibid., p. 86.
76 Hulme, *Speculations*, p. 126.
77 E. Pound, *Literary Essays*, ed. with an introduction by T. S. Eliot (Faber, 1960), p. 12.
78 R. Aldington, 'Modern Poetry and the Imagists', *Egoist* (1 June 1914), pp. 202–3.
79 T. S. Eliot, introduction to Pound, *Literary Essays* (Faber, 1960), p. viii; and E. Pound, quoted in M. Reck, *Ezra Pound: A Close Up* (Rupert Hart Davis, 1968), pp. 14–15.
80 C. K. Stead, *The New Poetic: Yeats to Eliot* (Hutchinson, 1964).
81 Quoted in Stead, *The New Poetic* p. 54.
82 Quoted in Stock, *The Life of Ezra Pound*, p. 159.
83 T. S. Eliot, *The Sacred Wood* (first published 1920; Methuen, 1972), pp. 147–9.
84 Ibid., p. 100.
85 Pound, *Literary Essays*, p. 4.
86 Pound, *Gaudier-Brzeska*, p. 86.
87 Ibid., p. 92.
88 *Blast* (1), p. 154.
89 Ibid.
90 Pound, *Gaudier-Brzeska*, p. 83.
91 Ibid., p. 85.
92 Ibid., p. 86.
93 *Blast* (1), p. 153.
94 E. Pound, 'The New Sculpture', *Egoist* (16 February 1914), p. 67.
95 E. Pound, 'Affirmations II: Vorticism', *The New Age* (14 January 1915), p. 277.
96 E. Pound, 'Affirmations IV: As for Imagisme', *The New Age* (28 January 1915), p. 349.
97 P. Wyndham Lewis, *Rude Assignment* (Hutchinson, 1950), pp. 128–9.
98 Ibid., p. 129.
99 *Blast* (1), p. 147.
100 Ibid., p. 82.
101 Ibid., p. 153.
102 See Pound, *Gaudier-Brzeska*, p. 45.
103 *Blast* (1), pp. 155–8.
104 Pound, *Gaudier-Brzeska*, p. 107.
105 Ibid.
106 Ibid., p. 29.
107 Ibid., p. 115.
108 Pound, *Literary Essays*, p. 5.
109 Pound, *Letters*, pp. 94, 117, 137, 141, 142.
110 Ibid., p. 78.
111 Pound, *Gaudier-Brzeska*, p. 91.
112 *Blast* (2) p. 34.
113 Pound, *Literary Essays*, p. 285.
114 Ibid., p. 288.
115 Pound, *Literary Essays*, p. 283.

Chapter 2

1 Quoted in P. Ackroyd, *T. S. Eliot* (Hamish Hamilton, 1984), p. 46.
2 Quoted by Aiken, *A Symposium*, p. 23.
3 E. Pound, *Letters*, p. 80.
4 E. J. H. Greene, 'Jules Laforgue et T. S. Eliot', *Revue de Littérature comparée* (July–September 1948), p. 369.
5 Pound, *Letters*, p. 226.
6 T. S. Eliot, 'Reflections on Contemporary Poetry', *Egoist* (July 1919), p. 39.
7 Ibid.
8 Greene, *Laforgue et T. S. Eliot*, p. 365.
9 T. S. Eliot, *Poems Written in Early Youth* (Faber, 1967), p. 26.
10 Jules Laforgue, *Oeuvres complètes*, 6 vols (Paris, Mercure de France, 1922–1930), Vol. v, *Lettres*, p. 26.
11 Jules Laforgue, *Poésies complètes*, ed. P. Pia (Paris, Gallimard, 1970), p. 85.
12 Laforgue, *Oeuvres complètes*, Vol. v, p. 21.
13 Eliot, *Poems Written in Early Youth*, p. 29.
14 All quotes, C. Baudelaire, *Oeuvres complètes* (Lausanne, La Guilde du Livre, 1967) Vol. 1, pp. 1258–1262.
15 Symons, *The Symbolist Movement in Literature*, p. 101.
16 Ibid., p. 110.
17 Laforgue, *Oeuvres complètes*, Vol. iv, p. 66.
18 T. S. Eliot, *Selected Prose*, ed. F. Kermode (Faber, 1975), p. 35.
19 Laforgue, *Poésies complètes*, p. 298.
20 Kenner, *Invisible Poet*, p. 6.
21 T. S. Eliot, 'A Commentary', *Criterion* (April 1933), p. 470.
22 Laforgue, *Poésies complètes*, p. 279.
23 See L. Gordon, *Eliot's Early Years* (Oxford, OUP, 1978), pp. 45–7. Some years ago I was refused permission to receive photocopies of these manuscripts, which are in the Berg Collection, New York Public Library.
24 Pound, *Letters*, p. 50.
25 Quoted in Gordon, *Eliot's Early Years*, p. 45.
26 R. Barthes, *S/Z* (Paris, Seuil, 1970), p. 146.
27 J. Lane, 'His Master's Voice? The questioning of authority in literature', *The Modern English Novel*, ed. G. Josipovici (Open Books, 1976), p. 121.
28 M. Arnold, *Poems: Narrative, Elegiac and Lyric* (Dent, 1900), pp. 235–8.
29 Quoted by Aiken, *A Symposium*, p. 23.
30 *Writers at Work: the Paris Review interviews*, 2nd series, introduced by Van Wyck Brooks (Secker, 1963), p. 82.
31 Pound, *Literary Essays*, p. 282.
32 All quotes, ibid., pp. 282–3.
33 Ibid.
34 Ibid.
35 Ibid., p. 25.
36 Ibid., p. 33.
37 E. Pound, *Collected Shorter Poems* (Faber, 1968), pp. 196–202.
38 Ibid., p. 247.
39 See M. Collie, *Jules Laforgue* (University of London, Athlone Press, 1977), pp. 87–8.

40 Pound, *Literary Essays*, p. 418.
41 Ibid., p. 419.
42 Ibid., p. 420.
43 E. Pound, 'A Study in French Poets', *Little Review* (February 1918), p. 7.
44 Pound, *Literary Essays*, p. 419.
45 Ibid., p. 420.
46 Pound, *Letters*, pp. 92–3.
47 Pound, *Literary Essays*, p. 420.
48 Laforgue, *Poésies complètes*, pp. 294–5.

Chapter 3

1 Pound, *Letters*, p. 294.
2 Ibid., p. 45.
3 Ibid., p. 203.
4 Pound, *Collected Shorter Poems*, p. 96.
5 Pound, *Gaudier-Brzeska*, p. 89.
6 Eliot, *Collected Poems*, p. 31.
7 Laforgue, *Poésies complètes*, p. 278.
8 Pound, *Letters*, p. 107.
9 Aiken, in *A Symposium*, p. 22.
10 Quoted in R. Ellmann, *James Joyce* (Oxford, OUP, 1965), p. 169.
11 Baudelaire, *Oeuvres complètes*, p. 1059.
12 J. Laforgue, *Moralités légendaires* (Paris, Mercure de France, 1954).
13 Laforgue, *Poésies complètes*, p. 284.
14 Pound, *Letters*, p. 223.
15 *Writers at Work*, pp. 84–5.
16 T. S. Eliot, *Collected Poems* (Faber, 1974), p. 48.
17 T. Corbière, *Les Amours jaunes* (Paris, Gallimard, 1973), p. 58.
18 See K. Weinberg, *On Gide's 'Prométhée': Private Myth and Public Mystification* (Princeton NJ, Princeton University Press, 1972), pp. 22–3.
19 A. Gide, *Le Prométhée mal enchaîné* (first published 1899; Paris, Gallimard, 1925).
20 T. S. Eliot, *The Use of Poetry and the Use of Criticism* (first published 1933; Faber, 1975) p. 69.
21 Gide, *Le Prométhée*, p. 50.
22 Ibid., p. 25.
23 Ibid., p. 80.
24 T. S. Eliot, 'Dans le Restaurant', *Little Review* (September 1918), pp. 12–13.
25 Eliot, *Collected Poems*, p. 64.
26 Ibid., p. 78–9.
27 Eliot, *Sacred Wood*, pp. 56–7.
28 Quoted in S. Spender, 'Remembering Eliot', *T. S. Eliot: The Man and His Work*, ed. A. Tate (first published 1966; Harmondsworth, Penguin Books, 1971), p. 59.
29 T. S. Eliot, 'Cyril Tourneur (1930)', *Selected Essays*, p. 192.
30 Eliot, *Collected Poems*, p. 50.
31 Kenner, *Invisible Poet*, pp. 70–1.
32 Ibid., p. 71.

Chapter 4

1 *Writers at Work*, p. 84.
2 T. S. Eliot, 'Professional, or . . .', *Egoist* (April 1918), p. 61 (signed with the pseudonym Apteryx).
3 See quote in Bernard Bergonzi, *T. S. Eliot* (Macmillan, 1972), p. 44.
4 Pound, *Literary Essays*, p. 437.
5 T. Gautier, *Emaux et Camées* (Texte définitif, 1872) ed. A. Boschot (Paris, Garnier, 1954), pp. 132–3.
6 Quoted ibid., p. L.
7 Joseph Frank, 'Spatial Form in Modern Literature', in *The Sewanee Review* (1945), Part I, pp. 221–40; Part II, pp. 433–56, Part III, pp. 643–53.
8 Ibid., p. 223.
9 Ibid., p. 229.
10 Ibid., p. 652.
11 Ibid., p. 653.
12 See Philip E. Tennant, *Théophile Gautier* (University of London, Athlone Press, 1975), p. 24.
13 Gautier, *Emaux et Camées*, p. XLIII.
14 Quoted Tennant, *Théophile Gautier*, p. 60.
15 Pound, *Literary Essays*, p. 282.
16 See Tennant, *Théophile Gautier*, p. 27.
17 Sartre, *Qu'est-ce que la littérature?* pp. 154–5.
18 Pound, *Letters*, p. 238.
19 Having mentioned it in 'In Metre', *The New Freewoman* (15 September 1913), p. 132.
20 Théophile Gautier, *Poésies complètes*, 3 vols, published by René Jarinski (Paris, Nizet, 1970), Vol. II, p. 207.
21 Eliot, *Selected Essays*, p. 424.
22 Previous quotes, Eliot, *Collected Poems*, pp. 51–2.
23 Previous references, Gautier, *Emaux et Camées*, pp. 74–9; pp. 115–19; pp. 11–18.
24 Eliot, *Selected Essays*, p. 296.
25 Gautier, *Emaux et Camées*, p. 76.
26 Pound, *Collected Shorter Poems*, p. 206.
27 Eliot, *Collected Poems*, p. 55.
28 See G. Smith, *T. S. Eliot's Poetry and Plays: A Study in Sources and Meaning* (Chicago, London, University of Chicago Press, 1974), pp. 40–2.
29 Eliot, *Selected Essays*, pp. 281–92.
30 Ibid., p. 287.
31 Eliot, *Collected Poems*, pp. 55–6.
32 T. S. Eliot, *The Waste Land: A Facsimile and Transcript of the Original Drafts Including the Annotations of Ezra Pound*, ed. V. Eliot (Faber, 1971), p. 23 (Hereafter referred to by the abbreviation *FWL*).
33 Gautier, *Emaux et Camées*, p. 93.
34 Eliot, *Selected Essays*, p. 286.
35 Ibid., p. 27.
36 Quoted Smith, *Eliot's Poetry and Plays*, p. 3.
37 Frank, 'Spatial Form', p. 652.
38 T. S. Eliot, 'Beyle and Balzac', *Athenaeum* (30 May 1919), pp. 392–3.

39 William Wordsworth, *Poetical Works*, (OUP, 1969), p. 462.
40 Previous quotes, Eliot, *Collected Poems*, pp. 46–7.
41 Frank, 'Spatial Form', p. 653.
42 Ibid.
43 Eliot, *Selected Essays*, p. 24.
44 Worringer, *Abstraction and Empathy*, p. 5.
45 Ibid., p. 7.

Chapter 5

1 D. Davie, *The Poet in the Imaginary Museum* (Manchester, Carcanet, 1977), pp. 81–3.
2 J. Espey, *Ezra Pound's Mauberley: A Study in Composition* (Faber, 1955), preface, un-paginated.
3 Pound, *Collected Shorter Poems*, p. 216. Subsequent references to *Hugh Selwyn Mauberley* as published in this edition are not footnoted.
4 See Espey, *Ezra Pound's Mauberley*, p. 99.
5 H. Kenner, *Ezra Pound*, (Faber, 1951), pp. 146–82.
6 Davie, *Poet in the Imaginary Museum*, pp. 83 ff. The main alternative reading, which is supported by some of Pound's own remarks about the sequence, as well as textual evidence, would see the first section as being 'Mauberley's', and thus employing his voice rather than the poet's. While this reading is persuasive as regards the first section, the problem remains that the voice of the first section of the poem seems to have no consistency with the individual described in the second part of the sequence. While perhaps it forces coherence on the poem, the Kenner–Espey reading does have the advantage of allowing critical debate, even though this is at the price of under-stating ironic possibilities.
7 Pound, *Gaudier-Brzeska*, p. 82.
8 Ibid., p. 89.
9 Gautier, *Emaux et Camées*, p. 3.
10 T. Gautier, *Mademoiselle de Maupin*, ed. A. Boschot (first published 1835; Paris, Garnier, 1955).
11 Pound, *Letters*, p. 139.
12 Pound, *Literary Essays*, p. 363.
13 Ibid., p. 409.
14 Quoted Tennant, *Théophile Gautier*, p. 16.
15 Pound, *Letters*, p. 98.
16 Pound, 'The Revolt of Intelligence', VI, *New Age* (15 January 1920), p. 176.
17 See E. Pound, *Selected Prose*, ed. W. Cookson (Faber, 1973), p. 364.
18 E. Pound, 'Paris Letter. August 1922', *Dial* (September 1922), pp. 333–4.
19 *Blast* (2), pp. 85–6.
20 Pound, *Letters*, p. 249.
21 R. Kipling, *A Choice of Kipling's Verse*, ed. T. S. Eliot (Faber, 1979), p. 164.
22 Quoted Tennant, *Théophile Gautier*, p. 10.
23 Pound, *Letters*, p. 248.
24 *Everyman's Book of Victorian Verse*, ed. J. R. Watson (Dent, 1987), p. 312.
25 Espey, *Ezra Pound's Mauberley*, p. 23.
26 Gautier, *Poésies complètes*, Vol. iii, p. 103.

27 W. M. Chace, *The Political Identities of Ezra Pound and T. S. Eliot* (Stanford, Stanford University Press, 1973), pp. 29–33.
28 P. Wyndham Lewis, *Time and Western Man* (Chatto, 1927), p. 87.
29 R. de Gourmont, 'The Roots of Idealism', in *Selected Writings*, translated G. S. Burne, (Ann Arbor, MI, University of Michigan Press, 1966), pp. 155–69.
30 See Espey, *Ezra Pound's Mauberley*, p. 51.
31 See Kenner, *Pound*, p. 176. 'Of course I moved among miracles', said Strether. 'It was all phantasmagoric.'
32 See Espey, *Ezra Pound's Mauberley*, p. 80.
33 Pound, *Literary Essays*, p. 399.
34 E. Pound, 'Affirmations . . . IV. As for Imagisme', *New Age* (28 January 1915), p. 350.
35 Pound, *Literary Essays*, p. 399.
36 R. de Gourmont, *The Natural Philosophy of Love*, translated with a postscript by Ezra Pound (The Casanova Society, 1926).
37 Pound, *Literary Essays*, p. 340.
38 Ibid., p. 341.
39 All quotes, ibid., pp. 340–3.
40 *Blast* (1), p. 153.
41 Pound, *Literary Essays*, p. 400.
42 Ibid., pp. 433–4.
43 Ibid., p. 434.
44 E. Pound, 'Through Alien Eyes, III', *New Age* (30 January 1913), p. 301.
45 Pound, *Letters*, p. 65.
46 E. Pound, 'Wyndham Lewis', *Egoist* (15 June 1914), p. 234.
47 E. Pound, postscript to de Gourmont, *The Natural Philosophy of Love*, pp. 169–70.
48 H. N. Schneidau, *Ezra Pound: the Image and the Real* (Baton Rouge, LA, Louisiana State University Press, 1969), pp. 165–6.
49 Ibid., p. 166.
50 Pound, *Letters*, p. 248.
51 Ibid., p. 234.

Chapter 6

1 P. Wyndham Lewis, *Tarr* (New York, Jubilee Books, 1973), reprint of unrevised 1918 edition.
2 Eliot, *Sacred Wood*, p. 121.
3 Ibid., p. 94.
4 Ibid., p. 92.
5 Ibid., p. 105.
6 Ibid.
7 Ibid., pp. 105–6.
8 Worringer, *Abstraction and Empathy*, pp. 23 ff.
9 Eliot, *Sacred Wood*, p. 111.
10 Previous quotes, ibid., p. 120.
11 Ibid., pp. 116–17
12 A. B. Kernan, *The Cankered Muse: Satire of the English Renaissance* (New Haven, Yale University Press, 1959), p. 11.

13 T. S. Eliot, 'Tarr', *Egoist* (September 1918), p. 105.
14 P. Wyndham Lewis, *The Wild Body* (Chatto, 1927).
15 Eliot, 'Tarr', p. 106.
16 Eliot, *Sacred Wood*, pp. 116–17.
17 Ibid., p. 117.
18 P. Wyndham Lewis, 'Inferior Religions', *Little Review* (September 1917), p. 3.
19 Ibid.
20 Ibid., p. 5.
21 Eliot, *Sacred Wood*, p. 112.
22 Lewis, 'Inferior Religions', p. 4.
23 Quotes, Eliot, *Sacred Wood*, pp. 112–13.
24 P. Wyndham Lewis, *The Wild Body*, p. 23. For ease of reference I have chosen to refer to the 1927 publication, although it is outside the period 1914–22, and offers revised versions of material Lewis had published previously. There are no fundamental stylistic *volte faces* in Lewis's career, and while there is a discernible strengthening of Lewis's use of 'impasto' verbal effects in the revised material, the techniques of external rendition in these stories are no more extreme than in, for example, the proto-drama *The Enemy of the Stars* published in *Blast* (1), 1914, pp. 51–87.
25 Lewis, *The Wild Body*, pp. 207–8.
26 Ibid., p. 6.
27 Lewis, *Tarr*, p. 28.
28 Ibid., p. 44.
29 Quotes, ibid., p. 45.
30 Ibid., p. 47.
31 P. Wyndham Lewis, *Rude Assignment* (Hutchinson, 1950), p. 151.
32 Lewis, *The Wild Body*, p. 4.
33 Eliot, 'Tarr', p. 105.
34 All quotes, T. S. Eliot, 'Reflections on Contemporary Poetry', II, *Egoist* (October 1917), p. 133.
35 Eliot, *Collected Poems*, p. 44.
36 *FWL*, p. 117. Eliot refers to 'the wronged Aspatia' in 'Elegy', a discarded lyric included in the *Waste Land* manuscripts.
37 See Beaumont and Fletcher, *The Maid's Tragedy*, Act II, scene ii, ll. 80–4.
38 Lewis, 'Inferior Religions', p. 4.
39 *The Tyro*, No.1 (*Egoist*, 1921), p. 2.
40 Lewis, *Rude Assignment*, p. 117.
41 P. Wyndham Lewis, *Wyndham Lewis on Art: Collected Writings 1913–1956*, ed. W. Michel and C. J. Cox (Thames, 1969), p. 187.
42 *The Tyro*, p. 2.
43 Eliot, *Collected Poems*, p. 59.
44 Ibid., p. 57–8.
45 *Blast* (1), p. 145.
46 Eliot, *Sacred Wood*, p. 110.
47 Ibid., pp. 115, 117.
48 Ibid., pp. 118, 119, 120.
49 Ibid., pp. 110, 112.
50 *FWL* p. xviii.
51 Lewis, 'Inferior Religions', pp. 6, 7.

52 Lewis, *The Wild Body*, p. 4.
53 Lewis, *Rude Assignment*, p. 118.
54 Lewis, *The Enemy of the Stars, Blast* (1), p. 87.
55 Lewis, 'Inferior Religions', p. 7.
56 See, in particular, the portraits from this period, such as 'Praxitella' (1920–1) (Leeds City Art Gallery), or the great portrait of Edith Sitwell, which was begun in 1923 and completed in the 1930s (Tate Gallery).
57 Eliot, *Sacred Wood*, p. 15.
58 de Gourmont, 'Success and the Idea of Beauty', *Selected Writings*, pp. 30–46. Originally published in *Le Chemin de Velours* (1901).
59 Ibid., p. 42.
60 Wyndham Lewis, *The Tyro*, No. 1, p. 4.
61 See R. de Gourmont, *Le Problème du Style* (Paris, Mercure de France, 1902), pp. 104–8.
62 Eliot, *Sacred Wood*, p. 58.

Chapter 7

1 Barthes, *Writing Degree Zero*, p. 8.
2 Ibid., pp. 19–20.
3 R. Barthes, *Le Degré zéro de l'écriture*, suivi de *Éléments de sémiologie* (Paris, Gonthier, 1965), p. 163.
4 Eliot, *Collected Poems*, p. 42.
5 B. C. Southam, *A Student's Guide to the Selected Poems of T. S. Eliot* (Faber, 1981).
6 R. A. Brower, *Alexander Pope: The Poetry of Allusion* (Oxford, Clarendon Press, 1959).
7 Ibid., p. 165.
8 *The Complete Poems of John Wilmot, Earl of Rochester*, ed. D. M. Vieth (Yale University Press, 1977), pp. 120–6.
9 A. Pope, *Collected Poems* (Everyman, 1975), pp. 339–49.
10 Brower, *Alexander Pope*, p. 285. See also pp. 282–318.
11 Quoted Southam, *A Student's Guide*, p. 49.
12 Brower, *Alexander Pope*, p. 48.
13 W. Wordsworth and S. T. Coleridge, *The Lyrical Ballads* (Henry Froude, 1911), p. 237.
14 J. Joyce, *A Portrait of the Artist as a Young Man* (Cape, 1966), p. 215. The phrase 'paring his fingernails' is itself intentionally excessive and somewhat tongue in cheek.
15 This lengthy epigraph was a late addition to the poem, which originally had as its epigraph the line that concludes Arnaut Daniel's words in the *Purgatorio*: 'Poi s'ascose nel foco che li affina.' (See Gordon, *Eliot's Early Years*, p. 98.)
16 Corbière, *Les Amours jaunes*, pp. 21, 28.
17 G. Pearson, 'T. S. Eliot: an American use of Symbolism', *Eliot in Perspective*, ed. G. Martin (Macmillan, 1970), pp. 83–102.
18 Ibid., p. 86.
19 Ibid., p. 88.
20 Ibid., p. 87.
21 J. Joyce, *Ulysses* (Harmondsworth, Penguin Books, 1969), p. 45.

22 T. S. Eliot, *Ara Vos Prec* (Ovid Press, 1920), p. 30.

23 Smith, *T. S. Eliot's Poetry*, p. 45.

24 P. Gray, *T. S. Eliot's Intellectual and Poetic Development 1909–1922* (Sussex, Harvester Press, 1972), p. 197.

25 T. S. Eliot, 'Kipling Redivivus', *Athenaeum* (9 May 1919), p. 298.

26 W. Benjamin, *Illuminations*, ed. with an introduction by H. Arendt (Fontana, 1973), p. 38.

27 W. Benjamin, 'Karl Kraus', *One-Way Street and Other Writings*, translated E. Jephcott and K. Shorter (NLB, 1979), pp. 258–90.

28 In Benjamin, *Illuminations*, pp. 219–55.

29 Ibid., p. 38.

30 Ibid., p. 39.

31 M. Edwards, *Eliot/Language* (Isle of Skye, Acquila, 1975), p. 17.

32 Eliot, *Collected Poems*, p. 65.

33 Kenner, *Invisible Poet*, p. 139.

34 J. Webster, *The White Devil*, Act V, scene iv, ll. 103–4.

35 P. Fussell, *The Great War and Modern Memory* (Oxford, OUP, 1975), p. 8.

36 See Arendt, *Illuminations*, pp. 42 ff.

37 Eliot, *Collected Poems*, pp. 115–16.

38 Quoted, Southam, *A Student's Guide*, p. 146.

39 W. B. Yeats, introduction to *The Oxford Book of Modern Verse 1892–1935* (Oxford, Clarendon Press, 1936), pp. xxi–xxii.

40 Eliot, *Collected Poems*, p. 47.

41 Pound, *Literary Essays*, p. 280.

42 Eliot, *Sacred Wood*, p. 48.

43 Pound, *Literary Essays*, p. 227.

44 Eliot, *Selected Prose*, p. 32.

45 Eliot, *To Criticize the Critic and Other Writings* (Faber, 1965), p. 16.

46 Ibid., p. 17.

47 E. Pound, *The Spirit of Romance* (first published 1910; New York, New Directions, 1963), unpaginated.

48 Eliot, 'Reflections on Contemporary Poetry', *Egoist* (July 1919), p. 39.

49 Pound, *Literary Essays*, p. 91.

50 Eliot, *Sacred Wood*, p. 49.

51 T. S. Eliot, 'Observations', *Egoist* (May 1918), p. 69.

52 T. S. Eliot, 'Verse Pleasant and Unpleasant', *Egoist* (March 1918), p. 43.

53 T. S. Eliot, 'Reflections on Contemporary Poetry', *Egoist* (September 1917), pp. 118–19.

54 Williams, *Marxism and Literature*, p. 116.

55 For a detailed treatment of Eliot's intellectual development, which discusses his paper on 'Primitive Ritual' and debt to Bradley, see P. Gray, *T. S. Eliot's Intellectual and Poetic Development 1909–1922* (Sussex, Harvester Press, 1972). See also M. H. Levenson, *A Genealogy of Modernism* (Cambridge OUP, 1984), pp. 176–89.

56 C. Eliot, *Savonarola, A Dramatic Poem* (R. Cobden-Sanderson, 1926), p. viii.

57 T. S. Eliot, *Knowledge and Experience in the Philosophy of F. H. Bradley* (Faber, 1964).

58 Ibid., pp. 141–53.

59 Ibid., p. 141.

60 Ibid., p. 166.

61 T. S. Eliot, 'Leibniz's Monads and Bradley's Finite Centres', *Monist* (October 1916), p. 571.
62 Eliot, *Sacred Wood*, pp. 49–50.
63 J. L. Borges, 'Kafka and his Predecessors', *Labyrinths* (Harmondsworth, Penguin Books, 1970), pp. 234–7.
64 See Barthes, *Writing Degree Zero*, p. 44.
65 Edwards, *Eliot/Language*, p. 44.
66 Eliot, *Sacred Wood*, p. 50.
67 Eliot, *Selected Essays*, p. 24.
68 Ibid., p. 26.

Chapter 8

1 T. S. Eliot, 'A Sceptical Patrician', *Athenaeum* (23 May 1919), pp. 361–2.
2 *FWL*, p. xviii.
3 See Gordon, *Eliot's Early Years*, p. 143.
4 See Pound, *Letters*, pp. 236–7.
5 James Joyce, *Ulysses* (Harmondsworth, Penguin Books, 1968), p. 45.
6 Eliot, *Collected Poems*, p. 39.
7 Samuel Beckett, *Malloy; Malone Dies; The Unnameable* (Calder, 1976).
8 Eliot, *Sacred Wood*, p. 57.
9 Eliot, *Sacred Wood*, p. 101.
10 Eliot, *Selected Essays*, p. 109–118.
11 Ibid., pp. 116–17.
12 See J. Dollimore, *Radical Tragedy: Religion, Ideology and Power in the Drama of Shakespeare and his Contemporaries* (Sussex, Harvester Press, 1984), pp. 231–46.
13 H. Adams, *The Education of Henry Adams* (first published 1918); (Boston, Houghton Mifflin, 1961).
14 Ibid., p. 268.
15 See R. Barthes, *Mythologies* (Granada, 1973), pp. 145–6.
16 Eliot, phrase in a letter to Herbert Read, quoted in *T. S. Eliot: The Man And His Work*, ed. A. Tate, p. 20.
17 Eliot, 'A Sceptical Patrician', p. 361.
18 Ibid., pp. 361–2.
19 Adams, *Education*, p. 451.
20 Ibid., p. 460.
21 Ibid., p. 35.
22 Lancelot Andrewes, 'Sermon of the Nativity: Christmas 1618' in L. Andrewes, *Sermons*, ed. G. M. Story (Oxford, Clarendon Press, 1967), p. 85.
23 Adams, *Education*, p. 238.
24 T. S. Eliot, *After Strange Gods* (New York, Harcourt, Brace, 1934), p. 20.
25 T. S. Eliot, 'The Preacher as Artist', *Athenaeum* (28 November, 1919), p. 1252.
26 J. H. Newman. *Apologia pro Vita Sua*, ed. M. J. Svaglic (Oxford, Clarendon Press, 1967), p. 111.
27 Eliot, *Selected Essays*, p. 72.
28 Ibid., pp. 130–1.
29 Eliot, *Selected Prose*, pp. 175–6.
30 Ibid., pp. 177–8.

31 D. Lodge, *The Modes of Modern Writing: Metaphor, Metonomy and the Typology of Modern Literature* (Arnold, 1977), p. 136.
32 J. Weston, *From Ritual to Romance* (Garden City, Doubleday, 1957).
33 See *FWL*, p. 13.
34 Ibid., p. 5.
35 Ibid., 'Editorial Notes', p. 127.
36 Ibid., p. 41.
37 Ibid.
38 Ibid., p. 55.
39 Eliot, *Selected Prose*, p. 241.
40 Eliot, *Selected Essays*, p. 405.
41 *FWL*, p. 129.
42 Ibid., p. 31.
43 All quotes, ibid., pp. 33–35.
44 Ibid., p. 31.
45 Gordon, *Eliot's Early Years*, p. 110.
46 Eliot, *Selected Prose*, p. 177.
47 T. S. Eliot, 'Lettre d'Angleterre', *Nouvelle Revue Française* (December 1922), p. 754.
48 Ellmann, *James Joyce*, p. 63.
49 Eliot, *Savonarola*, p. viii.
50 Eliot, 'Tarr', p. 106.
51 Eliot, *Selected Prose*, p. 64.
52 Eliot, *Selected Essays*, p. 16.
53 F. Moretti, 'From *The Waste Land* to the Artificial Paradise', *Signs Taken For Wonders* (Verso, 1983), pp. 209–39.
54 Ibid., quoting Levi-Strauss, p. 219.
55 Ibid., pp. 219–220.
56 Ibid., quoting Levi-Strauss, p. 221.
57 Ibid., p. 220.
58 Eliot, *Collected Poems*, p. 70.
59 Ibid., p. 82.
60 Southam, *A Student's Guide*, p. 97.
61 Ibid., p. 98.
62 Eliot, *Ara Vos Prec*, p. 30.
63 The title of A. Malraux's *Le Musée imaginaire* (Paris, Gallimard, 1965).
64 Moretti, 'From *The Waste Land*', p. 229.
65 Ibid., pp. 224–5.
66 Ibid., pp. 225.
67 *FWL*, p. 9.
68 W. Benjamin, *Charles Baudelaire: A Lyric Poet in the Age of High Capitalism* translated H. Zohn (NLB, 1973), pp. 139–40.
69 Ibid., p. 139.
70 Ibid., p. 141.
71 Eliot, *Collected Poems*, pp. 80–1.
72 Ibid., p. 82.
73 Spender, *T. S. Eliot*, ed. Tate, p. 48.
74 Ibid., p. 47.
75 Eliot, *Collected Poems*, p. 85.

76 Ibid., p. 86.
77 Eliot, *Monist* (October 1916), p. 572.
78 Eliot, *Selected Prose*, p. 164.
79 *Penguin Book of French Verse*, Vol. 3, ed. A. Hartley (Harmondsworth, Penguin Books, 1968), p. 96.
80 C. Belsey, *The Subject of Tragedy: Identity and difference in Renaissance Drama* (Methuen, 1985), p. 78.
81 J. Feteke, *The Critical Twilight* (Routledge, 1977), p. xii.
82 *Baudelaire*, ed. F. Scarfe (Harmondsworth, Penguin Books, 1964), p. 210.
83 W. Benjamin, *The Origin of German Tragic Drama* (Verso, 1985), p. 178.
84 Lewis, *Blasting and Bombardiering*, p. 250.

Chapter 9

1 Eliot, *Selected Essays*, p. 251.
2 Quoted Southam, *A Student's Guide* p. 26.
3 Eliot, *Collected Poems*, p. 65.
4 Ibid., p. 74.
5 Dante, *Purgatorio*, Canto V, l. 133.
6 Eliot, *Selected Essays*, p. 247.
7 H. Howarth, *Notes on Some Figures Behind T. S. Eliot* (Chatto, 1965), p. 73.
8 Eliot, *Selected Essays*, p. 250.
9 See Gordon, *Eliot's Early Years*, p. 98.
10 Dante, *Purgatorio*, Canto XXVI, ll. 140–9.
11 *FWL*, pp. 99, 101, 119.
12 Quoted Howarth, *Notes*, p. 278.
13 Quoted Smith, *T. S. Eliot's Poetry*, p. 141.
14 Eliot, *Collected Poems*, p. 95.
15 Andrewes, *Sermons*, p. 122.
16 Eliot, *Selected Essays*, p. 243.
17 Ibid., p. 239.
18 See E. Auerbach, *Dante: Poet of the Secular World*, translated R. Mannheim (Chicago, Chicago University Press, 1961); C. S. Singleton, *Dante Studies*, 2 vols. (Cambridge, Mass., Harvard University Press, 1970).
19 See R. Hollander, *Allegory in Dante's 'Commedia'* (Princeton NJ, Princeton University Press, 1969).
20 Eliot, *Collected Poems*, p. 121.
21 Ibid., p. 89.
22 Ibid., p. 101.
23 Southam, *A Student's Guide*, p. 134.
24 M. Barbi, *Life of Dante*, translated P. G. Ruggiers (Berkeley, CA, University of California Press, 1960), p. 19. The letter, which is mentioned by an early authority, has been lost.
25 Dante, *Inferno*, Canto I, l. 86.
26 Andrewes, *Sermons*, pp. 75–99.
27 Pearson, 'T. S. Eliot', p. 95.
28 C. Aiken, *Ushant* (New York, OUP, 'T. S. Eliot', 1971), pp. 215–16.

Conclusion

1 M. Holroyd, *Lytton Strachey: a biography* (Harmondsworth, Penguin Books, 1971), p. 774.
2 C. Bell, *A Symposium*, pp. 15–16.
3 Read, in Tate, p. 21.
4 Letter to Read, Tate, p. 20.
5 Holroyd, *Lytton Strachey*, p. 823.
6 ed. Tate, *T. S. Eliot*, p. 21.
7 Aiken, *Ushant*, p. 215.
8 ed. Tate, *T. S. Eliot*, p. 20.
9 T. S. Eliot, 'A Commentary', *Criterion* (April 1924), p. 231.
10 Letter to Read, *T. S. Eliot*, ed. Tate, p. 26.
11 Ibid., p. 22.
12 Pound, *Letters*, pp. 230–1.
13 See Lewis on Pound and Joyce in *Time and Western Man* (Chatto, 1927); or on Eliot in *Men Without Art* (Cassell, 1934); or Eliot on Pound in *After Strange Gods* (Faber, 1934), of which Pound was to comment, 'His diagnosis is wrong. His remedy is an irrelevance' (quoted, Chace, *Political Identities*, p. 222).
14 Pound, *Literary Essays*, pp. 403, 407.
15 Ellmann, *James Joyce*, p. 541.
16 Goldberg, *The Classical Temper* (Chatto, 1961).
17 H. Kenner, *Dublin's Joyce* (Chatto, 1955).
18 Ellmann, *James Joyce*, pp. 449–50.
19 *The Modern Tradition: Backgrounds of Modern literature*, ed. R. Ellmann and C. Feidelson (New York, OUP, 1965), p. 127.
20 R. Ellmann, introduction to S. Joyce, *My Brother's Keeper* (Faber, 1982), p. 23.
21 Smith, *T. S. Eliot's Poetry*, p. 38.
22 Pound, *Letters*, p. 234.
23 Lewis, in *Symposium*, p. 28.
24 Quoted in D. Gallup, 'T. S. Eliot and Ezra Pound: Collaborators in letters', *Atlantic Monthly* (January 1970), p. 60.
25 Kenner, *Invisible Poet*, p. 83.
26 Gallup, 'Eliot and Pound', p. 60.
27 T. S. Eliot, 'The Method of Mr. Pound', *Athenaeum* (24 October 1919), p. 1065.
28 Pound, letter: 'Mr. Pound and his Poetry', *Athenaeum* (31 October 1919), p. 1132.
29 Gallup, 'Eliot and Pound', p. 60.
30 Ackroyd, *T. S. Eliot*, p. 78. This is, of course, a slight example, and does not necessarily reflect on Eliot's ability to criticize Murray's translations of Euripides. For a more substantial analysis of Eliot's deployment of ostensible erudition, see F. W. Bateson, 'The Poetry of Learning', *Eliot in Perspective: a Symposium*, ed. G. Martin (Macmillan, 1970), pp. 31–45.
31 *The Diary of Virginia Woolf, Vol. 2, 1920–24*, ed. A. Bell (Harmondsworth, Penguin Books, 1984), p. 91.
32 Eliot, 'Kipling Redivivus', *Athenaeum* (9 May 1919) pp. 297–8; 'A Sceptical Patrician', *Athenaeum* (23 May 1919), pp. 361–2.
33 All quotes, 'Eeldrop and Appleplex', 1, *Little Review*, (May 1917), pp. 7–11; 2. *Little Review* (September 1917), pp. 16–19.

34 *FWL*, p. 31.

35 'Eeldrop and Appleplex' 1, p. 9.

36 Eliot, *Collected Poems*, p. 121, where the piece is subtitled 'Fragments of an Aristophanic Melodrama'.

37 T. S. Eliot, *The Use of Poetry and the Use of Criticism* (first published 1933; Faber, 1964), pp. 153–4.

38 Pound, *Letters*, p. 235.

39 Letter to Read, *T. S. Eliot*, ed. Tate, p. 20.

40 Quoted in *ibid.*, p. 60.

41 Ackroyd, *T. S. Eliot*, p. 15.

42 T. S. Eliot, 'The Latest Muscovite Menace', *Criterion* (June 1927), pp. 285–6.

43 T. S. Eliot, *For Lancelot Andrewes: Essays on Style and Order* (first published 1928; Faber, 1970), p. 7.

44 Ackroyd, *T. S. Eliot*, p. 41.

45 Wyndham Lewis, 'Early London Environment', *Symposium*, p. 24.

Index

All works are entered under the name of the author.